THE CULT OF THE MODERN

FRANCE OVERSEAS: STUDIES IN EMPIRE AND DECOLONIZATION

Series editors: A. J. B. Johnston, James D. Le Sueur, and Tyler Stovall

The Cult of the Modern

*Trans-Mediterranean
France and the Construction
of French Modernity*

GAVIN MURRAY-MILLER

UNIVERSITY OF NEBRASKA PRESS
Lincoln and London

Portions of this book originally appeared as
"Neither Reformers Nor *Réformés*: The Construction of
French Modernity in the Nineteenth Century," *Historical Reflections/Réflexions Historiques* 40, no. 3 (Fall 2014),
published by Berghahn Press, and "Imagining the Trans-
Mediterranean Republic: Algeria, Republicanism, and the
Ideological Origins of the French Imperial Nation-State,
1848–1870," *French Historical Studies* 37 (Spring 2014),
published by Duke University Press.

Library of Congress Cataloging-in-Publication Data
Names: Murray-Miller, Gavin, author.
Title: The cult of the modern: trans-Mediterranean France and the
construction of French modernity / Gavin Murray-Miller.
Description: Lincoln: University of Nebraska Press, 2017. | Series:
France overseas: studies in empire and decolonization | Includes
bibliographical references and index.
Identifiers: LCCN 2016029053
ISBN 9780803290648 (cloth: alkaline paper)
ISBN 9781496200297 (epub)
ISBN 9781496200303 (mobi)
ISBN 9781496200310 (pdf)
Subjects: LCSH: France—Relations—Algeria. | Algeria—
Relations—France. | Algeria—Colonization—History—19th
century. | France—Colonies—Administration—History—19th
century. | Social change—France—History—19th century. |
Nationalism—France—History—19th century. | Politics and
culture—France—History—19th century. | France—Politics and
government—19th century. | France—Intellectual life—19th century.
| BISAC: HISTORY / Europe / France. | HISTORY / Africa / North. |
HISTORY / Modern / 19th Century.
Classification: LCC DC59.8.A4 M87 2017 | DDC
303.48/24406509034—dc23
LC record available at https://lccn.loc.gov/2016029053

Set in Minion by Westchester Publishing Services.

For Morgan,
An antiquarian in his own right.

CONTENTS

ACKNOWLEDGMENTS

In his lengthy *Mémoires d'outre-tombe*, Chateaubriand described returning to Paris in the 1820s and reflecting on the personal significance of
each building and street he encountered in the French capital: a house
where he and his sister had spent their childhood; the Palace of Justice
that recalled his trial; the prefecture of police where he had served a brief
prison sentence. To walk the streets of the city was to revisit an intimate
past and history marked by familiar architectural sites and monuments,
each detail evoking a memory redolent of "the skein" of former days.

In certain ways, this books possesses a similar quality. It was written
over numerous years and in various places along the way. Sections and
chapters evoke specific times, people, and cities that are called to mind
in the act of rereading. In completing this work, I feel obliged to express
my sincere gratitude to those who made it possible.

The first draft of this work was written at the University of Virginia
under the guidance of Lenard Berlanstein, who unfortunately passed
away before its publication. Without his help and insightful commentary,
this book would not have been completed.

I would also like to thank Sophia Rosenfeld at Yale University who
oversaw the initial writing of this work in Charlottesville. Her continued
advice and support since I left Virginia has been deeply appreciated.

In addition, I am grateful to Benjamin Martin, whose early involve-
ment on this book while at Louisiana State University in Baton Rouge
has never been forgotten. Above all, he imparted to me the lesson that
good historians must also be good writers.

I am also grateful to John Powers and the History Department of Virginia Commonwealth University in Richmond. Later chapters of this book were revised in the office provided for me while I was teaching at the university. The deep sense of the past that Richmond evokes in its streets and public monuments furnished an appropriate milieu for the writing of history. I am equally indebted to Johannes Paulmann and Irene Dingel at the Leibniz Institut für Europäische Geschichte (IEG) in Mainz. I can still recall evenings sitting at my desk and listening to the toll of the cathedral bells from the square as I worked on the pages of this manuscript. The IEG's generous support during my nine-month stay in Germany provided a pleasant and stimulating atmosphere for the contemplation of the past while finishing this work. I would also like to express my thanks to Kevin Passmore and the History Department at Cardiff University where this book was completed. The department's deep sense of collegiality has been much appreciated since my arrival in the United Kingdom.

The extended time I spent in France while conducting research for this book was invaluable and it would not have been possible without the support offered to me by the École Normale Supérieure in Paris and the University of Virginia.

I would also like to thank my family for their persistent support over the course of my education and career. Writing this book would certainly not have been possible without them.

Lastly, I would like to thank Lara for all her support and assistance. Her discerning comments and attention to detail have played an essential part in the completion of this book. Moreover, her fascination with the past and nostalgia for days that are not our own remain, as always, a continuous source of inspiration.

THE CULT OF THE MODERN

Introduction

The Cult of the Modern in the Nineteenth Century

Residing in the French capital briefly during the early nineteenth century, the German writer Friedrich von Schlegel found Paris obsessed with what he described as "the fantastic caprice of ever-varying fashion." More than simply a critique on the lifestyles and tastes of Parisian society under Napoleon I, Schlegel's remark was a judgment on the French Revolution itself. The social and political transformations wrought by France's revolutionary experience in the late eighteenth century had, he believed, brought about a corresponding change in the sentiments and perspective of the country, commencing a period in which interests, just as much as politics, were subject to "the hasty revolutions of the fleeting day."[1] In Schlegel's estimation, the French suffered from an acute cultural amnesia as contemporary and momentary trends now took precedence over the historical and permanent, and this denouement was, he contended, a direct result of the political turmoil and upset that had radically transformed conventional understandings of time and society in the wake of the Revolution.

Although Schlegel's insights may have possessed a detached and analytical quality common to a foreigner's encounter with a society different from his own, such interpretations were certainly not lost on French observers. Over a half century after Schlegel's Parisian sojourn, the critic and philosopher Hippolyte Taine readily agreed with the observations made by the German intellectual. The French public interminably clamored for the "new, salient, and unexpected," he complained, while treating the past with disregard and boredom.[2] What was true of fashion was equally true of politics, in Taine's opinion. "We demolished the past," he claimed while speculating on the effect of the French Revolution, "and all had to be done over again."³ Severed from their roots, the French could only appreciate the transitory and contingent, seeing behind them a past of ruin and destruction with little consequence for the here and now. "In France, we are neither reformers nor *réformés*," the Saint-Simonian mystic Prosper Enfantin conceded in 1840. "We love new habits and have no desire for patching up old holes."⁴

Desire for novelty (*nouveauté*) encouraged a certain distaste for the old and passé, and this sentiment was as true of fashion as it was of physical places. Building projects during the middle of the century in French cities proceeded with little concern for the historic and familiar. Feeling nostalgic on a clement afternoon in the autumn of 1864, the journalist Victor Fournel decided to walk across Paris and revisit a small house that he had frequented on occasion in the past. "I wanted only to stroll by on the pavement slowly," he claimed, "raise my eyes to the third floor and look at the place." Arriving at the location, the journalist was appalled to find that where the building had once stood was now a vacant lot covered with a fresh layer of smoldering tar. "Even the street had disappeared," Fournel remarked in near disbelief as he surveyed the area.⁵ The experience of the writer and renowned gastronome Charles Monselet was hardly different. The Paris that he had come to know and love was quickly vanishing in the midst of state efforts to beautify and modernize the city: "day by day, the streets are disappearing, the buildings known for their history [*ancienneté*] and the memories associated with them are being demolished."⁶ The modern was, in Monselet's conjecture, a beast devouring history and memory that would, in time, efface all that had come before it.

Detached from the past, life, opinions, and perspectives in France became preoccupied with the "ephemeral, fugitive, [and] contingent"— elements that the critic Charles Baudelaire intimately associated with the advent of *la modernité*.⁷ Homilies to the modern and professions of faith in the "modern spirit" resonated among an entire generation and found expression in a variety of cultural, social, and political projects.

By midcentury, French outlooks revealed an infatuation with a cult of the modern, a trend first announced in the frenzied days of the French Revolution when politicians set out to break irrevocably with the past and create a radically new type of society with no historical precedent. In his *Dictionnaire de la langue française* published in the 1870s, the positivist philosopher and lexicographer Émile Littré listed the word *modernité* as a neologism dating from the late 1860s first coined by the literary critic Théophile Gautier.[8] In actuality, Gautier had employed the term at various times over the previous decade in his reviews, applauding works that were "of [their] time" and, by consequence, pregnant with elements of "modernité."[9] Yet Littré was, nonetheless, correct in accenting the word's neologic quality, identifying it as a distinct product of a culture and period captivated by all things new and modern. "Modernity immediately seduces us with its intrinsic charms deriving from a secret conformity with our tastes," admitted the literary critic René Doumic at the turn of the twentieth century.[10] For Doumic, a writer who came of age in an intellectual milieu where modernity not only symbolized an idea but a complete way of life and thinking, the appeal of *la modernité* was a given.

The extraordinary change and potential that nineteenth-century intellectuals and critics saw in their age have possessed an enduring legacy, one broadly understood as Western modernity. This phenomenon announced a "distinct and discontinuous" era in human history, a way of living and organizing society that was radically different from its antecedents.[11] It encapsulated the idea of a world torn asunder from its roots, "cut off from the past and continually hurtling forward at such a dizzy pace," as the poet Octavio Paz once remarked.[12] More than a century after men like Schlegel and Littré surmised on the meaning and import of modernity's implications for their own time, theorists and historians continued to adhere to basic assumptions that the changes experienced by Western societies between the eighteenth and twentieth centuries marked a fundamentally unique mode of thought and existence unlike any other. This modernizing drive provided the template for a vision of global order rooted in capitalist models of exchange, industrialized production, distinct cultural practices and forms of sociability that acquired a powerful "singularity" across time and space.[13] To invoke the modern was to invoke universal certainty, a monolith shaped by a particular idea of society read in terms of its dynamic and innovative possibilities.

Yet what we have considered modern is the product of a specific cultural logic that has prized and valorized this exact quality. It was nominally "modern" societies that first articulated the very concept, seeing in it a reflection of their own power, prestige, and eminence.[14] Rather than a condition, modernity has constituted a particular way of describing and talking about the world that is, in its very nature, self-referential. As John Camaroff has pointedly argued, "in itself, 'modernity' has no a priori telos or content." It is not an analytical category, but an ideological formation constructed and reproduced to revere certain practices and values while denigrating others.[15] Once modernity is stripped of its essentializing qualities, all that remains are the varying discourses, ideological forms, and cultural representations that give substance to this construction. The presupposed modern monolith vanishes, "melting into air," as Marx would have it. Until relatively recently, modernity was tied to an idiom of newness prized by cultural and social elites in the Western world.[16] In this respect, it has underwritten and sustained a particular type of discursive power capable of representing socially particular behavioral norms and values in universal and humanitarian contexts while furnishing a rationale for their forcible imposition on others.

This book is concerned with the creation and possession of modern time as it has been known to the West. It takes for its subject France, a society that has stood at the forefront of the mythmaking and imagining that gave birth to a putatively "modern" vision of the self and the world at large. The French Revolution witnessed the first truly modernizing agenda in world history as its authors attempted to establish and disseminate a radical program of reform committed to overthrowing all existing values.[17] Time was "turning a new page of history," as the republican Charles-Gilbert Romme confidently informed his contemporaries before the National Convention in 1793.[18] The revolutionary experience gave birth to a cultural discourse that would evolve over the coming years as movements and ideas increasingly validated themselves through claims to a modern inheritance. Democratic protests, colonial projects, and even aesthetic *modernisme* all bore marks of the modernist mentality that grew up over the following century. If France continues to symbolize an avatar of the modern, this verdict is largely the product of the ways in which the French have conceptualized themselves and their society.

The cult of the modern, therefore, proposes an analysis of nineteenth-century French politics and culture that attempts to take modernity on its own terms. Nineteenth-century France has traditionally epitomized the epicenter of the modern, whether in light of the nation's revolutionary inheritance or the various social and cultural developments that grew out of the period. It was the age of political and industrial revolutions, of large-scale urbanization programs, and the modernism of luminaries such as Baudelaire and Manet. Taken together, these details have contributed to a history of modernity that has ranged from assessments of artistic production and new modes of cultural experience to the roots of a "social modernity" associated with distinct forms of knowledge and administration appropriate to the rational organization of society.[19] Typically, the question of modernity has been one of origins. Numerous studies on nineteenth-century France have concerned themselves with pinning down the moment when modernity occurred or tracing its specific contours. Relatively less consideration has been given to questions of why the idea of modernity became so alluring to a widening French elite during this time or how this concept was iterated and reiterated within particular ideological frameworks and discourses.[20] Rather than seeking a genealogy of modernity, therefore, what is needed is a more informed understanding of the ways in which this concept has historically been imagined, reified, and deployed.

This analysis is especially instructive within the context of French politics and political life. From the French Revolution onward, the narrative of modern France has predominantly been communicated through a strong republican tradition linked to the country's revolutionary and republican nationhood. The battles between republic and monarchy that colored the postrevolutionary period have conventionally signified a "matrix" of the modern, a liminal period marked by incremental social, political, and economic transformations that came to realization during the early years of the Third Republic founded in 1870.[21] This notion of a postrevolutionary crossroads has underpinned a historical narrative equating the advent of the liberal and democratic republic with the definitive fulfillment of the nation's revolutionary and modern inheritance. Needless to say, this tradition of French history writing was shaped and influenced largely by successive generations of republican intellectuals who were ideologically inclined to see the republican state as the fulfillment of the modern telos. The fact that "modern" France continues to imply a republican France reveals more about the place and importance of modernity in French political culture and ideology than it does about the actual policies and practices that forged the French nation.

In light of this appraisal, a more nuanced understanding of modernity's performative function is required. During the nineteenth century, the subject of modernity was a leitmotif of French politics. Speaking in the name of the modern constituted a form of political action that was capable of legitimating a wide array of policies and platforms across ideological lines. The increasing importance French politicians and intellectuals placed on this concept corresponded to advances in democratization and imperial expansion, both of which exerted a crucial influence on political discourse and administrative practices in the country. Confronting the various challenges posed by popular suffrage and colonial integration necessitated organizing and structuring new forms of control and legitimacy accommodating a democratic and imperial society. In the cultural and political vocabulary of nineteenth-century elites, modernity became the dominant idiom for this process, furnishing the means for imagining and discursively representing a world that, although described in exceedingly universal and utilitarian terms, remained, nonetheless, consistent with elite values and aspirations.

While radicals during the French Revolution articulated their revolutionary program through a similar language, concepts like "modern society" and "modern civilization" acquired new contextual meanings and significance in the postrevolutionary period. Chronic domestic instability coupled with French expansion into North Africa after 1830 invested modernizing discourses with a distinct urgency and purpose as elites sought to reorder a fractured society. In many ways, Louis Napoleon Bonaparte and his Bonapartist entourage that came to power in 1852 set the tenor for this new style of French politics. Bonapartism exhibited an impressive ability to conjure the modern through bold speeches and spectacles. It dramatically wed modernity to a platform of national renewal and rehabilitation that proved effective at sustaining authoritarian government in an age of mass democracy. At midcentury, the revived Napoleonic Empire translated an infatuation with the modern into a dynamic political discourse and symbolism that contenders on both the left and the right found hard to discount. In the ensuing years, republicans and other political opponents were ultimately compelled to tailor their own ideological perspectives to the modernizing creed announced by the Bonapartist state and adhere to the cult of the modern.

This premise draws on recent reappraisals of the decade of conservative reaction following the revolutions that swept across Europe in 1848. The 1850s saw a new constellation of political alignments which prompted authoritarian regimes to endorse modernizing administrative and fiscal policies that inadvertently contributed to a resurgence of nationalist and democratic movements in the years ahead.[22] French historians now agree that the Second Empire marked a pivotal moment in which the roots of modern French democracy and political culture emerged.[23] However, changes in political practice were influenced and often shaped by political vocabularies and language that require further scrutiny. In examining how the politics of modernity influenced the period, this book deviates from earlier accounts concerned with the origins of social modernity in France. It suggests that rather than a determinant of social and political change, modernity was constitutive of the social relations and political projects that assumed shape over the course of the nineteenth century.

If an appreciation of modernity's imaginative properties holds the prospect of repositioning the Second Empire within the narrative of modern France, it also proposes a rewriting of this narrative across space as well. The Third Republic has enjoyed a status not only as the progenitor of the modern French polity but also as the chief architect of the modern French empire. The "civilizing mission" espoused by republican ideologues in the 1880s and the consequent acquisition of colonies across Africa, the Middle East, and Asia over the course of the following half century has constituted the necessary backdrop against which a mass colonial consciousness emerged in France. The result marked a significant transition from a nation that merely possessed colonies to a colonial republic that thought of and conceptualized itself in exceedingly imperial terms.[24] The French civilizing mission, an ideological program aimed at replicating modern European society overseas, traditionally provided a measure of continuity between France's own path to modernity and the subsequent modernization of non-Western societies. As a completed process in Europe, modern civilization was disseminated outward, reproducing the social and political forms of modernity throughout the colonial world, often in a violent fashion.[25] This narrative not only perpetuated one of the primary myths of the West's own modern origins and identity; it also distorted the fact that the colonial domain acted as a laboratory for many of the social and political projects that would be exported back and applied to European states under the guise of modernizing reforms.[26]

Considerations of the parallel nature of empire and European nation building have broadened our understanding of these processes in relation to one another. It is now recognized that external colonization abetted the production of domestic administrative techniques and types of knowledge within European societies.[27] Popular culture as well possessed an imminently imperial dimension that served to bridge the conceptual distance between metropoles and their peripheries. Propaganda, advertising, literature, and entertainment all contributed to the reproduction of imperial ideologies within the public and private lives of citizens.[28] The prevalence of empire in nineteenth-century culture and society suggests that imperialism was more than just a question of political action and policymaking. It transmitted notions of national identity, structured basic understandings of spatial and social difference, and gave expression to European ideals regarding the capability for human perfection and the generative role of the state in achieving them.[29] These inclinations were especially strong in France where a republican ideology prizing national unity and universal values lent itself to a particular style of imperial rule and empire building. Bolstering a polity vested in assimilationist principles and national association, France constituted an imperial nation-state as opposed to merely an imperial nation.[30]

The period between 1830 and 1870 has received comparatively limited attention in the making of this imperial polity. The result has been an acute underappreciation of the influence that postrevolutionary regimes exercised on either imperial policymaking or the core tenets that would underpin French colonial rule over the next century.[31] Throughout much of the nineteenth century, France was governed by liberal and authoritarian regimes that did not always conform to republican models of cultural and legal assimilation. These regimes, nonetheless, laid much of the foundation for future colonizing efforts, whether through creating intermediary administrative bodies that engaged different ethnic and religious groups or proposing strategies of cooperation with indigenous community leaders.[32] Although this brand of French "cosmopolitanism" deviated from republican precepts of universal rights and indivisible sovereignty, many of these structures continued to furnish a basis for colonial and domestic policies well into the twentieth century.[33] A closer examination of French nation- and empire building in the years prior to the Third Republic holds the prospect of expanding our understanding of France's often contradictory imperial polity and the concepts of nationality and citizenship that it influenced.

Much work has been done on the French Atlantic in critiquing revolutionary constructs of citizenship, democracy, and human rights in the eighteenth and nineteenth centuries.[34] Studies highlighting the particularities of the colonial Atlantic have revealed just how portable and flexible ideological principles and conceptions of national identity could be when applied within imperial contexts. For most of the nineteenth century, however, the Atlantic empire built upon slave labor and colonial plantocracies stood juxtaposed against a new vision of empire inspired by the Mediterranean, and social critics and policymakers of the day did not fail to draw stark contrasts between the two. The proximity of the Mediterranean region to continental Europe lent itself to greater metropolitan oversight and intervention than the distal Atlantic colonies. For this reason, North Africa played a key role in reshaping the imperial formations and practices of earlier regimes, redefining ideas of national boundaries, identity, and governance in the process as postrevolutionary thinkers responded to changes wrought by revolution and industrialization at home. By the early nineteenth century, the Mediterranean was already functioning as a laboratory for the administrative and modernizing policies of the First Napoleonic Empire.[35] France's entrance into the Ottoman Maghreb in 1830 and the subsequent creation of an Algerian settler colony only reinforced these tendencies as France established a permanent presence in the region that nurtured strong social and emotional ties to Europe. After 1830, metropolitan politics were increasingly projected onto Algeria in quite dramatic ways, resulting in the intertwining of imperial and domestic politics that influenced ideas of political leadership, militarism, republican virtue, and citizenship.[36]

This evolving interaction between imperial and national political culture provided the basis for *la France transméditerranéenne*, an abstraction upon which French values of universal liberty and national identity would be repeatedly projected and reified for national audiences over the course of the century.[37] Two years after the launching of the North African military expedition, imperial ideologues were already outlining an ambitious plan of conquest and national assimilation for the nascent Algerian colony. As Victor-Armand Hain, founding member of the Société Colonial de l'État d'Alger, wrote in 1832:

The time is not far off for us to believe that the [Barbary] Regency, governed by the same laws as the metropole, divided into departments will form a *France transméditerranéenne*. . . . Such an outcome will be worthy of a great nation, and our children will feel pride when, taking their first lessons in geography, they will be quizzed by the professor on the borders of their birth country and respond, while tracing their finger across the map: "France is bordered on the north by the Channel and the Pas-de-Calais and on the south by the great Sahara Desert."[38]

While Hain may hardly be considered a visionary or master architect of French colonial policy, his procolonial pamphleteering was indicative of a particular national-imperial mindset informed by a new sense of national mission and community stimulated during the years of the French Revolution. Although histories of French colonialism have traditionally made categorical and qualitative distinctions between a First French Empire centered on the Atlantic and the rise of the Third Republic's Afro-Asian Empire a century later, the interval between these two imperial polities suggests a more nuanced pattern of development than previously imagined.[39]

La France transméditerranéenne constituted a key ideological formation in a vision of empire that matured over the postrevolutionary period, an interim that David Todd has aptly labeled a "French imperial meridian."[40] The ambiguous status of Algeria vis-à-vis France prior to 1870, its proximity to the European mainland and its sizable settler and Muslim populations made Algeria at once a unique colonial territory and a model colony of France's revived empire. This contradiction was one of many framing the so-called Algerian question, which extended from questions of political integration and cultural assimilation to the limits of acceptance in the French nation itself. As a point of convergence for both national and colonial discourses, Algeria offers valuable insights into questions regarding how nineteenth-century individuals reflexively understood concepts of nationality, modernity, and the relationship between the French metropole and its colonial periphery. At once fashioned in the image of France *and* serving as an object against which French identity was constructed and projected, Algeria reflected the mythologies and tensions inherent within the idea of France itself to a greater extent than other French colonial domains.[41]

The years of the Second Empire marked an important moment in the making of this Franco-Algerian imaginary. Imperial efforts to consolidate authority and unite the country during the 1850s and 1860s paralleled attempts to establish French rule in North Africa. From the beginning, state modernization policies exhibited a trans-Mediterranean orientation that, in their most aggressive phase, translated into a Bonapartist civilizing mission straddling the Mediterranean. French "modernization" and North African "colonization" were, in this respect, interconnected processes, and this denouement permitted political and cultural elites to imagine the contours of a modern French nation and society in diverse and often expansive ways. Studies detailing the administrative arrangements and fluctuations of Second Empire colonial policies tend to lose sight of these wider parameters that framed Bonapartist politics and policies. A more critical examination of the modernizing acts undertaken by the imperial government provides a better understanding of the interwoven trajectories that guided Franco-Algerian social and political development at midcentury. Moreover, because colonialism offered an important channel for the articulation and realization of modernizing projects, Algeria figured prominently in the battles waged over modernity that played out during the period. Algerian modernization was championed by the Bonapartists just as much as their rivals; it served to justify the claims of metropolitans and spur colonists into action. As powerful symbols of the modernity coveted by French elites, colonization and the civilizing mission became fixtures of national political life. The politics of modernity helped establish and legitimate the framework for a trans-Mediterranean community that, by the end of the Second Empire, had acquired both republican and colonial features.

In focusing attention on these trans-Mediterranean currents, this book argues that during the years of the Second Empire modernity remained an imaginary construction that carried a variety of meanings and associations. The gradual pace of French economic growth matched with the persistence of traditional forms of labor and social relationships throughout the first half of the nineteenth century entailed that French modernization proceeded along a different path than that of Great Britain and the United States. The absence of the industrial "takeoff" familiar to Anglo-American modernization narratives permitted different groups to interpret the nature and scope of French modernity through divergent ideological perspectives.[42] Although Napoleon III promoted his modernizing program in an effort to unify a divided country, more often than not modernity proved a divisive subject. Radical and socialist opponents exploited the Second Empire's authoritarian policies and close ties with the clergy to fashion a revolutionary program of action promising an alternative vision of society organized around scientific and secular principles. Bonapartist modernity similarly came under fire from liberals and republicans who criticized the government only to tout their own platform of political and educational reform as the true cause of a new and "modern" France. Algerian settlers likewise employed the language of modernity to buttress claims of national inclusion and their vision of a French Algeria. The opposition that grew up under the imperial regime revealed the extent to which Bonapartist political discourse reoriented national politics, transforming an obsession with the modern into a common ideological currency.

In the fissures and commonalities it engendered, modernity remained tied to large issues of inclusion, identity, and power, eliciting questions of who had the authority to speak in the name of the modern and what attributes affirmed one's inclusion in a community with other nominally "modern" individuals. In its broadest sense, identity persuades people and groups that they are in some way identical, thereby establishing a conception of community and basis for collective action. This process is, by necessity, characterized by acts of confrontation and antagonism as subjects define and categorize themselves against putative outsiders.[43] Yet it equally fosters a sense of collectivity vested in "a powerfully imagined and strongly felt commonality."[44] Modernity contained—and continues to retain—these dual "grammars of identity" that simultaneously constructed social and cultural boundaries while effacing them through the promotion of a worldview and system of values deemed common to all.[45] It is this aspect of commonality that shaped an understanding of modernity as a multilayered, decentered, and spatially extended community connecting individuals across multiple points and frontiers.[46] In the democratic ambience of the postrevolutionary period, this sense of connection operated within political, national, and imperial discourses, offering a framework for the articulation of solidarity and alterity consistent with egalitarian and universal values. It was also this common sense of connection around which visions of a French people and nation united across vast swaths of space by a shared time, culture, and singularity would crystallize.

Placing the period of the Second Empire in a truly imperial context and assessing how conceptions of the modern defined French politics and political culture augers a rethinking of the general narrative that has underpinned France's path to modernity. As an early case study in the politics of modernity, the Second Empire stands as the backdrop against which the contours of modern France can be critiqued and accurately appraised. The confluence of colonial and metropolitan politics at mid-century came to be expressed in a new vision of a republican nation, one construed through democratic principles but that nonetheless rationalized forms of elite power and ethnic hegemony. Modernity became, in this context, encoded with forms of social and ideological domination that would structure French society well into the next century and give rise to the practices and discursive representations essential to the mythmaking and valorization of the French republican state.

1 Imagining the Modern Community

In 1867, Raimond de Miravals arrived in Paris from the Var, a Provençal department nestled in the extreme southeast corner of the country. A journalist by trade, Miravals was serving as a correspondent for *L'Echo du Var*, a local newspaper that had assigned him to report on the Exposition Universelle being staged in the capital that year. Like so many others who attended the exposition, Miravals expressed admiration for the industrial and scientific exhibitions flanking the Champ du Mars and rhapsodized on the "new era of civilization and progress" opening for humanity. The exposition inspired an appreciation for the inventive spirit of the modern era, in his opinion, demonstrating the triumphs made by industry and scientific advancement in the nineteenth century. "Man is never satisfied," he wrote. "The thirst for the unknown, the passion for travel, the rage for discoveries which each day breed uncertainties and invite new problems: I succumb to this constant inclination which is especially the inclination of the current century."[1]

Public reception of the exposition had been a chief consideration of the planning committee formed to organize the event. According to Victor Duruy, a leading committee member, the exposition was intended to bolster awareness of French industry and science and reveal to the world that "the innumerable riches of industry come out of the chemists' laboratory and the cabinet of physicians and naturalists like a river flowing from its source."[2] Educated individuals hardly needed to be informed of this fact, however, because science, industry, and manufacturing had already come to comprise a new trinity of progress in their minds, conjuring up images of a world rife with promise and unimaginable potential. "It is not an exaggeration to say that science contains humanity's future," claimed the theologian Ernest Renan, "that it alone can speak the words of destiny to him and reveal the way in which to reach his end."[3] Renan's veneration of scientific advancement epitomized the outlooks of many French intellectuals of the period. "Ask any good Frenchman what he understands by 'progress,'" wrote Charles Baudelaire. "He will answer that it is steam, electricity, and gas—miracles unknown to the Romans—whose discovery bears full witness to our superiority over the ancients."[4]

Pronouncements on "the era of civilization and progress" at hand and its superiority over past models were a veritable mantra of the nineteenth century. They gave credence to the idea of a new world pregnant with innovative and unprecedented possibilities. Yet such expressions of novelty were not simply reflections of a world in transition or an awareness of *la vie moderne* distinct from the past.[5] For all their exuberance and certitude, nineteenth-century critics and savants hardly surrendered themselves to "the inclination of the current century," as Miravals claimed. They actively promoted and publicized it, defending in the process certain value judgments and attitudes embedded within the tangle that was modernity. The fact that intellectuals and elites began to think and speak in terms of "new time" did not imply there existed some transcendental meaning or truth within their judgments or that modernity had simply arrived at a given time.[6] The increasing penchant to interpret the world in qualitatively different terms from the past and identify certain features and sensibilities as inherently "modern" stemmed from broad social and cultural influences that encouraged such perceptions. In an age that celebrated the modern, modernity was as much imagined as it was real. The ways in which this new time was imagined and made manifest are part of the historical experience of the nineteenth century.

Customarily, the birth of modern society has corresponded with the evolution of social and cultural practices readily attributed to classes rising to predominance in the nineteenth century, most notably those deemed "bourgeois." This group, although diffuse and often quite nebulous, has been considered one of the primary actors in the making of modernity. Simply stated, it has been assumed that modernity has its roots in the efforts and activities of middle class groups which, although possessing limited political power under ruling regimes, nonetheless exercised a broad influence on nineteenth-century society.[7] In this respect, *la vie moderne* has perennially amounted to *la vie bourgeoise*. This connection, however, deserves further scrutiny. Although modern society did connote a world defined by certain "bourgeois" interests and aspirations, the coupling of bourgeois life and modernity frequently obscures the more nuanced relationship that existed between social identity and time in the nineteenth-century French imagination, and to conflate the two concepts would be erroneous. As late as the 1840s, Prosper Enfantin could claim that modern society remained vague and ill-defined, and this at a time when "bourgeois" had become a common facet of public and social discourse in France. In Enfantin's estimation, modern society "demanded a new speech" if it was to become a salient and living idea.[8] The development and elaboration of this "new speech" that would convey and discursively possess modern time and society was still in the making at midcentury, and it would not be until the bourgeois social order underwent a crisis that prevailing views of modernity and modern society would become staples of French public and cultural discourse.

This is not to claim that modernity was an empty concept prior to the mid-nineteenth century. The ability of men and women to imagine themselves as subjects situated within modern time was, ultimately, dependent on the capacity to differentiate between past and present and make qualitative distinctions between these concepts. It is generally accepted that the French Revolution and Napoleonic Wars marked a critical moment in the making of this modern consciousness as violent political instability and military conflicts radically transformed European society within the span of a generation. Revolutionaries of the late eighteenth century set out to create a new order based on a division of "old" and "new" time that affirmed the French Revolution as a world-historical event. In rejecting the past and declaring the revolutionary republic a turning point in history, radicals conveyed both the regenerative promise and novelty of their cause. The Revolution was imagined as a rupture with the past that reoriented fundamental outlooks on the nature of time itself.[9] Europeans now saw themselves as modern individuals existing in a world quite unlike the one they had previously known. They were conscious of what Peter Fritszche has called the "melancholy of history" and saw fit to make distinctions between "modern" and "premodern" subjects that had implications for how they understood both themselves and others. The years of revolutionary upheaval not only allowed for the recognition of modern time as such; it allowed for the possibility of divergent times that reinforced the very qualities of the modern individual, creating modern subjects just as much as "strangers" to modernity.[10]

These dichotomies became the basis for social categories elaborated during the century and the power relationships that underpinned them. Distinctions between "then" and "now" were easily fungible with distinctions between "them" and "us," exhibiting a growing mindset evident in academic and scholarly discourse just as much as the general print culture and other media of the period. While the relationship between "bourgeois" and "modern" was not objective or even as clearly defined as has been supposed, groups associated with a nominal bourgeois class—journalists, writers, educators, and civil administrators—did, however, occupy important positions when it came to the capacity for transmitting information and knowledge.[11] They possessed the means of dictating and shaping the representations and logic of what was meant by "modern," a term increasingly associated with a set of ideas and attitudes representative of a "new time" shared with others. If French writers and thinkers were not necessarily using a new vocabulary, they were inscribing a revolutionary concept with new symbols and values specific to the postrevolutionary social environment.

This new speech developed a common language for the expression of particular social and political concerns, entailing that modernity signified more than just the awakening of a historical consciousness or the recognition of discontinuity with the past. Claims to modernity translated into real forms of power and authority in the present, a feature that the French Revolution and subsequent upheavals of the postrevolutionary era made evident. In a period characterized by democratization and imperial expansion, elites confronted demands for equality and greater political participation that threatened their authority. These conflicts cut across metropole and colony, eliciting debates on the nature of citizenship and the relationship between nation and empire. Modernity progressively constituted a response to this crisis as desires for stability encouraged political experimentation and the reconfiguration of elite leadership. By the late 1840s, the various pressures stirred by revolutionary politics and colonialism would converge in a social and political discourse relevant to the needs of a French imperial nation-state.

Bourgeois Order and Its Limits

Writing in the early 1870s, the anarchist poet Arthur Rimbaud lampooned the pretense and smugness of progressive bourgeois society with his sarcastic remark that in France "one must be absolutely modern."[12] This acknowledgment has been a familiar one: to be modern has entailed being bourgeois in some capacity. Yet was the bourgeoisie the historically consistent social group that such an assumption suggests? In France, the bourgeoisie never accommodated the strict social schema proposed by Marxist philosophy. Whereas Marx saw the bourgeoisie as an explicit class brought into existence by industrialization and the accumulation of capital, such socioeconomic interpretations did not necessarily gel with the realities of nineteenth-century French economic and social development.[13] Over the course of the century, French industry progressed at a relatively slower pace in comparison to Great Britain and the United States, and the preservation of more traditional forms of artisanal manufacturing matched with a primarily agricultural economy entailed that a bourgeois class controlling the means of production was largely absent in France.[14] This is not to suggest that the term bourgeois had no relevance. Indeed, the character and origins of the bourgeoisie were widely debated and speculated upon throughout the early nineteenth century.[15] Yet "bourgeois" rarely constituted the class of producers and entrepreneurs that Marx believed to make up the new ruling class in industrial society. Rather, it connoted a mark of social distinction that encompassed a broad array of French property owners, men of affairs, and political elites.[16] "The bourgeoisie is not a social class," the historian Jules Michelet aptly noted in 1846, "but a position within society."[17]

The social pedigree associated with the rubric "bourgeois" was, by and large, a product of the political environment of the mid-nineteenth century. The revolutionary inheritance with its mix of democratic ideals and political violence was a conflicted one in France. The sanscoulotte radicalism of the First Republic had given way to the Reign of Terror, revolutionary plots, and counterinsurgencies. The Napoleonic Empire established in 1804 temporarily managed to impose order on the country through a series of illiberal and martial policies before succumbing to military defeat a decade later. In the aftermath of revolution and empire, both new and established elites harbored strong misgivings over the practicality of democratic government while retaining mistrust for the "tyranny" that personal rule encouraged. Yet if they desired neither Robespierre nor Napoleon, many postrevolutionary elites were equally cool to the restored Bourbon dynasty which, in the words of Charles Maurice de Talleyrand, appeared to have "learned nothing and forgotten nothing" during its years of exile.[18] In July 1830, liberal opponents alarmed by the royal ministry's censorship policies and conservative manipulations rebelled against the government with the intention of establishing a progressive yet durable regime capable of balancing "liberty and order." These so-called Doctrinaires—Anglophilic politicians and journalists committed to constitutionalism and parliamentary government—found their representative in Louis Philippe, an heir to the Orléanist branch of the royal family who professed an attachment to the ideals of the Revolution and constitutional rule. Inviting Louis Philippe to ascend the throne and rule as a "citizen king," the Doctrinaires believed their modest revolution would inaugurate a new era of stability and reform as the so-called July Monarchy assumed power. To this end, new laws were enacted broadening the electorate to roughly a quarter of a million men, and the king exhibited an initial willingness to appease republican and royalist rivals in his public declarations. As the Doctrinaires wagered, only through a policy of moderation and reason would legitimacy be restored to French political institutions and royal authority.

From its inception, the July Monarchy was offered as a tenable solution to the political instability afflicting the nation. Seeking to curb the cycles of revolution and reaction that periodically destabilized French government, the Doctrinaires believed it essential to constrain popular participation and limit political power to a small class of moderate electors and office holders who, by virtue of their wealth, distinction, and education, would stand above the passions of *le peuple* and provide a bulwark against royal absolutism.[19] This middle course empowered an exclusive class of property owners and taxpayers with the vote. Yet legitimating an electoral franchise in which only one adult male in twenty-five was allowed to vote while professing a dedication to revolutionary principles could and did appear contradictory, inviting liberals to explain why certain citizens should enjoy political rights to the exclusion of others. Liberal ideologues consistently warned of the inimical influence that universal suffrage and social leveling posed, recalling the savagery and bloodshed that the Revolution had unleashed. "It is false that all men are equal," François Guizot, one of the foremost Doctrinaire spokesmen, explained. "They are, on the contrary, unequal by nature as by situation, by spirit as by body."[20] Emphasizing the "organic inequality" that existed in nature, liberals argued that not all possessed the necessary intellect and *capacité* to participate in public life. Education, wealth, and social distinction testified to an individual's ability to make judicious political decisions and conceptualize the greater social good outside of personal interest, and these qualities formed the basis of an open aristocracy that politicians and liberal critics associated directly with a new class rising to predominance in France, the bourgeoisie.[21]

In the discourse of classical French liberalism, "bourgeois" demarcated an exclusive social group with political rights derived from wealth. The mandatory poll tax required for voting and holding political office effectively restricted political power to a small minority of the population, with references to the bourgeoisie serving to justify the type of elite rule prescribed by liberal ideology. "We are the government of the bourgeoisie," the pro-Orléanist journalist and deputy Charles de Rémusat candidly proclaimed in 1834. "Without doubt, the revolution of 1830 has elevated the middle classes to a civil church [and] their true social rank."[22] Such pronouncements gave substance to claims of bourgeois primacy and power, defining a new aristocracy of probity and talent naturally suited for political leadership. "The bourgeoisie occupy the front of the stage in France," one critic bluntly put it in 1837, "just as democracy does in the United States."[23] Much as Sarah Maza has indicated, the French bourgeoisie was the product of a particular style of political discourse and language employed by July Monarchy liberals, one that constructed an image of the moderate and rational "bourgeois" individual to justify exclusive claims to power and authority.[24]

These claims to power, moreover, transcended social considerations in the nation proper. As a political philosophy, liberalism proved able to accommodate and adapt to existing social conditions in the greater French world where the principles of 1789 had been ambiguous at best. In the Atlantic colonies, slavery remained a linchpin of the Caribbean plantation economy. From the beginning of the French Revolution, the issue of slavery had been a prickly one, revealing inherent tensions between Enlightenment notions of natural rights and liberal perspectives on the sanctity of property enunciated in the *Declaration of the Rights of Man and Citizen*. In 1794, the revolutionary Jacobin regime issued an emancipation decree enfranchising the numerous slaves and *hommes de couleur* of the Atlantic colonies only to have Napoleon restore slavery once again in 1802. July Monarchy liberals were not averse to granting civil and political liberties to the property-owning free blacks and *hommes de couleur* of the islands, in essence extending the metropolitan *régime capacitaire* into the colonial domain. The gradual emancipation of slaves was not inconceivable either. The question, however, was how to implement such reforms without incurring the defiance of colonial slave holders and Creole elites fearful of any change to the racial hierarchies that structured colonial society?[25]

Although never attaining the widespread support found in Great Britain, the abolitionist movement had been gaining momentum in France since the late eighteenth century among liberal and social reformers. The slave revolts and violent racial struggles that had erupted during the Haitian Revolution persisted influencing French views on the slavery issue, which encompassed a range of opinions on specific economic and moral issues. Nonetheless, a general consensus was emerging that it was only a matter of time before the practice of slavery was officially ended.[26] Atlantic colonists (*colons*) routinely responded to abolitionist criticisms with warnings of the economic ruin and violent racial war that emancipation would unleash. For its part, the Orléanist government favored prolonging any decisive action for as long as possible so as not to roil the already strained relations between the Atlantic colonies and Paris.[27] Events like the slave uprising that broke out on Martinique in early February 1831 did nothing to alleviate anxieties and even appeared to validate planters' alarming predictions.[28] Serious consideration of additional colonial reforms or possible emancipation consequently languished in government circles, giving the colonial plantocracy a new lease on life. As notions of social inequality were synthesized with racial considerations and white rule across the Atlantic, the limitations characterizing the "bourgeois" revolution of 1830 became increasingly manifest.

If July Monarchy liberals accepted a world based on natural inequality and the social and racial divisions that codified it, they were equally becoming comfortable with the political forms of power that could rationalize such a system. During the First Empire and Restoration period, liberals had been leading opponents of imperialism, decrying it as the ultimate expression of tyranny and a deleterious influence on the mores of a free people. These views had been well-crafted criticisms of Napoleon and the authoritarian warmongering of the Napoleonic

Empire. By the 1840s, however, apprehensions over France's national standing and the acceptance of certain political realities had inspired a change of opinion, signaling the emergence of an "imperial liberalism" that encouraged support for empire and renewed colonial expansion.[29] Liberals began to accept imperial values, seeing them as a source of national regeneration and even an expression of the very revolutionary principles they were reluctant to deliver in practice. Imperial expansion, while often a violent enterprise, was increasingly celebrated for its commitment to promoting commerce and uniting diverse groups of peoples across vast tracts of space. As the French educator, writer, and Saint Simonian, Émile Barrault, asked in 1835, "Can the formation of an empire not be applauded where numerous regions and diverse races will be unified?"[30]

Barrault was not, however, reflecting on Martinique or the Atlantic world when he posed his question. For him, it was Africa and France's recent invasion of Algeria for which this question was of critical importance. In early 1830, France declared war on the Dey of Algiers following a series of escalating diplomatic disputes. Within a matter of weeks, Hussein ben Hassan's regency government had collapsed and a French military occupation was under way. The July Monarchy inherited the Algerian war, but it was quick to turn the African campaign to its advantage. Military victories and conquest furnished the new regime with a much needed source of patriotism.[31] With near Napoleonic fervor, King Louis Philippe spoke of spreading French "civilization" across North Africa and resolutely tied the government to this mission when on 22 July 1834 he impulsively annexed swaths of North African territory to the French nation rendering Algeria "a land forever French."[32] Political supporters, whether motivated by nationalist sentiments or fears of what abandoning Algeria might hold for French prestige, defended the turn to empire with similarly bombastic declarations. "Our right [to Africa] derives from the fact that we have a more advanced, peaceable, and humane civilization," insisted the deputy and journalist Prosper Duvergier de Hauranne in 1838. "If we recognize this right, we have no need for any other."[33]

The rhetoric coming from the Tuileries Palace and Chambers was indicative of a broader shift in public opinion on the subject of imperialism. The acquisition of the North African territories foreshadowed a new era of imperialism for France, one that necessarily invited a rethinking of standard colonial practices. Critics and journalists spoke freely of "modern colonization," insisting that imperialism could be harmonized with the enlightened and humanitarian ideals of the French Revolution. If the colonies in the French Antilles and New World relied on mercantilist business practices and plantation slave labor, the newly acquired territories in Africa offered a golden opportunity to set out on a new course. The idea that a colony constituted "a simple instrument of the metropole" was obsolete, the journalist Eugène Lerminier argued. France's new North African colony ought to stand as a symbol of "the new spirit" of the nineteenth century.[34] Slavery, a cruel and immoral institution, could no longer be justified, while mercantilism ran counter to the benefits of free trade. The demands of political and commercial liberty required, therefore, a new method and rationale for imperialism.[35] Rather than marginal possessions exploited by the metropole, colonies would be liberated and developed as France brought the benefits of civilization to the peripheries of its empire and the debased indigenous populations who inhabited it. "Let's not forget," Enfantin remarked when discussing France's new colonial mission, "that in our century, the legitimacy of our conquest, or at least our occupation of Algeria, can only be supported if we are the vigorous agents of African civilization."[36]

Being agents of civilization, however, by no means entailed acting civilly. The sudden collapse of the Algiers government plunged the region into a state of virtual anarchy, inciting fierce ethnic and territorial conflicts that French forces sought to contain.[37] The decision to transform Algeria into a settler colony and the introduction of European colonists—already some thirty-seven thousand by the early 1840s—into "pacified" areas along the coastal region only aggravated the situation. Fighting the French, native combatants employed calls to jihad and apocalyptic prophecy to mobilize Muslim resistance and obtain support from local notables and Sufi networks stretching across the Maghreb. As conflict escalated, the battle for Algeria was transformed into a clash of civilizations. In 1838, Colonel Jean Baptiste Bory-de-Saint-Vincent apprised the government on the deteriorating situation in his proposal for a state-sponsored scientific exploration, claiming, "The natives, of whatever race or religious belief, hold a strong hatred for the Europeans . . . [and] contempt for our civilization."[38] Members of the exploratory team experienced this hostility firsthand when they arrived in Algeria two years later. Prosper Enfantin, who was selected to accompany the team, watched in horror as a platoon of Arab combatants ambushed French forces outside Constantine. "I saw severed heads or bodies without heads," he wrote to a friend. "I saw the wounded, heard the cannons and the whizzing of bullets. . . . It sufficed to make me reconsider my love for this world and forget my dreams of changing it."[39] French reprisals were doubly brutal, with some 825,000 Algerian lives lost in combat and collateral casualties during the first Algerian War.[40]

As readers followed these military exploits and pitched battles in the newspapers, some observers felt obliged to point out that it was not only in Africa that civilization was at stake. In fact, threats to civilization could be found in the metropole among the swarms of rowdy laborers and conspirators bent on social revolution. The exclusionary practices and elitism of July Monarchy liberalism had done little to win over workers and republican sympathizers, groups symbolic of the unruly masses that the Doctrinaires firmly intended to bar from political power. Within its first year, the government demonstrated a heavy-handed approach in confronting its opponents by suppressing labor protests and driving republican movements underground. Despite these efforts, the reemergence of republican radicalism and angry workers protesting in the streets did not sit well with moderates who could recall the days of the Terror and Jacobin dictatorship. Writing in the midst of an ill-fated Lyonnais worker uprising in 1831, the journalist Saint-Marc Girardin spelled out the grave danger menacing the country, informing his readers bluntly, "The barbarians who threaten society are not in the Caucasus or the steppes of Tartary; they are in the suburbs of our manufacturing

cities."[41] Hannibal was at the gates, in Girardin's opinion, and civilization itself hung in the balance.

Over the coming decade such pronouncements readily found their way
into journals and social-scientific studies, corroborating and exaggerating
the threat posed by a poor and degenerate working class "whose lack
of education and precarious lifestyle place them in a state of dangerous
hostility to society," as the influential daily *Journal des Débats* reported
to its readers in 1832.[42] For postrevolutionary liberals, bourgeois morality and leadership comprised the surest guarantee of stability. It was a
bulwark against the passions of the mob and the necessary prophylactic
restraint on the twin threats of revolutionary terror and tyranny. These
outlooks lent themselves to a natural elitism, but also nurtured disparaging views of those outside the proprietary and moderate *juste milieu*
of bourgeois political society. With the ascendance of a class-based
system of rule came the criminalization of the poor, a view that depicted
the working classes and destitute as disruptive, pathological, and even
"barbarous."[43] With the Armée d'Afrique busy imposing civilization on
a savage African people, it hardly took a stretch of the imagination to
envision an analogous scenario at home where impoverished laborers
and social deviants conspired against the state and dreamed of avenging
themselves on society.

From its origins, the July Monarchy confronted a tenuous situation.
Militant workers and radicals challenged government authority in the cities; insoluble racial cleavages persisted in the Atlantic world while the
North African frontier simmered with ethnic and religious violence.
These challenges stabbed directly at the heart of a "bourgeois" social
order premised on the explicit recognition of inequality and difference.
By the 1840s, the various problems faced by the Orléanist regime were
pointing the way to a different type of French state and society, one
cutting across nation and empire that was difficult to reconcile with
the rhetoric and ideology of postrevolutionary liberalism. While the
concepts and discourses hinting at a new national-imperial outlook were
evident, they remained inchoate as French policymakers and statesmen

grappled with problems of inclusion, pacification, and social cohesion. Ultimately, as Orléanists resorted to suppression and preserving the status quo, sustaining the image of a liberal regime headed by a "citizen king" touted in 1830 became all but impossible. It was telling that Algeria came to figure more prominently in official proclamations and representations of the royal family over the years. The themes of military glory and order these images suggested were certainly more reflective of the government than the spirit of 1789.[44] Yet they were equally indicative of the diminishing gap between France and its colonial domains, a gap that Doctrinaire liberalism proved unable to bridge. "Algeria and the revolution of 1830 are inextricably linked together," Prosper Enfantin reasoned in 1840. "They are Siamese twins attached at the trunk that must either live or die together."[45] In the end, it was the latter that would prove accurate.

From *Capacité* to *Égalité*

In early 1848 the liberal order came under attacked on numerous fronts. The July Monarchy's repeated suppression of labor protests and republican movements during the 1830s and its refusal to sanction further electoral reforms succeeded in generating opposition to the egregious class rule favored by the Doctrinaires. A strong antibourgeois rhetoric grew up during the 1840s on the left that cast the bourgeoisie as a selfish and opportunistic class seeking personal profit at the expense of the people. Demands for political inclusion equally emanated from the various colonial territories where settlers who were denied civil liberties were subject to regimes reluctant to concede the basic rights granted to metropolitans. Calls for social reform and democratization increasingly brought into question the *régime capacitaire* as republican and socialist opposition movements became more vocal over the course of the decade. Poor harvests in the mid-1840s combined with labor discontent and an economic downturn beginning in 1847 only aggravated the situation. By February 1848, necessity and longstanding political frustrations came together in a toxic mix as workers and political opponents took to the streets in protest and Louis Philippe fled into exile.

The overthrow of the unpopular Orléanist regime on 24 February 1848 was greeted with enthusiasm as republicans stridently made known their intention of founding a society committed to equality and the pressing social issues of the day. From the Hôtel de Ville, the republican socialist Louis Blanc enunciated the objectives of the new government to be founded: it would provide jobs for all the destitute workers of France and ameliorate the egregious injuries committed against labor by the July Monarchy; universal manhood suffrage would be declared, inaugurating a new era in which people reaped the fruits of their work and communed with their fellow citizens.[46] As Baudelaire cynically observed, during the revolution "everyone built utopias just like castles in Spain."[47]

Calls for a more equitable society extended, however, deeper than just urban social grievances. Republican abolitionists, although a minority, wished to commit the new republic firmly to the cause of emancipation and racial equality, believing that republican institutions were incompatible with the persistence of chattel slavery still in practice across the French empire. Where the July Monarchy had vacillated on the issue of slavery, the new republic would be unwavering. Republicans had not been immune to the growing acceptance of imperial attitudes and values among French elites during the first half of the nineteenth century. Yet abolitionism was consistent with republican principles of universal citizenship and natural rights. It retained, therefore, an influence among certain republican clubs and circles that believed it essential to put an end to the "hideous ruins" of an old and brutal Europe out of touch with the enlightened and emancipatory currents of the century.[48]

Following the declaration of universal manhood suffrage in 1848, key republican spokesmen believed the moment was ripe for tackling the issue of colonial slavery head on and made known their intention to end all forms of slave labor on French soil. In early March, an emancipation commission headed by the radical abolitionist Victor Schoelcher was assembled, and on 27 April 1848, to the horror of colonial planters, all male slaves were declared citizens with equal legal and political rights. The decree immediately generated ripples in the Antilles and greater

Atlantic world. Within months of the ruling, *hommes de couleur* previously excluded from political life due to their African ancestry mounted heated electoral campaigns for seats in the National Assembly and local councils. In Martinique, attempts to delay the ruling provoked demonstrations as twenty thousand enslaved workers flooded the streets of Saint Pierre demanding the liberty promised to them by the republic.[49]

Cries for colonial reform also echoed closer to home that spring as French settlers in Algeria endeavored to capitalize on the revolutionary fervor and press their own demands on the metropolitan government. French expansion into North Africa had proceeded in an ad hoc fashion since 1830 with the military primarily supervising both security and settlement operations in the region. The status of the territory had increasingly presented a dilemma for policymakers during the 1840s as the settler population grew in number. Colonists never reconciled themselves to military rule, which regulated settlement and impeded civilian participation in Algerian affairs. Metropolitan republicans were among the most vocal critics of the colonial administration throughout the decade, proposing a policy of settler colonialism (*colonisation de peuplement*) as a means of liberalizing the colony's institutions and fulfilling France's "civilizing mission" in Africa. "It is civilian colonization that will realize the rapprochement of vanquished and conquering people," boasted the republican newspaper *Le National* in 1840. "In a word, this is what will lead the moral conquest of Algeria and secure it for France."[50] Such declarations naturally struck a sympathetic chord with settlers across the Mediterranean and encouraged them to believe a republican France would defend *colon* rights and interests.

Upon learning of the events transpiring in Paris, Algerian colonists immediately set to the task of organizing clubs and debating a course of action. According to Jouffroy d'Eschavannes, member of the Société Orientale, Algeria, like France, stood poised to enter "into the domain of revolutionary realities," presaging a greater union between the French metropole and the Mediterranean *outremer*.[51] Convoking an Algerian Commission in Algiers, colonists openly declared their support for the new republican regime, using the occasion to address long-standing grievances they expected the republican government to remedy.[52] Foremost was the issue of military rule that left settlers at the mercy of "the arbitrary actions . . . of a regime of exception," as one petition complained. In supporting the republic, *colons* were affirming their participation in the national revolution and their expectations of equality. The "principal mission" of the Second Republic was to recognize "the union of Algeria and France, its political, administrative, judiciary and legislative assimilation."[53] Proposing immediate assimilation (*rattachement*) with the metropole, colonists and metropolitan lobbyists requested an end to Algerian exceptionalism, insisting, as one *colon* publicist did in a patriotic appeal to his compatriots, "Frenchmen of the mother country and Frenchmen of Algeria, we are the same people!"[54]

In specific terms, assimilation meant not only establishing civilian institutions, but also extending the rights guaranteed to every citizen under the republic to French settlers. It was, colonial publicists urged, imperative to cultivate a "nationality" for the colonists and render Algeria "a *patrie* in place of a foreign land."[55] This process went beyond simple administrative assimilation. "The *patrie* is the soil, the family, the title of citizen, rights, duties and the affections which derive from them," argued Amédée-Hippolyte Brossard in a principled defense of *colon* enfranchisement. "Finally, for a child of France, it is the title of French."[56] Hoping to appeal to the republican sensibilities of the government in Paris, Brossard astutely framed his argument in the universal and isonomic language of republicanism, maintaining that "the title of French" and "the title of citizen" were closely linked if not synonymous. For Brossard and others, Frenchness was a quality obtained by virtue of belonging to a national political community, a conviction that wed colonial aspirations to firm republican principles. The Second Republic could not refuse French settler demands for assimilation and the basic rights of citizenship, the Parisian-based lobby La Société Algérienne noted that summer, "without failing its purpose."[57]

The hopes of colonial patriots were not disappointed. In March, the colony was granted the right to elect four deputies to the National Assembly and participate in national politics. Over the following months, the three Algerian provinces in the Tell region—Algiers, Constantine, and Oran—were recognized as administrative jurisdictions of France and permitted to elect municipal councils.[58] Algerian colonists, much like their metropolitan counterparts, were "taking in hand the most effective instrument, the strongest lever with which the democratic spirit has armed modern people."[59] Proclamations emanating from Paris similarly underscored the shared commitment to republican democracy exhibited by the new Franco-Algerian union. Yet metropolitan declarations went further. Addressing the National Assembly that September, the deputy Jacques Charles Brunet, a bibliographer turned republican politician, claimed that Algerian colonization warranted a special occasion for France. "Do not all great revolutions need at first to establish outside the country a grand monument for the future on which to imprint the seal of its principles and nationality?" Whereas the Jacobins and Napoleon had spread their messianic revolutions across Europe, in 1848 a pacific and less robust France could neither countenance nor afford to march across the continent disseminating its enlightened values. "Our revolution of 1848, whose principles are essentially pacific and productive," Brunet maintained, "can have for its theater only a vast field of colonization on which to apply all the lively forces that ferment in our *patrie*, all the general instincts that have made France the apostle of civilization in the world." Colonization and Algeria in particular would serve as "the monument" of the new revolution. As Brunet's cohort, the deputy Eugène Cordier de Montreuil, avowed, "Algeria is our raison d'être in this world for a people whose virtue has been otherwise extinguished and dead."[60] Algeria occupied a special place in the revolutionary élan and the republic it had founded, republicans contended. The colony was to be a testament to the democratic and nationalist ideals for which the Second Republic stood.

Yet if this new trans-Mediterranean fraternity was the embodiment of republican universalism, it was also suggestive of the colonial elements entering French social and political outlooks. The provisional government established in February set out to deal with the ever-troubling "social question," expressing sympathy for the plight of the French working classes and promising meaningful social reforms. The social legislation passed by the government appeared, however, too radical for elites and too costly to the peasants now making up a majority of the electorate. With dwindling funds, a deepening economic crisis and growing opposition, the provisional government soon found itself walking a precarious line. The closing of national ateliers—workshops set up to provide employment and financial assistance for destitute workers—to mollify public opinion served only to exacerbate the growing tensions between the republican government and working classes. By June, Paris was embroiled in a second revolt, this time divided along the lines of both social class and political ideology. Barricades were thrown up throughout the working-class districts of the capital as Parisian laborers cried out "To Arms!" declaring it was preferable to die on the barricades than to starve from hunger.[61]

As the so-called red days of June unfolded, Paris was thrust into a brutal class war that would leave a death toll of over 1,400 in its wake. Reactions to the event condemned it as a "new invasion of the barbarians," a war of the debased against the civilized and an attempt by the disinherited to "roll back civilization."[62] The participation of the Armée d'Afrique in subduing the June insurrection only heightened these colonial undertones. Generals Juchault de la Moricière and Louis-Eugène Cavaignac—both of whom had acquired notoriety serving in Algeria— were summoned back from North Africa just as the Parisian revolt erupted, and were given full powers to crush the rebellion by any means necessary. For the next six months, Cavaignac, de la Moricière, and other members of the Algerian command were hailed as the "saviors" of the republic and awarded key positions in the government to ensure order. French Algerian journalists could hardly fail to note the evident irony of the situation. As one writer for the Algerian daily *Akhbar* wryly commented, "France has not wanted to assimilate Algeria and now Algeria is on the verge of assimilating France!"[63]

In the following months, the implications of the June Days for Algeria became fully apparent. That fall, the National Assembly commenced debates on the prospect of sending unemployed French workers across the Mediterranean, arguing that "the colonization of Algeria is one of the most effective means at present of coming to alleviate misery [in our country]."[64] The colonial press enthusiastically supported the measure while intellectuals and politicians favorable to colonization in Paris took up the cause in the national press and chambers. Fears regarding demographic growth in the country and the threat idle workers posed to social order offered persuasive rationales for the plan. Legislation authorizing the transport of French workers passed that September, providing for the exportation of some twelve thousand Frenchmen to Algeria over the next three years. Republican policymakers had devised a politically expedient means of supporting colonization and putting an end to the social question in one stroke, ridding the capital of working-class militants in the process.[65]

Although republicans were quick to insist that the revolution of 1848 marked a rupture with the bourgeois order established in 1830, it was difficult to deny that the new republic was building on many of the institutions and policies that had been evolving under the July Monarchy. Calls for democratic reform and imperial expansion had produced social and political pressures that the liberal regime was ill-equipped to contain. The result was a revolution that reconceptualized ideas of national belonging just as much as national boundaries. Universal manhood suffrage implied an end to bourgeois privilege and the "organic" inequality endorsed by liberal ideologues, providing the institutional arrangements necessary for a democratic and imperial society. The Second Republic's egalitarian agenda abruptly overturned the social structures that had buttressed a hierarchical, imperial order built on class rule, racial inequality, and notions of natural leadership. It effectively annulled the language of social status and superiority employed by postrevolutionary elites, theoretically marking an end to the world of "bourgeois" favor and exclusivity. "The bourgeoisie is dead," Flaubert wrote while reflecting on the trend toward democracy taking place in the country. "It is now seated there among the populace."[66] Under the republic, égalité suffused French political speech and animated hopes that, following years of social conflict and fragmentation, the country could look forward to a new era of national revival and reunification founded on core principles of democratic equality, universal citizenship, and national unity.

This is hardly to imply that French elites became ardent democrats overnight. In most cases they continued to harbor a deep mistrust of mass democracy and popular participation. Yet the demands of a democratic political culture made defining a class of capable and natural leaders problematic. Whereas the political cartoonist Honoré Daumier had once described the bourgeoisie as "the new royalty," after 1848 social elites were forced to contend with a France that was exceedingly more democratic, diverse, and better-informed due to an expanding print culture.[67] Democratization necessitated a new type of elite distinct from the claims of natural inequality and social privilege familiar to classical liberalism. If elites intended to maintain their influence, they would have to devise a way of representing their interests through a language that could conceal existing social relations and represent politics and society without regard to division.[68] Consolidating a democratic-colonial order required a set of concepts and representations befitting an imperial nation-state. In the wake of the 1848 revolution, the idiom of modernity would enable this new style of speech.

Coevals and Strangers

French elites had a variety of concepts at their disposal when it came to reimaging the social order. Perceptions of change had been germinating in minds for quite some time, resulting in an accumulation of categories and concepts that could be drawn upon and deployed at will. Civilization, progress, class and race, modern time: this vocabulary was the product of changing outlooks and political experiments that had occurred over the course of a century. By the middle of the 1800s, these familiar concepts were being further elaborated upon through advances in scientific knowledge and industry. Europeans possessed the ability not only to think in terms of time and temporality, but to convey these impressions through a range of symbols and authoritative discourses capable of representing and organizing the social world.

In 1859, the magazine *La Vie moderne* invited its readers to reflect on the extent of change to which they currently bore witness, urging in a poem:

Time has doubled its course
Humanity rushes headlong
All the roads have become short
The ocean no longer has any limits at all.

Life was long in the days of old
On the slope it was dragged along
We now live more in one month
Than our ancestors lived in one year.[69]

Such sentiments were by no means confined to small magazines with suggestive titles like *La Vie moderne*. They found expression in a wide array of publications and genres. The poet Victor Hugo extolled the panorama of modernity he saw growing up around him, describing a world "whose arteries are railroads and whose nerves are electric wires."[70] Expressions of wonder could be and often were tempered with more melancholic reflections as well. Gazing upon a landscape of castles and crumbling monasteries, the conservative royalist Pierre-Simon Ballanche mournfully concluded that "these black towers crowned with crenellated stones must fall, these silent, tapering cloisters must be transformed into prisons or vast workshops for manufacturing. Our castles represent the time of knights and the feudal world. It is necessary that they disappear."[71] Flaubert captured the same sense of dislocation in his novels, albeit with more panache and artistic flair. In *A Sentimental Education*, he chose the image of Jesus Christ riding a steam engine through a virgin forest to symbolize these sentiments of rapid change and novelty, conveying the impression of an irrevocable break with standard traditions and perceptions.[72]

Reflections on the past and progress underscored the message that the nineteenth century marked a period of exceptional transformation. Writers spared no amount of ink when it came to detailing the modern landscape coming into sharp relief around them, mixing lamentations for a certain way of life coming to an end in France with admiration for the arrival of a new and vastly different era. Yet the world is not, as Leszek Kolakowski has noted, reflected and "reproduced" in words and texts; on the contrary, it is "appropriated" and actively shaped through them.[73] "Modern society" came alive through the words and imaginations of authors. Exposés, magazine articles, and illustrations functioned as vehicles for the spread of these new sentiments, outfitting readers with a vocabulary and contextual understanding that transformed the modern into a collective and shared experience. To sketch the contours of a nominally modern world through language and texts was to give it a definition and reality of its own that an educated and literate French population could identify with, relate to, and comprehend.

The textual nature of the modern signified, however, that it remained by and large the property of a narrow segment of the population. Books and newspapers were expensive in the nineteenth century. The average subscription rate for a journal cost between sixty and eighty francs at a time when agricultural workers earned no more than two francs and skilled workers no more than four francs per day.[74] Most publications remained beyond the means of workers and day laborers, even if they had the necessary literacy skills and leisure time to read them. As a primarily elite medium, texts reflected intellectual currents and topics of interest pertinent to educated society and readers. It was, therefore, unsurprising that convictions regarding the utility of scientific knowledge and the inexorable march of progress pervaded nineteenth-century print culture. Philosophical musings, reports on industrial innovations and the economy, descriptions of urban life and sociability: these subjects were both topical and attractive to an elite readership increasingly encouraged to view their world as the ne plus ultra of human endeavors and accomplishment.

"The true bond," Flaubert once wrote, "is that of language."[75] If "modern society" acquired its consistency in the realm of print, such representations similarly encouraged readers to associate and identify with these abstractions. To be "modern" implied participating in a certain culture and subscribing to a set of beliefs and practices shared by other like-minded individuals. Commonalities and mutual interests compelled people to think of themselves not necessarily as compatriots or social equals but as coevals inhabiting the same temporal and modern space.[76] Time, represented through a language of modernity, forged a bond between contemporaries, providing the basis for a type of imagined community that, constructed through the writings and declarations of cultural and political elites, became integral to one's identity, persona, and expectations. There could be no foreigners among modern men because modernity professed a certain uniformity of moral sentiments and common experiences that bound coevals across both space and time. The praises sung to "modern society" composed the backdrop of a new social imaginary complete with its own discursive forms that were increasingly becoming central to the mental universe and parlance of elite society.

The vista characteristic of the modern, continually produced and reproduced in the books and revues of the day, nurtured an understanding of the world that permeated the cultural discourse of nineteenth-century elites. In accenting the common culture and interests shared by "modern" individuals, educated elites were instructed to view themselves as coevals inhabiting a unique time different from the past. Such assumptions furnished a measure of social cohesions among a diverse stratum of society that defied the neat socioeconomic homogeneity familiar to Marxist interpretations of the bourgeoisie. In this outlook, change and progress constituted definitive features of a collective modern experience, but one largely exclusive to educated European society.

Arriving in the Gulf of Stora in 1860 to commence a six-week journey through North Africa, Charles Thierry-Mieg, an Alsatian inventor associated with the French textile industry, took note of the "uncultivated, savage, primitive, and inhospitable" environment surrounding him, "this desert that seemed condemned to perpetual sterility." Happening upon a throng of Arab tribesmen, he could not help but regard them with a sense of historical distance and detachment. "They are still in the Middle Ages," he recorded soberly, "their degree of civilization has remained the same. . . . Whereas we have progressed the Arabs have remained stationary."[77] As Thierry-Mieg presumed, the French and the Arabs inhabited two divergent and qualitative times, prompting him to differentiate between the modern and progressive time of Europe and the medieval and static time of the Orient. Drawing liberally upon anthropological theories and popular Orientalist stereotypes, depictions of the other routinely took the form of temporal distance, offering a mirror image of the modern self that cut across the axes of nation and empire, Occident and Orient.[78]

During the nineteenth century, learned societies and social scientific disciplines gave birth to the idea of the anthropological man, a construct rooted in a belief that humanity was "a distinct, observable and measurable object," as the naturalist Paul de Jouvencel claimed.[79] Savants hypothesized on the prehistoric migrations and evolutionary processes of the human species, often drawing conclusions based upon comparative racial traits and ethnological categorizations. Human origins, the anthropologist Louis Figuier argued in his influential work *L'Homme primitif* published in 1863, extended back millennia, tracing a vast history that had yet to be fully appreciated by modern science. The discovery of prehistoric "deep time" unearthed a distant human past, and in so doing effectively opened a chasm between contemporary man and his primitive antecedents.[80] Deep time also corroborated commonly held assumptions that human development and social evolution conformed to natural and universal laws. The technological and social disparities evident among different cultures reflected distinct levels of evolutionary maturity, which intellectuals and theorists of the period defined as "civilization."[81] "The differences between the human races living today," the naturalist Philippe Buchez explained in 1833, "are only the expression of differences in the states of civilization currently dispersed across the surface of the globe."[82] The world was best understood, savants argued, as a temporal mosaic in which less civilized and primitive societies coexisted alongside highly developed and modern ones. In a world configured through notions of temporal pluralism and unilinear evolutionary models, to encounter the primitive was tantamount to coming face-to-face with one's distant ancestry and traversing the centuries and millennia bounding a common human genealogy.[83]

It was through an understanding of the primitive that the possibilities of the modern came into sharp relief and assumed form, that individuals recognized themselves and their culture as eminently modern and superior. Yet while the modern individual may have believed himself to be centuries ahead of the savage, these conceptual distinctions often belied a troubling interdependence: the modern man needed the savage to imagine his own existence. Conceptually, these identities may have been mutually exclusive; in reality, however, they operated as part of the same discursive formation. Elite self-fashioning not only demanded a conception of the modern to valorize and celebrate; it equally required an object against which the possibilities of the modern could be projected and exemplified.[84]

Europeans applied the concept of civilization to make sense of a world that, on the surface, appeared characterized by an extensive racial, social, and cultural diversity. Yet by inscribing it within a discourse of time and natural development, references to civilization dissolved this heterogeneity within a generalized view of human nature and progress. In spite of its classical connotations, *civilisation* was still a relatively new concept by the middle of the nineteenth century, first appearing in the *Dictionnaire de l'Académie* only in 1798. Prior to the 1790s, the adjective *civilisé* possessed strong aristocratic connotations, with the "civilized man" (*homme civilisé*) commonly designating a cultivated individual typically of good aristocratic stock. It was precisely these aristocratic nuances that led Rousseau, Kant, and other *philosophes* to denigrate the civilized man, seeing *civilisation* as a corrupting force on the *bon sauvage*, or "noble savage" who, unlike his aristocratic counterpart, remained true to his natural state and human virtues.[85]

By the dawn of the nineteenth century, the *homme civilisé* was widely considered not only an individual of elevated manners and morals but also a bearer of superior cultural values and knowledge.[86] "The man who marches toward civilization," wrote the statesman Benjamin Constant in 1825, "seeks at once to reach out for what is elevated and rise above what is ignoble."[87] While primitive cultures remained in a deplorable state of nature, Europeans exhibited the unbridled potential of the *homme civilisé* who, through science and reason, relied on his higher intellect to organize his world and improve his condition. According to the diplomat and man of letters Édouard Alletz, civilization embodied nothing less than "the perfection of all man's faculties and the diminishing of life's suffering through reasonable means," qualities that reflected patently Occidental traits in his opinion.[88]

These laudatory appraisals of civilization reflected attitudes stemming from the Enlightenment and enhanced during the years of the Revolution and Napoleonic Wars. Marching into Egypt in 1798, Napoleon had declared his intentions of delivering the benefits of European civilization to Africa and spreading the Enlightenment to a fallen Oriental race. In the wake of the disastrous Egyptian campaign, Napoleon and his administrators applied this style of messianic conquest to the European continent, dictating the need to "civilize" peripheral Slavic and Eastern European ethnic groups recently incorporated into the empire. Naturally, this lofty civilizing rhetoric provided a convenient moral justification for imposing French rule on foreign populations, but it also indicated the newfound reverence for *civilisation* growing up among a generation instructed to see their nation as the bearer of superior values and an enlightened morality.[89] By the mid-nineteenth century, François Guizot could write with certainty on what he described as "the essence of modern civilization," enumerating "the scope of ambition," the "firmness of political thought," and the "clear understanding of the grandeur of man and the power that belongs to him. . . . All of Europe and most notably France has marched along . . . the same path of liberation and general progress. These paths have guided the people who have firmly engaged in a high degree of strength, prosperity, and grandeur that we call and that we have a right to call modern civilization."[90]

A resolute Doctrinaire liberal who served under the July Monarchy, Guizot logically enough identified these very same traits as definitive hallmarks of the bourgeoisie and its natural "capacity" for progressive leadership. If "bourgeois" implied a restrictive social identity and class that no longer comported with the dictates of a democratic French society, ostensibly bourgeois values were often expressed in universal terms through concepts like modernity and civilization.[91] Moreover, as identities increasingly became mapped and constructed according to concepts of time and temporality, labels such as "primitive," "savage," and "civilized" also reconfigured racial and social differences in new and vital ways.[92] The old language of bourgeois industriousness and capacity employed by liberal ideologues to justify their brand of class rule proved highly adaptable to the needs of subalternzation essential to ruling a colonial empire in a democratic age.

A decade after the abolition of slavery throughout the empire, the colonial reformer Edouard Hommaire de Hell gave his assessment of democracy in the Antilles, noting that the new citizens "more than ever . . . profited from the benefits of civilization."[93] Under the regime of slavery, Africans had been considered property with little attention paid to their moral or intellectual development. Emancipation had changed this fact. "Now that liberty has been granted to him, it is necessary to carry out with solicitude the means of moralizing this race, and to arrive at this aim there is only a single path: *work*." The imperative of moral improvement through work derived from general stereotypes shared by Hommaire de Hell that "the Negro [was] essentially lazy."[94] This same rationale had been applied to the free black populations of the colonies by republican reformers in the 1790s. While French republicans were inclined to speak the language of égalité, equality was never absolute. Much like the classical liberalism they abjured, republicans exhibited a similar tendency to evaluate citizens differently according to perceived moral and intellectual capacities.[95] Following the abolition of chattel slavery in 1848, former republican logics of exclusion were revived and elaborated on, as the imperative to moralize "savages" and prepare them for civilized life became the guiding precept of postemancipation colonial society.

Quick to declare slavery abolished, the Second Republic had shown less alacrity in enforcing the emancipation decree. Concerns over labor supply and exaggerated warnings from planters regarding the consequences that emancipation would pose to the economy and public order succeeded in stalling the process. As a result, few measures were seriously taken to integrate former slaves into colonial society.[96] Whites averse to emancipation found means of retaining their former dominance as efforts to preserve "public order" typically provided rationales for placing controls on newly liberated citizens. Compulsory work regiments and sharecropping practices left former slaves economically dependent on colonial elites just as social restrictions were enforced to preserve the old social order and constrain political expression.[97] Slavery may have legally ended in 1848, but subjugation and racial discrimination persisted in a variety of forms as emancipated "citizens" remained outside the social, political, and cultural life of the French empire.[98] Framing difference in terms of civilization and savagery, the modern and the primitive, elites discounted the racial and social inequalities that persisted to structure colonial relationships, reformulating them in temporal categories that, on the surface, upheld natural equality.

For most of the nineteenth century, French imperial ideologies tended to resist deterministic understandings of race. By necessity, French imperialism catered to views that emphasized man's capacity for improvement, thereby justifying the need for a moralizing and paternalistic French guidance.[99] Notions of "natural" inferiority were eclipsed by ideas of civilization and adaptability, stressing, as Hommaire de Hell did in 1859, that nature "bestowed its blessings on all people" and that "civilization alone" engendered differences between men.[100] As elites employed a language of time and social development to construct boundaries and convey distances they contributed to a vision of a monolithic modern community distinct from the superannuated and historicized formations found elsewhere.[101] Different cultures were interpreted as little more than artifacts destined to be effaced by the progressive movement of history, a process broadly construed as the colonization of primitive spaces by modernity.

Entering the colonies of the *outremer* commonly constituted traveling not only geographic distances but also temporal distances where the modern landscape of industry and urbanization disappeared in the premodern wilderness. "The philosophical traveler, sailing to the ends of the earth, is in fact travelling in time," the naturalist Joseph-Marie de Gérando explained, expressing an outlook that would become common to European colonial ideologies.[102] Making his way through the Arab territories between Philippesvilles and Constantine, the jurist Henri de Senhaux found only "deserted fields encumbered by old shrubs." The Arabs, he claimed, had left the land fallow, never settling or establishing farms due to their constant seasonal migrations and nomadic lifestyle. "The Roman ruins that you glimpse from time to time recall a past a thousand times more superior than the present," Senhaux stated.[103] Travel accounts and scientific observations during the century frequently described barren landscapes of desert, craggy precipices, untamed jungles, and crumbling edifices that stood in stark contrast to the familiarity of European capitals and cities partaking in industrialization.

One did not necessarily have to leave the continent to encounter these alien and exotic terrains either. The landscape symbolic of modern progress and industry vaunted by savants and politicians never extended far beyond the domains of French cities and towns, and *la France profonde*—the majority of rural areas making up continental France—could, at times, seem closer to the desolate and wild terrain of Africa than to Europe. Perceptions of rural autarky and backwardness suffused travel accounts through the countryside as rail and road construction opened up *la France profonde* to urbanites, and the inhabitants whom one found there could be just as savage and inhospitable as the milieu in which they dwelled. Observers regarded French rurals with the same detachment and distance applied to colonial subjects. Countrymen appeared too foreign and too different to be looked upon as compatriots or even equals. With their odd dialects that sounded more like "Chinese" than French and their peculiar customs, they were subjects seemingly culled from the pages of distant histories befitting anthropological speculation.[104] Observing the prandial habits, dancing, and festivities of Breton peasants in Rennes, Taine likened them to Arabs celebrating after a feast, remarking curtly, "mores remain very primitive here."[105] The culture and worldview of the French peasantry, much like the natives of the colonies, appeared archaic, unchanged, and reflective of a more primal age. In remarking on the stark divide separating urban and rural France, the liberal pamphleteer Eugène Ténot clearly saw "two juxtaposed people" living side by side on the national soil, "one burning with a new spirit, the other languishing in a former century."[106]

The recognition of pluralist and divergent times corresponded to a temporal geography that constructed and mapped the contours of national and global spaces. Metropole and colony or city and country-side constituted poles around which social and cultural differences were organized and articulated, circumscribing modern society within the limits of an industrialized and primarily urban milieu distinct from the peripheral premodern terrains populated by savages and foreigners. Yet, despite these telling spatial and geographic referents, the community of moderns never assumed the rigid territoriality that national and regional identities supposed. Social critics repeatedly maintained their convictions in man's ability for improvement and the uniformity of moral outlooks and common interests that bound "modern" and "civilized" coevals across time and space. "In the measure that civilization wins over the terrain, in the measure that its material and moral acquisitions propagate themselves," claimed one colonial journalist in 1865, "one sees, in effect, a certain community of sentiments, ideas, and habits establish itself among men. Civilized man ceases to be a foreigner from other civilized men, and the *patrie*, at first contained within the limits of a village or the walls of a city, extends until the limits of civilization itself."[107]

It is commonly assumed that the categories of race and nation that grew up during the nineteenth century dominated understandings of the social world during the period. Yet the recognition of an identity regime rooted in time and temporality often provided a countervision to these more reductive social identities. The modernity imagined by elites constituted a decentered and diasporic community extending across national and spatial frontiers. By its very nature, it was fluid and theoretically inclusive, reflecting the Enlightenment's belief in the universal perfectability of mankind through the certainty that the distance separating the modern *homme civilisé* from his vestigial antecedents, while vast, was not unbridgeable. Social evolutionary thinking remained premised on the belief that the savage could, under the proper circumstances, catch up with and be assimilated into the modern time of his superiors.[108] As one procolonial publicist alleged in 1867, "by adopting the methods employed by the people farthest along the path of progress . . . a retrograde people can make up the ground and diminish the sacrifices that lost time has imposed on them."[109] Phrased differently, primitivizing certain groups offered a moral rationale for imposing certain values and social practices on outside cultures.[110]

Such assertions manifested the logic of colonialism that furnished France with its overseas "civilizing mission," but the same primitivizing discourse used to construct colonial subjects was actively applied to the populations of the continent. The positive and concrete representations that sustained a belief in the modern were conversely hollowed out and emptied of content to construct modernity's others. What the modern and civilized man possessed and valued the atavistic savage lacked and disregarded, giving rise to identities that stood as mirror images of one another. "You'll find many prejudices to fight against here, Monsieur Bovary!" one of the townspeople advised the newly arrived doctor in Flaubert's novel. "Every day your scientific efforts will be blocked by people who stubbornly cling to the past, because many of them still resort to novenas, relics or the priest instead of naturally calling on a doctor or a pharmacist."[111] Such hackneyed notions found expression beyond the realm of literature and became commonplace descriptions of social and political realities in the nineteenth century.

In the age of rapid change, obdurately clinging to the past amounted to a complete negation of the ethos and mentality driving the modern world. Accusations of stasis and inertia slung at both rurals and colonial natives only served to further underscore the distance separating the novel and progressive time of moderns from the stagnant time of the other. As one author writing for La Vie moderne pointedly informed his audience in 1859, for the modern thinker "the absurd man is he who never changes."[112]

The Scourge of Barbarism

Images of rustic peasants stuck in their ways and colonial tribes steeped in primordial ignorance offered convenient representations against which themes of material advancement and social progress could be valorized and held up as models for emulation. Yet these impressions also informed actions and policies essential to dealing with groups deemed immature and even dangerous. Stubborn peasants and natives might be seen as obstacles to progress, but resistance could and frequently did assume more violent and confrontational forms that extended beyond mere caricature. Inclinations to distance coevals from strangers encouraged a concordance in national and colonial outlooks that had been maturing in France for at least half a century.[113]

The remaking of postrevolutionary society occurred in tandem with the onset of Algerian colonization, and these parallel processes created and mutually reinforced a distinct context and language for defining deviant groups and proposing solutions to disorder. The congruent objectives of social stability and colonial conquest encouraged the "colonialization" of national politics and security concerns as metropolitan and colonial officials alike came to see themselves as leaders obliged to assume responsibility for the rational and efficient management of unruly and subaltern populations.[114]

Perceptions of the colonial world frequently emphasized the violence endemic to non-European societies. According to Antoine Horner, a priest charged with overseeing Catholic missions in Zanzibar during the 1860s, law and order were alien concepts to the African continent where marauding tribes and family clans indulged in horrific acts of revenge and vicious blood feuds. "Africa is the country [*sic*] where tribal warfare reigns perpetually," he remarked, "where men are hunted as we hunt beasts in our own country."[115] In an address before the Corps législatif in 1861, Baron Jérôme Frédéric David, an influential adviser on the government's Algerian policy during the 1860s, painted a demoralizing picture of the Arabs inhabiting France's North African frontier. Criticizing opponents calling for a reduced military presence in Algeria, he urged

serious reflection on the nature of the Arabs, stating, "these are populations that know no other rules than violence . . . who are not familiar
with justice to redress their grievances."[116] The rampant lawlessness
and tribalism alluded to by Baron David and others underscored the
Hobbesian character of life found outside the sanctuaries of Europe.

Such views, however, were of relatively recent creation. By the time
of the French invasion, North Africa was scarcely a terra incognita to
educated Europeans. Long-standing commercial and diplomatic relations
between European and Maghrebi states had familiarized Enlightenment
scholars with the African Mediterranean, an area neither as exotic as the
Far East nor as "savage" as the virginal New World. By the dawn of the
nineteenth century, these diverse perspectives on the region had been
replaced with an exceedingly negative one shaped by French military
officials and savants disposed toward France's "civilizing" mission.[117] The
resistance encountered by French forces as they pushed through Algeria
encouraged accusations of savagery and fanaticism that, in turn, rationalized the use of extreme military force on native populations.[118] Colonial
conquest became synonymous with the eradication of "barbarism," a
conviction that emphasized the moral imperatives of colonial warfare.
"Subjugating barbarians is a useful act to civilization and can be beneficial
and laudatory if we elevate them to the level of a civil people," claimed
the jurist René Morin in 1854.[119] As Morin's injunction suggested, the
struggle against modern-day barbarism amounted to imposing political
and moral order on populations seen as inherently brutal and lawless.

As colonial warfare altered impressions of Arab society, it also aroused
underlying anxieties pertinent to the supposedly advanced and pacific
civilization enjoyed by the French. Scholars and Orientalists fascinated
with Pharaonic Egypt and Medieval Islam acknowledged that the East
had possessed impressive empires and complex civilizations in the past.
In tailoring civilizational discourse to the Arab world, critics drew on
Enlightenment narratives dating back to Montesquieu and Gibbon
centered on notions of civilizational decline. According to this theory,
societies either progressed toward civility or degenerated into barbarism.[120] Clearly a case of the latter, the Arabs had been stripped of their

"antique prestige," explained Henri Guys, a former French consul who had served out his tenure in Lebanon. A once admirable and accomplished civilization had, in his view, regressed and fallen prey to the brutalities of nomadic life and an irrational devotion to Islam.[121] This analytical framework explained the many deficient tendencies found in Arab society, but it also suggested that a civilized people could in fact devolve and descend back into a barbaric state. Civilization, in other words, was fragile and prone to decay, and one did not need to look to the Arab world to validate this assumption.

Nineteenth-century social critics and officials were not oblivious to the fact that major industrial centers offered examples of both the marvels and horrors of modernity. Describing Paris in 1852, Gautier expressed disgust at the deplorable living conditions and grime that could be found if one bothered to travel beyond the city center. "Three-quarters of the streets are only networks of black and fetid filth as in the times of the starkest barbarism," he claimed. "No traces of art or elegance . . . boxes of plaster with squares cut into them constitute what one calls a house in the nineteenth century, in this city that claims to be a modern Athens, the queen of civilization!"[122] These conditions certainly provided cause for concern, and not simply on humanitarian grounds either. "The persistence of base habits can be explained in part by the permanence of insalubrious and sinister quarters," wrote Charles Monselet. "The ugly calls forth the wicked."[123] Liberal fears of working-class protest and unruliness ran deeper than political exigency. A state-sponsored inquiry into pauperism conducted in 1840 spelled out the evident dangers posed by the "extreme misery" suffered by the urban poor on a daily basis, cautioning that the insalubrious environment and lack of education found among the working classes could provoke "a relapse into savagery."[124]

While industrialized labor was, in theory, a product of the modern society valorized by elites, the immediate environment, base habits, and squalid lifestyle of workers prognosticated an evolutionary reversal, effectively denying them a nominally "modern" identity. Applying the language and ideology of colonialism to metropolitans, these "savages of civilization" were reconceptualized as an inferior race, making indigent and *indigène* (native) practically synonymous.[125] The reformer Henri Lecouturier did not mince words when comparing the meandering existence of Parisian day laborers to nomadic Arab tribesmen, contending that the majority of inhabitants in the city owned no property of their own and frequently migrated from residence to residence in any given year. "Paris is a camp," Lecouturier summarized, "each of its houses a tent, and its population nomadic."[126] Lecouturier was writing in the aftermath of the June Days insurgency, an event that chillingly illustrated the exceedingly colonial dimensions of French domestic politics.

Security needs encouraged the colonialization of domestic administrative and bureaucratic practices, and over the next two decades the consolidation of state authority became readily interpreted in terms of colonial power and conquest. Traveling through Normandy in the 1860s, the English travel writer Henry Blackburn was inclined to view the primacy of Paris throughout the country as a virtual empire in its own right. Provinces connected to Paris by a growing network of rails and roads fed the capital just as colonies were expected to feed a metropole, Blackburn observed. "Let [the traveler] go . . . to the rail station at any port on his arrival in France and he will find everything—people, goods and provisions—being hurried off to the capital as if there were no other place to live in or provide for."[127] Taine was equally critical of the marked Parisian influence evident throughout the provinces. "The barracks, the magistrature, the university: nothing has proper roots. Everything is implanted." The local populations had even become reliant on the Parisian officials who attended to the day-to-day affairs of the communes and departments. "All the imbeciles, peasants, and petit bourgeois receive the *fonctionnaires* in the way that the Hindus would the civilians of the English Company," he scorned. "Without them, there wouldn't be any roads, justice, or schools."[128] "Colony is a word that can be extended to the [French] provinces," charged one writer in 1861 frustrated over the power and influence that Parisian administrators wielded in the countryside.[129]

The social and political concerns of the postrevolutionary period blurred distinctions between national and imperial topographies. The colonial moment inaugurated by the revolution of 1848 marked a key instant in this process as demands for universal citizenship and national unity brought metropole and periphery closer together. While politicians imagined an expansive French society rooted in core principles of democratic rights, equality, and a common nationality, social elites revealed a tendency to represent and organize this new society in terms that rationalized forms of control and leadership essential to ruling a democratic and imperial nation. If the present belonged to the march of modern progress and the triumph of civilization, this conviction scarcely implied that all men belonged to the age in which they lived. Civilization developed even if the majority of the population did not. In the realm of politics, the idea of the bourgeoisie as an imagined governing class may have been incompatible with the democratic impulses of 1848, but the ethics, ideals, and sentiments which had laid behind this cultural construction remained very much alive in the years following the Second Republic. Rejecting the explicit class rule and "natural" inequality prescribed by classical liberalism, modern coevals claimed authority through a universalizing discourse that was egalitarian in principle but elitist in practice.

In the terms prescribed by the language of French elitism, subaltern groups were faced with the choice of assimilation or social marginalization. In either event, the imposition of modernity implied that the new society to come would unconditionally belong, both socially and culturally, to a certain group bolstering urban forms of politics, knowledge, and sociability under the pretext of a universal modernity. The existence of social groups is dependent on the discourses and narratives that shape them.[130] After 1848, modernity offered a compelling language and story for conceptualizing a particular culture and lifestyle in temporal and historically specific terms. The idiom of newness that suffused French social and political discourse in the postrevolutionary period delineated the contours of a novel type of community that, while composed of numerous social actors and interest groups scattered across vast geographic distances, was, nonetheless, bound together through the realization of a shared time, worldview, and culture. Entrepreneurs, urban professionals and colonists, scientists and academics, journalists and men of politics composed the community of moderns standing at the forefront of history and progress. Universal in its scope and conceptualization yet emblematic of a minority of the population, modern society constituted the exclusive preserve of this new group invested with a mission to modernize the primitive and to conscript outsiders into the confines of civilized life.

2   State Modernization and the Making of Bonapartist Modernity

Arriving in Marseille in 1863 while touring France's southern provinces, Hippolyte Taine recorded his impressions of the recent building projects that had begun to transfigure the landscape of the port city significantly. The new monumental and sculpted houses lining the streets appeared, he claimed, "even more vast and magnificent than in Paris," outfitting the Mediterranean trading hub with a palatial affluence. Marseille exemplified the sudden boom in public prosperity stimulated by Emperor Napoleon III's Bonapartist government brought to power in 1851. While certainly not a Bonapartist sympathizer and commonly professing an indifference to politics, Taine was inclined to see the new Napoleon as a progressive and modern leader in light of the transformations occurring throughout the country at midcentury. "The emperor understands France and his century better than any of his predecessors," he candidly admitted.[1]

Such an impression derived, in part, from the rigorous self-fashioning of Bonapartist ideologues and propagandists who persistently drew attention to the regime's patently "modern" orientation in their public speeches and writings. Coming to power through an illegal coup d'état that overthrew the Second Republic, the Second Empire did not enjoy the security bestowed by popular legitimacy. From the start, the government was compelled to silence opponents and craft an identity for itself that might compensate for its questionable legality. National referendums carried out under universal manhood suffrage and ardent appeals to patriotism were employed to provide the regime with a semblance of legitimacy. However, it was Napoleon III's commitment to modernizing and rejuvenating French society that would remain a centerpiece of his government's political identity over the next two decades, providing a distinct discourse and rhetoric that was as attractive to elites as it was to the masses.

At its most elemental level, politics is a langue that seeks to mobilize ideas and construct a certain interpretation of reality, and Bonapartist modernity was no different in this respect.[2] Inheriting a country destabilized by chronic partisan divisions and social antagonisms, the architects of the Second Empire sought to assuage fears over France's political future by drawing the nation's fractious political elite and apprehensive business classes to a moderate government devoted to national prosperity and order. Although Bonapartist rhetoric at times exhibited a brazenly populist and nationalist nature, this populism never precluded cooperation with elites whose support was deemed essential to the regime's success. During the years of the Second Empire, modernity figured prominently in the new tenor set by Bonapartist spokesmen with terms like "modern society" and "modern civilization" saturating French public and political discourse. This common vocabulary and language conformed to the egalitarian impulses of post-1848 French political culture, offering a vision of society that was both universal and utilitarian. Yet it was also consistent with specific elite interests and power relations. In selling their vision of a modern French society to the public, Napoleon III and his supporters devised a means of representing and actively promoting particular social and economic interests in a political culture that celebrated equality and popular sovereignty.

Consolidating this identity entailed closely associating the actions of the government with its alleged modern character, obliging Bonapartists to represent and justify state policies as acts of "modernization." The July Monarchy had initiated a modicum of industrial and economic programs during the 1840s that catalyzed the boom years of the 1850s.[3] However, it was the Second Empire that received credit for many of these achievements as imperial spokesmen hailed the government's modernizing initiative as an unprecedented break with the past. Under Bonapartist rule, the advent of steam power, the adoption of new technologies in the manufacturing industries, and the laying of some thirteen thousand kilometers of operational rail line provided the impetus for systemic economic growth throughout the 1850s.[4] The state played a decisive role in this achievement by providing subsidies for manufacturers and railroad companies, carrying out large-scale public works, furnishing favorable terms for the acquisition of credit and contracting good relations with industrialists and major financial houses.[5] Through these policies, the government balanced elite interests with "the moral improvement and material well-being of the greatest number," as the emperor boasted.[6] Improvements in infrastructure and public utilities figured prominently in the modernizing and civilizing goals enunciated by the regime, illustrating the dynamic interplay between rhetoric, ideology, and policy that characterized imperial politics.

The building projects that Taine found so astonishing marked the most dramatic and controversial endeavor to instantiate this modernizing narrative. Over the nearly two decades that spanned the life of the Second Empire, statesmen employed a variety of forums and symbolic gestures in demonstrating the empire's supposed modern orientation. Building projects, exhibitions at industrial fairs, peons to the state's rail-building projects, and support for industrial development in the countryside all played an integral role in cultivating the modern and civilizing identity desired by the government. The talk of "civilizing" and "developing" that had characterized the liberal imperialism of the 1840s was being turned back on the French metropole, and this correlation between national and colonial objectives was made evident as the state's modernizing agenda progressed. Although the Second Empire demonstrated a preference for European trade and growth over colonial trade, France's new North African territory was also subject to industrial and urban development during the same period.[7] Presenting itself as a patron of French industry, the imperial government embraced the industrial ethos of the mid-nineteenth century and proudly flaunted its efforts to bring the material benefits of modern civilization to both France and its

Algerian possession separated by a body of water increasingly considered nothing more than a "French lake." As one *colon* journalist optimistically professed shortly after the new imperial regime was declared, "the time of monumental things has come for Algeria."[8]

For a government vesting its authority and power in the promise of a new and modern France, state policies became the concrete expression of this supposed modernity, equating the state's social and economic objectives with a process of modernization. From the act of modernizing sprang the raison d'être of the imperial regime and the authoritarian state apparatus over which it presided. In its objectives and scope, Bonapartist modernity constituted a national-imperial program and ideology that aimed to dazzle and entice just as much as transform the nation. The Second Empire presented itself as a forward-looking regime with an ambitious vision for the nation. Under the circumstances, modernity could be nothing short of monumental.

Announcing the "New Era"

A perceptive observer of nineteenth-century politics and society, the statesman Alexis de Tocqueville had few illusions when it came to diagnosing the ills of his country. The tensions generated by the French Revolution had never been adequately resolved. Revolts, coups, and civil strife persisted, leaving the nation acutely "coupé en deux," as he claimed. "Shall we ever attain a more complete and far-reaching social transformation than our fathers foresaw and desired . . . or are we not destined to simply end in a condition of intermittent anarchy, the well-known chronic and incurable complaint of old people?"[9] Tocqueville's question was an incisive one. Between 1789 and 1848 France had been governed by no fewer than six different political regimes, each promising to bring stability to the country in vain.[10] The Bourbon monarchy, restored in 1814 at the behest of the European powers, was toppled in 1830; the liberal Orléanist regime followed suit in 1848. Worker revolts sporadically plagued Paris during the 1830s and 1840s, culminating in the violence of the June Days. "All our political establishments, republic, empire, or monarchy, are provisional," Taine remarked, "like great sets of painted scenery that turn and turn about, filling the stage only to vanish or reappear as the occasion warrants."[11] Revolution had irrevocably shaken the foundations of French society. In its aftermath, the essential task, as Guizot noted, was not to "perpetuate society" but rather "reconstitute it" along new lines.[12]

Beset by social convulsions, political crises, and colonial wars, the Orléanists had neither effectively secured peace within the national domain nor promoted a conception of sovereignty that could unite the country. Consequently, this task would now fall to a Bonaparte. The collapse of the July Monarchy, the unpopularity of the provisional government's social programs and the subsequent June Days uprising all provided favorable circumstances for a Bonapartist revival in 1848. The myth of Napoleon—child of the French Revolution, champion of nationalism, and securer of French glory—retained a strong influence and popular appeal in the country.[13] Calls of "Vive Napoléon!" had been heard in 1830 following the overthrow of the Bourbon dynasty. Louis Philippe himself attempted to capitalize on these sentiments a decade later when he ordered the former emperor's ashes returned to France as a symbolic gesture of his dedication to the nation's revolutionary heritage. As the crisis of 1848 unfolded, the moment seemed ripe for a Bonaparte pretender and who better than his proud and progressive nephew, Louis Napoleon Bonaparte? "I am going to Paris," Louis wrote to his cousin from exile in London upon hearing of the outbreak of revolution. "The Republic has been proclaimed and I must be its master."[14]

Exploiting fears of proletarian violence and socialist radicalism, Louis announced his candidacy for the presidential elections schedule that December, presenting himself as a leader capable of restoring order and prosperity to a divided nation. The self-proclaimed "homme d'ordre" drew a wide array of support as his campaign gained momentum that winter. Conservatives saw him as an assurance against socialism. Moderate republicans associated the name Bonaparte with the ideals of the Revolution and national glory. The rural peasants, however, gave Louis Napoleon his widest base of support, believing Bonaparte to be a guarantee against the restoration of the ancien régime and a protector of the little land acquired since 1789. When all votes were cast, Louis polled nearly 75 percent of the total electorate, a sensational victory by any standard.[15]

Louis's commitment to moral and social order was first made apparent upon his assumption of the presidency as he assembled a ministry composed of monarchical notables, conservatives, and loyal Bonapartists. Licking their wounds after defeat in 1848, radical republicans and social democrats greeted the new government with contempt, making known their intention of seeking victory in the next presidential election four years later and establishing a "true" republic. Electoral gains in 1849 and 1850 gave substance to these aims, resurrecting the threat of the invidious *spectre rouge* that persistently haunted conservatives and moderates. With Louis's presidential term set to expire in 1852 and divisions between Legitimists and Orléanists preventing unified support for a conservative candidate, the revival of the "reds" appeared plausible. In 1851 conservatives attempted to amend the constitution and eliminate the article preventing consecutive presidential terms. The motion was defeated, however, when the National Assembly failed to attain the required three-quarters majority necessary to pass such a law. With few options remaining and a victory for the left a potential reality, Louis Napoleon followed in the footsteps of his uncle. On the eve of 2 December 1851, police were ordered to round up all suspected opponents in Paris as Louis and his inner circle staged a coup d'état in the name of public order. With the capital secured, the Bonapartists proceeded to use military force in suppressing republican strongholds in the provinces. In the years immediately following the coup, some ten thousand opponents would be forcibly resettled in Algeria, which was restored once again to military rule, putting an end to the civilian government created under the Second Republic.

Conservatives and moderates supported the illegal action, convinced that the promise of a strong government in the midst of a hostile socialism justified the infraction. The following year, Louis and his supporters held a national referendum asking the French people to affirm the official creation of a Second Napoleonic Empire. With political opponents either exiled or imprisoned and conservatives warning of the dire consequences that a vote against the proposed government would hold for the future of France, the motion passed. Louis Napoleon was declared Emperor Napoleon III. The new constitution established an authoritarian regime consisting of a national parliament, the Corps législatif, elected through universal suffrage, a senate appointed directly by the emperor, and a strong executive invested with the power to appeal directly to the French people through national referendums. Over the next decade, this combination of democratic politics and centralized authority, consisting of censorship, official appointments, and electoral engineering through officially sponsored candidates, would be used to consolidate the government's hold on power throughout the country.

The Bonapartist clan that seized control of the state in 1851 comprised a motley group, and Napoleon III was the first to recognize the diversity of opinion found among those in his inner circle.[16] A romantic disposed to progressive socialist theories in his youth, Louis had kept alive what he considered the "Napoleonic idea," which was not "an idea of war, but a social, industrial, and commercial idea—an idea of humanity," he contended.[17] Two disastrous coup attempts against the July Monarchy, a prison sentence, and exile may have tempered his former idealism but hardly his ambition. Although he spoke French with an awkward German accent from his years spent abroad in Switzerland, and his thin frame and refined appearance bore only a sparse resemblance to the squat, yet regal image of the famed French emperor, Louis never doubted the "destiny" that his birth presaged.[18] Much like his uncle, Napoleon III intended to close the great political rift that the Revolution of 1789 had opened and rally the nation to a moderate government with nationalist and liberal aims. Industry and trade were to be encouraged, drawing the middle classes and business community closer to the government and combating the severe economic conditions that stimulated the appeal of radical socialism.

Yet garnering support for the new government required convincing notables of the good intentions and orientation of the Second Empire, and Napoleon III's status as a parvenu estranged him from many of the influential social and political circles of Parisian society. The task of selling the empire to French elites fell to his half brother, Auguste de Morny, a former deputy under the July Monarchy and entrepreneur with close relations to the world of finances. "Raised in the upper echelons of Paris, having ties to all the eminent men of politics, literature, and art," Morny once boasted, "I, more than anyone else, was to give [the emperor] the precious education and council he required."[19] As Napoleon III's liaison to the world of French finances and politics, Morny believed himself indispensable to the emperor. Such expectations were, however, often bitterly disillusioned as his Orléanist sympathies and liberal convictions came into conflict with the policies touted by his half brother and men of his entourage. Morny did, however, remain faithful to the Second Empire in spite of the ideological quarrels that sprang up from time to time, and his active role in the government's financial policies buoyed confidence among French investors and entrepreneurs who came to equate the phrase "Morny est dans l'affaire" with a clear guarantee of profit.[20]

Morny's social grace and politesse stood in stark contrast to the gravity and insistence of Jean-Gilbert-Victor Fialin, the duc de Persigny. A former journalist and loyal devotee of the emperor, Persigny equated his dedication to the Bonaparte dynasty to a deep religious sentiment. Never modest, he considered himself the "Loyola of the Empire," a man invested with a sacred mission to spread the Napoleonic idea throughout France and the world.[21] "I have wanted all my life to marry the principles of the French Revolution to the ideas of grandeur and strength in the country," Persigny confessed to Louis Napoleon in 1848.[22] As one of Napoleon III's closest confidants, he was a committed Bonapartist who in various administrative positions throughout the 1850s and early 1860s worked to transform the Bonapartist cause into a national one that pledged to restore peace to the country and reaffirm French power abroad. According to the emperor, Persigny was the only true Bonapartist among those of his inner circle. "But," he added with some amusement, "he is [also] crazy."[23]

This mix of practicality, idealism, and patriotism found among the Bonapartist leadership never managed, however, to expunge memories of the coup or the government's questionable legal origins, leaving serious doubts as to the long-term viability of the Second Empire. Despite the popular mandate given to the regime by the national referendum of 1852, republicans and exiles were committed to keeping the memory of the ill-fated Second Republic and the "crime" of *Deux-Décembre* alive. From the start, the regime was confronted with a search for legitimacy. Evoking the glories associated with the Bonapartist dynasty and capitalizing on the popular Napoleonic myth offered a solution to the problem, albeit a limited one. Persigny, sensitive to the political significance associated with the Bonapartist name, urged prefects to exploit it whenever possible. Officials were instructed to "seek out the places where an old soldier of the empire or men who cultivate memories of the past may be found [and] address yourself to the Napoleonic sentiment of the people."[24] Public festivities commonly featured imperial eagles and large letter Ns adorning buildings. In 1852, Napoleon I's birthday was even made an official *fête nationale* in hopes of replacing the collective memory of the Revolution with that of the First Empire and the Bonaparte dynasty.[25]

Homage to Napoleon was, however, often complicated by competing efforts to build a broad consensus across political lines, an objective that frequently resulted in incoherent or contradictory policies. Government spokesmen discouraged a strictly political interpretation of the movement to distance it from the factionalism and political infighting associated with the July Monarchy. "The Napoleonic idea," as Louis Napoleon explained, "means to reconstitute French society, overthrown by fifty years of revolution, to conciliate order and liberty, the rights of the people, and the principles of law. . . . As it builds on a solid foundation, it rests its system on the principles of eternal justice, and treads under-foot the reactionary theories brought about by party excesses."[26] These were lofty principles, but also vague ones. Political historians have often struggled with Bonapartism's enigmatic quality when attempting to define its specific ideological character and import.[27] Officially, there existed no Bonapartist party. Supporters often classified Bonapartism as a national revivalist movement that transcended ideological divisions. Auguste de Morny did nothing to clarify this position when declaring before the general council of Puy-de-Dôme in 1862: "The Napoleonic sentiment is not an opinion. It is a religion."[28] Although the memory of Napoleon I and the Bonapartist name were powerful national symbols, Bonapartism itself had few dedicated adherents and lacked a solid ideological base to which the government might appeal.

In spite of this semblance of "permanent ambiguity," the Bonapartist leadership did work to organize the movement around certain concepts and perspectives that were more or less consistent, and in doing so furnish an identity for the new regime.[29] If Morny was reluctant to associate the movement with a political orientation, he was, nevertheless, insistent that the government was embarking on a "politique nouvelle" in 1851.[30] Hippolyte Fourtoul, who served Napoleon III faithfully as minister of education throughout the 1850s, agreed, claiming that the emperor had "opened a new era for France" that promised to transform the institutions, ideas, and habits of the country.[31] Officials may have been encouraged to appeal to a Napoleonic heritage, but the Second Empire was intended to be a quintessentially "modern" government, conforming to "the law of modern times," as the proimperial pamphleteer Charles Piel de Troismonts professed.[32] The self-proclaimed novelty embodied in the spirit and intentions of the imperial regime became a hallmark of imperial rhetoric. It furnished an ideological framework and script that would rationalize Bonapartist power and authority over the coming years as well as provide a measure of cohesion for a movement intent on rallying a broad array of support and political opinion. According to Persigny, the imperial government exemplified "the ideas, sentiments, instincts, and . . . even the passions of a new society" and was inspired by the "spirit [and] conscience" of the times to bring this social vision to fruition.[33]

Modernity figured prominently in the rhetoric and portrayals of the Second Empire as it worked to obtain support among liberals and moderates suspicious of a Napoleonic usurper. To alleviate these uncertainties, the Bonapartists leadership underscored the message that the "new society" it advertised would be compatible with expectations of stability and social order. Napoleon III reiterated his commitment to stimulating economic revival and national industries, abiding by his old maxim "to create prosperity is to assure order."[34] Yet the imperial program aspired to be more than just an economic policy. The revolutionary upheavals of the past had consistently threatened not only the financial interests of the upper classes but also their social primacy. Staunching the anarchic tide of socialism required social policies aimed at naturalizing the power relations and value systems that order required. The emperor did not conceal his intentions of instilling certain morals and codes of behavior in the French people, asserting it was imperative to "create new habits in accordance with new principles" if a durable society was to be founded in France.[35] Committed to modernizing both country and people, the Bonapartists coaxed support from elite social groups by ensuring that their vision of a modern France was consistent with elite interests and values. Under the Second Empire, Napoleon III assured, France would be "of its epoch" as the "the march of civilization" replaced the revolutionary disorder of the past.[36]

References to *civilisation* were a staple of Napoleonic rhetoric, and Bonapartist spokesmen emphatically stressed that to modernize France would correspondingly entail civilizing its people and taming the disorderly "passions" that consistently bred unrest. Enervated by over a half century of political upheaval and economic decline, France knew neither the security nor the prosperity promised by the fruits of modern civilization, they argued. The nation confronted turbulent political and social violence at home and a savage war of civilization in North Africa. Government, according to the new emperor, had to encourage "the necessary means . . . for advancing civilization," and this approach was as true of France proper as it was of its North African colony.[37] The Second Empire, Napoleon III famously declared, meant "peace," and peace meant curbing political extremism as well as *indigène* resistance. Napoleon III and his entourage saw themselves as both reformers and peacekeepers. Despite the division and odium incurred by years of political and social rivalry, the emperor never wavered in his certainty that the French people could transcend their differences and form a single, harmonious community. "If France is not completely homogeneous in its nature—it is unanimous in its sentiments," he declared before an audience in 1858.[38] In no uncertain terms, Napoleon III intended to pacify the French territory through the promotion of "progress, humanity, and civilization."[39] The dictates implicit in this *pax Napoléon* constituted the germ of a trans-Mediterranean civilizing mission.

The imperial leadership's reluctance to associate the Second Empire with any single political ideology or faction did not preclude the potential for unity. Modernization and remaking France in the image of a modern society were intended to form a common middle ground that was sensitive to elite concerns yet progressive and forward looking. Branding this social vision as *civilisation* incarnate furnished a moral basis for imposing it on others. Whether carried out pacifically or forcefully, civilizing the country amounted to a "moral conquest." "Civilization, although having for its aim the moral improvement and material well-being of the greatest number, progresses . . . like an army," Napoleon III explained. "Its victories are not obtained without sacrifices and victims."[40] The Bonapartist leadership fashioned itself crusaders committed to vanquishing the moral barbarism and savagery that impeded modernity's development. They were men endowed with a mission to modernize and civilize, a claim that effectively rationalized the use of force and violence against opponents as they tenaciously consolidated this "moral conquest." "Let's not forget," Napoleon III reminded in 1858, "the development of all new power is a long struggle."[41] As the bearers of modern civilization, however, the Bonapartists believed they were on the offensive in this struggle. As César Vimercati, an Italian nationalist and close friend of the emperor, stated in 1858, "In our day it is no longer the barbarian but rather civilization that has come to be an invading force."[42]

Modernization à Outrance

Giving a speech in Bordeaux in 1852 shortly after the promulgation of the Second Empire, Louis Napoleon candidly stated his objective of realizing a vigorous policy of economic renovation throughout the country. "We have an immense amount of uncultivated land to clear, roads to build, ports to dig out, rivers to make navigable, canals to finish, and our network of railroads to complete." These undertakings, he assured his audience, were how he "understood the Empire."[43] For the Bonapartists, the economic decline and slow pace of French industrial development during the first half of the nineteenth century had left France to flounder while other nations, particularly Great Britain, advanced. "Today steam and railroads are producing numerous marvels," Persigny insisted during a speech delivered in Roanne. "So as to ensure that we profit from all the benefits of these glorious inventions, so that we do not allow ourselves to be outpaced by the other nations of Europe, it is essential that not a single corner of French soil be bereft of these grand currents of richness and prosperity. In a word, French civilization is still incomplete; it is necessary to bring it to fruition."[44]

By the mid-nineteenth century, France was still a primarily rural country. The neoteric landscape of cities, factories, and railroads conjured by urban idealists was far removed from life in *la France profonde*. Farming methods and equipment remained traditional in most cases, with peasants suspicious or ignorant of new mechanized machinery and scientific advances in agronomy.[45] French cities and agricultural centers still proved susceptible to natural disasters, a fact made evident to all in 1856 when the Rhône, Loire, and Cher Rivers overflowed their banks. Crops in the region were devastated, while areas around the cities of Lyon and Tours were temporarily transformed into swamps. Large-scale crop failures only came to an end in France after the 1840s, culminating in the most devastating failures of 1846 and 1847, which caused widespread hunger in the country and fueled the discontent leading up to the revolution the following year. Epidemics also persisted to threaten the country, the most severe outbreaks occurring in the early 1830s and again in late 1848 when Asiatic cholera claimed more than nineteen thousand victims and provoked civil unrest in the capital.[46] Disease was particularly rampant in urban areas that were mephitic and unsanitary. In contrast, parts of "savage" Africa could be more salubrious. Visiting the Algerian village of Boufarik in 1860, Thierry-Mieg was staggered to discover that "the state of sanitation here is better than that generally found in France."[47]

Natural disasters, epidemics, and crop failures demonstrated that modernity's material benefits had yet to penetrate vast parts of the country. The "incomplete" nature of French civilization noted by Persigny was all too evident to urban observers and proved to be the norm rather than the exception. Coupled with political instability and social disorder, the problems facing France often paralleled those facing African societies where a disorderly "tribalism," outdated agricultural methods, and traditional forms of industry were commonly held up as indicators of the uncivilized and backward nature of Oriental life. At its core, the Bonapartist program prescribed a veritable civilizing mission for France proper, promising the order and prosperity befitting a modern people. In the opinion of the influential Algerian policymaker Ismael Urbain, "peace and work" were the means through which social and material improvement would be achieved, and this work was primarily the responsibility of the government.[48]

Urbain's conviction bore the marks of the Saint-Simonian philosophy to which he subscribed. He was one of many Saint-Simonians who associated themselves with the Bonapartist government after the coup. Henri de Saint-Simon, a political and economic theorist writing in the early nineteenth century, had professed a strong faith in Europe's new industrial civilization, which he believed to be the final and ultimate stage in man's progressive development. Society was to be a "truly organized machine," for it was only this type of society that would be able to establish an organic unity between industrial labor and the exploitative demands of modern capitalism.[49] An early forerunner of utopian socialism, Saint-Simon envisaged his system based upon scientific advancement and industry as the surest means of remedying many of the social ills afflicting Europe. "There exists only one common interest for all men," as he wrote in 1803, "that of the progress of science."[50] The task at hand was to harness the potential of the nineteenth century and forge "a great society of industry."[51]

The Saint-Simonians comprised a diverse group of individuals dedicated to the philosopher's theories of technocratic social organization. The emphasis on competent planning and bureaucratic regulation never amounted to a strict doctrine or belief system so much as a set of general principles and guidelines for the effective management of industrial society. As such, it proved highly adaptable to various schools of political thought and ideology, whether authoritarian, liberal, or republican in nature. The movement's appeal lay in its broad conception of a technologically advanced world administered and governed by savants, and it was, therefore, hardly astonishing that a generation of entrepreneurs and social critics enthusiastically took up Saint-Simon's gospel. Enthusiasts motivated by his vision of a society transformed through industry and rigorous social engineering rallied to the Second Empire, obtaining key positions in the military and civil administration as well as the French financial world.[52]

The nominal leader of the Saint-Simonian cult was Prosper Enfantin, a polytechnician and aspiring political economist whose stringent demeanor and aversion to liberalism often clashed with the socialist and revolutionary opinions of his cohorts. Upon Saint-Simon's death in 1825, Enfantin convoked a meeting of his followers in Ménilmontant, a rural suburb on the outskirts of Paris where his family owned a large house surrounded by pastures and farmland. There, the Saint-Simonians formed an isolated community practicing a daily regimen that bordered on the monastic. An eccentric disposed toward mysticism and unorthodox Christian beliefs, Enfantin cultivated an identity for himself as a quasi-holy man, taking the title of "father" to convey his new spiritual authority. During his time at Ménilmontant, père Enfantin used religious spectacle and impassioned speeches to inspire loyalty among his followers. As he consolidated his position at the head of the movement, he liberally reinterpreted the teachings of his former master in the process.[53]

Like many of his contemporaries, Enfantin contended that the French Revolution had eroded the foundations of European society. Advancements in industry and science over the course of the century offered the kernel of the new society to come, a society with little precedent in past models that demanded new forms of social and economic organization. "[The older generation] has only seen the past restored or demolished while the current generation has need of founding and constructing a new edifice," he wrote to a friend in 1840.[54] The architects of this new society were to be the cadre of savants and engineers who adhered to the Saint-Simonian philosophy: technocratic elites who, unlike elected politicians, possessed the knowledge and impartiality to govern in the interest of society.[55] "I am by necessity and by taste, I will say nearly by passion," Enfantin admitted, "a man of power rather than of liberty."[56] His authoritarian ideology sought nothing short of "constructing the future" through the management of industry and the moral reeducation of individuals, investing scientists and engineers with the power to reform society and place it on a rational foundation.[57] Building a new social edifice required "a very intelligent, vigorous, unitary, and even despotic power" capable of carrying out the "preparatory work" of reconstruction.[58] Likening parliamentary government to "a sepulcher filled with worm-eaten cadavers," Enfantin foresaw a strong and well-administered state as the only means of bringing forth the dynamic type of society he and his followers envisaged.[59] "To begin the organization of industry," he avowed, "it is necessary that the government give the example."[60]

Napoleon III was no stranger to the ideas of the Saint-Simonians, having been introduced to Enfantin's works during the 1840s.[61] Often styled as "Saint-Simon on horseback," the emperor adopted many of Saint-Simonianism's core tenets, taking to heart its insistence on the primacy of economics within politics, the importance of enlightened individuals in leading the work of social development, and the necessity of state intervention in initiating and implementing social and economic policies.[62] Governments alone possessed the resources and authority to bring about far-reaching and extensive social transformation, making them "the primary agent of all social organization."[63] In the purview of Bonapartist ideology, the state was not only envisioned as a constraint against disorder; it was a powerful instrument capable of shaping the contours of society and guiding progress. Outside of the state's administrative hierarchy, as Persigny was keen to note, there was "nothing but grains of sand without cohesion or common purpose."[64]

A resolute *étatiste* and principal apologist for Bonapartist authoritarianism, Persigny saw state-driven economic growth as the only feasible means of modernizing France. Perpetual instability since 1789 had undermined confidence in national finances and discouraged entrepreneurs and investors from engaging in large-scale industrial and commercial enterprises. "It is hardly surprising that in a country that has been subject to revolutions, emotions continue to be troubled by memories of the past," he remarked.[65] If individual initiative could not be counted upon, the state would have to assume responsibility for developing the national economy lest France be reduced to a second-rate power. "Modern societies" relied upon what Persigny considered the "intelligent organization" (*organisation savant*) of resources and labor.[66] Only through the application of "modern economic tools" could a people perfect "the instruments of pacific conquest," making their society competitive, robust, and, above all, dominant.[67] "The degree of a country's civilization," the emperor reminded, "is revealed by the progress of industry as well as its sciences and arts."[68] Work and productivity constituted the essential components of a civilization, and this conviction conformed to a vision of modernity read in terms of industrial and economic capacity.

In executing the practical work of modernization, the government ordered numerous surveys aimed at evaluating the industrial and agricultural capacities of the country throughout the 1850s. Officials were instructed to inspect dams and irrigation networks in agricultural centers vital to the national economy and suggest means for obviating flooding and other natural disasters detrimental to farming. Statistics on existing mineralogical resources were compiled to appraise regional mining and industrial capabilities while the real and potential agricultural production of departments was reassessed and reliable demographic statistics gathered.[69] The data were intended to give the government an informed idea of "the material situation of the state," as well as suggest possible ways of exploiting these resources and calculating the revenues expected from state-sponsored public works.[70] The bold initiative spearheaded by the government could, at times, even extend down to the local level. In the late 1860s, the Ministry of Agriculture, Commerce, and Public Works encouraged prefects to write up reports and make observations on regional and municipal expositions showcasing recent inventions and manufacturing techniques. These exhibitions, the minister Adolphe Forcade de la Roquette insisted, "serve the general interest and progress by contributing to the perfection of production, encouraging exchanges, and disseminating knowledge and well-being."[71] In the sweeping assessment of French industrial and commercial capabilities ordered by the imperial regime, no corner of the country was to be disregarded as officials scoured the cities and countryside to construct an accurate picture of France's economic and industrial potential.

In January 1860, Napoleon III publicly laid out an ambitious economic project for the country. Based on the statistical data gathered, the plan called for allocating funds for drainage and irrigation, providing credit to generate agricultural and industrial ventures, and, most important, continuing the construction of railroads and transportation routes that encouraged commercial exchange and production.[72] Rail construction constituted a centerpiece of the state's modernizing program. "If you want to form an idea quickly of the degree of advancement in a people's industry," the senator and former Saint-Simonian Michel Chevalier claimed, "don't look to gold or money, but to iron."[73] Indeed, iron rails were symbols of a new type of industry and economy, "that great industry of transports, which exercises a very decisive influence on the general prosperity," as one economist described it in 1866.[74] While the July Monarchy had given modest support to numerous small-scale and independent rail companies during the 1840s, the Second Empire envisioned a far grander scheme of interconnected transport networks stretching across the country.[75] As Persigny accurately remarked in 1861 when presenting his annual report to the Corps législatif, "the progressive development of our rail lines is today one of our most lively preoccupations and, it is necessary to say, one of the most legitimate for the populations of the Empire."[76]

While the government fused the array of small rail companies operating in France into six large companies and offered concessions to encourage construction and boost confidence in the new ventures, it also recognized the need for private investment and access to credit in financing railroads.[77] Thus, in 1853 Napoleon III authorized the creation of the Crédit Mobilier, an investment bank that purchased railway stocks and underwrote many of the major lines built during the 1850s. The bank was the brainchild of Émile and Isaac Pereire, brothers born of Portuguese immigrants who became leading entrepreneurs in France by midcentury. Having flirted with Saint-Simonianism during the years of the July Monarchy, the Pereires enjoyed access to many exclusive financial and political circles within the country and never hesitated to call upon former cohorts from their days as Saint-Simonians who might be in positions of power and influence. Profiting from these ties, the brothers gained the support of top government officials for the proposed bank, and within its first year the Crédit Mobilier financed the construction of three principal rail lines—the Midi Railroad, the Grand Central Railroad, and the French Eastern Railroad. The Pereires were not, however, the only entrepreneurs to capitalize on their Saint-Simonian connections. Edouard and Paulin Talabot, rivals of the Pereires, also obtained support from within the imperial government and in 1857 their Compagnie du chemin de fer de Paris à Lyon et à la Méditerranée was commissioned to build a line running along the major trade artery between the capital and the ports on the southern coast.[78]

If competition for state contracts was sometimes fierce on the continent, the same could not be said of Algeria. With the conquest of Kabylia in 1857, French authority was consolidated throughout the Tell Atlas region and native resistance temporarily quelled. The end of major combat operations offered France a chance to proceed with the "pacific conquest" of its North African territory. "The affairs of Algeria have thankfully entered a new period as the trials of war become rarer and have less importance than in the past," the military commander Ferdinand Hugonnet claimed in 1860. "The moment has come to preoccupy ourselves especially with pacific enterprises and the means of assuring the prosperity of the colony."[79] Plans for the development of a colonial economy were considered by the Algerian administration, and the necessity of rail lines occupied a central concern in a country with very few roads or navigable rivers. As the primary owner of Algeria's rich iron mines, Paulin Talabot expressed a marked interest in the project, envisioning a network of African rails transporting ore to the coastal ports and, subsequently, to France where it would fuel his growing industrial empire.[80] In 1860, the Talabots won the commission to build three initial rail lines in the colony and, by 1863, enjoyed a state-sponsored monopoly over Algerian rail construction, making their Compagnie des chemins de fer algériens the sole holder of all North African rail networks.[81] Although the initial rail lines proved to be short and slow, their creation nonetheless stood as a symbol of France's civilizing influence in Africa. Attending the inaugural ceremony of the Algiers–Blida railroad in 1862, Théophile Gautier clearly foresaw "an approaching future filled with promise opening for French Africa."[82]

The opening of new railroads always presented an occasion for pomp and ceremony with state-appointed officials lauding the achievements of the regime and blandishing the emperor. When delivering a speech at the inauguration of a new rail line running from Nantes to Lorient in 1862, the prefect of the Morbihan left little doubt as to who was responsible for the modernizing feats transforming the country. "It is to the Emperor, to his generous and patriotic plans, to his ardent love for all which can be useful to the country that we owe this complete network crossing Brittany in every direction."[83] As a potent symbol of modernization, rail construction epitomized the modernizing thrust endorsed by the imperial state. More important, it testified to an underlying logic that ran through the various projects spearheaded by the regime. It was through such "ameliorative practices" that the "chimeras" of radical and revolutionary transformation would be dispelled, Louis Napoleon had argued.[84] Unlike previous regimes, the Second Empire was attending to the hard and practical work of economic and material development. For government supporters, legitimate public authority could derive from practical efforts and sage policies favorable to progress and the public good. Modernization not only exposed the errors of foolhardy radicals and violent social change; it provided the Bonapartist government with a much needed source of legitimacy. As the emperor once insisted, the "best government" adapted "to the desires of the period" and modeled itself "on the existing state of society."[85] In publicizing its modernizing agenda, the Bonapartist clan intended to show itself as both pragmatic and of its time, offering a powerful rationale for Napoleonic leadership in the process.

Conveying the Modern through "Grand Measures"

Public addresses and ceremonies highlighting the accomplishments of the Second Empire constituted only one means of brandishing the modern and civilizing image coveted by the regime. Exhibitions organized by the state similarly offered an alluring theater in which to display to France and the world the work nurtured by the government. In an effort to emulate Britain's Great Exhibition staged in 1851, Napoleon III held his own International Exhibition on the Champs-Élysées in 1855, complete with displays of French industry and manufacturing housed in the newly built Palais de l'Industrie. More than a decade later, a second international exhibition—the Exposition Universelle—was staged in Paris to show "the complete representation of modern society in all its modes of activity," according to Victor Duruy, one of the exhibition's chief organizers.[86] Attending the exposition, Raimond de Miravals could not deny that France had been subject to an impressive transformation under the new Bonaparte. "After having exhausted itself on the glories of war and the glories of the past [France] has sought to inaugurate a new era built upon the glories of peace and the splendors of the future."[87] Busts of Napoleon III naturally adorned architectural designs in the exposition halls while the gold medals presented to the exhibition winners were embossed with the emperor's likeness. The Second Empire, these symbolic gestures proclaimed, stood for progress, industry, science, and prosperity.[88]

If exhibitions were fast becoming one of "the great rituals for celebrating the industrial world" in the nineteenth century, they were equally theaters in which to showcase the nation's "civilizing" influence abroad.[89] During the years of the Second Empire, the colonies attained greater public visibility alongside national representations of economic progress and innovation. Imperial officials consciously used expositions for the purpose of mobilizing interest in France's growing colonial empire, targeting both economic elites and the general public. Products from the colonies were put on display at exhibition stalls while placards reporting on state-sponsored public works and colonial economic projects aimed to attract investors and familiarize French audiences with the overseas territories. More dramatic exhibitions—such as the one staged at the Exposition Universelle of 1867, which regaled spectators with North African craft workers, African dancers, and Sudanese jewelers working their trade—attempted to create a mise-en-scène of the French colonial world, bringing what was far away close and demonstrating the achievements of French civilization in spectacular fashion.[90] Expositions, as Jules Duval observed in 1867, were a "magnificent spectacle" and a form of "popular education" that were coming to play an important role in nineteenth-century French national and colonial culture.[91]

At the international exhibitions hosted by the state, Bonapartist modernity was put on display for all to see. Yet one did not necessarily have to pay the admission fee at the Palais d'Industrie to comprehend the changes taking place in the country. Accompanying the economic transformation wrought by the regime was an extensive urbanization initiative aimed at drastically altering and revitalizing French cities. In 1853 Persigny selected the bordelaise prefect Georges-Eugène Haussmann to serve in Paris and direct the emperor's plans for renovating the capital. Prior regimes had overseen urbanization projects in the past, but they had typically been conducted in piecemeal fashion. Napoleon III envisaged a far more comprehensive project, one intended to beautify and enrich the capital of his modern empire. The imperious Haussmann was an ideal candidate for the job. As prefect of the Seine, he used the highly centralized Bonapartist state to restructure the city in accordance with the emperor's designs, opening up avenues to commerce, improving infrastructure, constructing a new sewer system, and remodeling entire neighborhoods. Old slums conducive to crime and disease were torn down and replaced with expansive boulevards and handsome buildings housing upscale residents and department stores (*grands magasins*). The cost of this massive project was estimated at an astronomical 2.5 billion francs, an unprecedented sum at the time.[92]

Imperial public works actively constructed and built the modern metropolis, and spectators were encouraged to view the new city as such.[93] It was primarily due to the efforts of the imperial regime that the cleric Antoine Arbousse-Bastide could extol Paris as the "capital of the modern world" during his trip in 1857.[94] As the principal locus of French industry and the depository of the major cultural and political institutions of the nation, Paris possessed "all the splendors and attractions of civilization," the economist Charles Lavollée boasted in 1865, echoing sentiments found in standard guide books of the day.[95] The demolitions and public works symbolic of the "new era" promised by the Bonapartist government became a familiar aspect of the modern experience remarked upon by writers and intellectuals. Laments over the demise of "old Paris" were mixed with reflections on the bewildering crowds and new style of public life encouraged by Haussmann's designs.[96] Parisians watched as familiar streets and neighborhoods were transformed into a sprawling construction site. "Everywhere houses in ruin, demolitions commenced, unfinished constructions, wooden gates, fences of dirty and disjointed planks, scaffolding blocking views, masonry and carpentry tools lying about," one critic complained.[97] Outside of Paris, urban modernization projects elicited the same perplexity. During his provincial travels, Taine was clearly impressed by the new Marseille with its seven-story apartment buildings, boulevards, wide streets, and stores. "It grows every day," he claimed, "building, demolition, stretching out to the hillsides and new ports. I saw it four years ago and it is now unrecognizable. . . . I have seen nothing like it except in London."[98]

Paradoxically, what urbanites might find unfamiliar in the new streets and buildings being erected in France often possessed an element of familiarity in French North Africa. Building projects in Algiers and other Maghrebi cities brought a discernible French character to urban areas as the old Moorish and Ottoman landscape began to disappear. The Marine Quarter of Algiers that housed the government offices looked like "a little rue de Rivoli," the painter and traveler writer Eugène Fromentin claimed in 1852. All the buildings reflected a noticeably Parisian style while on the streets a tourist could find cafés and French stores.[99] In the city of Bône to the west, Charles Thierry-Mieg discovered a similar phenomenon taking place by the early 1860s. "There are a few Arab streets, narrow, dirty, and lined with Moorish houses," he observed. "The others have all been enlarged with beautiful and looming European houses constructed on them."[100] Winding avenues bordered by Arab markets and Oriental facades could still be found in the city but they were increasingly relegated to small enclaves that French urbanization had yet to penetrate. "The Oriental has little by little been transformed into a modern city and the civilization of France has come to implant itself heroically in the heart of barbarism," declared the journalist Augustin Marquand in 1869 when assessing the government's building projects in Algiers.[101]

As Marquand stressed, imparting a French character to the cities of North Africa constituted an important aspect of France's civilizing mission. Employing teams of French architects and civil engineers, the imperial government worked to transform Algiers into a modern metropolis structured around investment and commercial exchanges that would, in time, nurture France's new imperial territory. In 1854, a Commission des Plans was created to consider proposals and organize the practical work of urban renovation. Under the engineer Charles Frédéric Chassériau, Algiers was transformed into the capital of France's new North African empire with promenades lining the bay, wide boulevards replacing the old, torturous streets and Parisian-inspired edifices supplanting the indigenous architecture.[102] Evaluating the plans for France's new colony in the late 1850s, Prince Jérôme Napoleon boasted that Algeria would stand as "the most beautiful conquest of the Second Empire" and "give the new government a great deal of prestige" as its efforts to bring the benefits of civilization to North Africa matured and bore fruit.[103] Inaugurating the new Boulevard de l'Impératrice completed in 1864, a spokesman for Morton Peto, the British firm contracted to carry out the work, praised the thoroughfare as a symbol of the imperial regime's commitment to North African development. "From these initial works," the representative proclaimed before a crowd of colonists and government officials, "it is obvious that the commerce of Algiers and the public in general will receive an immense advantage derived from the ease of communication between the port and the city and the sales that the stores on the boulevard will offer." The new city materializing on the Algerian coast epitomized the emperor's "ardent interest in the well-being and prosperity" of the colonial city.[104]

While the new urban landscapes brought investment and created cities reflecting the modern and capitalist ethos that the new regime claimed to embody, they also promised a measure of public order in a country agitated by years of social and political instability.[105] The narrow, medieval streets and working-class quarters of Paris that had consistently provided strongholds for urban insurrectionists were destroyed and replaced by wide public spaces easily accessible to troops and the gendarmerie.[106] Napoleon III was no stranger to the temperament of the French working classes that had risen up in 1848. As a self-proclaimed *homme d'ordre* he understood that the success of his regime depended upon neutralizing the threat of sporadic civil strife.[107] Building projects not only discouraged labor militancy by giving employment to workers in the construction trades; they equally relocated the more unruly elements of the population—namely, day laborers and the urban poor—to the urban periphery.[108] With the gentrification of Paris's center came new middle-class and upscale residents who could afford the higher rents of the newly constructed buildings. According to Victor Fournel, a writer critical of the government's urbanization initiative, Paris had been remade in the image of the conservative and empire-supporting bourgeois. "Today, when M. Prudhomme—proprietor, elector, expert juror, and captain of the *garde nationale*—climbs to the summit of the Vendôme column," he chided in 1865, "he looks majestically on Paris [and] sees . . . a city as august and majestic as himself."[109]

Attempts to relegate a "savage" working class to the margins of French cities were consistent with the more aggressive social engineering in

Algeria where newly arriving colonists supplanted the native inhabitants of Maghrebi cities.[110] Visiting Algiers in the 1850s, Fromentin could already recognize the segregation that would become a common feature of colonial society. "Not being able to do away with the Algerians we've left them with only just enough space to live in up on the belvedere of the old pirates."[111] The destruction of Moorish and Arab architecture and the dislocation experienced by many Algerians brought significant changes to the "profound and mysterious Orient that civilization must fatally invade in a very short time," as Gautier claimed.[112] The street bazaars had disappeared along with the Arabs who had once attended them; whole sections of Algiers existed now in name and memory alone; religious customs and cultural traditions were giving way to modern habits brought by the Europeans. "Proceeding by the principle of tabula rasa, civilization has begun by tearing down everything not in accordance with its tastes," Fromentin wrote cynically.[113] For the dramatist Ernest Feydeau, the results of colonization were disheartening as the exotic character of the Orient became eclipsed by a banal and unremarkable European landscape. "The Orient is disappearing," he lamented in 1860, "disputing the terrain step by step, but it is disappearing with its exquisite forms."[114]

Through the building projects undertaken by the Bonapartists, "modern civilization" acquired a geographic and spatial dimension within French territories that served to dramatically symbolize the extensive modernization promised by imperial statesmen. The English travel writer Henry Blackburn could not ignore the transformations evident in Rouen as he walked the city streets in the late 1860s. Provincial houses and medieval cathedrals indicative of the "old Rouen" were now lost in the midst of factories belching smoke, industrial cranes, and screeching locomotives. The quaint, provincial city Blackburn had visited on numerous occasions in the past was, he conceded, "disappearing like a dissolving view" before the new urban landscape erected by the disciplined army of administrators and civil engineers employed by the state.[115] The sense of transition that these new urban vistas inspired similarly extended to smaller towns where building projects and rail construction, while perhaps more modest than the large-scale urbanization taking place in major cities, were no less impressive. "Everywhere our villages are being transformed," a resident in the town of Bourges claimed in 1863. "Thatch is giving way to slate, walls are being raised, doors and windows are being enlarged [and] tiled floors are replacing mud."[116]

Although urbanization offered the most striking examples of Bonapartist modernization, it remained only one policy among many aimed at consolidating the modern identity communicated by imperial statesmen. Much like the building projects commissioned by the state, the development of national and colonial industries, the inaugural festivities celebrating newly laid rail lines and state-organized industrial exhibitions all attempted to convey and symbolize the "modern" spirit and orientation of Napoleon III's government. The pomp and pageantry associated with these events became regular facets of the "spectacular politics" habitually used by the emperor and his entourage to legitimate and boost support for the regime in an era of mass democracy.[117] As Napoleon III informed his cousin, Prince Jérôme, in 1852, "It is through small measures that one wins over individuals in the same way that it is only through grand measures that one attaches the masses to them."[118]

Yet the symbolism and panoply surrounding these events transcended mere public spectacle. The Bonapartist leadership used orations and state policies to highlight the government's self-proclaimed modern qualities. The discourse and rhetoric employed by the regime prefigured the context in which these actions and gestures were to be understood, endowing them with a quintessentially "modern" import and connotation. For a regime priding itself on its modern character, state policies logically translated into acts of modernization that subsequently validated the government's orientation and identity. Rather than a process, modernization offered a discursive framework for representing and legitimating certain types of political and social action. It was the act of modernizing that authenticated the rigorous self-fashioning of Bonapartist ideologues and, subsequently, furnished the rationale for the highly centralized and interventionist imperial state.

While historians assessing the democratic and national style of politics that came of age in France after 1848 have often spoken of the emergence of a "modern" political culture at midcentury, the political discourse that underpinned much of the Second Empire's policies suggests a slightly different conclusion.[119] Modernity and "modern society" were themes embedded in and elaborated through the political language of the period, exhibiting a *political culture of modernity* rather than an inherently "modern" political culture. Through the rhetorical devices used by politicians and corresponding acts of "modernization" carried out by the state, French politics rendered the modern social imaginary incarnate and palpable as the modernizing process came to insert itself directly into the daily life and experience of the nation. Rather than the unrolling of a universal process, modernization was the essential means of conjuring the modern, linking discourse with practice, and ideology with reality.

3   Civilizing and Nationalizing

In an exposé published in the summer of 1852, the political commentator Edward Warmington began his examination of French society with a familiar and by most standards commonplace narrative. Since 1789, the country had been torn apart by revolutionary antagonisms, public prosperity had dwindled, and faith in French government was increasingly diminishing with each fallen regime. "Our political divisions have degenerated into personal hatreds and hostilities," he apprised his readers, "and our differences of opinion have nearly made us forget our nationality, our interests, and our common duties." France required a government "suffused with a patriotic spirit," one that was "politically national and democratic," if prosperity and confidence were to be restored.[1] Neither erudite nor exceptionally shrewd in its analysis, Warmington's book nonetheless epitomized what historians have called the "Franco-French wars," the vicious political antipathies and partisanship that continued to plague French society long after the French Revolution's ambiguous conclusion.[2] The tenor of Warmington's rhetoric and the suggestive title of his book—*What Is Bonapartism?*—left little doubt as to the agenda it sought to advance and prefigured the objectives and political language that would remain central to the Bonapartist platform over the next two decades.

Although Bonapartist modernity defended and actively promoted the interests of French capitalism, Napoleon III always insisted that Bonapartism was, at heart, a "social idea" capable of uniting a divided nation. The architects of the Second Empire envisioned a form of social organization that an inherently cosmopolitan capitalist system structured by economic relationships and practices of free exchange and commodity could not realize. As Anthony Giddens has noted, "a capitalist society is a 'society' only because it is a nation-state."[3] A Bonapartist France might be capitalist in content but it was to be unquestionably national in form, according with the ideals of liberty and nationality first enunciated by French patriots in 1789. Pronouncements celebrating the nation's revolutionary legacy not only allowed the Bonapartists to represent the imperial regime as a national government and capitalize on the eminent mystique of the Bonaparte name; they were also essential. Napoleon III comprehended the situation facing his regime. The Second Empire would survive only by "assuring the future, by closing the era of revolutions, and by consecrating the conquests of '89."[4]

Under the *pax Napoléon*, peace and order would be restored as the old hatreds and ideological enmity stimulated by years of social and political unrest were effaced. Over time, the population would be instilled with the necessary values to sustain a liberal, democratic society. Liberty, according to Napoleon III, developed with the political education of a nation, "crowning" the political edifice "when time has consolidated it."[5] Only once a "new political generation, young, vigorous, and independent" came of age and replaced "the souls enervated by revolution" would France be fit to enjoy the fruits of true liberty.[6] Needless to say, this future generation would reflect a new type of individual inculcated with the values and patriotic ideals proper to the imperial regime. The advent of the Second Empire constituted a revolution of sorts, but one that intended to mold individuals and society pacifically and progressively, constituting what Persigny described as a "new political evolution."[7] "We come from revolutionaries," Prince Jérôme Napoleon Bonaparte, one of the more radical members of the Bonapartist clan, stated before the senate in 1862, "but honest ones."[8]

As "honest" revolutionaries, the Bonapartists fashioned themselves defenders of liberty and national self-determination, identifying these dual principles as the core ideological precepts of France's revolutionary heritage. The nationalist currents evident in Bonapartist rhetoric owed much to the political and intellectual atmosphere generated by the events of 1848 that inflected revolutionary and political discourse with an eminently national gestalt.[9] The pan-European revolutions of 1848 had set out to consummate the work of 1789 and emancipate nations from the oppressive yoke of monarchial tyranny.[10] Failure had not quashed the hopes of European republicans and nationalists, and the movements for national unification that emerged during the 1860s in Italy and Germany encouraged critics to believe that the ideals of 1848 were, indeed, still alive. "We must recognize that the time of nationalities has come, that it is the breath of their emancipation that shakes the old thrones and shatters the foundations of that old society," an anonymous French pamphlet stated in 1860.[11] The Bonapartist government remained sensitive to these currents and exploited every opportunity to express its commitment to the cause of European and in particular French nationalism. However, these nationalist aspirations went beyond validating the Second Empire's revolutionary credentials. In their speeches, imperial spokesmen frequently tied the Bonapartist state to a set of traditions deemed "natural" to the French people and soil. Efforts to indigenize the Second Empire and associate it with a primordial Gallic nation went hand in hand with the revolutionary identity it encouraged, producing a specific brand of nationalism that spoke to both left and right while coating the imperial government in a patina of national legitimacy. If the Bonapartist were inaugurating a revolution, it was often difficult to tell on what side of the political spectrum this revolution lay.[12]

Bonapartist nationality policies would also see this revolution brought to North Africa during the 1860s as the emperor breached the troublesome "Algerian question." Napoleon III endeavored to use Algeria as a symbol of his sincerity to the cause of national liberation, bolstering an explicitly Arab national identity intended for France's Muslim subjects. While the promotion of Arab nationality was in line with the spirit of the imperial regime, efforts to spread the Bonapartist revolution to the North African frontier proved highly problematic and, ultimately, brought to light many of the inherent contradictions at the heart of the state's nationality policies. As statesmen and officials grappled with the tensions between national identification and cultural diversity, two competing logics of Frenchness and the nation emerged that were not easily reconcilable. Political and cultural forms of nationalism were often promoted at will, resulting in a contradictory and, at times, incoherent ideology centered on *nationalité* that attempted to make sense of a French society that was diverse while in theory unified.

Bonapartist modernity aspired to modernize both state and people, and the promotion of *nationalité* represented a distinct form of modernization employed by the government. Attempting to achieve order through force and violence had only served to add salt to old wounds in the past, leaving the country divided along regional, political, ethnic, and confessional lines. Suturing these divisions necessitated a unifying idea, and to this end the Bonapartist leadership readily placed the concept of national association at the heart of its modernizing program. According to Napoleon III, national unity constituted "a holy cause" that had "the sympathies of the civilized world" as it consolidated its moral conquest over human barbarism and savagery.[13]

Janus-Faced Nationalism

"I am going to fight for Liberty, not for a party," the young journalist Philippe Faur claimed in 1848 as he welcomed the collapse of the July Monarchy that February. "From men and parties I expect nothing. My hopes are in the action of Providence, in a religious transformation to regenerate society."[14] Disillusioned with the interest-driven politics and elitism of Orléanist liberalism, Faur, like many of his contemporaries, zealously placed his faith in the new revolution's promise of national unity and revival.[15] In the wake of the June Days, Louis Napoleon proved adept at appealing to this widespread desire, bolstering a nationalist platform that catered to a yearning for solidarity and a sense of national mission lacking in postrevolutionary politics. A nation-builder and exponent of national liberation abroad, he was representative of the nationalist ambience prevalent in post-1848 Europe, a period in which the idiom of *nationalité* came to suffuse the political discourse of both the left and right.[16] "Nationality is the real religion of France," one critic remarked in 1861. "It is more than a principle or sentiment. At present, it is an unyielding instinct."[17] For imperial ideologues, *nationalité*, a concept pregnant with indigenous and historical connotations, was the vital center of the community, the lifeblood of society, and the primordial substance of the individual. "A people possess force," Napoleon III reminded his followers, "only by virtue of their nationality."[18] Such pronouncements became ubiquitous as the Bonapartists consolidated their power, making *nationalité* a rallying call of the new imperial regime.

Taking their cue from the emperor, propagandists for the new government played upon fears of national dissolution and lauded Napoleon III as the savior of the French nation. "French nationality no longer existed," the political writer Charles Piel de Troisments remarked when recounting France's turbulent history since 1789. "Napoleon III has given it a new life."[19] The Napoleonic parvenu embodied the "sentiments and providential instincts" of the French people, as one writer insisted.[20] "Before [the Empire] rallied all the forces of the nation," proclaimed Persigny with typical patriotic flair, "it was born in the cottages of the people."[21] Such nationalist rhetoric equally extended to Napoleon III's foreign policy and was especially encouraged in garnering public support for the government's Italian and Romanian policies in the 1860s. A particularly admiring pamphleteer blandished the emperor for his keen understanding of nationality's importance in the modern era. "The world moves along this path, proceeding more surely and quickly because it has found in Napoleon III, who understands its aspirations, its pilot."[22]

While Second Empire politics exhibited a brazenly nationalist tenor and attitude focused on the cult of the emperor, nationalism itself was nothing new to French politics. The concept of *la nation* already possessed a long history rooted in the intellectual and political culture of the ancien régime.[23] Many Enlightenment thinkers looked askance at the growing talk of "patriotism" in the mid-eighteenth century, preferring worldly cosmopolitanism to the "prejudices" nurtured by national identification. "It is sad that often in order to be a good patriot one is the enemy of the rest of mankind," Voltaire despaired. For his part, he was inclined to reject the senseless worship of the fatherland (*patrie*) and serve humanity as a "citizen of the world."[24] Although a tradition of cosmopolitanism retained an appeal among French intellectuals throughout the nineteenth century, maintaining the status of a world citizen became increasingly difficult in an age of proliferating national identification.[25] The revolutionary nationalism of the late eighteenth century proposed a new type of community that redefined established understandings of identity and territory across the continent.[26] National association implied that "France is, and must be, a single whole" as the revolutionary Emmanuel-Joseph Sieyès declared in September 1789.[27] More specifically, it was a unity constituted through the collective will of a sovereign people. Much as Rousseau and his republican acolytes anticipated, a nation was understood to be a political community formed of individuals invested with equal rights and, theoretically, partaking in the general will through an active civic participation.[28] The Napoleonic Code issued in 1804 may have muted these democratic elements, but it continued to adhere to egalitarian principles, equating *nationalité* with legal equality and the rights enjoyed by all French citizens.[29]

Declarations of natural and universal rights gave substance to the idea of a French national community, but these principles also rested upon broader ideals that transcended national boundaries. In the most radical phase of the French Revolution, republicans endeavored to carry the revolutionary élan across Europe, declaring that the ideals of Liberty, Equality, and Fraternity were not only French, but those of humanity and civilization in general. French national identity was, from its origins, tied to a universal and inclusive rhetoric that identified France as the repository of common values and aspirations.[30] "In England, Germany, Italy, and Spain there is expressed only the destinies of England, Germany, Italy and Spain," the republican Hippolyte Marlet claimed in 1854. "In France the destiny of mankind is expressed."[31] The jurist Jean-Gabriel Cappot expressed as much in his study on nationality, insisting that while other nations were composed of distinct groups that "retained the name of their race and the mark of their nature as a form of protest . . . France alone truly represented a unity, a nationality."[32] Despite Cappot's belief in French universalism, he, like Marlet, could not resist the temptation to attribute something definitively French to this universalism. "Undoubtedly, every great nation represents an idea important to universal man," the historian Jules Michelet would write in 1846. "But, good God, how much more true is this of France!"[33]

This distinctly French character noted by writers like Michelet hinted at a second idea of *la nation*, one diverging from civic and universal understandings. From the early years of the Revolution, a certain tension was evident within concepts of nationality.[34] The civil code of 1804 may have defined the nation in accordance with the rights of the citizen, but it concomitantly laid out more restrictive criteria regarding who in fact was to be considered part of the nation. Under article nine, French nationals were determined by jus sanguinis and residency requirements were established for foreigners and national minorities living within the country.[35] Although tied to a language of universal rights and citizenship, nationality was not a concept reducible to purely political and legal categorizations and over time became divorced from an overtly democratic-revolutionary context. During the Restoration and July Monarchy, liberals suspicious of popular sovereignty made distinctions between "civil" and "political" rights that favored legal rather than democratic ideas of citizenship.[36] They similarly endorsed a vision of the nation stressing historical and organic unity that judiciously marginalized the importance of the Revolution in favor of continuity with the past.[37] In contrast to the abstract and often cosmopolitan outlook of the *philosophes*, the postrevolutionary generation cultivated an appreciation for the particular historical experiences and cultural influences that shaped the character and mentality of a people. "Every people has its distinct genius," affirmed Taine, "that is why each people has its distinct history."[38]

Whereas revolutionaries interpreted the nation as a violent rupture with the past, postrevolutionary generations were inspired by desires to endow nations with a history and genealogy, eliciting a search for origins and "aboriginal essence."[39] This obsession with roots could extend down to the most elemental levels of society, cultivating an appreciation for the cultural specificity of the varying regional localities constellating the country—the *pays*. Nineteenth-century provincial elites wrote local histories, staged regional exhibitions, and encouraged the promotion of a localism rooted in the familiarity of provincial life and the individual's emotional attachment to both *pays* and *nation*. This vision of a France symbolizing "diversity in unity"(*variété dans l'unité*) frequently ran counter to the top-down nation-building policies endorsed by state authorities. Yet it did resonate with many liberals and conservative notables of the postrevolutionary period seeking alternative means of restructuring French society. More to the point, localism spoke to the romantic desire for an intimate and organic sense of belonging that linked local forms of experience, patriotism, and culture with the nation.[40]

If thinkers of the eighteenth century prized the universal equality and unity associated with revolutionary nationhood, their successors emphasized the unique, the historical, and the indigenous. With its focus on customs handed down over generations, language, and organic social development, romanticism inscribed nationality with an ethnological and particular content that did not always rest easily alongside its revolutionary counterpart. National essentialism encouraged the "culturalization" of peoples and societies, producing a discourse that could be just as reductive and exclusionary as the variants of biological racism taking hold in the nineteenth-century social sciences.[41] Indeed, as Stuart Hall has argued, cultural differentialism constituted one of "racism's two registers," producing a discourse in which cultural distinctions seamlessly merged with categories of biological and racial difference.[42]

In their veneration of nation and nationality, Bonapartist spokesmen frequently made little distinction between the varieties of nationalism they promoted, seeing fit to employ one or the other model as the occasion warranted. In the wake of the coup, statesmen were keen to emphasize the revolutionary and democratic orientation of imperial politics, insisting, as Persigny did, that the Second Empire was built upon "the principles and ideas of the Revolution of 1789."[43] The principal goal was to transform the illegal government into a popular one. Universal manhood suffrage, won by the people in 1848, was maintained even if the Second Republic was not. In 1852 the Bonapartists held a referendum asking the nation to go to the polls and either approve or reject the creation of the imperial state. With political opponents exiled and polling closely monitored, the Second Empire received the popular mandate desired by the leadership. The people had empowered the government through a single vote, "clear, simple, and understood by all," providing a democratic foundation for a regime that had violated the republican constitution and installed itself through military force a year earlier.[44] Popular approval, according to Napoleon III, was the "first guarantee" of a people's liberty, giving the nation "the right to choose the government that suits it."[45] In affirming the institutions and laws that presided over the nation, the French people were expected to view the state as an expression of their collective ambitions and values. The Bonapartists had made the French people "masters of their own destiny," as Persigny later explained, rendering the Second Empire the fulfillment of the nation's democratic and revolutionary ideals and the purest manifestation of the general will.[46]

The revolutionary and popular dimensions of Bonapartist nationalism owed much to the efforts of Persigny, a man of moderate republican conviction whose loyalty to the Bonapartist cause was incontestable. Whether through his use of the press and pamphlets to slander political opponents or his insistence that prefects encourage displays of popular support for the empire during public ceremonies and speeches, Persigny played an instrumental role in creating a Bonapartist movement capable of appealing to the great majority of French citizens over the fractious political elites of the country.[47] His populist inclinations were never radical in substance, and although he understood the utility of appealing to the masses over the political classes, he also understood the danger in alienating social elites. Persigny sought to define a Bonapartist program that was revolutionary and popular in spirit but capable of instilling trust in French notables. As minister of the interior during the 1850s and early 1860s, he dedicated himself to incorporating former politicians and statesmen into the government through appeals to patriotism and national devotion. "Do not neglect any occasion for convincing them that the country could profit from their wisdom and experience," he once advised prefects, "and remind them that while it is noble to reflect fondly on the past, it is still nobler to be useful to their country."[48]

The allure of a Bonapartist government, Persigny believed, was in its synthetic nature just as much as its revolutionary heritage. The French Revolution had left a legacy of sharp ideological division. There were "four or five nations within the nation," Persigny claimed, each identifying with different political principles and heritages believed to be incompatible.[49] Yet with its ambitions of establishing a Bonaparte dynasty at the head of the nation, the Second Empire could appeal to Legitimists while its dedication to order and prosperity curried favor with liberals. The commitment to universal manhood suffrage central to republican ideology was, moreover, shared by the government, holding out the possibility of rallying moderate and conservative republicans to an imperial state with a liberal and progressive orientation. Representing a "vast fusion of old opinions," the Second Empire could, in Persigny's opinion, potentially reconcile the old political hatreds dividing the nation and form a "great national party" attractive to both the masses and political society.[50] Owing to its broad appeal, Bonapartism offered the most solid foundation for a truly liberal France. "Between the monarchial habits of eight centuries and the republican form—the natural aim of all political perfection—there can still be an intermediary phase," Persigny claimed, "and I [think] that the blood of Napoleon, inoculated in the blood of France, could prepare a completely liberal regime better than all others."[51]

The marked republican and revolutionary nationalism that colored the speech of Bonapartist spokesmen remained, however, tempered by a persistent mistrust of popular participation. Napoleon III and his entourage never repudiated their commitment to the principle of national sovereignty, yet they also made it clear that the new empire would not perpetuate the revolutionary turmoil that had enervated the country. The regime intended to wage war on the forms of "savage liberty" that imperiled order and to develop the values and habits conducive to "the liberty of civilized people."[52] To this end, it was first necessary to "discipline the parties" and extirpate the source of conflict, advised Morny. Political groups would be reined in and inflammatory newspapers and extremist elements suppressed.[53] In time, the old rivalries would dissipate as the French people came to see themselves as compatriots bound by a common culture and national sentiment. In combating that "savage liberty" inspired by radicals, Bonapartist liberty endeavored to remove politics from the civil sphere, offering a robust and interventionist state committed to national prosperity and public welfare as an alternative to the unruly factionalism of party rule.[54] Parliamentarianism was discouraged on the grounds that it was particularly English and, therefore, alien to the temperament and character of the French people.[55] "The formation of English nationality has proceeded from totally different means than those followed for the formation of French nationality," Louis Napoleon pronounced in 1851 when presenting his constitution to the nation.[56] It was unfeasible just as much as unnatural to expect France to follow the English model of representative government. For the emperor as well as his most faithful followers, "national character" was the essence of any successful polity, necessitating a government derived from French traditions and customs. "The theory that seeks to impose the same forms of liberty everywhere," Persigny contended, "is as contrary to history as it is to reason."[57]

From its origins, therefore, the Second Empire was identified with a primordialism distinct from the nation's revolutionary tradition. Liberty was "susceptible to all forms," Persigny claimed. It varied with "the social state, history, and thousands of other circumstances of climate, race, and place" that formed a nationality.[58] Rather than an English-style parliament, France required a strong central authority. The French state, first created to suit the needs of the absolutist monarchs and subsequently used by the revolutionaries to carry out their agenda of radical reform, had evolved with the political development of the nation. What Persigny styled "the spirit of centralization" was natural to the French nation, for it was the state that had traditionally arbitrated between rowdy factions and defended public authority against the violence of the masses.[59] For an *étatiste* like Persigny, the heavy-handed bureaucracy maintained by the Napoleonic government conformed to this time-honored and native model of governance just as the democratic liberties guaranteed by the regime adhered to the nation's revolutionary heritage. By "submitting to the nation the principles of a constitution derived at once from the traditions of leadership belonging to his race and his own informed reflections," Napoleon III had, Persigny boasted, "elevated a monument" to France built upon "the natural foundations found on its soil."[60]

In cultivating a native identity for the government, imperial officials relied heavily upon a discourse of national particularism that associated the state with a certain history, set of traditions, and even ethnic identity. This was not the universal language of the French Revolution speaking, but rather the primordialism familiar to conservative and right-wing ideologues. Bonapartist populism spoke to the nation's revolutionary nationhood, placing the government on a popular footing. Yet these elements scarcely concealed the government's more illiberal and authoritarian elements. The highly centralized and interventionist state that, ultimately, constituted the instrument of the Bonapartist civilizing mission found its legitimacy elsewhere in the traditions of royal leadership and state authority that had forged the historical character of the nation. While studies on Bonapartism and the Second Empire have frequently stressed the national tenor of imperial politics, the evident contradictions and paradoxes replete in this nationalist agenda have yet to be fully appreciated. In French political discourse, arguments rooted in long-standing cultural associations and historical experience were liberally blended with a universal and revolutionary nationalist ideology vested in a language of rights, citizenship, and civic participation.[61] "To understand what we are it is necessary to know what our fathers were," Napoleon III asserted.[62] This verdict included not only understanding the revolutionary inheritance left by the nation's forefathers. It encompassed the historical lineage and patrimony extending down to the bedrock of the historical nation.

The Bonapartists certainly employed the idiom of *nationalité*, but they inscribed it with a dualism, imparting a Janus-faced character to French nationality, which was at once universal and particular.[63] These inconsistencies spoke to the acute need for legitimacy, whether to efface the illegal foundations of the regime or justify the actions of an illiberal, modernizing imperial state. Yet if the promotion of *nationalité* sought to validate the Second Empire, it also conformed to the modernizing impulses of the regime, promising an end to the "savage" conflicts of the past. Nationality was, in the final assessment, the mark of a modern people, a conviction that appeared self-evident as the government turned its attention to the project of nation building in Algeria.

Not a Colony "Strictly Speaking"

Walking through the streets of Paris in the spring of 1852, a spectator might have encountered a curious sight: Arabs dressed in military uniforms with the Croix de la Légion d'honneur pinned to their open burnoose. In preparation for military festivities scheduled to be held at the École Militaire that May, Louis Napoleon summoned a half dozen Arab military commanders from Algeria to the capital. The prince president's intentions were not only to reward the native commanders for their service to France in North Africa where they had fought valiantly alongside the Armée d'Afrique. The celebration, staged seven months before the revived Napoleonic Empire, would be presented to the people for approval, clearly possessed value as a tactful piece of Bonaparist propaganda. It permitted Louis Napoleon to demonstrate his support for the nation's "civilizing mission" in Africa and to warm the public to a Napoleonic restoration. As guests of the state, the commanders and their retinues were free to visit museums, attend the opera, and tour the city, much to the amusement of Parisian onlookers. Over the next two months French newspapers carried regular updates on the comings and goings of the exotic visitors, noting their cosmopolitanism, sociability, and European demeanor that stood in stark contrast to the stereotype of the "barbaric" Arab. "There were numerous women with them who have clearly adopted French habits and values and taken to wearing our style of dress," *Le Presse* informed its readers.[64]

On the day of the festivities, throngs of Parisians gathered to watch as the Algerian commanders received Napoleonic eagles among fluttering tricolors and artillerymen spanning the length of the Champ de Mars. Recounting the festivities, the journalist Henry Chauvin was less impressed with the decorated warriors than with the young men in their retinues donning western garb and speaking French. "These others belong to the young generation of natives who are familiar with our institutions and laws and who have witnessed their racial antipathies and religious prejudices dwindle due to contact with us," Chauvin admired. "They have only known fidelity to us and one can only attribute their influence and example to the progress that we have imprinted on the Arab population."[65]

Chauvin's adulation for France's "civilizing" initiative was representative of the national and colonial mentality growing up in the country. Since the Revolution, French engagements with religious and ethnic minorities had been inconsistent. The revolutionaries insisted that "foreign" communities living within the country must be subject to the civil code, thereby precluding minority groups from forming a "nation within a nation," as Napoleon would later brand French Jews. Despite certain efforts to dissolve ethnoreligious subgroups and integrate their members into the nation as individual citizens, the First Empire in fact tolerated ethnic minorities, establishing state institutions that worked with different ethnic groups and retained particular religious and customary laws in civil affairs. The *consistoires israélites* created in 1808 to liaise with Jewish notables and rabbis were matched by similar attempts to coordinate relations with Arab, Italian, and Polish refugee communities arriving in France during the early nineteenth century. This "cosmopolitan" polity in which the state acted as an arbitrator between various ethnic communities was continued under the Bourbon Restoration and would not be seriously challenged until the early 1830s as growing alarm over "foreigners" in the country and the Algerian conquest prompted a more xenophobic nationalism.[66] The nationalist resurgence of the late 1840s reanimated traditional republican demands for assimilation and national uniformity, emboldening colonialists to call for the creation of L'Algérie Française and the assimilation of North Africa's "barbaric" Oriental races.

Seeking to bolster popular support for his government, Louis Napoleon catered to these aspirations in the spring of 1852 by presenting the public with a spectacle assuring his commitment to assimilating and civilizing France's North African subjects. Yet over the next decade, the Second Empire's colonial aspirations would undergo a considerable transformation and, in many ways, revert back to the old "cosmopolitanism" of the First Empire. Foreign policy objectives in Italy and Eastern Europe compelled support for national liberation movements in these regions, publicly committing the emperor to the principle of national self-determination. Moreover, the nativism touted by the government proved difficult to square with demands for colonial assimilation. If the political institutions and practices of the Second Empire were deemed legitimate by virtue of their supposed Gallic character and profound connection to the French people and soil, how was the government to consider the North African borderlands inhabited by a sizable Muslim population? Overt assimilation fit neither with the government's interpretation of *nationalité* nor with the emperor's support for the "sacred cause" of national liberation, and by the early 1860s Napoleon III had begun to sing a different tune, replacing the language of assimilation with that of "regenerating" a fallen and moribund Arab nationality. "When France placed its foot on African soil thirty-five years ago," he declared during an official visit to Algiers in 1865, "it did not come to destroy the nationality of a people but, on the contrary, to lift this people from an old oppression."[67]

As the government's *politique de nationalité* reached a crescendo during the 1860s, the value of Algeria was difficult to ignore. Support for Arab nationality certainly reinforced the Second Empire's image as a champion of national liberation; yet it also served to validate the brand of nationalism that imperial ideologues like Persigny claimed was integral to the government. The confluence of these two ideological positions revealed an increasing penchant to represent the modernizing impulses of colonialism as a trans-Mediterranean program of national revival and nation-building. "France, which especially sympathizes with the idea of nationality," the emperor stated when clarifying his position on the Algerian question, "cannot justify to the world the dependence in which it is obligated to hold the Arab people if it does not impart the benefits of civilization and lead them toward a better existence."[68]

From the start, the North African campaign had been marked by shameful acts of looting and vandalism. Muslim cultural artifacts, monuments, and architectural relics were systematically removed during the first wave of the conquest, and the July Monarchy hardly found it in questionable taste to display them like trophies in the galleries of the Louvre.[69] Just as little consideration was shown to the native inhabitants as military personnel occupied mosques and Muslim cultural centers and rapidly converted them into hospitals or garrisons for military use. As late as the 1860s, certain sections of Algiers continued to resemble a French barrack. The novelist Alphonse Daudet found the city filled with "military men, more military men, and always military men but not a Turk in sight."[70] Charles Theirry-Mieg was astounded to find the palace of the Algerian dey being used as a French garrison. The colorful wall murals had been covered by whitewash, he complained, and the grand terrace now sported an office for the sale of tobacco.[71] Native inhabitants who had fled the invading French forces returned to find their homes occupied by European residents and their farms sold off to land speculators. Possessing few means of redressing their grievances, North African proprietors had little choice but to sell their land and buildings to foreign buyers at a fraction of their actual value.[72]

In addition to military appropriations, mosques were also allocated to Christian missions or transformed into churches to accommodate the arriving European settlers. The majority of established religions outside of Islam lacked sufficient buildings in which to worship and in certain cases public offices were temporarily offered as spaces to hold services on the Sabbath. Typically parsimonious when it came to doling out funds for the construction of new churches in the colony, the government found it more practical and economic to relocate religious groups to existing mosques.[73] In any given Algerian city, newly minted Christian iconography could be found adorning the minarets and walls of mosques while chiming bells rather than the Islamic *adhān* summoned the faithful to worship. In 1841, the Abbé Bargès, a French Catholic inspired by dreams of re-Christianizing Africa, extolled the opening of the Cathedral of Algiers, remarking, "a cross sits at the summit seeming to triumph over the thousand crescents that surround it on all sides."[74]

Whether due to the needs of security or the demands of confessional groups, Muslim centers of worship were significantly affected by the arrival of the French.[75] With mosques closed indefinitely, transformed into churches or converted for military use, Islamic educational institutions and bureaucratic channels did not remain immune to the effects of war and conquest. A report delivered before the Chamber of Deputies in May 1847 warned of the disastrous consequences that would result if the current policy was continued. "Around us the lights have been extinguished, the recruitment of men of religion and law has ceased. That is to say, we have rendered Muslim society much more miserable, more disorganized, more ignorant, and more barbaric than it was before contact with us."[76] More than two decades later, some critics found little improvement in the situation. In a speech given before the Oranais general council in 1869, the commander of the province, General Édouard-Jean-Étienne Deligny, reminded that Algerian Muslims continued to experience acute social dislocations. "As a new civilization is imposed on them and their social order is undermined, [the natives] find their ideas cast into disorder and their material interests attacked."[77]

If war and military occupation severely disrupted Algeria's Muslim communities, the influences of the newly arriving colonists on the natives appeared just as devastating. Although colonial ideologues commonly flaunted the image of the virtuous and hardworking *colon* as the agent of European civilization in Africa, the realities of Algerian life usually paled in comparison with the ideal. Colonial settlements possessed all the vices that European society had to offer. "The village is a small city and has all the faults of one," the polemicist Clément Duvernois complained in 1858. "Despite their small size, one can find not one, but three, four, and five cabarets."[78] In European settlements, prostitution, drunken carousing, and gambling made up familiar aspects of colonial life, and the pernicious influence of these European imports on the natives was plain for all to see. Encountering a Berber outside of Jemmapes, Thierry-Mieg was appalled by his brazenness and overtly European demeanor. "He was the type of *indigène* that we have civilized, possessing all our vices without our qualities," he remarked sardonically. "He spoke with ease about the cabaret where he went to get drunk or play billiards and cards with the Europeans."[79] Rather than spreading civilization, colonists appeared more adept at disseminating bad habits and moral debauchery among Muslims. The influential publicist Frédéric Lacroix was not being facetious when he deemed such depraved colonists "professeurs d'absinthe."[80] The traditional sobriety and piety that many French observers associated with Islam appeared to be under siege as European tastes and forms of entertainment proliferated throughout Algerian towns and cities. "It is a very distressing sight," Ernest Feydeau remarked while watching Arabs sitting at French cafés in Algiers, "to see them publicly imbibing glasses of absinthe and aping the manners of their vanquishers under the pretext of civilization."[81]

While the unscrupulous seizure and sale of native property and flagrant disregard for indigenous residents in the major cities of the Tell raised questions as to whether or not France was indeed exercising a supposed "civilizing" influence on Algeria, the influx of European colonists posed a particular concern for the military command. Excepting the brief interlude of the Second Republic, Algeria remained under the war ministry and the Armée d'Afrique that assumed responsibility for the overall governance of the colony and administration of the native populations. Commanders understood that land-hungry settlers had the potential to generate conflicts with native communities as colonists spread further into the interior and attempted to establish themselves in tribal areas. Having pacified the native resistance after nearly thirty years of combat, military officials cautioned that unbridled European settlement might reignite ethnic tensions in the predominantly Arab and tribal territories of the south. To obviate this threat, the military placed restrictions on the areas open to colonization, relegating the growing *colon* population to the coastal zones north of the Tell Atlas Mountains. The boundary lines distinguishing the nominally Arab territories from the northern civilian provinces of the settlers established a framework for the dual administration of the two colonial populations. In the Tell, a government of civil servants attended to the European colonists while in the Arab territories the military exercised virtually unchecked authority over the indigenous populations.[82]

The institutionalized segregation enforced by the military remained the lynchpin of France's Algerian policy throughout the nineteenth century. This strategy was recommended by an array of military officials and civilian observers, among them Prosper Enfantin who in his lengthy tome on Algerian colonization noted the utility of cordoning off the bulk of native inhabitants.[83] "The first condition, the absolute condition of organizing the Muslim natives is to *separate them from us.*"[84] A conquered people could not be expected to adopt the social conventions and institutions of a foreign power immediately. Old customs and traditions would have to be modified over time and the vanquished populations slowly integrated into the new society created by the French.[85] Algeria was composed of "two distinct societies" and it was essential to recognize that the "diversity of races and nations [constituted] different needs," the former governor general, Viala Charon, urged.[86] Attempting to implement a uniform policy capable of accommodating both the Europeans and natives was, officials argued, imprudent. "It is necessary to lead [the Arabs] successively and progressively in receiving our civilization," the government spokesman on Algeria Baron Frédéric David explained in 1861. "Yet it is a chimerical idea to believe that today policies could be extended outside the civil territories, treating the Arabs . . . as one treats a European population."[87] This outlook was informed by practical concerns over control and authority, as well. Subduing native resistance during the first two decades of the French invasion had required upward of 100,000 troops, and directly subjecting Algerian natives to French rule threatened once again to stoke the flames of revolt.

The concept of a native administration was by no means novel and in fact looked back to Napoleon I's abortive Egyptian campaign of the late eighteenth century. Occupying the Nile Valley in an effort to strike a blow against British commercial interests in the Near East, Napoleon had overthrown the Mamluk sultanate in 1798, leaving him in possession of a diverse and, by French standards, "uncivilized" Oriental population resistant to foreign rule. The French opted for a policy of indirect rule over the local communities, turning to sheikhs, Coptic elites, and Islamic ulemas in an effort to stabilize the country. Presenting himself as a liberator, Napoleon pledged to "regenerate" the Egyptians and transform them into a modern and enlightened people. Yet attempts to rally the Arabs and Copts against their Mamluk overlords proved futile, and by 1800 Napoleon's army was being driven out of the region by local resistance movements. In spite of the obvious failure that loomed over the brief Napoleonic occupation, the Egyptian campaign nevertheless prefigured the ideology and practice of nineteenth-century French colonialism, outlining both a method and moral justification for a new brand of "enlightened" imperialism.[88]

These lessons were taken to heart by the Armée d'Afrique as it overtook Algeria, perpetuating a veritable Napoleonic tradition. Although notorious for violent policies against Muslim combatants on the battlefield, Thomas Robert Bugeaud, governor general of Algeria from 1840 to 1846, experimented with the idea of subduing resistance through cooperative efforts. "Select the most influential [natives] to govern in our name," he strategized, but "don't give them enough power to become dangerous."[89] To accomplish this aim, Bugeaud created the Arab Offices (Bureaux Arabes), a special division within the military administration to serve as a liaison between Muslim notables and the French administration. Through the Arab Offices, the military implemented a form of indirect rule based on the Egyptian model, effectively monitoring the actions of tribal leaders, supervising Muslim judicial and religious institutions and enforcing taxation.[90] Sheikhs and local notables were permitted to retain some of their traditional autonomy in their communities while the qadi—Muslim judges practicing Sharia and customary law—continued to preside over civil courts within their respective jurisdictions. By exercising a measure of indirect control at the local level, the Arab Offices successfully used native authority to curb outright resistance and fortify the tenuous *présence française* in North Africa.[91]

For idealistic officials, the Arab Offices represented more than a tactical provision; they were vehicles for the diffusion of French modernization. Officers and military spokesmen readily encouraged this impression and, following the end of major combat operations in the 1850s, increasingly presented the "civilizing" work performed by the Arab Offices as a rationale for prolonging military rule in the colony. Bureaux officers took credit for introducing Muslims to the practices and procedures of state administration and eroding the feudal Arab tribalism that estranged native communities from modern society. "Absolutist sheikhs" were being transformed into *fonctionnaires* and learning to serve the interests of the French regime.[92] The Arab Offices were a vital link between the natives and Europeans, reminded the former bureau commander Ferdinand Hugonnet in 1858. They demonstrated France's commitment to "pushing the *indigène* race along the path of progress and civilization" by providing justice, maintaining order, and encouraging local participation.[93] Three years later, Ismael Urbain, a military translator who would soon became one of Napoleon III's most influential policy advisers on Algeria, reiterated the mission of the army in North Africa and its significance for the future: "In the zones where the Muslims are the majority and where our civilization has not yet planted deep roots, it is the army that must apply French institutions in the most effective measure and prepare the natives for their entrance into the civilian territories."[94]

It was fitting that an *homme de couleur* from French Guiana would present himself as a tenacious defender of native interests in Algeria. Born in Cayenne in 1812 from the union of a *colon* planter and creole mother, Ismael Urbain was no stranger to the ambivalence and exclusion that characterized European colonial societies in the nineteenth century. Declared illegitimate by consequence of the laws prohibiting interracial marriage in Guiana, Urbain's status as a "man of color" estranged him from both white society and the native community in the colony. Divided between two worlds by dint of his mixed blood, he was denied a place in either. "Men of color are not white," he conceded in a youthful poem. "They are not black. They are not slaves nor are they masters."[95] The isolation and displacement experienced early in life would exercise a profound influence on his more mature thinking, nurturing a profound sympathy for the alienation that colonial subjecthood imposed.

As an *homme de couleur* educated in France, Urbain saw himself as a product of two divergent and even oppositional worlds characterized in the binary terms of Occident and Orient familiar to the nineteenth century. Owing to his mixed blood and composite identity, he expressed a personal obligation to serve as a mediator between East and West and work toward reconciling these two civilizations historically locked in conflict. This aspiration encouraged him to seek employment in the Armée d'Afrique as a translator and plunge into "the immense ocean of Oriental life" accessible in North Africa.[96] It equally prompted his conversion to Islam. "I thought that in giving to the Muslims such a great testimony of sympathy for their beliefs I would dispose them to welcome me with more confidence, to listen to me, and to reduce their aversion to the ideas of the Occident." Urbain never fully renounced his Christian beliefs in spite of his conversion and consciously appropriated a polytheistic identity that he reconciled in his association as a Frenchman. "I am at once Christian and Muslim because I am French, and this title is for me, at this moment, the most elevated religious and civilized qualification."[97] Both Occidental and Oriental, black and white, Christian and Muslim, Urbain stood as a living testament to French universalism and its capacity to transcend reductive religious and racial identifications. Through artful self-fashioning, he crafted an identity that was cosmopolitan, pluralistic, and civilized: an idea of Frenchness incarnate, as Urbain understood it.

This conviction in France's universal attributes, much like his ambitious goal of uniting East and West, were products of the Saint-Simonian education Urbain had received while living in Paris during the early 1830s. Urbain became introduced to the cult through pamphlets lent to him by a friend. "Within the first hour [of reading them]," he later claimed, "I became a fervent apostle of the Saint-Simonian religion."[98] The camaraderie and fraternity cultivated among the Saint-Simonians at Ménilmontant was a welcome change for a man accustomed to living at the margins of society, and the Saint-Simonian vision of a new world order driven by industrial and scientific progress—the "one common interest of all men," as the great master Saint-Simon had proclaimed—appealed to a generation hungry for change.[99] Above all, Urbain was intrigued by the movement's comprehensive scope, its religious-like veneration of progress, and its increasing insistence that the Orient was to play a crucial role in the coming transformation of human society. In 1833, he accompanied leading Saint-Simonians on an expedition to Egypt with the intention of assisting the progressive-minded khedive Muhammad Ali in his modernizing reforms.[100] While the khedive regard this unsolicited foreign aid with suspicion and the expedition ultimately came to nothing, the Egyptian venture did little to dispel the cult's messianic ideology or its zealous dedication to advancing their cause beyond Europe. "What is essential for France to undertake without delay," Urbain's mentor and friend Émile Barrault urged in 1835, "is a great deployment of industrial activity abroad."[101]

That Barrault considered this reconfiguration of the global economy an explicitly French enterprise was quite telling. Enfantin and his aco-lytes may have sermonized on the universal applications of industry and humanity's collective destiny, but they never considered this trans-formative project anything less than a national mission. Embracing the spirit of the Enlightenment and inspired by a messianic impulse to spread universal principles of liberty and fraternity, France possessed the necessary cultural capital and humanitarian values to direct man's progressive evolution and suffuse it with a unity of purpose. "Today," Enfantin avowed in 1840, "the French prophecy is universal. It is for the Orient as much as for the Occident, for the Muhammadan as for the Christian. It is association, the *affamilation* of people."[102] As Enfantin indicated, the new world on the horizon was, ineluctably, to be a world remade in accordance with the values and ideals of the French nation.

The Saint-Simonian conception of humanity was, by all standards, abstract, partial to sociological generalizations, and often dismissive of cultural difference. Yet quite paradoxically, these universal pretensions coincided with a pronounced appreciation for cultural relativism and disdain for Eurocentric narcissism.[103] In light of the unique features and cultural particularities Oriental societies possessed, Enfantin warned that France could not simply promulgate its beliefs and systems like a pedantic educator. There existed, he assured, "a future proper to the Orient" that could not be made in Europe's image.[104] "The Orient is not in a state of tabula rasa or total disintegration," Barrault concurred. "If the Orient wants to draw inspiration from the genius of the Occident today it does so not to be a copy, an imitator, a parody, or an eternal student. It does it in order to add to its own nature and manifest itself with its originality."[105] Much like the antinomies informing prevailing conceptions of nationality in France, Saint-Simonianism was premised on a set of contradictory principles that defined man and society in both universal and particular terms. At its core, it advocated a novel type of imperialism aimed at spreading European values and forms of social organization to "primitive" societies while simultaneously claiming to remain sensitive to their distinctive cultural and historical characteristics.

Despite claims to French technological and cultural superiority, Enfantin nevertheless maintained that France could not assume that it had "everything to teach and nothing to learn."[106] The implacable forces of global commerce, military expansion, and cultural exchange were sowing the seeds for a dynamic world civilization built upon the ruins of the old, effete social order currently in a state of disintegration. "The civilization of the Occident, today mixing with the effervescent and disorderly civilization of the Orient, is destined to enliven it and be enlivened in turn," Barrault prophesized. "From this mixing will come a rejuvenated civilization no longer oriental or occidental but rather human."[107] Enfantin welcomed the oriental influences that would no doubt spring from France's North African venture, believing that the French would renounce the materialism and selfish individualism besetting modern Europe and adopt the communal ethics and spirituality prevalent in the East.[108] Was it too absurd to imagine "a France a little Bedouin, a little rustic . . . or perhaps a little pasha," he asked while speculating on the contours of a world revitalized through cultural intercourse, mutual interests, and collective harmony?[109]

As he acquired greater influence in the Algerian administration over the 1840s and 1850s, Urbain drew upon the ideas and inherent contradictions of Saint-Simonianism in formulating a new North African policy committed at once to France's "civilizing" enterprise and the equitable treatment of Maghrebi natives. He rejected the plan of colonization and cultural assimilation favored by staunch imperialists, seeing it as both impractical and contrary to French interests. "We preoccupy ourselves too exclusively with introducing a European population in Algeria," he wrote in 1842. "Yet pushing the natives into the desert will only serve to inflame the hatred and sentiments of vengeance that, in the heart of a vanquished people, are sometimes muted but never entirely extinguished."[110] Not only did unbridled Gallicization hold the prospect of inciting native resistance; the very idea of overt assimilation ran counter to Urbain's understanding of France. Stalwart nationalists may assert that a French Algeria implied giving it the same institutions and cultural identity as the continent, but for Urbain, this unity promised nothing more than a "general uniformity."[111] The France that Urbain identified with could not be distilled so easily into reductive understandings of culture and identity. His France was a rich and diverse mosaic of customs, languages, and people united by common values. "Can we still not distinguish the diversity of its origins in the different provinces despite the fact that France is one of the most homogeneous nations in Europe today?"[112] France embodied a natural and organic diversity, according to Urbain—that classic sentiment of "variété dans l'unité" appreciated by postrevolutionary thinkers. What set his views apart from the mainstream of French nationalism was, however, a willingness, at least in theory, to extend this celebration of diversity to non-European peoples.

This outlook formed the kernel of an alternative vision of Algeria that would find support among a loose-knit group of former Saint-Simonians entrenched in the military bureaucracy and publishing industry. Touting his program as a native policy (*politique indigène*) opposed to national chauvinism and assimilation, Urbain attacked the strategy of settler colonialism, insisting it was naive to believe that France could "suddenly change the habits, customs, and laws of a population."[113] A more effective course of action was to abandon compulsory assimilation and chart a course for Algerian Muslims "in line with their normal development, linking their past, present, and future."[114] "For each individual as for each group there is a point of departure and a particular aim," Urbain contended. It was vital "to consult the traditions and memories of each and all" in formulating social and political policies.[115] Much as Bonapartist ideologues in France avowed, government, if it was to be considered legitimate, must be indigenous and accord with the historical development and customs of the people it represented. To proceed otherwise was not only to invite disaster; it would mean flouting the sacred principle of *nationalité* central to France's revolutionary heritage.

Urbain's nativism framed the Algerian question as one of national rights and oppression, and in doing so invited reflection on what France's "civilizing" initiative in North Africa actually implied. Frédéric Lacroix, a well-connected Parisian journalist supportive of Urbain, ridiculed the state of affairs in Algeria, insisting that in yielding to the desires of a small minority of settlers and nationalists France had sacrificed its claim to "moral conquest." Recounting examples of the abuse and exploitation settlers meted out on Algerian natives, Lacroix did not hesitate to draw a comparison to the demoralizing slave regimes of the West Indies. "France believes that by emancipating its slaves it destroyed racial antipathies and that there are no longer either serfs or pariahs within its limits," the fiery polemicists railed. "This is an error. Pariahs and serfs may no longer be found in the distant colonies but they are at the door of the metropole two days from Marseille. . . . The prejudices that once separated whites from the black race in the Antilles are today projected onto the Arabs in Africa in all its violence and blindness."[116] France, passionately outspoken for the cause of oppressed nationalities abroad, nonetheless appeared willing to countenance the suppression of an Arab minority on its very soil, making it no better than the absolutist Habsburgs or Russian tsars. It was, Lacroix concluded, a matter of conscience and principle to support the cause of Arab nationality in Algeria, to declare without reservation: "Algeria will never become a French Poland!"[117]

Emphasizing and, at times, even exaggerating the racial antipathies that threatened to violently divide Algerian society, Nativists painted a dismal portrait of the Maghrebi Arabs as an oppressed nationality suffering under the yoke of a foreign power. This assertion, hardly shared by all, armed officials with a convincing rationale for limiting civilian governance and maintaining the Armée d'Afrique's presence in North Africa. Although major combat operations had ceased and native resistance was temporarily suppressed, the military administration was now obliged to defend the Arab population from the European settlers. "I believe that the Arabs need to be protected and cannot be delivered to the designs of the colonists," argued Baron Jérôme David when discussing the role of the military in the colony.[118] Unlike the colonists, the military possessed an intimate knowledge of Arab society acquired through direct experience and the Arab Offices' regular interaction with local communities. Few Frenchmen, Ferdinand Hugonnet argued, "had lived the Arab life of the tribes ... [and] showed themselves to be sympathetic to the natives or desirous of studying their needs and aptitudes in a consistent manner. In a word, very few have sufficiently put on the Arab burnoose to observe all the movements of heart and spirit that interest these populations."[119] The centrality of the Arab world to the authority and ideology of the Armée d'Afrique encouraged various military officials and Bureaux officers to lend their support to Urbain's native policy and the cause of Arab nationality. As Charles Nicolas Lacretelle, a general stationed in the northwestern district of Sidi Bel Abbès, opined in 1868: "France does not conquer a people to precipitate their ruin but rather to improve their lot and accelerate their progressive march."[120] This task could only be achieved, the argument ran, under the military's benevolent supervision.

The premise of Algerian nativism rested upon the claim that Maghrebi Arabs had in fact conserved the distinctive traits of their nationality despite centuries of foreign rule and oppression. In this context, Urbain and his allies were proposing to revitalize a defunct Muslim society and invest the "old Orient" with a new life that accorded with the organic and natural elements of the Arab people. Looking back to the medieval

Caliphate, Lacretelle believed that the Muslims of North Africa could, with the aid of France, once again reclaim this glorious heritage and enter upon the path of progress first laid out by their ancestors. "The blood that flows in the veins of our Algerians is the same as the Arabs during the first age of Islam," he affirmed, "[and] what their forefathers were, the Arabs of our day can and must become again."[121] Urbain concurred: "Among the Arab race there are all the necessary elements to constitute a nation, not by the models of European nations, but an Oriental and Muslim nation that will take from our civilization only what its faith, mores, and character permit it to assimilate."[122]

Allusions to Arab nationality and "regenerating" a fallen people pervaded Nativist rhetoric, invoking both the old Napoleonic imperial ideology and the emancipatory nationalism prevalent in the period. Nativists saw themselves engaged in a project to create both a *patrie* for France's Arab subjects and a Muslim *pays* bound to the nation. Yet the prescribed formula of civilizing through nationalizing central to Urbain's plan often undercut the supposed cultural relativism upon which it rested. The notion of "regenerating" Arab nationality was always more ideological fiction than reality. "Arab" constituted a generic term applied by French administrators to a diverse and heterogeneous North African population and, consequently, carried little currency among native groups who neither spoke Arabic nor identified with an Arab ethnicity.[123] In deeming Algeria an "Arab" territory, French officials were, in actuality, working to create the very Arab nationality that their cultural and political policies claimed to represent and protect, in the process authorizing the wholesale Arabization of various non-Arab groups such as the Turks and Berbers. In 1861, Baron David illuminated the contradictions at the heart of the nativist proposal when he openly applauded the military's intention of "creating what had not previously existed, the Arab nationality that has begun to appear."[124] Although Urbain candidly admitted that concepts of nationhood and nationality were European imports, stating that "nationality, as it is known to Europe, still remains only a latent idea among these populations divided into tribes attached to diverse and hostile origins," he nevertheless continued to believe that national identification, when pursued with consideration for the "normal development" of a people, signified a universal stage in humanity's social evolution.[125]

"The idea of progress," Urbain wrote in 1861, "implies multiplicity but at the same time unity in the human destiny."[126] This sentiment both constituted the crux of Urbain's native policy and, ironically, undermined its very foundation. Endeavoring to inculcate an Arab national consciousness among the Algerian *indigènes* and revive a decadent Oriental civilization, Nativists relied upon a conception of Arab modernity defined in exceedingly Eurocentric terms, imposing revolutionary constructs like nationality and the nation-state on a society estranged from Europe's revolutionary experience. Regenerating Arab nationality amounted to a policy of "assimilative regeneration" that at once recognized the Arabs as a culturally distinct group while intending to "civilize" them in accordance with European norms.[127] Urbain, like many of his contemporaries, equated Frenchness with civilization itself. He never doubted the universality that French values purportedly embodied or their potential for transcending the varieties of human diversity and experience. He also never doubted his cultural relativism either, perennially affirming the notion of "harmonic multiplicity" that French nationality was best suited to realize.[128]

Blending cultural nationalism with universalized notions of civilization and progress, Nativists saw little conflict in cultivating indigenous and particular forms of national identification while integrating them into an expansive and exceedingly cosmopolitan idea of Frenchness. Fostering a common set of "ideas and needs" among the North Africans, as Lacroix argued, offered a just basis for the "moral conquest" of Algeria. "The development of human reason" was "perfectly compatible with Muslim piety," he assured, leaving little doubt that the Algerians could adopt the civilized qualities of the French without disowning their own culture and heritage.[129] "We do not seek a religious conversion that offends conscience and provokes social convulsions," Urbain declared. "We only ask that the natives rally to our civilization, which will surround them and entice them with numerous benefits."[130] Blind to the contradictions contained within a policy at once seeking to pre-serve and revolutionize Muslim society, Nativists prided themselves on resolving the evident conflict between France's expansionist ambitions and its revolutionary political culture, synthesizing them in the idea of a Franco-Arab Algerian society.

In theory, the *politique indigène* proposed to reconcile the divergent civilizations of the Occident and Orient though the progressive associa-tion of Algeria's European and Arab inhabitants. With time and proper guidance, an ethnically diverse population would be molded into a single community that was neither European nor Arab but French. French universalism would receive its true baptism in Algeria as ideals of tolerance and equality united French, Europeans, and Muslims into a single people.[131] Reflecting on this ambitious plan in 1864, General Yusuf Vantini anticipated the day when Algeria would see "the last remains of racial antagonism disappear." A Muslim of Italian origin who participated in quelling native resistance during the conquest, Yusuf had witnessed firsthand the carnage and ethnic violence that had destabilized Maghrebi society following the collapse of the Ottoman dey. Now, thirty years later, he was willing to believe that the ethnic warfare and tribalism of the past was finished and that from the "racial ensemble" of a reconstituted Algerian society would come "the most useful and durable progress."[132]

The growing recognition of Urbain's native policy was, moreover, not lost on the government in Paris, especially as Napoleon III himself began reflecting critically on France's North African quandary. Fruitless Algerian policies and unremitting disputes between colonists and the military had provided a source of endless frustration for French governments since the conquest. "Poor Algeria!" exclaimed the emperor. "We have attempted a great many systems, none of them successful."[133] Seeking a tenable administrative solution capable of mollifying the grievances of Algerian colonists on one hand and the military regime on the other, Napoleon III began drawing counsel from Nativist proponents such as Baron David and Lacroix, both of whom subsequently introduced him to the works of Urbain. Nativist pamphlets detailing the racial tensions and deplorable conditions of Algerian Arabs appealed to the emperor's sympathies for oppressed nationalities while the *politique indigène* accorded with the spirit and ideology of Bonapartist *nationalité*. Within Urbain's ideas, Napoleon III saw a potentially bold policy consistent with his sense of Napoleonic grandeur. Transforming the *politique indigène* into an official ideology, Napoleon III would present himself as the savior of Arab nationality, the benefactor of the oppressed, and the protector of Algerian Islam.[134]

Prior to the emperor's endorsement, the Nativist platform had been confined to a small group of military officials, politicians, and journalists concerned with the issue of Algerian reform. In early 1863, however, the situation shifted dramatically. Following months of private deliberations and cabinet meetings in Paris, Napoleon III galvanized military officials and the settler community in February with a formal declaration outlining a new course of action. Addressing a public letter written in French and Arabic to the acting governorgeneral Aimable Jean Jacques Pélissier, Napoleon III declared that Algeria was not "a colony strictly speaking, but rather an Arab Kingdom (Royaume Arabe)." "The natives, like the colonists, have an equal right to my protection and I am the Emperor of the Arabs just as I am the Emperor of the French." It was imperative, Napoleon III urged, "to convince the Arabs that we have not come to Algeria to oppress and steal from them, but rather to deliver the benefits of civilization." "The first condition of a civilized society," he continued, was "the respect for the right of each," entailing that native property rights had to be guaranteed by the state and respect for their religious beliefs strictly upheld.[135] In the coming months, Algerian natives would be promised access to positions within the colonial administration, voting rights in local elections, and freedom of religious worship. While Algeria may still have been a land "forever French," as King Louis Philippe once declared, it was not, according to the emperor, to be a land solely dominated by the aspirations and interests of a small French minority.

Embarking for Algeria in May 1865, Napoleon III drove home the new course favored by his government, leaving little doubt as to the incentives behind his Arab Kingdom policy. Delivering a speech to apprehensive colonists in Algiers, he implored them to have "faith in the future." "Attach yourself to the earth that you cultivate like a new *patrie* and treat the Arabs in the places where you live like compatriots."[136] For colonists, however, this injunction was difficult to fathom. Having maintained customary and traditional legal codes in Algeria for both ideological and practical reasons, the imperial government continued to uphold natives' rights to practice Sharia and Hebraic law in civil affairs. While this conformed to the state's commitment to religious tolerance and respect for indigenous and "natural" institutions, it entailed maintaining separate and distinct legal systems for the Europeans and Algerian natives, respectively.[137] Yet French nationality, as prescribed by the Napoleonic Code, rested upon the premise of equality before the law, reflecting the revolutionary assertion that a French national was one subject to the unitary laws that governed the nation. If the natives remained subject to a different legal system, could Europeans be expected to think of them as compatriots? Moreover, if they were considered French nationals, did this entitle them to citizenship and political rights?

Urbain fully acknowledged that the Islamic faith posed an obstacle to Muslim enfranchisement. "Because the natives will not allow a radical separation between the spiritual and temporal, because their culture and religious dogmas are in contradiction with our codes," he conceded, "they should not be invested with the title of French citizens."[138] France could hardly compel Muslims to repudiate their faith and espouse a secularism alien to their traditions, Urbain reasoned; yet it could not invalidate the basic principles upon which its society was founded either. Under the circumstances, citizenship would have to be a personal choice for Algerians rather than a universal condition. Only once the "civilizing" influences disseminated by France had taken root and the Qur'an became a purely religious book and not a text for civil legislation could Muslims be considered for citizenship.[139] For Urbain, however, the question of citizenship was, ultimately, secondary. The primary question was how to make the natives French, and this had more to do with nurturing shared interests among the two populations of the colony and attaching them to a new *patrie* than it did with political rights. The objective behind the Arab Kingdom was, in Napoleon III's view, to establish "perfect equality between the natives and Europeans."[140] To this end, Muslims were to be granted access to positions in the civil bureaucracy and made eligible for state benefits, privileges reserved exclusively for French nationals in principle. Native integration—the cornerstone of Urbain's envisaged Franco-Arab society—hinged, therefore, on the nationality question, which, according to Urbain, was independent from questions of political rights.[141]

These assertions, like the Arab Kingdom itself, were highly controversial. While protest from the settler community and colonial lobbies was to be expected, opposition from within the military was becoming more vocal, especially at the level of the high command. The recently appointed governor-general, Patrice de MacMahon, did not conceal his doubts regarding the state's encouragement of Arab nationalism, a policy that was, in his view, as counterproductive as it was dangerous.[142] Tensions only escalated that June when Napoleon III drafted a memo to MacMahon and confirmed his personal support for Urbain's program with the succinct pronouncement: "The Arabs are French since Algeria is a French territory."[143] Following a series of debates in the spring of 1865, a formal senatorial commission was called to address the thorny issue. On 14 July—Bastille Day—the senate ruled in favor of conferring French nationality on Algerian Jews and Muslims by virtue of *jus soli*. This blanket naturalization marked a clear victory for Urbain and his hope of attaining "the fusion of the two races in civil equality, freedom of religion . . . [and] tolerance for mores while bringing [the natives] more into line with our civilization."[144] In more specific terms, the resolution officially endorsed his policy of native integration by determining formal procedures through which Algerians might acquire French citizenship once they had obtained a sufficient level of civilization. Upon learning of the senate's verdict, Auguste Vital, a doctor, former Saint-Simonian, and colonial publicist stationed in Constantine, wrote to Urbain and congratulated the efforts of his longtime friend, candidly remarking, "Your ideas have received baptism through their application."[145]

Yet if the Arabs were French, the ruling of 1865 confirmed them so only as nationals, not citizens. Algerian *naturalisés* were not obliged to submit to the French civil code and, therefore, continued to retain their special status under traditional law, upholding the conviction that citizenship must be a personal and individual choice.[146] While Muslims were recognized as French nationals sharing in the nation's "great political unity," as Urbain claimed, their legal status continued to affirm their attachment to an external community, rendering them nominal Frenchmen bereft of the civil and political liberties accorded to citizens.[147] Long-standing and overly generalized assumptions regarding the incompatibility of Islam and secular society came together within a discourse of rights, French law, and national belonging to sanction the creation of an ethnopolitical colonial order.[148] Legal categorizations distinguishing between *citoyen* and *indigène* revealed the persistence of classical liberal thinking and its logic of exclusion, providing a criterion through which ethnic and racial conceptions of difference were simultaneously effaced and reaffirmed to suit colonial rule.

If 14 July 1789 marked the birth of the French political nation and citizenry, exactly seventy-six years later to the day, French politicians and policymakers declared an end to the Rousseauian revolution. The conception of *nationalité* enshrined in the civil code was abandoned as legislators acknowledged a distinction between French nationals and French citizens that would possess ominous implications for the future. Unmoored from a political and legal context, *nationalité* became a distinct concept in its own right, yet one that proved to be exceedingly elastic and labile. Urbain's hope of realizing a cosmopolitan, tolerant, and multicultural vision of France in North Africa always rested uneasily with his desire for unity and national affiliation. In the end, these two objectives proved irreconcilable and, under the republican state that came to power in the last decades of the nineteenth century, it would be the latter principle that would win out to the detriment of Algeria's native inhabitants.

The Exigencies of Time

Revolution or Evolution? Such was the question that Bonapartist modernity raised. Through a mix of democracy and patriotism, Bonapartists managed to craft a revolutionary identity for themselves, one that flouted the radicalism of extremists and called for a return to the core values of the nation's revolutionary heritage. Yet despite appeals to past Napoleonic grandeur and the principles of 1789, the Bonapartist movement demonstrated a strong commitment to creating a novel type of society that was in many ways distinct from past models. The senatorial ruling of 1865, inspired in equal measure by revolutionary ideas of equality and currents of postrevolutionary nationalism, indicated the extent to which the intellectual and political milieu of the mid-nineteenth century encouraged a rethinking of France's revolutionary heritage and offered alternatives to imagining a nominally "modern" France consistent with the realities of postrevolutionary politics and colonialism. Revolutionary in spirit but not necessarily action, the imperial government sought to implement what the minister Adolphe Billaut described as a "pure, honest, and conciliatory revolution, at once prudent and progressive."[149]

The twin principles of *Nationalité* and *Unité* provided the substance of this conciliatory revolution amounting to a Bonapartist trans-Mediterranean civilizing mission dedicated to forging a modern nation from the debris of fallen regimes, continuous political upheaval, and social collapse. Nationality occupied a central role in the state's "modernizing" agenda as officials and ideologues outlined a policy of modernizing through nationalizing, applicable to both continent and colony. Pacifying populations, and constructing this envisaged modernity could not, however, be achieved overnight. "Progress is an evolution, not a revolution," Urbain once remarked, dictating that time was essential to allow the work of progress to mature and bear fruit.[150] "Time alone," Persigny averred in 1858, "can bring about the reconciliation of parties that have for so long divided France."[151] The same could be said of North Africa where colonial officials engaged in the work of reconstituting a society torn asunder by war and lingering enmities. Creating an Algerian society, much like creating a French one, could only come about through sensible policies, modernizing acts, and patience. "Societies do not transform in a few days," the prime minister Eugène Rouher acknowledged in 1868. "Time, labor, and daily efforts are necessary so that a nation with ossified institutions can gradually be united, fused together, transformed, and absorbed by a new civilization."[152]

Yet time was not a luxury the imperial government could afford. With the resurgence of a republican movement and growing opposition in the Corps législatif during the 1860s, the Bonapartists found themselves in a precarious situation. Increasingly pressed to defend their policies in the press and before the national legislature, the government could only implore patience and understanding as its ambitious plans gradually came to fruition. "In a society as shaken as ours by numerous revolutions," Napoleon III urged during the opening session of the legislative assembly in February 1859, "time alone can fortify convictions, remake characters, and generate political faith."[153] The question remained, however, whether indignant republicans and democratic reformers would give the Bonapartist government the time required to bring its vision of society to completion.

4 The Crucible of Modern Society

Marseille's Cathédrale Sainte-Marie-Majeure sits upon the coast facing out toward the vast Mediterranean Sea. The towering Byzantine-inspired construction has stood as a symbol of France's enduring Catholic identity in a maritime region historically situated at the crossroads of the Christian–Muslim frontier. In the autumn of 1852, Louis Napoleon arrived in the city to lay the cornerstone for the newly commissioned cathedral. Two months before the declaration of the Second Empire, the prince-president of the republic adeptly intended to use the public ceremony as a means of rallying Catholics to the Bonapartist cause and thereby ensure a popular base of support for the future government. "My government, I say it with pride, is perhaps the only one that has supported religion in itself," he declared after laying the ceremonial keystone. "It does not support it as a political instrument or to please a party but only by conviction and by love for the good it inspires and the truths that it teaches."[1] The import and meaning of the message was clear: the Bonapartists, while revolutionary in spirit, were not anticlerical. Catholics, as well as all confessional groups, could expect to find a friend in Louis Napoleon, a man who, according to the minister Adolphe Billaut, considered religion "one of the social bases on which morality and civilization rests."[2]

Promoting his platform of reconciliation and unity, Napoleon III persistently sought to extend a hand to religious moderates and draw them closer to a government nominally committed to the principles of the Revolution.[3] This rapprochement between church and state not only aimed to soothe the confessional tensions that had agitated the country for over half a century; it was also a Napoleonic tradition tracing its origins back to the Concordat of 1801 when Napoleon I placed state controls over religious institutions in the country.[4] According to Napoleon III, the Second Empire abided by the same "principle of religious freedom" as its predecessor, and as the ruler of a multiconfessional empire he was obliged to serve as the protector of France's faithful.[5] Not forgetting that "the great majority of French are Catholic," the emperor showed no reservations in making appeals to the millions of Muslim subjects that inhabited French soil. Presenting himself as a new sultan to his Algerian subjects, Napoleon III incorporated Qur'anic verses into his speeches and encouraged France's Muslims to consider him a benefactor of *dar al-Islam*, the refuge of all practicing Muslims. "[These speeches] have provoked and led some to believe that the Emperor might well not be a Christian as previously supposed," one colonist amusingly noted in 1865. "He is familiar with the Qur'an and not afraid to cite it."[6]

Napoleon III's ability to craft and project multiple identities may have been one of his most appealing qualities, but it could also prove difficult to ascertain where the self-fashioning ended and the actual man began. Speeches and public spectacles assumed the air of a masquerade, and this ambiguity could and did come to extend to the Second Empire itself.[7] Yet in the wake of 1848, supporting religion while cultivating a modern identity proved tricky. Hardline Catholics riled by the June Days vented their contempt for the liberal and scientific movements hailed across Europe as definitive triumphs of modern society. "What about those who find modern society wrong, who estimate that this fantastic—and perhaps imaginative—entity is rife with the most iniquitous pretensions?" the Catholic polemicist Louis Veuillot asked in 1866.[8] For Catholics who saw the secular and nationalist facets of modernity as both alienating and heretical, modern society could, indeed, seem more fantastic than real at times. Religious militants like Veuillot prided themselves on their resistance to the "modern spirit" and the ruses of blasphemers spreading profane ideas under the pretext of "modern society." For conservatives, there could be no middle ground when it came to accepting the trappings of modern society. As expressions of support or disdain for modernity assumed poles around which antagonistic political and social identities were constructed, the Second Empire found itself confronting an identity crisis. If Napoleon III fancied himself a patron of science, industry, and the modern spirit, he equally imagined himself as a peacekeeper and unifier. These twin objectives appeared, however, increasingly contradictory as "modern" and "traditional," "secular" and "religious," "old" and "new" became highly politicized and contentious terms.

Committed to a policy of tolerance and reconciliation, the Second Empire encouraged a measure of diversity within French public life that often ran counter to hard-line demands for conformity from both the left and right. The government's support for religion had dovetailed with conservative aspirations for "moral order" and consequently gave Catholics a more pronounced public identity in the country. Napoleon III similarly showed a willingness to accommodate Muslims publicly prior to announcing his Arab Kingdom policy in 1863. As early as 1852, he had made conciliatory gestures aimed at warming North Africans to French rule. Upon meeting the Islamic scholar and vanquished resistance leader Abd al-Qādir at the Palais Saint-Cloud that January, Louis Napoleon treated him with an air of dignity befitting his notoriety in the Muslim world and permitted the bête noire of the Armée d'Afrique to carry out the traditional Islamic *salāt*. "Today, for the first time ever," the official broadsheet *Le Moniteur* declared, "the Palais de Saint-Cloud heard the prayer of a Muslim."⁹ The Nativist policies of the 1860s, with their emphasis on Islam's historical place in Arab national life and religious tolerance, certainly marked a continuation of the emperor's accommodating stance toward Maghrebi Islam, but they were never completely removed from more general attitudes regarding the compatibility between confessional identity and French national life held by the regime.

To quell the vicious battle between Reason and Revelation unleashed during the eighteenth century, the Second Empire intended to arbitrate between these warring camps and unify a divided country around common nationalist sentiments. It has often been forgotten that for most of the nineteenth century in France, the relationship between religious institutions and the state was more often than not interdependent rather than antagonistic. Postrevolutionary governments commonly made use of religious values and church institutions for the purposes of upholding public order and providing social services to the community.[10] In this respect, Bonapartist support for revolutionary ideals coupled with its responsiveness to religious opinion did not appear contradictory in principle. It was primarily the events and political atmosphere of the late 1850s and early 1860s that brought the government's modern identity into question. As rightwing Catholics increasingly came to articulate an identity in opposition to modern society and opponents of the regime adopted a confrontational stance in defense of French values and modernity, the government found it problematic to sustain a platform that was at once revolutionary and conciliatory. Attempts to retain a middling position translated into appeasement and inactivity as North African *colons*, reformers, and radical student protestors expressed their grievances in terms that fundamentally challenged the integrity of the government. In the ensuing debates surrounding issues of national education, colonization, and the role of religion in public life, the identity and legitimacy of the imperial regime was clearly at stake as protest movements during the 1860s coming to the defense of "modern society" brought into question the ideological premise underpinning Bonapartist modernity.

An Unsentimental Education

Tensions between modernity and religion in France have tended to be most dramatic in the classroom, a feature of French national culture that has extended right up to current controversies over the wearing of the Islamic hijab in public schools. Prior to the Revolution, the Catholic clergy served as the moral educators of society, administering schools that were attended by a select few of the aristocratic elite. At the tail end of the eighteenth century, the Directory championed the notion of freedom of education (*liberté de l'enseignement*),which effectively removed religious influence over education and gave nominal academic liberties to teachers. Possessing only disdain for these reforms, clerics persistently clamored to reestablish their control over schools. From the First Empire through the July Monarchy, the struggle between lay and clerical control over education remained a contentious issue and in 1833, with the passing of Guizot's legislation supporting national reforms in primary state schools and a secular curriculum for citizens, the clergy found itself on the losing side of the debate. Spurred into action, Catholics placed education at the center of their program in an effort to compete with the state for the hearts and minds of the coming French generations.[11]

Debates over education took place against the backdrop of evolving outlooks concerning the role of schools and the functions of educational institutions in the nineteenth century. Since the Revolution, state schools have persistently been held up as "modernizing" institutions in France, a feature made most evident in the education reforms carried out under the Third Republic. The republican education system established in the 1880s is largely given credit for replacing the collective and oral cultures of the rural French peasantry with a written, individualistic, and uniform "modern" one.[12] Yet a uniform culture ultimately meant a national culture, entailing that state schools were not just modernity's reformatories; they were equally the place in which modern national identities were cultivated and internalized, an instrument for transforming "peasants into Frenchmen," to use Eugen Weber's turn of phrase.[13]

Imperial officials were neither indifferent to the linguistic and cultural diversity found throughout the country nor oblivious to education's potential in effacing these differences. As Napoleon III's minister of public instruction, Victor Duruy, informed him in 1866, "I intend to undertake the most energetic activity in primary education and . . . exercise the lofty methods avowed by civilization and equality to extend our national language."[14] Reluctant to foot the bill for obligatory primary education, however, and seeking to allay Catholic fears of a state monopoly over education, the Second Empire did not actively pursue a national education system comparable to the one created by republicans later in the century. In light of the chronic social ills and divisions afflicting the country, imperial officials were more inclined to view education as a prophylactic against insurrection and a means of turning rebellious and "savage" groups into productive members of society. In its annual report to the legislature in 1863, the government contended that primary instruction should "respond to the true demands of our time" and vigorously disseminate "all the elementary notions proper to enriching both intelligence and work among the laboring classes in the cities and countryside."[15] As Duruy maintained, "the social question is essentially a question of education." His conviction that education constituted a vehicle for social and ideological reform was, moreover, understood as an empire-wide project. Having served as a rector in Algeria for the military administration during the 1850s, Duruy was aware of the evident parallels between social reform at home and the nation's African civilizing mission. "It is necessary to contain the Arabs by the sword and win them over through material interests but we can penetrate their ideas and, by consequence, their mores only through education," he advised the emperor. "Your ministry of public instruction has a great task to fulfill in the colony as well as the metropole."[16]

The slow turn toward mass education over the course of the century was representative of the new power dynamics endemic to what one historian has labeled the "Age of Control."[17] Rather than simply developing knowledge and imparting erudition, schools began to function as institutions of "social reproduction" where the values, forms of knowledge, and normative behavioral codes of society were to be instilled and reinforced in young minds.[18] In a France destabilized by aggressive ideological and social conflicts, reformers hailed education as the corrective instrument that would promote social cohesion and produce the type of individual befitting the stable and productive society envisaged by French leaders. Duruy's remarks on the French working class were revealing, if not ominous: "they ignore that we have become bourgeois through order, work, and economy. It is necessary to teach them."[19] The sprit and intention underpinning such sentiments was not, however, all that different from Prince Jérôme Napoleon's stance on North African natives in 1858: "We are in the presence of an armed and tenacious nationality that it is necessary to subdue through assimilation."[20] While reputedly aspiring to "enlighten" and "modernize" the population, education remained closely associated with questions of social assimilation and order, exposing the patent "colonial" character of nineteenth-century French education institutions.[21]

From the beginning of the Bonapartist ascension in 1851, education was employed in promoting the government's modernizing agenda. Selected to head the Ministry of Public Instruction in 1852, Hippolyte Fortoul announced his intentions of renovating French higher education by establishing courses in technical instruction and making French universities receptive to the needs of "modern societies through a fuller organization of the teaching of science, the source of the wealth and political supremacy of nations."[22] More than a decade later, however, such promises had yet to materialize. Conservatives saw the education system as a crucial weapon in consolidating Bonapartist power and were inclined to agree with reactionaries that revolutionary ambitions were nurtured by student agitators and wayward educators. Accusations that schools and students had fomented the disorder of 1848 were primarily fictions endorsed by conservatives and clerics with little basis in reality. Student activism in the 1840s had concerned itself with issues of academic autonomy and education reform, remaining largely aloof from overt political concerns on the whole.[23] As one critic later charged, the restraints placed on education after 1848 constituted "a spiteful reaction against secular instruction" and nothing more.[24]

The events of 1848 imbued Catholics with a new crusading spirit that was publicly encouraged by the Vatican. The salute of cannon fire that marked the beginning of Pope Pius IX's reign in the summer of 1846 had signaled an exuberant optimism in Rome over the prospect of a new liberal era for the Church. Warmly referred to as Pio Nono, Pius IX had outlined a papal agenda intent on reconciling the Catholic Church with the democratic ambitions of the age. Granting a constitution and pressing his desire to reform the papal bureaucracy, he was hailed as the "liberal pope." "The events in Rome are such to delight us all," wrote the Piedmontese official Massimo d'Azeglio. "The appearance of a Pope who has entered the realm of moderate liberalism is a fact of new and immense importance."[25] This optimism was, however, quashed in 1848 when Italian nationalists challenged the temporal powers of the pope and declared a secular Roman republic, forcing Pio Nono into exile. The extreme nationalism and anticlericalism of Italian republicans was a sobering slap in the face that was not to be forgotten when he was restored to power in 1850 with the aid of none other than France's new president, Louis Napoleon. Returning to Rome, Pio Nono renounced his former liberalism and urged a systematic opposition to the degenerative forces corrupting Europe.[26] The papacy's retreat to conservatism was made explicit in 1864 when, provoked by Italian unification and the progressive sentiments infiltrating the clergy under the banner of "Liberal Catholicism," Pius issued his notorious *Syllabus Errorum* (Syllabus of Errors). In no uncertain terms, the Holy See asserted "it is an error to believe that the Roman Pontiff can and ought to reconcile himself to and agree with progress, liberalism and modern civilization."[27]

Taking its cue from Rome, the French clergy stepped up its opposition, blaming the violence and disorder of the June Days on the absence of religious instruction in lay education. "All the disasters of 1848 came from contempt for religious authority," seethed the Abbé Gouget, who accused the middle classes of accepting an education that cared nothing for God and encouraged support for socialism and other profane ideas.[28] In the aftermath of revolution, Catholics exploited social anxieties, insisting that the danger residing in state-run institutions had to be checked by fervent religious instruction. As the Abbé Hébert-Duperron, an education inspector at the Académie de Besançon in the Jura, claimed in 1859, there was now an obligation to spread "healthy and religious ideas" throughout French communities, "forming docile children . . . , citizens devoted to order and the country, and Christians faithful to God."[29] Ironically, clerics came to support the once revolutionary notion of *liberté de l'enseignement* in their campaign to challenge the state's monopoly over primary education and make Catholic schools competitive with state institutions.

Always sensitive to public opinion in the country, Louis Napoleon proved receptive to Catholic demands. Although averse to the position taken by right-wing ideologues, he was not above courting conservative support for his election to the presidency in 1848 and perceptively understood that his electoral platform of social order could be joined with Catholic concerns over education. That year, he met with Charles Forbes René de Montalembert, a man of moderate political conviction who, as the leader of the influential Parti Catholique, enjoyed significant clout in the Catholic community. In return for his endorsement in the presidential campaign, Louis promised to support the freedom to teach if elected and break the state monopoly over education. The stratagem worked as planned, with Catholic leaders throwing their support behind the Bonapartist candidate that winter and effectively sealing an alliance with the state against the pernicious forces of socialism and revolution.[30] True to his word, the following year Napoleon made good on his promise, ordering his minister of public instruction, the Legitimist Count Alfred de Falloux, to assemble a commission and draw up new legislation. Composed of reactionaries and religious reformers, the commission set out to limit the scope of primary and secondary education and allow religion a more direct influence on national curricula. The Falloux Law (*loi Falloux*), as the legislation became known, passed in March 1850. Under its guidelines, Catholic schools were given a virtual carte blanche while state schools became subject to rigorous inspection. In addition, religious officials were selected to oversee the important *baccalauréate* examination required for entrance to the universities, with the state reserving the right to inspect all schools in order to guarantee conformity of instruction.[31]

Although secular in principle, the Bonapartist regime saw the utility of drawing Catholics and the Church closer to the state. It held the prospect of luring the provincial notables faithful to the royal Bourbon dynasty and the Catholic Church closer to the Bonapartist cause. The government also expected clerics to support imperial polices in return for their privileged status, an expectation that became problematic in later years.[32] Yet the so-called alliance of Moral Order cemented under the Second Republic was never the counterrevolutionary cabal opponents insisted, nor were state polices necessarily beholden to an overarching reactionary agenda either. The *loi Falloux* scaled back the anticlericalism of previous administrations by allowing Catholic instructors who had not attended state-run schools (and hence not received official diplomas) to teach in public and private institutions. It allocated mandatory seats on educational councils for religious officials and sought to make religious schools overall competitive with state institutions. The intent was to protect the independent status of religious educational institutions in the country against secular interference and furnish a basis for reconciliation between Catholics and secular authorities. While ultraconservative ideologues could and certainly did use this arrangement to their advantage, support for religious instruction remained consistent with Bonapartist efforts to end the cultural rifts inherited from the Revolution and reintegrate Catholics back into French national life.

Desires to minimize conflict in education were similarly evident in the realm of higher education not subject to the Falloux legislation. Wary of the freedoms permitted to the French *université*, the government targeted the institution after 1852 as part of the general consolidation of Bonapartist power. Carrying out this task fell to Hippolyte Fortoul. A former art critic and Saint-Simonian, Fortoul was a moderate who had curried favor with the emperor through sycophantic overtures. Convinced that "detestable doctrines" had contaminated the national education system, he believed the state was compelled to battle the "secret peril" threatening French universities and set out to undermine the autonomy of the universities.[33] Fortoul stacked the governing Conseil with his own men to ensure that higher education was "directed by a single hand," guided by a "unity of direction" and, above all, compliant to the state.[34] To this end, the minister of public instruction appropriated the power to design academic curricula and appoint or dismiss professors at will to ensure that public instruction was "in harmony with the same principles of the new government."[35] According to Fortoul, pedagogical lectures were to be "dogmatic and purely educational."[36] "The proper mission of universities is to teach the most undisputed parts of human knowledge," urged an official circular. "It is not to encourage the inventive spirit nor propagate discoveries that are not fully verified."[37] The constraints placed on higher education in the name of social order impelled instructors to give insipid lectures to an apathetic audience. The effect, as Ernest Renan commented, lowered educated men "to the ranks of public entertainers."[38]

Reducing secular interference in religious schools and encouraging an anodyne curriculum in state institutions failed, however, to produce the desired social order and tranquility the Bonapartists anticipated. The regime proved unable to rein in rightwing clerics, and as Napoleon III's foreign policy drove a wedge between the government and its Catholic support, the alliance of the early 1850s showed signs of strain. The emperor's patronage of Italian nationalism, aimed at bringing a weak and unified Italy under French influence, placed the government in a precarious situation when Italy demanded the annexation of Rome and the Papal States. Catholics condemned support for an Italian nation-state, and often took their opposition directly into the pulpit. Clerical resistance became so great that prefects were ordered to shut down pro-papal journals and arrest clergy members caught insinuating politics into their sermons. Beginning in 1861, Persigny set out to break up prominent Catholic societies and organizations operating outside of the government, specifically targeting the Société de Saint-Vincent-de-Paul, an influential association dedicated to charitable works and social Catholicism with networks extending throughout the country.[39] Intransigent clerics responded to this harassment by fulminating against the government's profane foreign policy and even comparing the emperor to the Antichrist.[40]

The reactionary stance of Pope Pius IX and his virulent diatribes against "modern civilization" equally posed a problem for the Bonapartists. The Syllabus of Errors seemingly validated anticlerical opinion that the Catholic Church was nothing but a medieval relic out of touch with "the modern spirit."[41] It was now beyond doubt, the liberal journalist Edmond Scherer seethed, that the Church was not only a "foreign element in our civilization but also a rebellious element that modern society seeks to assimilate in vain."[42] How could a government priding itself on its commitment to nationality and modern society lend its support to a religion and Church blatantly hostile to the cause of national liberation and "modern civilization" in all its guises? The growing obduracy of the papacy and Catholic radicals put Napoleon III in a hazardous position. With critics assailing the Catholic crusade against modern society, the identity of the Second Empire was now placed in question. In an intellectual and political atmosphere where it was becoming necessary to choose sides and declare one's self either for or against modern society, clerical resistance became a thorn in the side of the regime that threatened to undercut its dual objective of religious tolerance and national unity.

Civilizing Natives or Secularizing Muslims?

Navigating between the poles of secularism and religious tradition was no easier when it came to administering the population of more than two million Muslims inhabiting French soil. While Napoleon III's efforts to present himself as a patron of *dar al-Islam* may have evoked memories of his uncle's attempt to cast himself as a "Muhammad of the West" a half century earlier in Egypt, Algeria did present a unique case in which the tensions between religion, modernity, and education intersected in novel ways. Having suppressed Muslim resistance during the initial conquest, the military administration understood all too well the incendiary implications that confessional politics could assume in the colony if left unchecked. Muslim leaders periodically used calls to jihad and chiliastic prophecy to rally supporters and forge political alliances with their brethren against the French infidel. In the early 1840s, the emir Abd al-Qādir had solicited aid from influential Sufi orders and generated a wide-spread resistance movement in the west that took nearly a decade to suppress. No sooner was Abd al-Qādir's rebellion put down than further revolts sprang up in the Kabyle territories and the Sufi-dominated Za'atsha. In the process of suppressing these movements, the military quickly discovered that local religious authorities were actively fueling Muslim resistance and assisting in recruiting combatants against the French.[43]

The links connecting Muslim educators and Islamic authorities to the resistance reinforced strong mistrust for the Qur'anic schools and mosques operating independent of French supervision. In 1865, Baron

David denounced madrassas as bastions of Islamic militancy and warned of the dangers that would result if native education was not effectively subordinated to French oversight. "Without exception," he charged, "the methods of instruction given in these establishments encourage a belief in the superiority of the Muslim and contempt for the infidel."[44] Filling impressionable minds with fresh prejudices and hatred, educators imparted their message of defiance to Muslim youths, cultivating a wild "fanaticism" that, according to one journalist, undermined peaceful coexistence in the region.[45] Following a revolt led by sheikh Ouled Sidi in 1864 that roiled southern Oran, Auguste Vital was inclined to put credence in the ubiquitous accusations of Muslim fanaticism levied by colonists and officials. "There are still those magic words that goad [the Muslims], and every time someone speaks to them of nationality, Islam, and the Holy Land to be purged of the infidel they are ready to march."[46]

Prior to the French invasion, the regency of Algiers possessed neither a unified administration nor central education system. Customarily, instruction was the prerogative of local communities, with Muslim children attending schools affiliated with mosques or receiving secondary education abroad in Tunisia or Cairo. Education curriculum varied from school to school and region to region, but in general Muslim learning remained centered on religious instruction given by ulema at madrassas, Qur'anic schools dedicated to studies in theology, Sharia law, and Islamic pedagogy, or through local *awliya'* (marabouts) who dispensed religious and legal advice in independent schools. These institutions were responsible for producing the ranks of judges, officials, and educators who presided over Maghrebi society and, therefore, became a primary target of the French administration as it attempted to consolidate its control and influence over Algerian communities.[47] These security objectives were, moreover, broadly consistent with the modernizing thrust of French colonial ideology and ideas of African conquest as a French national mission. "We have declared our intention of applying the French Revolution to the Arab people," General Louis-Christophe-Léon Juchault de la Moricière declared. "Unfortunately, the Muslims have only seen this act as a brutal attack on their religion and an absence of faith."[48] As the Revolution that had begun in Europe spread to North Africa, the Muslim world, as many French administrators saw it, was now poised to enter its own struggle between Reason and Revelation, as the architects of the future battled against the prophets of the past.

During the first years of the conquest, the state opened schools intended to provide the children of European colonists with a French curriculum and education, anticipating that native elites would eventually succumb to the pressures of assimilation and seek to promote the advancement of their children through French institutions. These so-called *écoles mutuelles* failed, however, to attract students and remained largely unpopular among Algerian Muslims.[49] With native elites unwilling to accept the French curriculum and language, certain military officials expressed reservations over reopening mosques and sending children to the madrassas before French authorities had a chance to thoroughly purge and reform the education system. In the opinion of Captain Jean-Auguste Margueritte, a seasoned soldier and administrator in the Armée d'Afrique, it was "better to allow the Arabs to follow their natural inclination to learn nothing."[50] By the closing years of the July Monarchy, these attitudes had begun to change as officials came to accept the inevitability of developing specific institutions attractive to Muslims. "Islam is not absolutely impenetrable to enlightenment," a state-ordered committee of inquiry reported in 1847. "It has often permitted certain sciences and arts at its core. Why not seek to make them flourish under our empire? Let's not force them to attend our schools, but help them to rebuild theirs, to multiply the men of law and religion that Muslim civilization cannot do without any more than ours can."[51] This approach developed over the coming years set the tenor for the Nativist policies to come, outlining a program aimed at renovating and restructuring the Muslim education system and bringing about what Urbain later described as a "slow initiation into our habits and mores."[52]

In the summer of 1850, a series of decrees authorized the creation of six Franco-Muslim schools (*écoles françaises-musulmanes*) in the colony. The reforms signaled a new effort on the part of the French state to influence the indigenous education curriculum and establish an administrative apparatus capable of monitoring and controlling Muslim pedagogy. They also reflected growing outlooks among French political and cultural elites regarding the utility of education in molding young minds.[53] "It is with the children that it is necessary to start," as the anthropologist Louis Pierre Gratiolet explained. "It is in the nascent generations that the seeds of civilization will be planted."[54] Urbain agreed, arguing that the school was "the hearth where the boy [was] transformed into a man."[55] In the perspective of prominent Nativists, influencing Muslim education offered an effective means of transforming the population and slowly integrating them into colonial society. The Bonapartist propagandist Eugène Fourmestraux summed up these arguments concisely in 1866 when defending the government's education policies in the colony: "By developing the intellect, education works to lower the barriers between two peoples separated by differences in customs and beliefs."[56]

The development of a native education system complemented the military's segregationist policies and demonstrated a further willingness to cooperate with local Muslim notables "for political reasons and in the interest of conquest."[57] Yet because the purpose of these reforms was tied to issues of security rather than purely academic concerns, officials argued that native education ought to be the exclusive preserve of the military. The authority of the state education ministry was to be limited exclusively to French and European education in the civilian provinces. This arrangement ensured the primacy of the Arab Offices over native affairs and extended the dual civilian-military administration into the realm of education.[58] The *écoles françaises-musulmanes* founded after 1850 prescribed a twofold curriculum for native youths, offering instruction in both Arabic and French. Muslim instructors gave religious and grammar studies while courses in language, mathematics, and the sciences were run by French officials. This double curriculum both encouraged the development of the Arab national identity supported under the Arab Kingdom program as well as placed controls on Muslim educators. French officials were responsible for supervising the new madrassas charged with imparting a traditional Qur'anic education to children while the Arab Offices attended to the recruitment of native instructors and school masters with the objective of curtailing the spread of Islamic "fanaticism" and subjecting Islamic educational institutions to state surveillance. The objective was to create a curriculum that was at once familiar to Algerian natives yet accountable to colonial administrators, establishing an allegedly "indigenous" education system that would ideally produce a cadre of native bureaucrats and educators compliant with French authority.[59]

In tandem with these efforts to place administrative controls on Muslim education, the military endorsed a second curriculum aimed at promoting secular studies and professional training. At the behest of Urbain and other Nativists, the governor-general Jacques Louis César Alexandre Randon authorized the creation of the *collège arabe-français*, an institution opened in Algiers in 1857 and later replicated in Constantine and Oran. The *collèges* were intended to initiate natives into a French-inspired curriculum and prepare them for admission to the colonial lycées attended by the Europeans. The courses offered at these colleges focused on scientific learning and the development of industrial skills essential to integrating natives into the colonial economy.[60] In Randon's estimation, the *collèges* would "spread instruction throughout the tribes . . . and make it accessible to the elevated classes of Arab society, whence it will descend to the masses."[61] Urbain similarly lauded the new institution as a bastion of progress, claiming that the specialized and secular education they offered would develop the "agricultural and industrial habits" of the natives and pave the way for the advent of an Arab "middle class" traditionally stymied by conservative Muslim notables and religious authorities content to preserve the status quo.[62]

Despite this ambitious program, state efforts proved largely unsuccessful. Local elites regularly protested against French instruction while Muslim pedagogues resented the administration's attempts to curb their autonomy. The *écoles françaises-musulmanes* set up in the Arab territories remained consistently unpopular among Muslims, with only some 1,300 students attending them throughout the colony by 1870.[63] These figures were even more disappointing in reality since the number of registered students reported by officials did not take into account high absentee rates. It was not uncommon for French teachers to give instruction to two or three Arab children during any given class session while the instructors at the *collèges arabe-française* more often than not found themselves delivering lectures to a primarily European student body.[64] Suspicion and resentment for foreign institutions were not, however, the only factors discouraging native attendance. In designating North Africa an "Arab" territory, French administrators failed to take into account the ethnic diversity of Maghrebi society, subjecting non-Arab populations such as the Berbers and Turks to an education given in Arabic and partial to an Arab culture to which they could not easily relate.[65]

If Algerian natives saw the military's policies as intrusive, the European population in the colony was inclined to view state education initiatives as too passive. Catholics and missionary groups operating in North Africa were among the fiercest critics, seeing the military's efforts to promote Qur'anic education as anti-Christian and profane. As the "eldest daughter of the Church," France was called upon to bring civilization to Africa and, as the Catholic historian Jean-Joseph François Poujoulat proudly declared, "reconstruct the edifice of the Christian faith" after centuries of Muslim dominance and desuetude.[66] Espousing a strong crusading rhetoric that cast the French invasion in terms of reconquest and re-Christianization, Catholic spokesmen envisioned a reborn Christian Africa under French rule, and education was one of the key instruments in "regenerating" the region's Christian heritage.[67] In this war between Christian civilization and Muslim barbarism, missionaries were soldiers in a "Catholic army . . . devoted to the moral conquest of our African possession," according to the priest Antoine Horner.[68] Missionary objectives ran counter to Nativist aspirations of creating a Franco-Muslim Algeria. Catholics were among the most vocal detractors of the segregation and "tolerance" practiced by the military, ridiculing Islamic schools as strongholds of Muslim fanaticism and anti-French sentiments. In 1867, the newly appointed archbishop of Algiers, Charles Lavigerie, spelled out the Catholic position clearly: "It is necessary to renounce the errors of the past, to cease sequestering those of the Qur'an as has been done for a long time and continues to be done in a futile effort to create a so-called Arab Kingdom."[69]

Military officials could brush off these criticisms because, in reality, they posed little danger to the administration's integrity. The minister of war Alphonse Henri d'Hautpoul revealed the flimsy position of Catholic opponents when remarking in 1850: "I ask you if we can command three million Arabs and Kabyles with a black habit?"[70] Yet this did not mean that missionaries and clerical officials were innocuous. Catholic proselytism had the potential to ignite sectarian conflicts between Muslims and Christians in the colony and imperil public order. Officials repeatedly emphasized the importance of circumscribing missionary activities and prohibiting them from the territories attended to by the Arab Offices. Catholic polemicists in turn stepped up their opposition to Nativism and the Arab Kingdom, applying pressure on both the colonial administration and the emperor to end the segregation that sequestered natives from the colony's Christian population.[71] Reflecting on the tense atmosphere in his *mémoires*, Ismael Urbain accused Catholic militants of dividing Algeria into two hostile camps and seeking to foment a veritable holy war in the colony. "Reconciliation and sympathetic relations between the two races had become impossible," he recalled sadly. "It was necessary to choose and take social positions with the Christian French or the Muslims."[72]

Yet religious conflict was not the only obstacle to Nativist designs. Settlers assumed an equally critical stance against the military administration, albeit for reasons distinct from those of Catholic polemicists. Faced with the pressing and more immediate concerns posed by Algeria's underdeveloped economy and lack of skilled labor, *colons* saw little value in debating the merits of religious instruction. What use did religion serve when the majority of colonists sitting on the rural municipal councils were illiterate and lacked a basic knowledge of arithmetic?[73] How could *colons* be considered "agents of civilization" in North Africa or even be expected to take an active role in the affairs of the colony, critics argued, if they continued to remain uneducated? Émile Thuillier, a radical republican deported to Algeria in the early 1850s, showed his anticlerical colors when it came to colonial reform and heaped scorn on religious officials ill-suited to attend to the practical needs of the colony. In his opinion, the vapid instruction given by priests was insufficient for turning out the type of productive and energetic individuals required to colonize and develop North Africa. "Neither the confessional priest concerned with directing young souls nor the religious-minded, who have all the confidence in the world regarding their students, can inspire in [our children] the true sentiments and responsibility befitting the new existence that awaits them."[74]

Thullier was representative of the republican and liberal outlooks germinating in the settler community under the Second Empire as political exiles and deportees averse to Bonapartism adapted their ideology to the situation in the colony. Anticlericalism encouraged consideration for the practical skills and knowledge essential to colonial modernizing and often translated into sharp critiques of state policies. Frustrated by the slow pace of economic growth in the colony, the journalist Clément Duvernois chided the government's feeble industrial policies, which had failed to either attract metropolitan investors or establish a viable colonial infrastructure. These shortcomings underscored the dire need for an education curriculum composed of courses in economics and management that would produce homegrown elites knowledgeable in the practices and theories of market capitalism. "Public instruction exercises a remarkable influence on production as it turns out competent individuals prepared to take the lead in useful enterprises," Duvernois reminded his readers in 1858.[75] In 1868, the newspaper L'Echo d'Oran reiterated Duvernois's point, stating its support for a secular and "special" education curriculum that would promote the interests of the colony. "Give to the masses that demand it the means of acquiring a positive instruction that conforms to individual needs and social interests," the paper urged. "It is through these methods that we will come to form honest citizens."[76]

As contentions over secular and religious instruction divided public opinion during the 1860s, the colonial administration found itself square in the middle of this emerging conflict. Inspired by lofty ambitions of spreading civilization across Africa, many officials sympathized with *colon* demands for progressive educational institutions, believing, as one official claimed, that France's civilizing influence must "[open] minds to the marvels of modernity" and combat superstition and ignorance.[77] Conversely, however, promoting or forcibly imposing a European-inspired education curriculum on the native populations clashed with the ostensible cultural relativism and tolerance adhered to by military officials and Nativists. Much like the Bonapartist government in the metropole, colonial officials were confronted with questions of how to minimize conflicts between Reason and Revelation while shaping an education system that was at once progressive yet tolerant of religious traditions and specific cultural practices. This end was to be sought in a policy that would expunge religious zealotry and inspire what General Nicolas Theodule Changarnier deemed "a more rational direction" within Islamic pedagogy without directly imposing foreign influences on Muslim teaching methods and forms of knowledge.[78]

For colonists, however, these measures signified nothing short of accepting "Islamic barbarism." In an open letter to the prefect of Algiers in 1860, Clément Duvernois frankly admitted that preserving the authority of the ulema and marabouts would only fan the flames of resistance and exacerbate sectarian strife. "Believe me, Monsieur," he urged, "the spirit of tolerance does not guide the partisans of all things Muslim in Algeria."[79] A *colon* professing a staunch dedication to France's civilizing mission, Duvernois avowed that "the day the French flag was hoisted above the walls of Algiers, a new era was inaugurated for all of Africa."[80] Yet the progress promised by French rule required resolve and dedication. The first step was combating the refuges of Muslim sterility and savagery, the Qur'anic schools. "Far from spreading enlightenment [these schools] perpetuate religious prejudices among the vanquished and distance them from the vanquishers," he inveighed.[81]

Duvernois's convictions of French superiority and unyielding hostility toward Muslim culture constituted popular themes in an emerging *colon* ideology that could, at times, appear just as fanatical and intolerant as the alleged "prejudices" and "hatreds" harbored by Algerian natives. Muslim religious authorities and educators were commonly accused by colonial polemicists of propagating a medieval religious mentality that encouraged resistance to progressive change, accusations that justified marginalizing Muslim cultural elites and suppressing Islamic religious institutions.[82] In the view of the colonial publicist Henri Verne, Islam was "the largest obstacle to the fusion of the two races." Social accord between the indigenous and European populations would continue to be a vain dream unless the state committed itself to purging education of its religious influences and encouraged a secular curriculum.[83] Wilfrid de Fonvielle concurred in 1860, arguing that such a policy would "calm the religious susceptibilities of a people who attach too much importance to the exterior forms of their sect."[84]

An amateur scientist and republican journalist deported to Algeria in 1851 after the Bonapartist coup, Fonvielle neither concealed his disdain for the dogma and irrationality that religion inspired in man nor wavered in his beliefs regarding the importance of education for a progressive and democratic society. He spurned the efforts of Catholic missionaries and Islamic clerics alike, asserting that "in this environment of confused opinions" religion only served to inflame passions and jeopardize civilization. Lest the French state assume an active role in assuaging religious hatreds and nurturing a commitment to secular ideals in the coming generation, Algeria would, Fonvielle warned, remain plagued by chronic instability and internecine struggle. "Each religion has its temple [in Algeria], but humanity continues to lack one. The school [will be the place] where all young Algerians, whatever the color of their skin or nuance of their faith, receive a common instruction."[85]

Reason and science offered the foundation for a mutual education encompassing all Algerian children, and Fonvielle was not alone in insisting that "taught side by side [and] learning something as essential as science" the future generation would "forget the sad prejudices of their fathers" and come to see themselves as a single people.[86] Victor Duruy came to a similar conclusion during his work in Algeria in the 1850s. Aware of the confessional divide distancing Europeans from Muslims,

Duruy posited that science alone held the prospect of social unity and "achieving the moral conquest of these three million men whose hostility is a continual danger to us."[87] Despite this promising insight, Duruy soon became preoccupied with affairs in the metropole, leaving the question of colonial education in abeyance. Writing in 1858 at a time when Napoleon III was examining possible alternatives to military rule in the colony, Duvernois used the opportunity to attack the army's support for Qur'anic schools, remarking sharply, "these establishments cannot contribute greatly to the spread of enlightenment" in Algeria.[88] His indictment of Muslim pedagogy digressed into an attack on the segregationist policies of the military regime tout court. By isolating Muslim children from the colonists and abandoning them to the tutelage of religious extremists, the military failed to recognize that "continual contact with the Europeans at an age where prejudices have not yet taken root habituates them to not consider us as enemies."[89]

As a modernizing and civilizing force, education was expected to temper religious extremism through the cultivation of reason and scientific knowledge. Its potential to foster sociability across ethnocultural lines rendered it "the most energetic instrument of pacification and racial fusion" in Duvernois's estimation.[90] Yet if colonial critics noted the social utility of secular instruction, whether in combating "fanaticism" or promoting social unity, there was little question that secularizing the education curriculum ultimately meant Gallicizing it as well. In a typical criticism of native segregation published in 1869, the pamphleteer Arthur Ballue expressed his support for mixed schools "where all religious speculation [would] be severely curtailed." "When the reason, intelligence, and judgment of the Arabs has been developed through study they will understand what our true superiority consists of."[91] Enlightenment and the cause of civilization may have furnished *colons* with a rationale for cleansing education of its dogmatic and medieval influences, but such perceptions were never detached from questions of power and ideological hegemony on France's North African frontier. If the future of the colony was imagined in terms of state schools imparting scientific learning and practical skills to European and Arab students, this future was arguably one in which Islamic cultural elites were severely marginalized, if not irrelevant.

The "New Generation"

By the 1860s, the Second Empire's attempts to chart a middle course and encourage a pluralist policy had, ironically, contributed to rather than reduced conflict. Moreover, this was only the first in a growing number of problems facing the regime. With the opening of a new decade, the prosperity and stability that the Second Empire had ushered in was rapidly waning. An economic downturn generated by ill-conceived trade agreements, large deficits resulting from the government's public works projects, and the revival of political rivalries in the Corps législatif indicated that the halcyon days of the 1850s were coming to an end. "In the past ten years, never has France faced such a worried situation," one Bonapartist dignitary commented in 1862. "The great party of order is disorganized, there is anxiety everywhere, and a sort of silent agitation is creeping throughout the country."[92] Following the coup in 1851, Napoleon III had carried out an effective purge, driving republicans underground and confining their movement to the local level. "[The republicans] lack cohesion," one official reported in 1854. "The suspicion, which exists even between the most militant, prevents them from establishing a united group influenced by the same ideas."[93] Yet in 1857, the government was shocked by the election of five moderate republicans to the Corps législatif. The victory of *Les Cinq*, as the five deputies became known, portended a revitalization of the republican movement, and in 1863 republicans made further electoral gains in Paris, this time returning former Forty-Eighters (*quarante-huitards*) who did not hide their loathing for the government.

The weakening of the clerical alliance and the growth of political opposition had a sobering effect on the emperor, indicating the need for a shift in the government's political orientation. Hoping to mend fences with disaffected liberals, Napoleon III searched about for a suitable minister of public instruction, one who was progressive yet moderate. In 1863, he settled on Victor Duruy, a former teacher and academic inspector who had served in both Algeria and Paris. A confirmed Deist, Duruy was not antipathetic to the applied sciences and, while serving in North Africa, had promoted scientific education as a means of diffusing religious tensions in the colony. With religious conflicts currently agitating French society, cultivating an appreciation for scientific rationality in young minds, although controversial, was not altogether undesirable, especially if carried out slowly and pragmatically so as to usher in a "quiet revolution." To achieve this objective, however, Duruy realized that the imperial government could not continue to pander to Catholic reactionaries. He expressed his misgivings to the emperor bluntly: "The bishops are closely linked to the Pope and his polices, which are in absolute contradiction with the institutions of modern society."[94]

A proponent of modernization, Duruy believed it essential to devise a curriculum capable of developing the applied sciences and technical skills that sustained industry, the motor of economic and "moral" progress. New industrial needs required a novel type of education, one capable of fostering "a new spirit and new men" in the country.[95] Despite the opposition of clerics, the imperial government, in his view, was not theoretically at odds with the demands of reformers, offering hope that his reforms could be sufficiently realized. The question, however, was how to endorse such measures without further estranging Catholics or offending religious sensibilities. Unable to devise a pragmatic solution, the emperor and his entourage of conservative ministers preferred to appease Catholic reactionaries rather than sanction liberal reforms that could possibly endanger the government's authoritarian policies. In spite of Duruy's hope of inaugurating a "quiet revolution," he found his freedom of action hampered by staunch conservative opponents and the emperor's futile attempts to please everyone.

Upon taking up his post in the ministry at 110 rue de Grenelle, Duruy announced his intention of reversing the damage done during Fortoul's administration.[96] No sooner was he in office, however, than a controversial situation presented itself. In 1862, Ernest Renan, a theologian recently elected to the Collège de France, gave the first lecture from his forthcoming book *The Life of Jesus.* Intent on presenting a humanistic history of Christianity, Renan went as far as to deny the divinity of Christ and attributed the working of miracles to apocryphal accounts by the apostles.[97] After delivering his lecture, he was suspended from the *collège* by the education ministry. With the government desiring to mollify clerical acrimony and reaffirm its Catholic support, it could scarcely tolerate such a contentious subject being taught in a state institution. Renan was defiant, however, and continued to give private lectures attended by students at his own home. In 1863 he published his *Life of Jesus*, which, by the following year, had gone through ten editions and sold some fifty thousand copies, much to the government's chagrin.[98]

The conflict soon mushroomed into a controversy as Catholics unleashed a venomous criticism of Renan and Duruy, and fiery arguments erupted in lecture halls. Although a supporter of academic freedom, Duruy disdained instructors prone to controversy, abiding by a personal maxim of "first order, then liberty." Judging it imprudent to give in to the demands of the clergy outright and generate a cause célèbre that would give Renan "the baptism of persecution," Duruy pressed the government to proceed delicately with the matter. His suggestion was, however, ignored in favor of appeasing Catholic opinion and Duruy was compelled to dismiss Renan from his post. Much as the minister had anticipated, Renan's dismissal provoked student protests in support of academic freedom and free thought, obliging Duruy to enforce his prerogative despite their disapproval.[99]

The Renan affair set the tone for Duruy's troubled career as minister of public instruction. Reviled by conservatives and attempting to initiate a slow but progressive reform policy, he became the target of both the left and the right, at once appearing either too conservative or too radical depending on the critic. With Catholic extremists and student activists constantly seeking to exploit academic contentions for their own ends, grievances had the potential to escalate into controversies quickly, and Duruy found himself reacting with a heavy hand when it came to divisive ideas arising in the universities. Student protests rose throughout the 1860s in response to the regime's unpopular education policies. Writing in 1862, a vice-rector at the Académie de Paris complained of the growing disorder he noticed in schools, claiming that unruly students "fashioned themselves apostles of skepticism and materialism."[100] Support for science and materialism was rarely apolitical in nature, according to the official. Due to the "pernicious influence" of militant student activists, French higher education was quickly becoming a veritable breeding ground for dangerous ideas and radical political ideologies.[101]

While the police and imperial authorities expressed concern over the growing radicalism in schools, various liberals and democrats interpreted the politicization of French youth as an auspicious sign.[102] Following the favorable mention of former republican luminaries in the pages of the student newspaper *Journal des Écoles* in 1862, the *quarante-huitard* Edgar Quinet sent a personal letter of gratitude to the paper's editors from exile in Switzerland. "It is natural that old men will support their own, and it is often their single consolation," he wrote. "But when the young in their turn conserve and recall such things and men in their fresh memories, lifting them from obscurity, then it is certain that moral life continues, that truth persists to germinate in passionate hearts, and that we may still hope and believe."[103] The republican Jules Simon similarly offered words of encouragement to the student movements taking shape in France, remarking, "What makes youth so magnificent is its enthusiasm for all great causes."[104]

What the socialist Benoît Malon deemed the "veritable awakening" of French youth marked the advent of a new movement directed by young middle-class elites committed to reform and political opposition.[105] Student newspapers became the chief organs of this protest movement, with editors circumnavigating the imperial censors of the *commission d'examen* while they remained in print. Most of the papers had a short existence, with many of the editors having their presses shut down by government officials or finding themselves serving brief prison sentences for the publication of unauthorized material. Charles Longuet, editor of *Les Écoles des France*, received a four-month prison sentence in 1864 before relocating to Brussels and launching his second and more successful journal, *La Rive gauche*. Georges Clemenceau, a medical student and journalist in the 1860s who would become a leading republican politician and eventually premier during the Third Republic, narrowly avoided arrest one afternoon when authorities appeared at the door of his residence on the rue du Bac where he kept an illegal printing press. He managed to conceal the criminal device from the police at the time of their visit but the following day it was moldering at the bottom of the Seine.[106]

Clemenceau had already served a short sentence in Sainte-Pélagie prison for his underground political activities and had little desire to return there. Others, however, were not as lucky, nor did they necessarily want to be. Sainte-Pélagie became a popular meeting place for like-minded student radicals, and serving a prison sentence was in some cases considered a badge of honor and a testament to one's dedication to the cause of liberty. As the young Blanquist Gaston da Costa boasted when reflecting on his arrest in 1867, "through my polemics I was talented enough to earn my first prison sentence and a fine of two hundred francs."[107] Attempts by the imperial regime to root out and discipline young militants often had the unintended effect of strengthening their ideological resolve and further associating demands for academic freedoms with the broader call for political liberty that had begun to enliven political opponents. Noting the uniformity of purpose and shared hostilities expressed by French students during the 1860s, Charles Longuet did not hesitate to proclaim that he and his cohorts constituted a "new generation" possessing its own aspirations and mission distinct from the past.[108]

Although stressing generational solidarity, Longuet was not blind to the "diverse tendencies" existing among the various student groups. He was especially troubled by the discrepancies he saw arising between militant Jacobins on one hand and democrats averse to "excessive and outmode displays of force" on the other.[109] United by shared revolutionary and republican aspirations, activists remained, nonetheless, divided over the issue of how exactly to inaugurate this extensive social and political transformation. For a radical like Gustave Tridon, a Parisian law student notorious for fraternizing with Jacobin terrorists and waxing lyrical on the "men of blood" who orchestrated the Great Terror in 1793, political struggle was, in its very essence, a violent enterprise befitting men of stern will and iron conviction. "The Revolution can only be accomplished by force," he declared in 1865, "and that force is in us."[110] Yet not all democrats subscribed to these extreme opinions, and even a radical like Longuet admitted that certain "concessions" would have to be made on the part of militants if the student movements hoped to retain a unity of purpose.[111]

Tridon and his ilk made up one of the most extreme and militant camps within the student resistance. They pledged their allegiance to the notorious Jacobin revolutionary Louis Auguste Blanqui, a shadowy figure considered the scourge of bourgeois society whose repeated incarceration as a political prisoner over the decades had earned him the sobriquet *l'enfermé*, the "imprisoned one." The prominent activist and friend of Longuet, Paul Lafargue later claimed that Blanqui "provided the revolutionary education" for his generation, an assessment that proved quite accurate in light of the events that would unfold during the 1860s and early 1870s.[112] Convinced that "the nineteenth century will only justify itself through science," Blanqui nurtured an aggressive appreciation for materialism and atheism in his young acolytes. Science was the definitive weapon in the battle against Catholic dogma and clerical authority; violent rhetoric and revolutionary action the true politic.[113] His followers took these words of wisdom to heart as the aged Jacobin reared a fresh generation of political militants whose strong dedication to social revolution and terrorist tactics would prove exceedingly difficult to tame.[114] In light of the Blanquist faction, Longuet's hope of softening extremist opinions within the ranks of the student movements and discouraging violence would have to be able to trump the influences of notable revolutionary icons and build a radical platform capable of drawing the support of insurrectionists and more temperate activists alike.

The "new generation" promoted by Longuet and his followers constituted a rallying call to French youth. It intended to forge a common identity and purpose across ideological lines and orient the student movements around a set of core republican values. This new generation, united by its loathing for servitude and intellectual tyranny, was carrying on the traditions of French student activism and collectively paid homage to its forbearers by continuing the revolutionary struggle, in Longuet's opinion.[115] Despite the fact that the student activists of the late 1840s had rarely expressed support for revolutionary ideas and remained cold to overtly political concerns, Longuet understood the importance of constructing a past and common heritage.[116] Cultivating an identity that students could associate with necessitated locating it within a specific cultural context and fostering solidarity through appeals to tradition and acts of collective memorialization. Veneration for the past was, however, coupled with conceptions of rupture and discontinuity to highlight the revolutionary and novel character of the student movement. One could have accused Longuet of insincerity when his newspaper *La Rive gauche* declared that while their predecessors abided by the credo "God and *Patrie*," the current generation proudly obeyed a new one: "Reason and Fraternity!"[117]

As brothers in arms, students upheld a tenacious devotion to the cause of free thought, identifying schools and universities as the definitive battlefield on which the coming revolution would either be won or lost. "Education is the supreme salvation [and] solution to all the problems of our time" a student petition drafted in 1867 declared.[118] Drawing upon Blanqui's notion that education constituted the only "real revolutionary agent," Paul Lafargue echoed the teachings of his mentor when affirming "revolution must be social and not political, and education is the most powerful revolutionary force I know."[119] Faithful to their republican principles, activists vented their spleen at clerical influence over French education. Religion instilled subservience and "a profound disgust for terrestrial affairs" in young minds.[120] A new generation now demanded enlightenment. In the opinion of the neurological student Albert Regnard, the debates over faith and reason had reached a fever pitch, and it was now essential to take sides in this struggle. For Regnard and his generational coevals, the choice was simple. "All men of progress are for materialism today," he affirmed. "On our flag, one reads progress through science."[121]

Science constituted a core ideological tenet of the new generation, vaunting a modern identity that student activists proudly celebrated to demonstrate their break with established traditions and beliefs. "Our light is human science . . . our criterion is human reason and our principle is human law," wrote a student journalist in 1865.[122] More forceful, the Blanquist Germaine Casse declared before an international student congress in 1867 that youth had let out its "war cry" while "the entire past trembled."[123] His generation stood for science and freedom, Casse insisted, and it was, he added, willing to wage war against the forces of intellectual and political oppression to attain them. "We are strong and young," claimed Tridon, "we have a hunger for bread and ideas, for justice and science. . . . Why should we continue to wait? Do we not have a faith, Atheism; a goal, Justice; a method, Revolution?"[124] Science and revolution produced an intoxicating mix in the thoughts and writings of student activists speaking on behalf of a new generation, and their message sought nothing less than to expose "the radiant image of the approaching future" built by the "great revolutionary work" calling forth a new republic, as La Rive gauche informed in 1865.[125]

This social vision was not merely a French vision either. According to many leading publicists, student activism possessed a continental purview offering a future in which "all men, united by science, marched in common accord toward the definitive conquest of liberty."[126] In an antiwar proclamation scripted in the midst of the Austro-Prussian conflict in 1866, students made an impassioned appeal for solidarity among Europeans, urging that the time had come for the youth of the continent to detach itself from the "old world" on the verge of collapse. "United and marching together," Europe would cast off the slough of the past and accomplish its "sacred mission, the mission of the nineteenth century."[127] International student congresses held in Belgium during the 1860s emboldened hopes that the "cult of science" and democratic aspirations germinating among a younger generation might consolidate the "fraternity of schools" from Lisbon to Saint Petersburg, promoting peace and liberty across Europe.[128]

These dreams of an irenic and cosmopolitan Europe certainly played upon the minds of various student activists as they made their way to Liège in 1865 to attend a student congress. In a letter drawn up to advertise the congress in the foreign press, the organizers invited students from across Europe to discuss "the question that touches us most directly, that of education." Emphasizing the cosmopolitan intentions of the gathering, the announcement unequivocally stated: "The congress of Liège will not be a gathering exhibiting a passionate political agenda. It calls for calm and fraternal deliberations from young men coming from all schools, all sects, all parties, as well as all countries."[129] In mid-October, Parisian students set up an organizational committee to make plans for attending. With Lafargue sitting on the committee, it was no surprise that invitations were extended to the Blanquists, who readily saw the gathering as a public forum to make their ideas known to France and Europe despite the request for "calm and fraternal deliberations."

The opening of the congress on 29 October began with controversy, to the dismay of the organizers. At the inaugural ceremony, national representatives were asked to march into the hall carrying their respective flags as a symbolic gesture of European unity. As the procession of flags proceeded and the national colors of each country were hung beside one another, the Blanquists delegation entered the hall carrying a black flag. As they marched through the room, students exchanged puzzled looks. When one student asked what the black flag signified, the Blanquists replied, "the mourning of French liberty." Mortified by the behavior of his compatriots, the French student Paul Giraud-Cabasse sent for the standard tricolor to be hung among the others and requested that the black flag be removed. The Blanquists protested, remarking sullenly, "France's flag was red. . . . There was no need for those stripes added by tyrants."[130]

The Blanquists' allusion to the *drapeau rouge* of the Jacobin Republic and their insistence on using the congress as a platform for nationalist polemics and political criticism prefigured the events that would transpire over the next three days. Once debates got under way, the Blanquists attracted much of the attention with ribald antics and inflammatory declarations. Stating his contempt for established religion, Lafargue went on to denigrate the current intellectual atmosphere in France and proclaim his dedication to scientific materialism. Affirming that science was the "tremendous narrative undertaken by man against God," he continued his harangue, declaring: "Science doesn't deny God. It does better. It renders him useless. . . . War of God! That is progress!"[131] Tridon joined in the tirade, lauding science and the French Revolution as the destroyers of an insidious Catholic dogma that, although once powerful, was diminishing day by day. "The struggle at the moment is between man and God," he insisted, "between the future and the past."[132]

The flagrant antireligious diatribes announced in Liège were intended to buoy the spirits of radical free thinkers and repulse moderate and Catholic sensibilities, and they had their desired effect. The Bonapartist newspaper *Le Pays* deplored the "implacable and savage war" preached by the young radicals across the Belgian frontier, writing them off as "furious madmen."[133] The Catholic press was no less critical and, as expected, exploited the spectacle to illustrate the poisonous ideas circulating through French universities. The liberal Catholic journalist Gustave Janicot implored moderates to maintain their principles of tolerance in spite of such vicious attacks mounted by extremists, commenting sullenly that "such radical, audacious and subversive doctrines as these have not been heard since the worst days of our revolutions."[134] "The fact is nobody believes in the red specter anymore," the writer Edmond About opined that December. "It was necessary that a half dozen young men, in an unhappy escapade that we would like to attribute to their age, have served to furnish a pretext to those who refuse us our liberty!"[135]

As About indicated, the "unhappy escapade" brought a conservative backlash and a deluge of comments disparaging the inimical influences that liberty and free thought posed to social order. Demands for more rigid controls over French schools echoed in the press. The events at Liège also delivered a powerful blow to Longuet's hope of effacing the ideological divisions within the student movements and transforming student activism into a progressive and revolutionary force committed to broad social change. If the solidarity of the "new generation" proved to be illusive following the Liège fiasco, Blanquist radicalism had equally torpedoed the campaign for peace and European fraternity. The astringent nationalist rhetoric and irreligious attitudes of extremists was clearly in

conflict with the irenic and cosmopolitan ideals extolled by the spokesmen of Europe's "new generation," driving a further wedge between the
leadership of the student movements.

The events in Belgium did not go unnoticed by imperial statesmen
infuriated by the public show of opposition. In December, the Counseil
Académique of Paris summoned the student participants, but only a
single person bothered to acknowledge the summons. This refusal to
appear incensed the council, which summarily expelled seven students
for desecrating the national flag and attacking the "principle of social
order."[136] The authoritarian manner in which the proceedings were
handled brought criticism from liberal opponents and greater demonstrations of resistance from students.[137] Once news of the expulsions
became known, protests broke out in the Latin Quarter as indignant
demonstrators disrupted lectures and openly heckled professors. The
constant disturbances prompted the government to send in the police
to maintain order, and the sight of armed officers only aroused further
protests that resulted in street brawls between students and the police.
In such a heated atmosphere, students were forced to show identification
cards or matriculation papers in order to enter academic buildings, and
by late December classes were canceled altogether.[138]

While Duruy's reluctant decision to dismiss unpopular academic
officials and the coming of winter recess brought a reprieve, the open
resistance to the state reflected poorly on the imperial government.
Coming to his post in 1863, Duruy had hoped to promote science and
industry through education reform, giving an impetus to Bonapartist
ambitions of forging a modern French society. Within two years, however, Duruy's idealism had been quashed, as students, educators, and
radicals denigrated the education minister as yet one more example of
Bonapartist obstinacy and parochialism. Lambasting the Second Empire
as the embodiment of an "old" and moribund society that conspired
with clerics and impeded scientific advancement, radical republicans
and student activists stridently declared themselves representatives of a
"new generation" imbued with the spirit and resolve necessary to found
the modern society the Bonapartists could not. The politicization of the

Second Empire's education policies provided young militants with the opportunity to construct and articulate a new identity that bolstered resistance to authority and nurtured a strong commitment to the radical republicanism that Napoleon III had set out to purge from the country. As was evident, by the middle of the 1860s the master narrative of Bonapartist discourse was beginning to unravel as a revived republican movement began to speak in the name of modernity.

The Vague Monster Everyone Calls "Modern Society"

In her study on colonial education, Yvonne Turin has claimed that the preservation of Qur'anic schools and the institutionalized segregation imposed by the military administration in Algeria gave rise to what she accurately describes as a "double culture," one that remained a defining feature of French Algerian society right up until decolonization.[139] Yet as French officials attended to madrassas and vetted Muslim educators, the metropole was contending with its own "double culture" of sorts, one given official recognition in 1850 with the passing of the *loi Falloux*. The cultural divide between Catholics and secularists ran deep within French social and intellectual life, and the conflicts surrounding education at midcentury were a microcosm of these larger ideological splits. "The more I look at everything, the more I am convinced that there are only two parties in France, the clerics and the liberals," Taine claimed, and many would have agreed with him.[140] On the North African border, these divides were infused with existing racial and ethnic tensions that distinguished Europeans from Muslims, colonizers from the colonized.

As a unifier, Napoleon III intended to suture these divisions through a platform of "forgetting and reconciliation" that extended to the government's education policies.[141] Bonapartist modernity rested upon the premise that an ambitious program of state-driven development and reform could effectively remake individuals and rally them to a progressive, tolerant society. This aspiration ran through the various civilizing and modernizing discourses espoused by the regime. In its various incarnations, Bonapartist modernity promised stability, prosperity, conciliation, and social fusion. These themes cut across nation and empire, contributing to an image of a trans-Mediterranean French community unified, ultimately, through the modernity and progress delivered by a new Napoleon.

The problem, however, was that modernity also proved divisive. In the nineteenth century, the question of modern society stood at the center of various cultural conflicts in which there appeared very little ground for compromise. The schism between implacable clerics and liberals noted by Taine persisted. Colonists upheld their intransigence to a hostile and inferior indigenous Muslim culture. In the conflict-ridden atmosphere of the 1860s, professions of faith in modernity tended to accent existing cleavages as critics challenged "traditional" authorities through appeals to modern society and secularism. For the most radical thinkers, uniformity rather than tolerance was the panacea, eliciting calls for an overtly secular and national education curriculum that would advance modern society as they understood it. The discords of the period were charged by what Louis Veuillot deemed the "vague monster that everyone calls 'modern society.'"[142] It was, moreover, this same "vague monster" that stalked the imperial regime. Rather than pacifying these contentions, the government found itself embroiled in them as it attempted to steer a middle course. The tensions emerging within France's national and colonial policies at midcentury were producing a common set of criticisms that reformers on both sides of the Mediterranean could direct toward the regime, calling into question the modern identity it coveted.

5   Old Ends and New Means

During the month of February 1853, the lawyer and future politician Émile Ollivier visited the salon of Marie de Flavigny, Comtesse d'Agoult, better known to Parisian circles by the pseudonym Daniel Stern. In attendance at Agoult's soirée were some of the future luminaries of the republican opposition, of which Ollivier was one. Since the coup of 1851, Agoult's Maison Rose on the upper Champs-Élysées provided a regular meeting place for ostracized political elites. There they were able to discuss politics and social issues without fear of interference from the imperial police. "The general mood of these meetings," Ollivier noted, "is full of sadness and boredom for present things, fear rather than optimism for the future."[1] This dark period marked, indeed, the nadir of republican fervor. The Republic had been lost in 1852 with the promulgation of the Second Empire, and the republican cause itself was in a state of disarray, with many of its leaders driven into exile or forced underground by Napoleon III. "The word *order*," complained the republican Edgar Quinet from Switzerland in 1860, "has been used to morally extirpate all those who have pledged themselves to liberty, and it is in the name of democracy that we democrats who have shown their true colors are now morally assassinated."[2]

Despite the sense of despair and stagnation that characterized the republican movement in the early 1850s, frequent meetings and constant dialogue between republican elites would provide the roots of a republican renaissance in the following decade. Writing from exile in

1869, the philosopher Jules Barni claimed that "the republican idea is accepted today, and the thing itself is awaited. Sooner or later it will arrive, and it will be up to us to make it live."[3] Such optimism was nearly unimaginable a decade earlier when republican ideas remained confined to the small salons hosted by socialites such as the Comtesse d'Agoult. The reawakening of the republican spirit was the product of a new generation of thinkers, self-proclaimed "young republicans" (*jeunes républicains*) who worked to distinguished themselves from the older generation of *quarante-huitards* that had presided over the failure of the Second Republic. By focusing attention on respect for law, the promotion of progress, and the creation of a modern and democratic political state, young republicans would successfully construct a new political identity that at once stood poised between the extremes of both radical Jacobinism on one hand and Bonapartist authoritarianism on the other.

Since the Revolution, French republicanism had been associated with a democratic and nationalist program opposed to the traditions of royal authority and subservience symbolic of the ancien régime. Its ideological outlook stressed a commitment to a vision of man and society that was, by its very nature, "modern." Radicals hailed the advent of the First Republic in 1791 as the birth of a new era in human history, transforming the drama of the Revolution into a "mythic present" through the manufacture of new rituals, public celebrations, and theatrical speeches.[4] During the years of the July Monarchy, revolutionary aspirations for political and social equality found common cause with disenfranchised workers and socialist militants, tying republicanism to the protests and unrest that regularly beset the government throughout the 1840s.[5] The dangers of a socialist movement speaking in the name of "the people" became evident in 1848 when workers and radicals took up arms against the state, resurrecting the "traditions" and "borrowed language" of their revolutionary forbearers, as Marx saw it.[6]

Young republicans desired to shun the troubling legacy of violence and instability left by the Jacobin Terror and June Days. This goal required outlining a vision of republican society that ceased to equate modernity and revolution. Taking their cue from their Bonapartist rivals, they made broad appeals to the heritage of 1789 while expressing disdain for the revolutionary ideology that consistently marginalized support for the republican cause in the country. Young republicanism drew upon a variety of established discourses, combining aspects of liberalism, philosophy and sociology to accommodate a moderate political agenda. Although speaking in the name of the modern society first imagined by revolutionaries in the late eighteenth century, republican moderates during the 1850s and 1860s firmly identified themselves with a new social vision at odds with the extreme egalitarianism and violent methods adhered to by radicals. As the republican and positivist philosopher Émile Littré claimed, the Terror was "the specter that looms over the republic."[7] It would be men like Littré who contributed to outlining a vision of republican modernity that transcended the revolutionary experience and provided a framework through which a moderate brand of French republicanism could be reimagined and articulated.

The desire for a more practical republicanism cleansed of its revolutionary connotations had much to do with the emergence of a new republican elite that, after 1848, endeavored to make the republican idea palatable to a broader segment of the middling classes—which the republican Léon Gambetta would later deem the "the new social stratum" (*nouvelle couche sociale*)—coming of age under the Second Empire. The Bonapartists had successfully managed to rally support in the early 1850s with their promise of order and prosperity. By the end of the decade, however, ballooning deficits incurred by state spending and the lack of parliamentary controls over the budget provoked demands for greater government accountability and a more liberal polity overall. "People are now less fearful of the idea of liberty in France than they are of growing public expenses," Clément Duvernois sardonically noted in 1863, summing up the new political ambience.[8] Young republicans keenly sought to exploit this growing discontent. By formulating a political program that blended positivist themes of science and progress with democratic values, they aimed to attract influential men in French political and financial circles to their cause. This objective entailed defining a vision of society that not only discouraged political violence, but comported with the interests and intellectual outlooks of the new class of urban elites distinguishing themselves in French society.[9]

Salons like those hosted by the Comtesse d'Agoult, recreational societies, Masonic lodges and, eventually, even the chambers of the national legislature offered opportunities for republicans to ingratiate themselves with the prominent political figures and entrepreneurs of the day. Sociability and frequent exchanges between elites over the course of the 1850s and 1860s contributed to a growing sense of trust, familiarity, and cooperation between politicians and men of affairs. These settings equally brought together republicans and progressive liberal thinkers who, increasingly disillusioned with the policies of the imperial government, did not conceal their desires of forming an oppositional front capable of forcing liberal concessions from the Bonapartist regime.[10] Much like republicans, liberals recognized the need to redefine their own political identity by the early 1860s if they intended to attract new supporters and win seats in the Corps législatif. Whereas republicans were haunted by the specter of the Terror, liberals remained burdened by the legacy of division and illiberal politics left by Guizot and the Doctrinaires. As republicans and liberals mutually began to reassess and reject the "traditions" and conventional tenets of their respective political cultures and ideologies, both camps revealed a willingness to work with former political rivals and foster cooperation through adherence to common principles and a shared language centered on themes of freedom and modern society.[11]

French political history has typically highlighted the ideological divisions separating republicans and liberals during the nineteenth century. Whereas French republicans drew upon Rousseauian notions of community and the rights of the citizens, liberals characteristically spoke out in defense of particular interests and individual liberties.[12] These divisions are easy to uphold if one focuses on extreme examples, whether the conservative liberalism of Guizot or the intolerant republicanism of Robespierre and the Jacobins. Although liberals and republicans certainly had their own distinct political cultures and histories in France, the years spanning the Second Empire testified to the fact that these two cultures were not impenetrable and, in reality, subject to a great deal of cross-pollination.[13] Under the Second Empire, republicans became critics "of a liberal type," as the historian Pierre Rosanvallon has argued, revealing a growing accord between the two political camps that would continue into the years of the Third Republic.[14] Classical liberalism was a reaction to the radical democracy and popular politics of the French Revolution and, as such, retained a strong mistrust of the people. Liberals favored parliamentary debate over popular activism and believed that public opinion, when confined to the pages of elite journals and publications, manifested the true voice of reason. They never quite reconciled support for emancipatory values with more immediate concerns of public order and authority.[15] While revolutionaries inspired by Rousseau had set out to remake society and invest it with political purpose, liberals contended that politics and society were mutually constitutive elements. Politics reflected social and commercial realities; it could not create them outright.[16]

This fundamental distinction between the political and social was, however, becoming blurred by the middle of the nineteenth century, especially as republicans came to espouse a more sociological perspective in their outlooks. "The true man, the real man is he who lives in society and by society," the republican theorist Étienne Vacherot explained in 1859. "Properly speaking, it is not society that is the abstraction and the individual the reality. To the contrary, it is society that is real and the individual the abstraction."[17] That republicans and liberals could find common ground and speak a similar political language was hardly shocking. French liberalism and republicanism did possess common ideological roots in the principles of 1789, and despite the political divergence between the two camps during the postrevolutionary period French liberalism never fully abandoned its republican heritage, retaining a patent concern with political liberty and the moral character of the citizen.[18] This variant of "republican liberalism" witnessed a resurgence under Bonapartist rule in France among a rising generation of political thinkers eager to define a "new" liberal platform.

In spite of their abhorrence for the July Monarchy and the exclusionary regime erected by Guizot and his allies, republicans could find some wisdom in the teachings of their Doctrinaire adversaries. The rationalist liberalism of the Orléanists had set out to inaugurate a new art and technology of government capable of subduing the revolutionary tide and bridling popular sovereignty. For Guizot, in a democratic and revolutionary age, authority could no longer be considered independent of society. On the contrary, power had to be built into prevailing conceptions of the social, establishing hierarchies and behavioral norms that were natural and indisputable. "The true methods of government are not in the direct and visible instruments of the action of power," he wrote in 1821. "They reside in the heart of society itself and cannot be separate from it."[19] Put otherwise, society was a construction shaped by ideology just as much as an object in its own right. If a stable postrevolutionary order was to be established in France, it could only be conditioned by and constituted through a form of discursive power capable of instilling new values in the population and making "society" a living idea.[20] Framing their political critiques in terms of "modern society" under the Second Empire, self-proclaimed democrats and partisans of liberty followed in the footsteps of their Bonapartist rivals, promising a vision of a new and dynamic type of society that they alone could deliver.

Republican Modernity and the Positivist Republic

The ideological divisions that had come to light among French student activists in the early 1860s proved to be a portent of things to come among republican circles in general. As with Longuet and his hope of rallying supporters to the idea of a "new generation," republican elites speaking for "modern society" looked upon radical fringe groups like the Blanquists with aversion. Even the most militant political thinkers within such circles, such as the passionate Jacques Pyrat, criticized the tactics employed by radicals. "Raoul Rigaul, Germain Casse, both of whom terrify the bourgeoisie," seethed Peyrat, "[these types] have strayed quite far from our ideas."[21] Having learned from the painful experience of 1848, republican thinkers recognized the need to dissociate themselves from the socialists and Jacobins who had driven the country into the arms of Louis Napoleon and the Party of Moral Order. The threat revolution posed to property owners and financial interests made it anathema, a point strongly emphasized in the criticisms of insurrectionary methods by republicans. Giving a speech in his native Loiret, Adolphe Couchery used the opportunity to remind his audience that "for us all revolution would be ruinous. Our lands would lose value; our capital invested in enterprise would be swallowed up in the tempest. No! Never a revolution."[22]

Contrary to the revolutionary materialism touted by radical student activists and militants, young republicans argued that modern society must be considered in light of the certainty that sociological and scientific knowledge offered. "There is only one thing which could serve as the foundation for a truly human society," declared the lawyer and aspiring politician Léon Gambetta, "and that is science."[23] This strong belief in the value of science and scientific rationality produced, in turn, a new political realism in the writings of republican theorists. No longer could action be guided by strict ideology or idealism; experimentation, analysis, and flexibility—what would become known as "opportunism" under the Third Republic—were perceived to be the new principles needed in bringing forth the republic and promoting social order and progress. "The young republicans . . . possessed a horror of sentimental chimeras," professed Juliette Adam, a woman of strong republican conviction, "understanding that they could no longer judge each fact according to a formula, but only according to its possible results."[24]

Many of these ideas derived from the writings of Auguste Comte and his philosophy of Positivism, which had a strong influence on republican circles during the 1850s and 1860s. Comte himself had initially conceived of his philosophy as a natural corollary to republicanism, stressing Positivism's revolutionary heritage, the need for rationalism in politics, and a belief in morality as a guide for political action. That republicans and positivists could find common ground was, therefore, not surprising.[25] Republican aspirations were in accord with the dictates of positive philosophy, as a young positivist noted. "The republic is the form of government that, by its sheer elasticity, is best adapted to the incessant modifications of modern time."[26] Republican interest in Positivism became so extensive during the Second Empire that Juliette Adam complained discussions at her salon were constantly occupied with the natural "agreement between positive philosophy and republican ideas."[27]

An intellectual movement led by the eccentric polytechnician and former Saint-Simonian Auguste Comte, Positivism prescribed a philosophy vested in scientific knowledge and empirically verified data opposed to metaphysical and abstract reasoning."[We] regard the search after what we call *causes*, whether first or final, as absolutely inaccessible and unmeaning," Comte contended in his manifesto, stressing that one can "only try to analyze correctly the circumstances of their production, and to connect them together by normal relations of succession and similarity." Causality was beyond the realm of human intellect because its existence could not be verified through directly observed phenomena. It was, according to Comte, "insoluble and outside the domain of Positive Philosophy."[28] As one of his most dedicated followers, Émile Littré, explained, Positivism was a "philosophy of science" concerned with "general facts [and] fundamental truths" beyond theological and metaphysical speculation. Its intention was to divide the world and knowledge into two spheres, "one known, the other unknown," and advance a new philosophy predicated upon scientific law.[29]

The appeal of a philosophical system grounded in verifiable and scientific knowledge sprang from more general social anxieties pervading postrevolutionary French society and culture. Social critics throughout the mid-nineteenth century frequently gave bleak prognoses of the nation's future when addressing the troubling disorder and severe skepticism they believed were agitating the country. "Societies are cracking, minds expanding, and among all this the old teachers of the world have ceased to serve, to help," the political theorist Charles Dupont-White lamented in the mid-1860s.[30] The anarchist Pierre-Joseph Proudhon was not alone when suggesting that "the century [awaited] a new light" to replace the "old logic" and mentalities no longer capable of structuring and comprehending a world turned upside down.[31] For Comte, the "intellectual anarchy" permeating the postrevolutionary world constituted "the great political and moral crisis" of the age. The only means of assuaging this crisis was to advance new principles anchored in forms of knowledge that were pure, irrefutable, and homogeneous.[32]

At its most fundamental level, Positivism held out the promise of epistemological uniformity, proposing a single set of values and assumptions propagated by the new priest of the nineteenth century, the savant. In the views of leading positivist philosophers and theorists, pluralism was symptomatic of decadence and disorder, inviting "the confusion of principles [and] the excess of viewpoints."[33] As the positivist Félix Aroux insisted, "the perfection of civilization" required "moral, intellectual, civil, political, and economic homogeneity."[34] This perfection rested upon a denial of subjectivity, prizing unity above a fissiparous individualism that encouraged anomie and skepticism. Once it was generally accepted that scientific knowledge alone offered man access to truth, the precision of science became undeniable. It promised a unitary and verifiable form of knowledge that excluded divergent beliefs or opinions.[35] Science and freedom of conscience were incompatible with one another, according to the positivist critic Hippolyte Stupuy. "One allows the play of the imagination while the other subordinates all to observation."[36]

The totalizing premise of Positivism rested on the authority of what Littré deemed "the rationalist principle."[37] It refused to recognize religious or metaphysical speculation as just, for "wherever [science] extends its hand, it uproots the supernatural and replaces it with the natural."[38] Such extreme rationalism could appear disenchanting and perfunctory when confined to philosophical debate. Yet once the spirit of Positivism was "rightly understood," Comte contended, it led to an aspiration far beyond scientific curiosity: "the object, namely, of organizing human life."[39] In proposing what Comte considered a "social physics," Positivism asked men of science to turn their microscopes onto the social organism and unearth the natural laws governing society.[40] "Science in general and the newly constituted social science in particular will become the driving force in the government of human affairs," predicted the doctor

Louis-Adolphe Bertillon in the late 1860s, "just as the mechanical, physical, and chemical sciences are in industrial work."[41]

As the social organism became the object of scientific scrutiny, a conception of society in its totality would be formed that would, in turn, engender new social sentiments; self-seeking individualism and egoism would be replaced by collective concerns and an appreciation for the general social good. "To the Positivist," Comte wrote, "the object of Morals is to make our sympathetic instincts preponderate as far as possible over the selfish instincts, social feelings over personal feelings."[42] In outlining the role and mission of the positive "sociologist," Littré stressed the savant's desire to make social phenomena intelligible and render service to humanity's progressive development: "Kings, people, assemblies, bodies [and], parties create events. The sociologist makes them into experiences. He fulfills his office and duty when he illuminates what, step by step, advances that social evolution, which, as spontaneous as it is, needs to be directed if we desire . . . that future development be better than past development and bereft of disasters and travesties."[43]

With their concern for moral and social questions, positivists naturally turned their attention to politics. While Comte himself was attracted to the Bonapartist platform and its promise of order and social harmony after 1852, prior to the coup of *Deux-Décembre* Comte had openly associated his philosophy with the republican cause. Positivism identified with the ideals of 1789 and saw the Revolution as a profound moment in world history, both central themes within French republican ideology. Comte also believed that a republican form of government was best suited to realize the goals of his positive system. "By concentrating all human forces of whatever kind in the general service of the community," he claimed, "republicanism recognizes the doctrine of subordinating politics to morals." Republicanism was an ideology imbued with a moral sentiment, Comte believed, making it compatible with the tenets of Positivism. "The direct tendency, then, of the French Republic is to sanction the fundamental principle of Positivism, the preponderance, namely, of Feeling over Intellect and Activity. Starting from this point, public opinion will soon be convinced that the work of organizing society on republican principles is one which can only be performed by the new philosophy."[44]

Yet if Positivism was conceptualized as a variant of republican thinking, Comte was quick to dissociate his ideas from the more radical strain of Jacobinism. Indeed, the most dangerous obstacle to Comte's envisioned social regeneration was posed by the intransigence of radicals, men he deemed "professors of the guillotine." By persistently relying on revolutionary tactics to bring about social and political transformation, Jacobins and other extremists effectively retarded progress and forced order to take a reactionary form. "The only effect really produced by this party of disorder," he remarked, "is to serve as a bugbear for the benefit of the retrograde party, who thus obtains official support from the middle classes in a way which is quite contrary to all the principles and habits of that class."[45] His examples were drawn from the struggles of 1848 when the specter of radical socialism after the June Days led to the formation of the conservative Party of Moral Order.

In addition to jeopardizing progress, radicals also stood accused of putting their faith in "metaphysical utopias," which they sought to create through violent and undemocratic means. By employing principles central to the new sociological outlook of Positivism, it was, Littré maintained, feasible to conceptualize the "sociologically impossible," replacing utopian and metaphysical schemes with rational and empirical speculation. A practical approach to social issues could be achieved guided by rational means and moderate ends.[46] "The legitimate republic, if we understand it to be the better arrangement of social forces, will come forth only through experience," claimed Littré. "In other words, through a gradual perfecting of what exists with the aid of reflection by political leaders and the suggestions of sociology."[47] By stressing the relationship between the principles of Positivism and the establishment of a democratic republic in France, Littré presented the germ of a new republican attitude that was moderate and defined by reason. More important, it was not beholden to rigid ideological precepts, in his opinion.

Coming from a Parisian family committed to republicanism both during and after the French Revolution, Littré had been inculcated with a respect for the democratic and enlightened values of republican thought at a young age. A dedicated follower of Comte during the 1840s, he subscribed to his mentor's beliefs in progress and science's potential to offer solutions to the pressing social problems of the age. "Among the men of today," he stated, "we are moving toward the propagation of enlightenment attained by the works of science, and through this propagation, a corresponding improvement in social relations."[48] While Littré broke with Comte in the early 1850s as his mentor turned to Bonapartism and increasingly espoused a more mystical variant of Positivism that Littré accused of being "subjective" and groundless, the young scholar did not reject the core tenets that had structured his philosophical education.[49] From 1852 onward, Littré sought to promote a program that synthesized Positivism and republicanism. In 1867 he founded *La Philosophie positive*, a journal spotlighting political and intellectual critiques that became a forum for republican and liberal theorists enamored with the potential of a "positive politic."

"The positive philosophy dictates that the aim of social development is the human ideal in which natural laws constitute salutary rules, humanity a beneficent spirit, and history a means of substantiating belief," Littré apprised his readers in the premier issue of *La Philosophie positive*.[50] The political tenor of the journal grappled with issues from French politics to foreign policy and European affairs, consistently accenting the role that scientific education and progress played in the modern world and in the growing political opposition in France. With its focus on sociopolitical debate, the publication firmly inscribed Positivism with a political dimension, transforming it from a philosophical movement into an ideological outlook with a progressive and republican orientation. It offered a comprehensive vision for a new type of democratic and innovative society reflecting modern man's collective aspirations. As Hippolyte Stupuy instructed readers of *La Philosophie positive*, the essential task at hand was "to reconstruct the whole" in the wake of traumatic revolutionary upheaval, adding, "if we are to have the Revolution enter a phase of organization and conciliation" it was necessary that "politics become a positive science."[51]

True to his positivist beliefs, Stupuy argued that the basis for a "positive politic" meant investing governance with a pronounced sociological orientation. The problem, as he saw it, derived from the revolutionary fallacy of popular sovereignty. Parties consistently spoke in the name of "the people," giving rise to an "anarchic confusion of opinions and desires." As an object of postrevolutionary political discourse, "the people" had become an "elastic" term capable of legitimating any political position. If politics was to become stable and consistent, it was essential to replace the abstract man with a "true" and real idea of man derived from scientific and social analysis. Once political actors took account of how man functioned in and engaged with his social world, "the people" would cease to be a discursive figment, Stupuy argued. What politics required was a clear understanding of the socially real and possible.[52]

The brand of "scientific" republicanism promoted by Littré and his cohorts resonated among republican circles, indicating the growing desire among moderates to impart a spirit of scientific realism to republican thinking. "It is in palpable realities, in science, in industry, in the mathematical rigor of positive truths that [the revolution] has found its force and built its strength," Daniel Stern claimed in 1862.[53] Rather than "vague propositions," republicans needed to introduce a "scientific spirit" into government, insisted Gambetta, a young admirer of Auguste Comte and his philosophy. "We need a method and a system," he claimed, and a scientific approach offered both in his opinion.[54] "Politics is not, any more than philosophy, an abstract science in which one proceeds a priori," Émile Ollivier explained when addressing the Corps législatif in 1870. "Politics, just as and even more than philosophy, is an experimental science."[55]

The new scientific realism espoused by republicans offered a language and theoretical framework around which a moderate brand of French republicanism could be constructed and conceptualized. It stood in stark contrast to the "blood-drenched fury" exemplified by the Jacobins and republican socialists.[56] In their condemnation of the revolutionary adventurism upheld by radical traditionalists, Littré and Comte highlighted the central dilemma republicans faced at midcentury: the revolutionary ideology of republicanism, born from the experiences of 1791 and the National Convention, was an obstacle to creating a mass movement. Until the revolutionary element was purged, the republican cause would remain relegated to a limited group of followers. As Comte stressed, the ideals of 1789 had to be upheld in working toward order and progress and the revolutionary tradition of republican mythology abandoned.

Exorcising the Ghosts of the Past

One didn't necessarily need to be a positivist in order to appreciate the perceptive insights of thinkers like Comte and Littré. By the early 1860s, similar views were evolving among republican theorists and critics, many of whom expressed doubts regarding the practicality of modeling a political movement on rigid philosophical paradigms.[57] Charles Dupont-White, a political writer with ambiguous republican leanings, warned against putting unwavering faith in attractive and fashionable ideas, finding them, on the whole, perfunctory and overly dogmatic. In his opinion, philosophy appeared neither "suitable to modern complexities" nor capable of "furnishing the oracles necessary to soothe the spirit."[58] Demands for more calculated and moderate forms of political engagement did not always translate into a full-fledged acceptance of Positivism's philosophical program, as the remarks of the seasoned republican Edgar Quinet made apparent. Although convinced of the need for a "new generation" of republican leaders to break with the traditions of Jacobin terrorism, Quinet never imagined this new leadership succumbing to the "spiritual tyranny" he found implicit in Comte and his followers.[59] Nonetheless, Quinet was one of the most strident advocates of a nonrevolutionary brand of republicanism and an acerbic critic of the violence and force valorized by Jacobin militants.

A *quarante-huitard* serving out his exile in Switzerland, Edgar Quinet addressed the subject of republican methods head-on in 1865 with his book *La Révolution*. In it, he argued that the French were consistently obliged to either accept or reject the Revolution tout court, never once considering that the principles of 1789 could be upheld without embracing

Jacobinism or the Terror. "It is said that the Revolution is a Great Whole that it is necessary to accept or reject indiscriminately, without deliberation," Quinet chided. "What! Without criticizing, without discernment, make a single mass of virtues and crimes, of light and darkness, adhering to it without bargaining over it, eyes closed." Condemning Jacobin terrorism and the evident despotic elements embedded within republican political culture, Quinet accused those harboring radical aspirations of dooming the republic in France to repeated failures. In his assessment, the Republic had been won in February 1848 only to be undermined by the extremism of the June Days. No progress toward a republican form of government could be made in France until republicanism was cleansed of its ideological zealotry and violence. "We will only establish [the Republic] by forming new generations," Quinet counseled, "who, breaking absolutely with the idolatry of force, carry with them the spirit of humanity that the world calls for without doubt, but is still very far from possessing."[60]

Writing to a friend in late 1865, Quinet confessed that his book was "written from the first to the last line in the spirit and passion of liberty, to which I have sacrificed everything. The value of this work is to awaken the public spirit and conscience!" Much as intended, the publication of *La Révolution* ignited a controversy within republican circles and stimulated heated debates over the meaning of France's revolutionary and republican heritage. Radicals spurned Quinet's attempt to brand patriots upholding the revolutionary tradition as enemies of the republican cause and sharply reminded readers that it was the Jacobins alone who saved the Revolution.[61] Even Émile Littré, who concurred with Quinet's reproach for the revolutionary carnage of the 1790s, flatly rejected the author's insistence that the acts of terror committed by the revolutionaries were criminal. "I have not called it a crime and I will not call it that," he reposted in a strong defense of his republican conviction.[62]

Yet for others, Quinet appeared "a sacerdotal soul" and "a priest" dedicated to reviving the spirit rather than the living memory of the Revolution.[63] Defending Quinet's work before his cohorts in the national legislature, the young lawyer Jules Ferry capitalized on the opportunity to breach the subject of republicanism's woeful past in a public forum. "Jacobinism is no longer an arm of war but a peril," he declared, "because it represents among us something sadder than the memories of the scaffold: the prejudice of the dictator." Jacobinism, much like Bonapartism, symbolized tyranny and dictatorship, and by linking the two, Ferry skillfully attempted to adumbrate the contours of a new republican movement and identity in opposition to both radicals and imperialists. Neither Robespierre nor Bonaparte represented "justice," he insisted, adding that "democracy can only accept a tradition of justice."[64] Rather than adhering to a murderous and outdated revolutionary tradition, Ferry called on his fellow republicans to abandon the past and embrace a new platform respectful of law and liberty.[65]

Quinet's plea to renounce the errors of the Revolution while celebrating its ideals struck a chord with many republicans. "That doctrine which states that the end justifies the means, if favorable in appearance, is disastrous," warned Jules Simon. "Its inevitable effect would be to destroy public order and unleash the anarchy of the will."[66] Émile Ollivier, soon to be the leader of the parliamentary opposition under the Second Empire, saw the need to adopt a more moderate political attitude, envisioning a "conservative" republic more than a decade before Adolphe Theirs would popularize the phrase in his attempt to sell Orléanists and royalists on the Third Republic. "It is necessary," Ollivier wrote in 1857, "to render the republican principle conservative in that it is progressive and distinguished from its purely revolutionary element."[67] "What is needed for governance in France is violence in speech and moderation in action," summed up the fiery Gambetta.[68]

Reacting against the brutal tactics of republican revolutionaries, young republicans endorsed the use of reason in outlining practical policies. "I am convinced that reason alone must indicate the possibilities of politics, religion, and art," claimed Ollivier. "I no longer consider sentiment a compass that designates direction . . . like an intermediary through which the facts of reason are communicated to the ignorant and feeble-spirited."[69] In 1855, the journal L'Avenir, a periodical focused on literary and philosophical topics that attracted a sizable republican audience, proclaimed its dedication to the rationalist spirit, declaring "we believe in the sovereignty of reason and its omnipotence."[70] By emphasizing reason and condemning revolutionary aspirations, moderates were consciously affirming their respect for legal precedent over mob violence, asserting that politics, by necessity, was a rational and scientific enterprise. "Politics is nothing other than philosophy," Simon offered. "Its condition is to be practical or not be at all."[71]

By its very nature, revolution could not constitute a political strategy let alone found a stable and durable society. As Stupuy explained in 1870, revolution was an essentially destructive enterprise. Its purpose was to raze a decayed and defunct society, making it a tragic but necessary phase in the larger scheme of social reconstruction. "No doubt popular sovereignty will prevail," he wrote. "But—and here is the coming peril—when a majority hostile to the old order overtakes its antagonists, will it be capable of establishing a new order? In a word, is it a solution or only a method?"[72] In Stupuy's assessment, revolution was required to dismantle the old and level the ground for the building of the new. Taken to its logical conclusion, his argument dictated that the work of revolutionaries had already achieved its ends and could not, therefore, serve any purpose other than to obstruct the current rebuilding process. Stupuy consciously transformed the Jacobins into historicized subjects who stubbornly refused to accept the finality of their mission and recognize inconsequence in a postrevolutionary world. While the needs of society had changed and progressed, the revolutionaries sadly remained stationary, appearing little more than specters from a bygone era that continued to haunt the present.

"It is necessary to forget the bloody memories that the times carried off without return and that revealed the dolorous price of universal emancipation," Jules Simon proclaimed in 1865.[73] According to Littré, historicizing the Revolution was vital to purging French politics of its revolutionary fetish. The Jacobins of the 1790s had attempted to create a radically new society, one severed from historical continuity and oriented explicitly toward the future. Such an idea was not only foolish in Littré's opinion, but fallacious. "No century can turn toward the one preceding it and say 'you are not my father,'" he rebuked. The development of any society was an "uninterrupted chain" that could not be disrupted or broken, and the Revolution, like any other social phenomena, possessed deep historical roots extending back beyond 1789 or the founding of the First Republic. It was, Littré argued, essential to break with the idea of that "mythic present" perpetuated by revolutionary ideologues. To understand the Revolution in the *longue durée* of French national development and social evolution was, in his final analysis, the first step toward "finding a path between the revolutionary spirit and the retrograde spirit."[74]

Such reasoning was a far cry from the rhetoric of violent rupture endorsed by radicals and sounded more in line with the appraisals of conservative liberals like Taine who reproached the revolutionaries of 1789 for abandoning history and custom in their zeal to create a new world. The fascination with novelty remained, in Taine's opinion, one of the most detrimental influences of the nation's revolutionary experience. "We rarely regard the past, the possible, the practical," he criticized. "We willing perceive what must be rather than what can be. We don't think of making a government for the French that we are but for the abstract man that is within us."[75] Scolding the *philosophes* for their "unjust hatred" of the past and "bizarre desire" to separate themselves from their fore-fathers, Guizot likewise declared that "our time is not a deviation from our past, an extemporaneous accident, a foreign inconsequence."[76] In their denunciation of revolutionary politics, republicans were begin-ning to resemble the reactionary liberals who heaped scorn upon the Revolution despite claiming to recognize the validity and wisdom of its principles. In fact, with their emphasis on moderation, political debate, and the "sovereignty of reason"—a term itself popularized by Guizot and the political thinkers of his generation—the camp of young republicans resembled Orléanist Doctrinaires with their motto of "neither revolution nor counter-revolution."[77]

If the revolution of 1848 struck a blow to the elitism and limited suf-frage sanctioned by July Monarchy liberals, the cause of French liberalism was by no means dead in the country. Much like republicans, liberals were conscious of the need to revamp their image and bring their theories into line with current political circumstances. Doctrinaire notions of *capacité* and "bourgeois" authority had marked liberalism as antidemocratic and self-serving, and liberals had no illusions that these impressions would have to be corrected if they intended to play an active role in French political life. Mass democracy demanded a "new liberalism" removed from the traditions and theories of Orléanism. "The new liberalism, formed from the most diverse elements, attaches itself, it is true, to the principles of 1789," wrote Edouard Laboulaye in 1863. "But as a political party it is in no way of the past. It was vanquished neither in 1830 nor in 1848. It has neither regrets nor old memories nor retrograde notions."[78] Laboulaye's declaration of a "new" liberalism was timely. With elections to the Corps législatif scheduled for late 1863, liberals were hard-pressed to devise a new platform capable of appealing to voters. Between the revolutionary rhetoric of the Bonapartists and the new pragmatism of republicans, liberals found it troublesome to distinguish a clear political identity for themselves. "With revolutionaries for conservatives and moderates for revolutionaries we will have neither the voice of wisdom nor the voice of the mad," observed Charles de Rémusat.[79] A prominent Orléanist during the July Monarchy who had willingly supported the "bourgeois" monarchy, Rémusat was, nonetheless, convinced that electoral gains would come about only if liberalism demonstrated an ability to acclimate to the changing political environment. "The cause of liberty is in a new situation," he claimed in 1863, "and there would be little wisdom in narrowly engaging it in the links of the past."[80]

Signaling their departure from the past, aspiring politicians and liberal theorists grudgingly paid lip service to the universal suffrage and culture of equality that they had traditionally sought to keep at bay. "The liberal party sincerely accepts universal suffrage as a guarantee of liberty, as a means of government, and as an instrument of political education," conceded Laboulaye. "Far from seeking to weaken it, it wants to strength and clarify it."[81] According to Clément Duvernois, an influential journalist in liberal circles who had made a name for himself through his scathing criticisms of the military regime in Algeria during the 1850s, the acceptance of universal suffrage signified a reorientation of liberalism's basic objectives. While the Doctrinaires had sought to blunt democracy with claims of bourgeois primacy, the new generation, he insisted, was obliged to "reconcile the people and the bourgeoisie, and demonstrate that authority and liberty [were] not, as is believed, antipathetic to one another."[82] "The day that the government called on the universality of the citizens to go to the polls it delivered to France en masse the recognition of its political capacity," Duvernois maintained.[83] While men like Tocqueville and Guizot had greeted the coming of mass democracy in the wake of the June Days with pessimism and dejection, a decade later, such presentiments appeared old-fashioned. "The cause supported by the liberal party," declared the political critic Ernest Duvergier de Hauranne in 1869, "is the cause of democracy itself."[84]

In shrugging off the legacy of the July Monarchy, self-proclaimed "new" liberals had to confront the accusations of factionalism and political rivalry that imperial statesmen consistently attributed to the former Orléanist government. The Bonapartists denigrated the partisanship of the "old parties" as an impediment to democratic government in the country. In response, liberal supporters stressed that they were neither a close-knit faction nor a party of the bourgeoisie intent on promoting narrow and self-serving interests.[85] Writing in 1868, Agénor Bardoux, a Parisian law student who within a decade would be awarded a ministerial post under the Third Republic, called on all men dedicated to the cause of liberty to abandon party politics in the name of shared principles and aspirations. "We are all for liberal government where the country is master of its own destiny. We are not indifferent to labels, but for us they are secondary."[86] "We prefer the triumph of an idea to the triumph of a party," Duvernois proclaimed, "because we love liberty in itself and for the good it can promote, because we prefer progress by reform to progress by revolution."[87] With the Bonapartists assailing parliamentary politics on the grounds that it was divisive and an Anglo-American import, liberals were forced to assert their commitment to principles over party. The refashioned liberal party was not, Laboulaye insisted, a "small sect narrowly attached to the letter of a symbol," but rather "a universal church with a place for anyone who believes in liberty and seeks it out."[88]

Unlike legitimists who demanded the return of the monarchy and republicans who saw the republic as the teleological end of man's progress, liberals spoke for certain principles and practices rather than a specific political form. Despite the fact that Louis Philippe had labeled his government a liberal regime, there remained no fixed model or particular reference point in the past that gave liberals their political identity.[89] "Monarchy, assemblies, republic, empire, royalty whether legitimate or quasi-legitimate—all have fallen," claimed Laboulaye. "Only a single thing has remained: the principles of 1789. Is that not a supreme lesson?"[90] Much like the Bonapartists and republicans, liberals laid claim to the inheritance of 1789, insisting that the ideals of the Revolution were not the sole heritage of a particular party or faction.[91] Writing in 1863, the editors of the *Revue des Deux Mondes* frankly affirmed that "the liberal system pursues . . . the complete realization of the noble program of our revolution: *liberté, égalité, fraternité*." Yet going further, the authors explained, "on this slogan, we have allowed the word liberty to rust. Fraternity has effaced it, leaving only a fine residue in France that is barely noticeable, cold and impenetrable to the general sentiments that animate societies."[92]

For liberals, *Liberté* constituted the primary tenet of the new opposition. As one journalist remarked, while equality was an "intimate element" of French national life, the "habits of liberty" remained chronically underdeveloped in the country. Liberty was an alien concept to the French, prompting the author to admonish: "It is our illiberal habits that have killed LIBERTY in us."[93] The colonial journalist Arnold Thomson was of the same opinion. "We have abused the word *democracy* to such an extent over the past twenty years that in reality we no longer know what it means. There was a word that once summed up the opinions of all friends of progress and the emancipation of the people, and this word was LIBERTY."[94] Liberal critics sharply rejected Bonapartist assertions that national sovereignty constituted the firmest guarantee of a people's freedom. The Bonapartists "confuse liberty with universal suffrage," reminded one journalist. "The existence of universal suffrage is not liberty. It is only one of its manifestations."[95] According to the editor of *Le Temps*, Edward Scherer, it was as astonishing as it was embarrassing to think "that liberty, after all our attempts, has still not managed to be successfully established in France. . . . What is missing in France is the very notion of liberty itself," he informed readers in an editorial column as elections approached in 1863.[96]

Declarations emphasizing a commitment to liberty above all and the principles of 1789 echoed the new tenor espoused by republican elites during the 1860s. Eugène Pelletan extolled his fellow republicans as the partisans of "maximum liberty" (*liberté à outrance*) who demanded "liberty, complete liberty, and nothing less than liberty!"[97] In his political tract discussing the opposition in 1868, Jules Simon applauded the growing acceptance among politicians and critics that liberalization was the most pressing concern of the day. "France, enlightened by its latest misfortunes," he wrote, "finally understands that liberty alone can give it prosperity and repose. Let's realize that it's not a question of a small or large sum of liberty, but total liberty."[98] Liberals like Duvernois believed it was imperative to convince the nation that liberty and authority were not "antipathetic to one another," and the same could be said of moderate republicans. Simon sounded very much like his liberal contemporaries when professing that "politics consists precisely of conciliating authority and liberty in a just measure."[99]

As the political historian Mark Hulliung has suggested, the republicans of the 1860s learned to "speak the language of liberalism."[100] Yet if young republicans proved willing to liberalize the republican polity, new liberals equally demonstrated a readiness to espouse a language of republicanism. In distancing themselves from the reactionary theories of Guizot and the Doctrinaires, liberals came to accept popular sovereignty and the political realities of mass democracy. Coming to terms with democracy did not, however, necessarily imply accepting equality, especially the extreme social and political egalitarianism endorsed by socialists and radicals. In spite of the various pronouncements embracing universal suffrage and recognizing the political *capicité* of the masses, liberals remained partial to elite rule, professing that educated, talented, and industrious individuals were best suited for the responsibilities of competent leadership and, within a free society, would naturally rise to the top. "Liberty has a false air of aristocracy in giving precedence to the human faculties, by encouraging work and the economy," Laboulaye explained in 1863. "It brings out natural or acquired superiorities. It elevates talent and wealth. It creates characteristics and raises personal nobility."[101] Universal political rights did not translate into natural equality. Power was to remain in the hands of reasonable and capable individuals making up an elite class tolerable to a democratic society.

Antiegalitarian sentiments were not wholly remnants of a reactionary liberal ideology. Reiterating the suggestions of Comte, positivists unabashedly awarded social primacy to savants, insisting as Comte had that a progressive society required enlightened individuals to moralize and edify the populace.[102] Drawing upon liberal notions of *capicité* and Positivism's support for a technocratic elite, republicans stressed the need to foster what Jules Simon deemed "an aristocracy of probity and talent" capable of occupying positions of leadership in society.[103] This "aristocracy" was neither a privileged class invested with political rights à la Guizot nor an intellectual oligarchy à la Comte but rather an open aristocracy composed of men reflecting the values, interests, and sensibilities of a new cultural and political elite. "Universal suffrage only nominates the legislature," Eugène Pelletan claimed in 1867, "or, to put it another way, it gives the power of public speech to the intellectual elites of the country by virtue of their reputation and experience."[104] If conservatives perpetually harped on the inherent dangers of democracy, republicans sought to assuage such fears, insisting that popular sovereignty did not mean abandoning society to the uneducated and volatile majority. "Sovereignty must only exercise itself through material and sensible instruments," Ollivier affirmed. "I believe these instruments are not the *kings*, but all and each, by means of *some people*, the most capable and charismatic. In this sense, and not otherwise, do I accept the sovereignty of the people."[105]

"Politics," Simon argued in 1868, "consists of reconciling authority and liberty in an exact measure."[106] This resolution between power and freedom culminated in a form of elite democracy that was acceptable to both liberals and moderate republicans, promising a politics that was progressive yet stable, democratic yet conducive to social order. Defining a style of democratic elitism contributed to the rapprochement between liberals and republicans, but it equally demonstrated how transformative the years of the Second Empire were for the two political factions. Following the disasters of the Second Republic and the founding of a popularly approved Napoleonic Empire, both groups comprehended the necessity of redefining their respective political movements and reformulating their core ideological tenets to compete with the Bonapartists. In constructing new political identities, liberals and republicans set out to exorcise the ghosts haunting their pasts, whether these menacing specters were the bourgeois elitism of Guizot or the revolutionary violence of Robespierre. Casting off the slough of past traditions and practices, liberals and republicans came to emphasize the novelty of their movements, describing them as "young," "new," and "modern" by comparison.

These descriptive terms also played into the oppositional politics of both groups. Allusions to the youthful and quintessentially "modern" qualities that spokesmen attributed to their respective movements always invited commentary on the allegedly superannuated and obsolete character of the Bonapartist state.[107] It was telling when in 1863 Jules Ferry rebuked the martial ethos and dynastic ambitions touted by Persigny, professing that the statesman's outlooks revealed that he belonged to "a different time than ours."[108] Ferry's indictment easily extended to the Second Empire itself. A relic of absolutism, the imperial regime would never abandon its desire to preserve the "antique throne," the liberal Prévost-Paradol contended. He believed, however, that the moment had come for France to "pass from an immemorial despotism to the liberty that agrees with modern time," and this crossing into the realm of the modern was, he maintained, the mission of the new generation coming of age in the country.[109] In 1863, Laboulaye concluded his criticism of the imperial government with a declaration of faith in the country's desire for change and transition. "Today the time has come to be finished with the errors of another age," he announced confidently.[110]

In the diatribes and polemical writings of opponents, Bonapartist modernity was inverted, transforming the self-consciously "modern" imperial regime into a living anachronism. Although mutual discontent with the imperial regime and desires for greater political liberties offered favorable circumstances for a liberal–republican rapprochement during the 1860s, the growing unity among imperial opponents was not simply limited to shared objectives. In dismissing the supposedly "modern" identity promoted by the Bonapartists as mere self-fashioning and calling for reforms in the name of modern society, liberals and republicans developed a common language of opposition that struck at the very foundations of the Second Empire. Developing a shared discourse not only facilitated compromise and conformity of opinion when it came to particular issues; it likewise fostered a common identity with which disparate political groups and factions could readily associate. In bolstering support for the idea of a "new generation" reflecting the aspirations and values of the future, dissident political elites determinedly affirmed themselves as coevals inspired by sentiments and interests that transcended ideological lines. According to liberal and republican opponents, it was they, and not the atavistic Bonapartists, who represented the spirit and ethos of a new society. Appropriating "modern" identities proved effective in challenging the legitimacy of the reviled Bonapartist regime just as much as it did in softening ideological differences. It was the common struggle against Bonapartist atavism and the collective effort of founding a modern French society that provided a consistent measure of ideological unity binding a diverse opposition.

Breaking with the Revolutionary "Tradition"

Generational solidarity had a powerful appeal in the mid-nineteenth century and offered the various democratic and oppositional movements growing up in France a means of distinguishing themselves in terms that were attractive to the public. Influential newspaper editors, political spokesmen, and activists consistently emphasized the gap between those who clung to old ideas and those called to action by the "modern spirit," insisting, as the publicist Edward Scherer did in 1863, that "Another generation is coming of age and old concerns are now replaced by new aspirations."[111] Such declarations were never entirely divorced from a political context, as critics of varying persuasions invoked the ideas of a "new generation" to encourage and strengthen the evolving rapport between disaffected liberals and republican moderates. "Forget your old resentments, hatreds, and dissensions," the liberal journalist and pamphlet writer Eugène Ténot proclaimed in his appeal to his generational coevals. "Is the flag of liberty not vast enough to shelter all of you under its folds?"[112] Calls for collective action and conciliation continued into the coming years, giving substance to claims that a changing of the guard was in the process and the reign of youth would soon replace the senescence of a twilit order. "There is now in France, and everywhere," the art critic Théophile Thoré observed as early as 1857, "a singular inquietude and irrepressible aspiration toward a life essentially different from the life of the past."[113]

Thoré's remark not only summed up the new ambience emerging in French by the late 1850s. It also indicated the important place the republican revival occupied in shaping perceptions of change, for in that year Émile Ollivier, an emerging leader within the young republican movement, delivered a shock to French political society. Since 1852, inveterate republicans and embittered exiles had committed themselves to a policy of political abstention in demonstrating their opposition to the illegitimate Bonapartist regime. This tactic effectively sequestered republicans from public life and contributed to the movement's noticeable quiescence throughout much of the decade. Vowing never to be "chained by tradition," Ollivier broke ranks with the *abstentionnistes* in 1857 and encouraged a small number of republicans to run for election to the Corps législatif.[114] He correctly saw that inaction and silent protest would achieve nothing and that reestablishing republican governance in the country would only come about through sound policies and political participation. Garnering support from opposition journalists,

Ollivier and four other republicans successfully defeated the candidates endorsed by the imperial government. Although the victory of *Les Cinq* drew sharp criticism from *abstentionnistes*, the entry of the five deputies into the Corps législatif gave moderate republicans a public forum in which to transmit their ideas and political program on a national level. As Ollivier anticipated, the election of 1857 gave a new life to the movement, outlining a course of action that was consistent with the goals of republican centrists and conducive to developing relationships between republicans and liberals over the course of the next decade.

By the early 1860s, it was evident that republican ideology and practices were in a state of transition as young republicans endeavored to carve out a path between revolutionary violence and crippling resignation. Previously, it had been the liberals who supported parliamentary politics with their contention that relegating political action to certain institutional settings offered the best means of combating popular political activism. By the end of the 1850s, however, a growing number of republicans were coming to express an appreciation for the wisdom of their liberal predecessors. As Dupont-White indicated in 1863, liberty could only take the form of a "representative regime" fostering rational public debate and the political integration of citizens. "When political liberty takes this form, when opinion is organized in this manner it produces a precious effect that signifies the acceleration of progress."[115] Such pronouncements ran counter to the logic of Jacobinism and Bonapartism, both of which favored the unanimity of the general will and direct democracy over the plurality of political opinion.[116] Yet Jules Ferry revealed the young republicans' willingness to reconcile parliamentary formalism with Rousseau's veneration of direct civic activism. "Let's not forget that fundamentally we can only be a government of opinion," he claimed before the Corps législatif in 1869. "We represent our citizens and seek to interpret their interests. In order to draw inspiration from their ideas and needs, it is a necessity that becomes more imperious each day for us to associate the entire nation through its interests [and] affairs, in the collectivity as well as the particular."[117]

The growing acceptance of parliamentary government among republican elites and their willingness to work within established institutional settings signaled an important change in the political practices of republicans. This change was, however, the product of a broad ideological transformation taking shape during the years of the Second Empire. In a political culture that prized novelty and the modern, republicans were obliged to reformulate their ideological discourse and find a language suitable to describing and constructing a vision of republican modernity acceptable to political and social elites. Purging republican ideology of its fetish for violence and revolutionary action was of primary importance. Positivism provided an intellectual justification for the secular, dynamic, and ultimately totalizing social vision that republican ideologues increasingly championed under the banner of "modern society."[118] Yet Positivism constituted only one variant of republican discourse under the Second Empire, and while its principles and implications could be wed with other strains of republicanism, it did not necessarily furnish republicans with a comprehensive discourse and ideology. One did not need to subscribe to the ideas of Comte and Littré to recognize the threat posed by republican radicalism. The repudiation of Jacobinism spanned a range of republican cultures and became one of the chief hallmarks of a reinvented and nominally "modern" brand of republicanism.

The language of temporality and "tradition" employed by moderates and centrists reinforced the notion of a postrevolutionary republican modernity severed from its revolutionary origins. "We can no longer accept all the traditions imposed by the Revolution with closed eyes, as the Catholics accept, without deliberation, the creed and formula of ecclesiastical authority," Quinet advised in 1865.[119] Construing Jacobinism and revolution in terms of a republican "tradition" allowed moderates to contrast revolutionary adventurism with their own "modern" identity, classifying Jacobinism as passé and alien to modern sensibilities and interests. It was against the dark past of the Revolution that "young" republicans established a sense of self, but these same affirmations of youth and novelty equally played into the rhetorical and ideological attacks on Bonapartist authoritarianism. According to young republicans, Bonapartism and Jacobinism were two sides of the same coin, reflecting a political mentality predicated upon despotic and illiberal principles. Speaking before a crowd of Algerian colonists in Constantine, Jules Favre condemned both radical extremism and Bonapartism as "revolutionary" movements inimical to modern liberty. "The revolutionaries are those who proclaim in their official harangues an absolute respect for the will of the people while refusing them the right of associating and hearing one another, who do not want to protect liberty or the sanctity of the home against the omnipotence of *fonctionnaires*, who incite factional disputes and who, by consequence, deliver society to the caprices of arbitrary power."[120] As Favre's denunciation of the Second Empire made evident, for republican opponents Jacobinism and Bonapartism manifested the revolutionary tyranny of the past.

Through opposition to revolutionary politics and authoritarian despotism, republicans successfully appropriated a nonrevolutionary, democratic, and "modern" political identity for themselves. The idea of a postrevolutionary republican modernity acquired coherence and lucidity as "young" republicans distanced themselves from the "old" and retrograde political parties that consistently thwarted the advancement of liberty in France. Divesting modernity of its revolutionary context and connotations did not, however, signify a renunciation of the Revolution and 1789, a fact that moderates were careful to communicate in their writing and speeches. "Our political education is long in coming, but it is nonetheless advancing," declared the republican historian Léonide Babaud-Laribière in 1866. "[The] excellence of the great principles of 1789 is better appreciated, and everyone understands that these principles are the safeguard of the wealth and happiness we have conquered at the cost of so many efforts."[121] Like Napoleon III and the Bonapartists, republicans pledged to uphold the ideals of the Revolution while relinquishing tactics of violence and terror. Although the revolutionary élan and spirit would continue to inform ideological assumptions and animate French political life, it would not, republicans sternly argued, provide a template for political action and decision making. The objective, according to

Ollivier, was "to make the republican principle as conservative as it is progressive and remove from it its purely revolutionary element."[122]

Through allusions to modern society and the ideals of 1789, the young republican movement draped a nonrevolutionary and in many ways conservative ideology in revolutionary garb. Republicans recognized the necessity of keeping the revolutionary spirit alive while simultaneously defining a stable postrevolutionary social order. By reconceptualizing modern society, moderates were able to offer what the Revolution had promised—the promise of modernity—while pursuing an elitist program capable of drawing support from liberals and conservatives. With republicans and liberals starting to speak the same language, it was now crucial to consolidate this emergent unity through a program of action addressing specific issues and common points of concern. "If France is to be revived," Quinet claimed in 1861, "it will be by examples as well as actions."[123] Following Ollivier's decision to make republicanism an active force once again in French political life, action now implied winning over allies and delineating policies capable of translating an imagined modern French society into a living idea.

6 Republican Government and Political Modernization

In the immediate aftermath of the June Days, Henri Lecouturier, a political critic and self-identified republican "realist," offered his assessment of the worker protests and violent civil war that had shattered the unity of the country and endangered the viability of the infant Second Republic in one demoralizing blow. Reprimanding "idealists" who "[spent] their time searching in the shadows of the future for the ideal republic of their dreams," Lecouturier issued an ominous warning that he urged his compatriots to heed if they desired to see France remain a republic. The romantics and extremists who sought to revolutionize society with bold gestures or, even worse, the sacrificial blood of their political enemies were a cancer on society. They not only eroded the base of republican virtue in the country but repulsed the great majority of honest citizens who desired nothing more than equitable government and peace. Founding a durable republican democracy in France demanded more than just haughty declarations; it required initiative and progressive action. "The Republic ceases to be a utopia when it is in [our] mores and something more than just a name," he claimed.[1]

The dispiriting collapse of the Second Republic in 1852 bore out Lecouturier's caveat. The breakdown of public order and the slaughter of French citizens in the streets of Paris some four months after the founding of the republican regime cast a pall over the new government, one from which it never completely escaped. Rather than the heroic people's revolution of February, the Second Republic became memorialized in the butchery of June, making it difficult for republicans to construct a founding mythology for the regime. Republicans' inability to create a set of new and meaningful political symbols and public ceremonies to represent the state was equally disappointing, leaving little wonder that a charismatic Bonaparte brandishing heraldic imperial eagles and evoking memories of the nation's glorious Napoleonic past could found an authoritarian government with popular support.[2] Even prior to the election of Louis Napoleon in December, Lecourturier had been capable of understanding that a government must be more than just a mere political form if it wished to command the loyalty and respect of its citizens. It had to be a living idea and a way of life, a lesson that republicans would not dare ignore the next time around.

With strident declarations and impressive public spectacles, the Bonapartist government had managed to win over followers and sustain support. Its modernizing program promised national unification and renewal to a fractured country, transforming an elite vision of the world into a veritable cult adhered to by citizens and civilized alike. Republicans may have abhorred the imperial regime, but they could not deny the power and appeal that Bonapartist modernity possessed. They too adhered to the cult of the modern so effectively channeled by their rivals, adapting it to their own ideological proclivities and the currents of postrevolutionary politics. Lacking the power and dynamism of the imperial state, however, opponents were pressed to devise alternate strategies of modernization outside the grand spectacles staged by the Bonapartists. Instead, they turned their attention to politics, civil society, and individual emancipation, subjects closely associated with the revolutionary heritage celebrated by democrats and repeatedly invoked in their criticisms of Bonapartist "despotism." Reminding that the course of the French Revolution had yet to reach its foreordained conclusion, opposition members insisted that they, rather than the Bonapartists, would be the ones "to apply the principles of the Revolution in their entirety" and found, by consequence, a new and modern order in the country.[3]

Conveying the modern through symbols and narratives required, however, furnishing counternarratives as well. Although opponents successfully used both the Jacobins and Bonapartists as foils in crafting a political identity for themselves, these juxtapositions were less convincing outside the explicit context of political opposition. Reformers turned their eyes instead to the countryside, finding there a vast population estranged from the modern society they valorized. Distinctions between urban and rural France had a well-established precedent in the country. Medieval histories related tales of the indigenous Gallic tribes conquered and ruled by the Romans. Romantics and nationalists interested in unearthing the roots of an authentic French nation in the early-nineteenth century put stock in these old ethnic genealogies and mapped them onto the present. France was a country made up of "a conquering race and a conquered race, vanquishers and vanquished," as François Guizot explained in 1820.[4] Liberals and conservatives critical of the country's revolutionary nationhood were especially keen to emphasize continuity with a prepolitical Gallo-Roman nation. "Despite the French Revolution there have always been two peoples in France," wrote Taine, "the Gauls on one side and the body of Latin *fonctionnaires* mixed with the debris of the German aristocracy on the other."[5] This story of two primeval and conflicting races was reinforced through ethnographic surveys and anthropological studies over the century as differences between a historic Romano-Germanic aristocracy and a subjugated class of Gallic peasants became central to narratives of the French nation's historical evolution.[6]

During the Second Empire, political opponents would elaborate upon and reconfigure these narratives, wedding them to a domestic reform program with putatively modernizing objectives. Most striking were the ways in which quasi-colonial notions of temporality and assimilation were grafted onto former understandings of ethnic and racial difference. Distinctions between a depraved peasantry and French ruling class provided a framework for demarcating "modern" and "archaic" identities, and throughout the 1860s reformers readily employed such categories to define the boundaries and substance of a modern politics and political platform.[7] Often exaggerated and erroneous, portrayals of French rurals did serve an important ideological function. As the antithesis of the modern individual, the coarse and ignorant peasant was viewed as "uncivilized" and morally deprived, and as such not logically expected to possess agency in a nominally modern society. Reformers found a collective sense of mission and purpose in calls to "educate" and moralize a barbaric peasantry, entailing that the creation of a modern democratic republic in France was never divorced from the civilizing process. As Alice Bullard has noted, "the moralizing project" of the French republic comprised an essential part of its "imperial character."[8] Expressed through temporalized identities and dichotomies of civilization and savagery, republican modernity was easily fungible with the practices of colonialism as rural populations were transformed into citizens through a process of internal colonization.[9]

The imaginative nature of these stereotypes elicits scrutiny on many of the unstated presumptions underpinning ideas of "modern" politics and democracy that modernization theorists and liberal critics have proved reluctant to abandon. Political modernization has typically rested on assumptions that modern democracies are driven by broad sociocultural influences and evolutionary social change.[10] Yet this political "modernization" often translates into a process of political "homogenization" between urban and rural spheres, one that can hardly be considered a natural evolution. The journalist Eugène Ténot, one of many advocates of modernizing the French countryside, reasoned accordingly in 1865, informing his fellow reformers that "ideas take their course only when they find men to carry and propagate them."[11] Modernization was a program actively pursued and encouraged by political elites who were seldom reticent when it came to declaring their intentions. "Democracy is not a natural phenomenon or the spontaneous product derived from the genius of a people or race," Étienne Vacherot wrote in 1859. "It is, like all political societies, and perhaps even more than other political societies, the slow and laborious work of civilization."[12] Much like the civilizing and modernizing language central to Bonapartism and French colonialism, liberal–republican discourse exhibited a similar ideological striving for modernity, one centered on themes of democratization, civic activism, and citizenship that intended to mold a new type of society and individual.

A Country Shrouded in "Intellectual Midnight"

Following the collapse of the Second Republic and the advent of a popularly sanctioned Napoleonic Empire, democratic opponents struggled to make sense of the turn their nation had taken. One culprit was "civic virtue," or rather the absence of it. Republican and liberal critics chalked up the rise of imperial authoritarianism to a lack of "liberal mores" and educated voters in the country. Bonapartist *étatisme* and the passivity it inspired in citizens was one of the chief obstacles to establishing a true democracy in France, they contended. Years of centralized authority and rule by an overbearing state had transformed the French into what the liberal Royer-Collard described as overly-regulated population (*peuple d'aministrés*).[13] "France, people say, is habituated to relying on the state," Laboulaye lamented. "I know that this is our feebleness."[14] The antidote to this chronic passivity was the creation of a new type of citizen befitting the needs of representative liberal government. For young republicans loath to recognize Bonapartist rule, it was essential to nurture civic virtue in the populace and rehabilitate the French people.

The young republican movement of the 1860s was part and parcel of a general period of reflection taking place among republican elites. During the 1840s, republicans had flirted with notions of populism as they worked to enfranchise the majority of people who did not meet the property and financial qualifications to vote under the July Monarchy. This populism sprang partly from Romanticism's interest in folkloric culture and idealistic belief in *le peuple* as the truest embodiment of the nation. Republicans of the 1840s enthusiastically spoke of reviving the nation through the collective action of the people and founding a social republic imagined as the mirror image of the oligarchic *juste-milieu* in power.[15] Yet with the coming of the Second Republic, many republicans found their expectations shattered. The declaration of universal manhood suffrage in 1848 empowered the countryside with the vote, making the peasants an imposing three-fourths of the overall electorate. If republicans had supported mass democracy under the assumption that the will of the people was infallible and naturally inclined toward the social good, reality presented a sobering reappraisal.

To the horror of democrats, the newly enfranchised peasantry voted for conservative notables who mounted a formidable opposition in the National Assembly. The turn away from the revolutionary élan of February 1848 was made explicitly manifest at the end of the year with the election of Louis Napoleon, an ominous portent of the popular support that the Bonapartists would use to legitimate their illegal seizure of power three years later. Following the debacle of the Second Republic, various critics became wary of the populism that had played a central role in the ideology and political program of French republicanism since the days of the Revolution. As the rise of Napoleon III and the Bonapartists demonstrated, universal suffrage could be used to buttress authoritarian government, suggesting that democracy did not necessarily guarantee liberty. Moreover, Bonapartist statesmen bolstered a nationalist and democratic platform that attracted republican moderates and *ralliés* to the Second Empire.[16] Bonapartism not only co-opted republican sympathizers but, more important, employed the langue of French republicanism against republicans.

While disgruntled republicans were quick to parcel out blame for this failure on an ignorant peasantry enamored with a Bonapartist pretender, the reality was quite different. The years of the Second Republic profoundly impacted rural politics and society in France. In building support for their platform of social reform between 1848 and 1851, democratic-socialists had carried out an effective campaign in the countryside and successfully forged a broad republican collation composed of rural workers, tradesmen, and urban political elites. Although Louis Napoleon's police frequently disrupted republican networks, the efforts of republican socialists during the years of the Second Republic did win over supporters in regions situated in the south and center of the country, establishing strong and enduring bases of republican support in the provinces.[17] The extent of this rural republicanization was made manifest in late 1851 when

Louis Napoleon and his accomplices overthrew the elected government. The major theaters of resistance to the Bonapartist seizure of power came not from Paris, where Louis Napoleon had taken preemptive measures to thwart opposition, but from the countryside. Organizing resistance through regional networks and secret societies, peasants took up arms in defense of the Second Republic, staging, as one historian has called it, "the most serious provincial uprising in nineteenth-century France" with over a hundred communes participating in insurrection. Following the restoration of order, the great majority of rebels either jailed or deported came from the countryside as the Bonapartists attempted to purge the insidious "red" republicanism simmering in the provinces.[18] Despite the fact that republican ideas had penetrated rural politics, urban republicans under the Second Empire saw fit to point the finger for the failure of the Second Republic at the mass of peasants who came out to vote in favor of the Second Empire in 1852.

In the following years, republicans abandoned the cult of the people that had long been a cornerstone of republican ideology. The grim situation facing republicans in the 1850s compelled reassessment and inspired a greater appreciation for the new realities that popular sovereignty posed. Democrats typically drawing their support from urban areas were politically marginalized in a country where the majority of citizens—some 70 percent at midcentury—lived outside of cities. Jules Ferry was correct when he claimed that politicians and publicists residing in cities knew only "the France that we are familiar with, that we see and that touches us." "But," he solemnly continued, "there is another France that, for the past fifteen years, liberals have hardly taken note of and that the liberals of the future will do well not to forget: it is the France of the peasants."[19]

The opposition's poor electoral showing outside of cities did not necessarily indicate that the provinces were the bastions of imperial support that disillusioned republicans assumed them to be. With the bulk of the former republican leadership in exile, rebuilding the networks that had spanned urban and rural centers under the Second Republic proved exceedingly difficult. Republican abstention also had a pronounced influence on electoral support, with high absentee rates at the polls allowing conservative candidates to take local and national elections with very little contest.[20] The damaging effects of abstention had become so grave by the early 1860s that the seasoned republican Louis-Antoine Garnier-Pagès commenced a whistle-stop tour through sixty towns and villages in 1862 in an effort to convince republican supporters that abstention was a futile enterprise. While republicans did occasionally do well at the local level in some departments, victory at the national level proved more challenging, especially as republican candidates in the provinces tended to be former *quarante-huitards* who, associated with the disasters of the Second Republic, failed to attract sufficient support among rural voters.

In spite of efforts to attract greater support outside of French cities, a disorganized republican movement matched with the strong social networks maintained by conservative notables and parish priests in the countryside typically made for poor electoral showings in these areas by members of the opposition. The building projects and urbanization initiative spearheaded by the government also had an effect on electoral trends, stimulating a rural exodus that witnessed young men flocking to the cities in search of work. Urban migrations between 1852 and 1870 served to relocate the journeymen and colporteurs who had traditionally circulated radical literature and ideas earlier in the century, diminishing the channels through which republican propaganda had once been disseminated.[21] Under the circumstances, the majority of oppositional democrats found themselves virtually shut out of the provinces, leaving democrats and reformers to speculate on the chasm separating the two parts of the French population.

"One wants liberty, the other ignorance," Eugène Ténot, editor of the popular journal *Le Siècle*, opined in 1865, "one is discontent, the other complacent; one wants liberally, the other docilely." In the provinces, he insisted, one found a "primordial ignorance" and natural inclination toward subservience that brought into sharp relief the "antinomy between the people of the cities and those of the country."[22] Romantics of the early nineteenth century may have expressed admiration for the Gallic purity of the peasant, celebrating him as the repository of the

French traditions and customs that gave the nation its unique culture and identity. By the middle of the century, however, critics were inclined to see things quite differently. The rustic virtues and simple conventions of the French peasant once celebrated by intellectuals were replaced with degrading images of rural poverty and misery or astringently ridiculed as a formidable barrier to social progress. Writing to a friend in 1862, Edgar Quinet claimed he was not astounded by the nation's support for the Bonapartist pretender, stating that servitude was the condition most natural to the habits and mentality of the French. "In all its years, [France] has never known anything else [but bondage]," he assailed. Servitude was "its tradition, its habit, its old atmosphere," while liberty, "that true life," remained to be realized.[23]

Pronouncements on the ingrained docility and customary deference of peasants were hardly more than excuses to justify the poor performance of oppositional candidates in the provinces, but critics liberally employed such arguments as vehicles for illustrating larger ideological positions. Commenting on the source of this provincial subservience, Grégoire Wyrouboff singled out the swarms of clerics and parish priests operating in the countryside, giving vent to his rabid brand of republican anticlericalism. "In the priest there is a habit of domination and in the people a habit of obedience deeply rooted for centuries," he complained. Spreading science, that "element of civilization," offered, in his opinion, the best means of combating this deplorable state of affairs and liberating an enslaved peasantry from the authority of medieval institutions and mentalities.[24] Declaring that "Catholicism and despotism are brothers," Vacherot similarly asserted that a religion preaching submissions and docility contradicted true liberty and could only serve as an obstacle to developing free and democratic institutions in the country.[25] "Humility, confidence, obedience, imposed faith," charged Jules Simon, "all of these phantoms from an abolished world cannot be brought back or exist without folly in the milieu of our modern world governed by reason and politics, and of which the first and last word is the sovereignty of the people."[26]

The servility that republicans believed entrenched in the provinces constituted the root of the despotism that France, despite its numerous revolutions, remained unable to depose. Liberty, hailed by Laboulaye as "the common patrimony of civilization," had yet to be established in a country that ironically prided itself on being the fountainhead of western civilization.[27] Accustomed to centuries of despotic monarchial rule, the French were fundamentally ill-prepared to make rational political decisions or even comprehend the duties and responsibilities that democracy incurred. According to Ferry, the peasants' understanding of legality and justice remained "in an almost savage state." With his "naive fatalism" and ingrained deference to traditional authority, the peasant made no distinction between just authority and arbitrary power, leaving him to accept the judgments of his social betters and the power of the state without question.[28] Ténot concurred. "Due to a longstanding tradition of despotism the sovereign always appears to [the peasant] as the absolute master, the Oriental despot whose will is law."[29] The "Oriental" character Ténot associated with provincial mentalities was telling. The rudimentary intelligence, superstitions, and social resignation routinely assigned to North Africans did not appear all that distinct from the majority of French one might encounter in the remote provinces, and political elites concerned with the nation's moral character increasingly came to apply the demoralizing language of colonialism when referring to their metropolitan compatriots.

Accusations of social atavism went well beyond the submissive and deferential nature of the peasantry. They extended into the very heart of French rural society itself. Much like colonial *indigènes*, French rurals were impugned for their regional tribalism, which discouraged larger social associations and confined interests to immediate and contingent needs. The political consciousness of the peasantry remained severely immature, assuming a "local, narrow, self-serving, and timid" character that could not make sense of the larger national community to which they belonged, Ferry contended in 1863.[30] If Arabs stood accused of lacking a national consciousness, French peasants were hardly any better, possessing only a rudimentary idea of shared national interests or a national identity. "Each village is a clan," Michel Chevalier had remarked in the late 1830s after a visit to the eastern Pyrenees, "a kind of state with its own form of [local] patriotism."[31] For political reformers, this clannish aspect endemic to rural life presented a thorny impediment to forging a national and democratic polity. Like the "primitive" tribal social organization of North African Arabs, the parochial forms of sociability found in the provinces had to be dissolved in accordance with the needs and dictates of modern society. As Wyrouboff bluntly put it in 1868, it was now necessary "to wipe out the past and change ideas and mores."[32]

In framing their modernizing program, liberals and republicans aimed to radically alter rural society, and the veritable means to achieving this end were first and foremost providing a political education for the mass of French languishing in a depraved state of "degradation and barbarism."[33] Ignorance in a people was, Charles Dollfus professed, akin to an "evil weed" that, when left to grow, corrupted independence and resulted in "moral barbarism."[34] Extirpating the seed of this barbarism was not only desirable but essential, he urged, lest France repeat the fatal error that had precipitated the downfall of the Second Republic. "A nation like ours armed with the universal vote cannot afford to play blindman's buff with liberty," Dollfus cautioned in 1861.[35] The advent of universal suffrage had exposed the menacing "intellectual midnight extending throughout the countryside" first noted by Louis Blanc in 1848.[36] The experience of the Second Republic left no doubt that the most essential task at hand was to create a new type of individual in the provinces. "As long as the political education of a people is not complete," Vacherot apprised, "universal suffrage remains impractical and cannot be fully realized."[37]

Allusions to rural savagery and the patriotic duty of the "enlightened" to spread the light of civilization into the darkest and most remote provinces of the country revealed the increasing penchant of French political elites to think in colonial terms. The advent of universal suffrage encouraged such perceptions as elites confronted questions and concerns regarding the incorporation of the masses into national politics. If the overwhelming majority of newly enfranchised citizens had constituted a virtual unknown for democrats in 1848, by the 1860s liberals and republicans believed they had a more informed, if jaundiced, idea of what lurked outside the cities and were repulsed by what they found.[38]

La France profonde, with its static time and moral barbarism, bore all the marks of the colonial other. As such, the peasantry appeared little more than raw human material to be worked upon and modified, a premodern and colonized people deprived of an identity and culture of their own.

The harsh critiques of rural society doled out by opponents were more often than not polemical in nature and aimed at discrediting the influence of the government's economic and building projects in the provinces. Taine, whose depictions of the natives in southwest France during the mid-1860s were hardly flattering, revised his initial impressions of rural life later in the decade, noting in a letter to a friend that the peasantry appeared to be financially better off and less rustic than in the past. "They are contracting certain middle-class ideas," he reported, "indulging in some comforts . . . thinking of the future and beginning to read newspapers."[39] During the years of the Second Empire, improvements in transport networks, urbanization, the growth of national markets, and the steady rise in the price of agricultural products had begun to generate wealth in certain sections of the country and encourage greater contact with the outside world.[40] Opponents averse to acknowledging the regime's accomplishments certainly found utility in reproducing the conventional images of rural savagery, but perpetuating these caricatures also possessed more constructive purposes as well.

Appropriating the dominant idioms of Bonapartism and tailoring them to the platform of the opposition often proved a more dynamic strategy than directly challenging the master narrative of Bonapartist modernity. In effect, the opposition and the government began to use the same vocabulary, and yet in doing so the picture that emerged in the parlance of the opposition began to look distinct from the state-monitored and capitalist-oriented society touted by imperial ideologues. Just as Persigny had insisted when promoting the government's program of economic modernization, French civilization appeared "incomplete." Yet its fulfillment was not necessarily to be found in rail networks winding through the country or factories spouting plumes of smokes. The task of modernizing and civilizing France entailed working directly on the vast majority of the French, enlightening them and familiarizing them with the practices of debate and association essential to the development of liberty, that "glory and force of civilized people."[41] "Do you not see," asked Victor Hugo, "that the old world has a fatal flaw, an old soul—tyranny, and that into the new world that is about to descend necessarily, irresistibly, divinely, a young soul—liberty?"[42] Republicans certainly did see the truth of Hugo's testament and were intent on expunging this "old" despotism lying at the heart of rural society. To do so, however, would require a distinct type of acculturation centered on political practices and the making of new citizens. As Ténot tersely put it, the time had come "to set the peasant straight."[43]

Decentralization and "The Art of Making Men"

By what means, however, were the peasants to be "set straight"? As a counterbalance to the despotic and insular politics of the countryside, democrats stressed the importance of active civic engagement. As Paul Cottin, a citizen from Ain who claimed to "take politics seriously," affirmed in 1868: "Public life is necessary because it is indispensable to the free exercise of rights, which are themselves nothing other than the exterior accomplishments of our individual needs."[44] Liberty was meaningless if citizens continued to remain atomized and detached from the currents of national life. "To attach citizens to their political privileges it is necessary to habituate them slowly to public life by associating them through the affairs of the commune, the department, the Church, the hospice, and school," Laboulaye admonished. "It is necessary to make them understand these particular liberties that, in modern society, touch upon a great part of sovereignty."[45] The Bonapartists use of popular sovereignty to prop up an illiberal and illegitimate government had clearly demonstrated that "in a country like France there could be no greater danger than the detachment of citizens from their proper affairs," as Jules Favre claimed.[46] The antidote to imperial "Caesarism" was to be found in refining the intellectual faculties of Frenchmen through education and, subsequently, nurturing a conception of citizenship and national belonging that would draw the disaggregated mass of peasants from their social and cultural isolation.

In encouraging robust civic engagement as an antidote to the apathy that fed despotism, liberals and republicans stood in stark opposition to Bonapartists who stressed the necessity of the centralized state in combating the degenerative forces of social revolution. Since the first days of the Second Empire, Bonapartists had shown an incorrigible suspicion of local government and political activism. If not properly monitored by the authorities, communes and municipal offices elected under universal suffrage could become potential havens for dangerous radicals and enemies of the regime, especially in the larger urban areas where republican clubs and associations had thrived during the Second Republic. Hoping to expunge political contentions and factional rivalries from local political life, the Bonapartists clamped down on the administrative and conciliar organs of the French communes in the name of public order and unity, subordinating municipal governments to the Ministry of the Interior. Prefects appointed by the state wielded great political influence and authority at the local level. They selected mayors without the approval of local constituents and manipulated universal suffrage during national elections by supporting state-sponsored official candidates, men who had curried favor with imperial officials and who would faithfully carry out the policies of the government, even in the provinces farthest from Paris.[47]

In this restrictive political culture, the roles of civic councils and municipal officials were significantly marginalized. "The members of the municipal councils are really *fonctionnaires* who have nothing in common with their citizens except for the expenses they impose on them," Jules Favre reproached in 1867 during a speech before the Corps législatif.[48] The relative independence and authority once enjoyed by representative councils and municipalities under the July Monarchy and Second Republic had become eclipsed by the central administration in Paris with the cadre of bureaucrats and state-appointed civil servants virtually doubling between the years 1852 and 1870.[49] Political opponents condemned the bloated imperial bureaucracy and maligned imperial officials, painting them as public icons of the Bonapartist despotism they reviled. Prefects became especially popular targets during the 1860s as democrats assailed the "excessive centralization" sapping the vitality of the country and leaving it "ideally mediocre."[50] "Distant despots obeying the orders of another despot, the prefect either ignores the particular interests of the commune or overlooks them for political or personal reasons," Charles Renouvier criticized. "[He] is in no way entrusted with defending the great moral, intellectual and material interests of those he administers."[51] Depicted as listless and incompetent, imperial officials were vilified as instruments of state authoritarianism who deferred to the wishes of their bureaucratic supervisors "without any responsibility to the public."[52]

"It has become quite common to blame the prefects, to incriminate them on the slightest acts, to envelope all of them in a general condemnation," the journal *L'Europe* reported in 1865 when summing up the mood of growing discontent. Local officials appointed by the ministry appeared "imposed on the commune, and for that reason, often become very unpopular."[53] Public disapproval of "excessive centralization" was not lost on imperial officials who remained conscious of the adverse effects that municipal appointments and the policy of official candidature had on public opinion. In 1863, Napoleon III directly addressed the issue in the midst of the government's waning popularity, claiming that centralization had become overly burdensome for the regime. "The incessant control of the administration on almost every matter," he complained, had become the "raison d'être" of the Empire in the public's view.[54]

The extensive scope of state intervention in French public life was a familiar grievance of liberals like Alexis de Tocqueville and Benjamin Constant who saw centralization as an acute threat to liberty and civic virtues in the country. On coming to power, the Bonapartists played upon these liberal concerns, publicly supporting a policy of state decentralization while simultaneously employing the heavy-handed imperial bureaucracy to implement the government's economic plans and clamp down on opposition. "Centralization makes up the force of France while rendering the hand of power everywhere," Persigny wrote in 1854. "Yet," he continued, "it is necessary not to overexaggerate its application and strip local authorities of all initiative." In his opinion, centralization had destroyed the sense of individual initiative and responsibility in the country, substituting "apathy in place of action, listlessness in place of decisiveness." Decentralization promised to give prefects and local authorities a more active role in political affairs, resulting in an effective administration that would encourage the formation of "men of government."[55]

This view was reiterated in ministerial memorandums drafted over the course of the next decade. Officials incessantly warned of the consequences that the state's unnecessary interference in local affairs had on the general popularity of the government. Policy initiatives should be more mindful of the "terrain and local customs" of specific localities and official candidates chosen with greater care and the interests of the local electorate in mind.[56] Although the Ministry of the Interior defended its prerogative to nominate official candidates, it did not reject granting local officials "complete freedom in selecting candidates" when the election posed "no political significance" for the government directly.[57] The growing consensus among officials frustrated by ineffective administrative channels and prefectorial dependency on the capital prompted debates on whether to curtail bureaucratic overhaul and allow civil servants more influence in shaping and directing policies. Prefects familiar with the interests and issues of the departments they administered, the reasoning went, were better suited to address local concerns and the day-to-day affairs of their respective populations than ministers issuing directives from Paris.

The prospect of decentralization first materialized in the late 1850s, and surprisingly it was the colonial administration in Algeria rather than continental France that provided the litmus test for reform. In an effort to appease critics outraged by the malfeasance and near-autocratic rule of the colonial regime in North Africa, Napoleon III announced a radical policy change in June 1858 aimed at diluting the power of the military and bringing the French colonies under a unitary state administration. Selected to head the newly commissioned Ministry of Algeria and the Colonies was Prince Jérôme Napoleon, a member of the Bonapartist inner circle known for his strong republican sympathies. Assuming his new post, Prince Napoleon supplanted the office of the governor-general and appropriated the portfolios of the various ministerial bodies that had hitherto directed Algerian affairs. From the start, civilian administrators were to be given a more pronounced and direct influence over colonial policymaking and the native populations.[58] Writing to the emperor that August, Prince Napoleon assured that the new colonial ministry would "carry out modifications in the organization of public powers in Algeria" and "accord to the local authorities a freer and more direct action, permitting them to administer with more independence and responsibility."[59]

Making good on his promise, he authorized the reestablishment of general councils (conseils généraux) in Algeria with the intention of allowing civilian administrators greater control over departmental budgets, land transactions, and the allocation of funds for infrastructure and public works. These general councils were not, however, to be subject to popular mandate, with councilors selected personally by the emperor from "among the most capable landowners, industrialists, and merchants of Algeria." Turning to the role of civil servants in the colony, Prince Napoleon criticized the curtailed powers of the prefects under military rule and wrote it off as "a system where one drafts reports on everything but makes decisions on nothing." To augment the authority of state-appointed administrators, he called for extending the scope of their powers within their respective departments, insisting that "if there is, in effect, a country where local power must have a certain independence it is Algeria where everything is subject to special conditions."[60] True to the guiding principles of state authority and administrative control shared by his Bonapartist cohorts, Prince Napoleon's colonial reforms never planned to reduce state power or democratize representative bodies; rather, they intended to allow state-appointed administrators "a greater latitude" of action in local affairs.[61]

Lasting a mere sixteen months before an imperial decree dashed the hopes of the settler community and reinstated military rule over Algeria in late 1860, the abortive colonial ministry brought to light the limits and shortcomings implicit in Bonapartist notions of decentralization and administrative reform. The *étatiste* ideology of prominent Bonapartists refused to countenance the attenuation of state authority in economic and political affairs, upholding the conviction that a strong state alone furnished the means of promoting social progress and the development of modern civilization throughout France. In Bonapartist parlance, decentralization implied freeing the cadre of state-appointed *fonction-naires* and officials from the constraints of bureaucratic formalities and Parisian oversight. It sought to encourage competent and patriotic men amenable to the government to act with greater resolve and independence in carrying out their responsibilities. Reducing bureaucratic supervision did not, however, entail surrendering state jurisdiction over municipal and local offices and, least of all, subjecting them to popular elections.

Opponents skeptical of the Second Empire's dedication to reform were quick to label the government's talk of decentralization as nothing more than rigmarole intended to gloss a naked authoritarianism with a patina of liberalism. "The government and the opposition do not speak the same language," Simon charged before the Corps législatif in 1865. "The word 'decentralization' does not mean the same thing for the government as it does for us."[62] Attempts to outline a reform policy consistent with the government's authoritarian principles and shelter municipal offices from democratic influences furnished political rivals with a crucial opportunity to lay bare the specious logic and deceptive promises of the imperial regime. "Neither the communes nor the departments are more free," Ferry complained when assessing the situation in 1863. "It is only the prefects who have been emancipated."[63] By the late 1860s, attacking Bonapartist *étatisme* constituted a mantra for all self-proclaimed partisans of liberty, rendering calls for decentralization and democratization a key source of unity for an opposition movement composed of various political and ideological persuasions. Criticism of imperial centralization became so pervasive that numerous republicans endeavored to warm conservatives to the idea of a republic by portraying it as the antithesis of the Bonapartist state. "Rather than suffocating municipal freedoms under a system of administrative centralization," Jules Barni pledged, "the republican state will favor their development."[64]

Calls for greater municipal liberties and decentralization became a popular form of protest for the opposition during the 1860s, one that brought forth a series of reflections on the meaning of "modern" democracy and citizenship in France.[65] Favre was not alone in his claim that municipal freedom provided the firmest guarantee of liberty in the country, contending that where municipal freedom did not exist there could only be "the subjugation of citizens." "Everywhere that liberty is respected, municipal liberty reigns [and] everywhere that liberty perishes, municipal liberty is sacrificed," he maintained. "To some extent, the social state of a people, in terms of its political, moral, and intellectual freedom can be measured by its municipal liberty."[66] Yet liberals and republicans both realized that reducing state power in a country accustomed to constant bureaucratic oversight and intervention would have minimal results unless citizens were prepared to take an active role in their own affairs. The simple process of administrative restructuring proposed by the Bonapartists offered little in this respect, Clément Duvernois argued. Decentralization could be successfully implemented in France only if accompanied by "the extension of individual liberties."[67]

Having made a reputation for himself in Algeria as a fierce critic of the military regime during the 1850s, Duvernois migrated to France following the dismantling of the civilian ministry headed by Prince Napoleon and the suppression of his newspaper *Algérie Nouvelle* in 1860. From Paris, he continued to rail against the pernicious influence of excessive centralization and authoritarianism, adeptly tailoring his criticism of the colonial administration to the larger issue of metropolitan liberalization and democracy. Contesting claims that a strong state accelerated the march of human progress, Duvernois warned of the inimical impact that *étatisme* and concentrated authority had on the social development of a people. "Far from proceeding from the growth of the state," he argued, "progress consists in substituting our vast association with distinct and independent ones, in developing the sentiment of individual responsibility through emancipation, and, finally, by diminishing everywhere the role of the state."[68] Centralized authority was a poor substitute for individual initiative, and its long-term implications would constantly oblige the state to assume "an extensive, equitable, economic, and charitable nature to compensate for the individual."[69] Lacking vigor and self-initiative, the French were accustomed to being taken care of and attended to in almost all aspects of their life, a condition that would only encourage stagnation, despotism, and decline over the coming years. "Today," he advised, "the great misfortune of our situation is that the public spirit seems . . . relegated to Paris while the provinces remain disinterested in politics. Excessive centralization is the principle cause of this inactivity while the insufficiency of liberty is equally responsible for this lethargy."[70]

Yet all was not lost in Duvernois's opinion. The remedy to this deplorable situation was to be found in stimulating the "public spirit" and encouraging passive citizens to become engaged in political life. If the imperial government could not be counted on to carry out a policy of decentralization that would emancipate the provinces from the tutelage of Paris, it was necessary to infuse the peripheral territories of the nation with a new life supplied by local journalism and civic political participation.[71] As Jules Simon had averred in his address to the Corps législatif, opponents of the Empire were, indeed, speaking a different language than their imperial rivals when confronting the issue of decentralization. In contrast to Bonapartist desires to streamline the state bureaucracy and produce more independent-minded *fonctionnaires*, liberals and republicans welcomed decentralization as an expansive and transformative process that would nurture self-reliance and foster a sense of civic virtue noticeably absent in imperial *étatisme*. "Decentralization, in its most natural sense, is to reduce certain central attributes of power and restore them to the individual, to the commune, [and] to the body of citizens," as Laboulaye explained in 1863.[72]

Under the Bonapartist yoke- the commune was "only a collective peasant vegetating in poverty and dependence," Ferry accused.[73] These conditions fomented the stagnation and ingrained obedience detrimental to the "public spirit." Conceptions of decentralized authority and active citizenship touted by liberals and republicans rested upon a conviction that public participation in municipal life would integrate the individual into the community and the larger nation, cultivating a strong social consciousness and civic ethos lacking in France. "The commune is the primary school of governmental science," the republican deputy Pierre-Joseph Magnin claimed. "Attaining the power of administering their own commune will allow citizens to comprehend the price they must attach to the public sphere . . . [for they] will take a livelier and more ardent interest in the welfare of the locality and the village rather than in the great concerns of the state."[74]

Creating this new type of citizen necessitated, however, complementary changes in sociability and a style of life altogether distinct from the autarky rife in the provinces. As Duvernois insisted, only through "the practice of civil liberties" would individuals come to acquire the habits and routines essential to "the practice of political liberty."[75] Within the purview of the new civil society envisaged by democrats, journals, and daily periodicals, what Laboulaye hailed as the "forum of modern people," occupied a particularly significant role.[76] During the course of the nineteenth century, the reading of newspapers increasingly became a familiar feature of urban sociability, amounting to a "ritual of public life" for educated French elites, according to Jeremy Popkin.[77] Newspapers could be found everywhere in French cities by the middle of the nineteenth century: on streets corners, in kiosks, at train stations and cafés. "When one wants news, one finds it in the journal that he prefers or buys the closest one at hand," noted Jules Simon.[78] The splenetic Baudelaire summed up the popularity of nineteenth-century journal reading appositely when remarking that newspapers had become "the disgusting *apéritif* that the civilized man [took] with his breakfast every morning."[79] Whether one expressed admiration or revulsion for the new medium, journalism and newspapers clearly symbolized an integral facet of modern life in public discourse.

For all its rhetorical allusion to modern society and civilization, however, the Second Empire assumed a cautious stance when it came to the press. Committed to destroying factionalism and the seditious ideas that fueled disorder, Napoleon III empowered the government with strong discretionary powers over the press, assigning imperial censors the task of monitoring political journals and reporting any writing considered inflammatory or contrary to public morality. Although Persigny assured critics that "all serious and sincere opinions" would be allowed to publish freely, the imperial government placed controls on the press by requiring editors to obtain official approval in order to publish and extending favorable treatment to proimperial dailies. Punitive measures consisting of fines and imprisonment were used to weed out undesirable opinions and relegate political opponents to the margins of the public sphere.[80] Political journals were nothing more than "a society of capitalists surrounded by a certain number of talented writers," in the words of the journalist and deputy Adolphe Granier de Cassagnac, and, therefore, merited the state's suspicion.[81]

A writer for the pro-Bonapartist journal *Le Constitutionnel*, Granier de Cassagnac was not being overly facetious in labeling newspapers a medium of capitalists and elites. Up until the last quarter of the nineteenth century, liberal elites dominated the French newspaper and publishing industries, with most journals serving as organs for their political views and opinions. It was, therefore, natural for liberals to be among the staunch defenders of the free press in France. "Public opinion" typically meant liberal opinion. In addition to serving as a medium for liberal ideas, newspapers also played a central role in the ideological outlook of classical liberalism. Not only did they represent a virtual public forum in which the "voice of reason" could be expressed; they equally provided the only "legitimate" arena outside of government where politics could be discussed and engaged. By confining the legitimate expression of political opinion to parliament and the press, liberals endeavored to avoid more popular forms of political activism and restrict political power to the educated classes.[82]

Imperial censorship marked a break with this core tenet of liberalism, and liberal-republican opponents did not hesitate to symbolize their commitment to liberty by vociferously defending journalistic freedoms and extolling the press as a "necessary tool of modern civilization."[83] "The use of the periodic press is so profoundly entrenched in the mores of modern people, and particularly in France, that it is impossible for any government or revolution to wipe it out," declared Prévost-Paradol.[84]

Bristling at the restrictions imposed on free speech and public opinion, critics attacked state policies that hampered suspect journals with high fees and censorship controls while extending privileges to proimperial publicists. "Rather than allow [newspapers] to penetrate the masses, you have rendered the press an aristocratic institution at a time when aristocracy no longer exists," Simon charged.[85] Refusing to capitulate to the shadow of tyranny that had descended upon the nation, Simon maintained his optimism that liberty and justice must ineluctably prevail. "The time approaches," he claimed before the Corps législatif, "where all fictions and all barriers are going to finally disappear, and where the critic, the true sovereign of democracy and modern societies, will reign absolute."[86]

Simon's principled defense of free expression stemmed from his conviction that the press was "the singular organ [reflecting] the intellectual and moral life of a country."[87] More than merely the views of opinionated writers and editors, journals constituted, according to fellow republican Eugène Pelletan, the "daily confession of the nation," offering a space where France itself was capable of being "entirely assembled as though in a public place."[88] As a reflection of the political nation, therefore, newspapers occupied a principal role in the shaping of public life and association, providing the people with the "political education" needed for a healthy democracy.[89] It was in the pages of daily periodicals that individuals were informed about politics and society, came to recognize their common interests with compatriots, and acquired their identity as citizens. In the purview of liberal-republican ideology, journals were a powerful medium for the dissemination of ideas among the populations of the countryside and, more important, a key vehicle for the process of political modernization envisaged by democrats.

"If you want to forge a political nation that knows its responsibilities and can defend its rights," Laboulaye advised, "speak to the citizens about their interests every day."[90] The creation of a political society required nourishing a civic spirit and injecting new life into a rural world believed stagnant and dead. This denouement entailed introducing the countryside to new types of socialization and urging men estranged from civil society to appropriate the habits and practices central to an urban and modern milieu. Political elites saw this initiative to transform and assimilate the countryside as a primary duty, contending that failure would render the cause of liberty a dead letter in France. "The small cities and multitude of towns stretching across the countryside will become ardent hearths where the democratic idea will shine," Ténot exclaimed with the zeal of a missionary.[91]

Unable to deny political rights to citizens on the grounds of inferior intelligence and lack of "capacity" as the previous generation of liberals had, the next generation of political thinkers was quickly coming to understand that the incorporation of the people into national politics necessitated familiarizing individuals with the values and practices that could buttress and sustain a stable democratic political order. Political modernization did not, therefore, imply a process of democratization tout court in the minds of liberals and republicans. Rather it implied universalizing a certain type of political acumen and the practices associated with it. In more general terms, this strategy translated into a process of democratizing elite values and interests and acculturating the mass of French inhabitants scattered throughout the rural periphery. Much as the republican intellectual Henri Allain-Targé contended in the 1860s, the essential task was "to raise the thirty-five million brutes who [made] up the nation to the level of active citizens and enlightened patriots," of transforming them, in other words, into the type of men befitting a society conducive to order, economic expansion, and representational government.[92]

This form of politicization outlined a practical means of synthesizing elite control with democracy through an emphasis on homogenization and assimilation. Yet imposing values and nurturing new social and political practices in a democratic age required, in turn, new forms of power and influence outside of force and violence. Modernity signified the embodiment of this novel type of power, equating the imposition of certain values and cultural norms on others with the benefits of "modernization." Modern society and the correlative act of modernization through which it was to be realized not only provided the justification to shape society and individuals in accordance with particular interests, but structured the very symbols, representations, and meaning of a new social reality. It became the essence of a lived experience, assuming a normative and irrefutable quality that would, in time, command French citizens to think of themselves as a modern and civilized people. Rather than an evolutionary or social process, "political modernization" actively created a new center of social and political power for a democratic age.

"The art of making men and citizens is the primary function of a democratic society," the political theorist Étienne Vacherot claimed in 1859.[93] This sentiment expressed, ultimately, the guiding principle of a reformulated republican ideology that found its purpose in a modernizing and colonizing agenda. By the late 1860s, critics began to express optimism that it would only be a matter of time before their vision of French society bore substantial fruit. "It is not difficult to perceive," Léon Gambetta declared in 1870, "that not only in the cities, but in the countryside as well, there is a political fermentation penetrating into the lower classes of the population."[94] For republicans like Gambetta, this emergent society marked the horizon of the new republic, one that had been constructed through words and language during the years of Bonapartist rule but which dedicated republicans never doubted would one day be translated into a definitive reality. By the end of the Second Empire, the efforts of young republicans had synthesized the republican idea with the liberal ambitions of French elites, making it acceptable to a broader segment of the country's political classes.[95] "We shall see it, we shall see it . . . our Republic," Pelletan exclaimed in 1868, "a beautiful social and political future will flow from the ugly task we are carrying out at this time."[96] Prior to its declaration in 1870, the Third Republic already constituted a living idea in the minds of its founders.

7 Toward the Trans-Mediterranean Republic

In August 1857, young republicans had cause to celebrate as the results of the Parisian runoff elections were announced and the victory of *Les Cinq* confirmed. As friends and cohorts gave their felicitations and sent congratulatory notes in the coming days, Jules Favre, one of the five republican candidates set to take a seat in the Corps législatif, was noticeably absent. As the ballots were being counted, Favre surprisingly left the capital for the Algerian city of Oran to plead a case in the local *cour d'assises*, one of the French law courts set up in the colony to try criminal offenses. The trial in question involved Auguste Doineau, a captain in the Armée d'Afrique and commander of the Arab Office in Tlemcen charged with malfeasance and secretly orchestrating the assassination of the Muslim notable Ben Abdullah. Pleading his case before the Oranais court, Favre used the scandal to condemn the military regime and, by association, the imperial government, insisting that the *Affaire Doineau* exposed the authoritarian character of the colonial administration and its preference for personal power over justice and liberty.[1] "If what occurred in Tlemcen is indicative of all the Arab Offices, then it is necessary to eliminate or profoundly reform them as quickly as possible," Favre boldly charged.[2]

The tenor of Favre's diatribe and the timing of his arrival in Algeria were not insignificant. With the entrance of *Les Cinq* into the Corps législatif set to give a political voice to republicans, it was essential to find issues capable of building an opposition platform and attracting reform-minded allies. Concerned with the progress of the nation's civilizing mission being carried out in the colonies, Favre had come to Oran believing that Algeria could provide republicans with a possible forum for promoting their ideas and demonstrating their disapproval of the government. He even confessed that recent events in Algeria and the incessant grievances of colonial settlers held the potential of cementing a "common cause" between metropolitan democrats at home and disaffected Algerian *colons* across the Mediterranean.[3] From the very beginning of the republican resurgence, Favre and a select number of other republicans were capable of recognizing the importance that the Algerian question had for national politics in general. More to the point, Favre's visit revealed the first indications of a political strategy aimed at integrating colonial concerns into the broader issues of liberty and state reform championed by republican spokesmen on the continent, setting the stage for a possible trans-Mediterranean opposition movement spanning from Paris to Algiers.

This idea was neither idealistic nor necessarily novel, and even perpetuated a long-standing republican tradition. During the First Republic, the Jacobins had extended national citizenship to the Atlantic colonies while in 1848 republicans resurrected the ideal of universal French citizenship with the abolition of slavery throughout the empire and the recognition of the new Algerian provinces as de facto French departments. In both instances, a Bonaparte had undermined the promise of broad inclusion championed by republicans. Despite the vicissitudes of national and colonial policy since the Revolution, the French republics had both been national-imperial regimes committed to the principle—if not the practice—of universal citizenship. The rhetoric of French republicanism remained indebted to an ideological tradition of colonial integration and national unity that republicans of the 1860s would continue in their fight against the Second Empire, a feature often overlooked in accounts of the republican opposition of the period. In more specific terms, the short-lived Second Republic marked the beginning of a national and political discourse focused on Algeria that increasingly became integral to the language and ideology of French republicanism on both sides of the Mediterranean.

In light of the vicious anti-Semitism and racism that became staples of colonial politics in Algeria, *colon* commitment to republicanism has often been considered questionable. Settler support for the republic, critics claim, was pragmatic rather than ideological, entailing that colonists tolerated republican governance only as far as it upheld the repressive institutions and racial hierarchies that buttressed white European rule.[4] Although the racism and xenophobia rife within settler outlooks cannot be denied, the notion that colonial republicanism was merely a metropolitan export stomached by the settler population out of practical concerns is in need of reevaluation. The year 1848 proved instrumental in fostering a culture of republicanism in the colony, one that drew upon both local and metropolitan influences as it developed. Between 1848 and 1851 some twelve thousand French laborers were transferred to North Africa under the Second Republic followed by an additional six thousand to eight thousand *transportés*, radical workers and republican insurgents exiled by Louis Napoleon after the coup.[5] While idealized hopes of transforming political prisoners and urban workers into colonial farmers proved largely elusive, this influx did fuel existing republican sympathies and nurture anti-Bonapartist sentiments among the colonial population. *Transportés* equally served as an important conduit between metropolitan political circles and settler communities throughout the following decade.[6] The raw elements of an Algerian republicanism were already in place as the young republican movement gained traction in France. Writing in 1860, the *transporté* Wilfrid de Fonvielle asserted that the ambitions of radicals were "devoutly conserved" among the colony's French population. "They have not grown indifferent to the plight of humanity or to the success of their doctrines because they have abandoned Europe to establish themselves in a less agitated environment," he claimed, indicating that the republican spirit had by no means been extinguished in North Africa with the downfall of the Second Republic.[7]

In the early 1850s, Napoleon III had demonstrated a tepid commitment to Algerian assimilation through a policy of *colonisation departmental*.

Intended to attract colonists to the region and infuse Algerian life with a sense of provincial patriotism noticeably absent among *colons*, these projects authorized the construction of settler communities directly modeled on French towns and cities.[8] The institutional framework of 1848 was, moreover, left intact, allowing for a civilian administration monitored by the government in the settler territories. The creation of the colonial ministry under Prince Napoleon in 1858 had sought to empower the existing general councils and prefectures to a greater extent while equally retaining government control over official appointments. Yet in 1860, these reforms were significantly scaled back and the office of the governor general reestablished, subjecting local offices in the civilian provinces to military authority once again. Although the return of the colonial military regime did not signal a complete rupture with the former policies of civilian administration, the governor general did enjoy wide-ranging powers, including the nomination of prefects and representatives sitting on the general councils. This arrangement effectively sidelined *colon* opinion outside of the small number of colonial notables favored by the regime, granting the military a strong influence over local policies and state spending in the civilian provinces.[9]

Despite tensions between military and civilian authorities, administrative assimilation had, for the most part, proceeded apace during the 1850s, witnessing the creating of new subprefectures and the expansion of civilian institutions in areas inhabited by European settlers. The announcement of the Arab Kingdom and the promotion of an Arab nationality in the colony, however, officially signaled the cessation of these initiatives. *Colon* critics rankled by their lack of political rights and the government's Nativist policies came together under the banner of *L'Algérie Française*, mounting an opposition campaign that republican elites were well-positioned to use and encourage for their own ends by the 1860s. The commonalities and consensus that developed between republican circles and colonial activists throughout the decade would effectively transform the "Algerian question" into a national one as *colons* increasingly came to apply the terms of republican modernization to the colony. Under the Second Empire, the politics of modernity brought

Algeria into the mainstream of national political life once again, crystallizing an idea of *la France transméditerranéenne* that would play a significant role in the brand of republican colonialism to come.

The Struggle against Oriental Primitivism

In February 1863, reports of protests in the major cities of the Algerian Tell began to trickle in to the office of the governor general from the various prefectorial bureaus. Recording his observations of agitated colonists in the streets of Constantine, the doctor Auguste Vital remarked that "the beautiful days of 1848 returned as people prepared to leave behind them the legal monotony and partake in a fevered and disordered existence."[10] The cause of the disorder concerned the publication of Napoleon III's letter to General Pélissier on 6 February outlining the government's intentions of recognizing the colony as an Arab Kingdom. The revolutionary overtones of the situation were not lost on Frédéric Lacroix, who noted with mild sarcasm that Algeria could now claim its own "day of the barricades" (*journée des barricades*). For a Nativist like Lacroix, the event hardly possessed the same popular and insurrectionary implications observed by Vital. Where Vital saw the reawakening of Algerian political life, Lacorix saw only a "violent explosion" of settler racism.[11]

These conflicting interpretations mapped two distinct ideological positions that were becoming central to Algerian politics under the Second Empire. Whereas Nativists desired to integrate North Africa's Muslim population into a nominally multicultural Franco-Algerian society, colonists demanding cultural and administrative assimilation with the French metropole demanded an end to colonial segregation and a more vigorous colonizing initiative. The declaration of the Royaume Arabe had made the divergent objectives of these two platforms evident. Disgruntled colonists assailed the military for perpetuating Oriental barbarism and officials fired back at their critics with accusations of racism and religious prejudice. "The publication [of the emperor's letter] and the commentaries that accompanied it generated a profound disquiet among the European population," General Patrice de MacMahon, the governor-general of Algeria from 1864 to 1870, recalled in his memoirs. "Establishing an Arab Kingdom had a strong impression on them."[12]

While the "day of the barricades" that threw the colony into a momentary state of crisis quickly dissipated, the "strong impression" that the emperor's declaration had on *colons* did not. Questions regarding the viability and significance of an Arabized French territory would continue to agitate Algerian politics for the next seven years. "In Algeria and France," the polemicist Auguste Warnier fulminated in 1865, "[there is] a raucous party more Arab than the Arabs that has shown itself disposed to sacrificing everything, even the interests most dear to France, in order to arrive at the creation of a so-called Arab Kingdom."[13] The Nativists were not only sacrificing "the interests of their *patrie* and civilization" out of a "hatred for European society," one *colon* petition accused, but were demanding that France "abdicate its civilizing role."[14] An Arabized—and hence Orientalized—Algeria embodied all the connotations of that old and barbaric world beyond the pale of Europe's modern horizon. At a time when modernity established a powerful rationale for inclusion and exclusion, the emperor's announcement that Algeria be considered an Arab Kingdom was a stinging affront to colonist desires for integration with France proper. It summarily cut *colons* asunder from their coevals across the Mediterranean and erected social and cultural boundaries threatening the very foundation of a French Algeria. "All those devoted to the prosperity of the colony, to the grandeur of France, and to the progress of civilization will understand that the moment has come for us to act together," the republican *transporté* Alexandre Lambert urged. "We must seek what will unite us. To act otherwise would make us accomplices to the deplorable doctrines that seek to perpetuate barbarism here."[15]

Colonial journalists and activists were quick to present the Algerian situation in stark terms, contrasting the patriotic *colon* dedicated to progress and civilization with the authoritarian military regime bent on perpetuating Arab barbarism across North Africa. Yet these divisions were always more imagined than real. The image of the *colon* touted by polemicists tended to obscure the diversity of a settler population consisting of aristocratic landowners, middling entrepreneurs and merchants, small-scale agriculturalists, and various insular immigrant communities.[16] Social and national differences provided a major obstacle to cohesion within settler communities, and opinions regarding colonial assimilation and the detrimental influence of the military were hardly shared by all.[17] *Colon* signified a cultural rather than an explicitly social category, one that assumed greater saliency as colonial activists attempted to mobilize support for their vision of an *Algérie Française* tied culturally and politically to the European continent. In their opposition to Nativists, *colon* agitators sought to imbue settlers with a collective sense of purpose and furnish the base of a common Algerian identity uniting a settler population consisting of French, Italians, Greeks, Maltese, and Spaniards, groups nominally categorized by the colonial government as "European" for administrative purposes but which, in reality, possessed little formal unity. Appeals to civilization and modernity offered a potent means of dissolving these existing ethnonational differences and imagining a new class of people bound by a shared culture, worldview, and spirit of innovation distinct from the native tribes.

In publicizing this identity, activists aggressively took aim at the putative "civilizing" initiatives of the government's policies. Encouraging Arab nationality was, Alexandre Lambert insisted, delusional, since the Arabs possessed neither a national identity shaped by deep historical roots nor a shared national consciousness. "To mention an Arab Kingdom is to speak of the thousands of *douars* and tribes continually fighting, pillaging, stealing, and killing each other without cause," he scoffed.[18] *Colon* criticism was practically unanimous on this point, noting the lack of solidarity and tribalism rampant among Maghrebi natives.[19] "There are no intimate relations and solidarities that constitute a *nationalité* [among the native tribes]," Jules Duval observed. "The idea of a *patrie* is unknown to them."[20] Although maintaining that "in the name of humanity" the natives were entitled to property, good administration, and equitable treatment, "in the name of nationality" they had a right to nothing, he insisted.[21]

If *colon* opinion leaders criticized the Arab Kingdom as an ethnographic fallacy, they equally questioned its moral premise. Rather than "civilizing" the natives, the military permitted indigenous populations to fester under a feudal regime dominated by religious zealots and tribal sheikhs. According to Andrieux, editor of the *Courrier de l'Algérie*, the Arab world was marked by "opulence without limits above and the most wretched proletarian misery below." By preserving the inequalities and traditional social hierarchies of the tribe, the military administration only served to perpetuate these miseries. "You are not the friends of the Arab *people*," he charged. "You are the friends of the aristocracy, a feudal order a hundred times more severe than ours ever was that allows a minority to devour the multitude!"[22] Opponents argued that efforts to safeguard traditional Arab society constituted an obstacle to developing a modern, liberal Algeria, not to mention a blemish on France's identity as the bearer of enlightened and progressive values. According to the author and colonial newspaper correspondent Henri Verne, the government's policies were misguided and left much to be desired from a nation consider the vanguard of liberty and human progress in the world. "Can we hope to be moving along the path of social and political progress when, as partisans of democracy in Europe, we leave tribes under the oppression of powerful leaders and support a completely feudal system?"[23]

With its tribal mores and "feudal" hierarchies, Arab society was depicted as the antithesis of the progressive spirit and productivity emblematic of Europe. The nomadic lifestyle and collective ownership practiced by Arab tribes amounted to a chronic idleness and "horror of work" that left the earth "sterile in their hands," portending stagnation and widespread underdevelopment for the entire colony.[24] Land was not viewed as a commodity in Maghrebi societies and ownership was commonly understood in terms of conserving family patrimony rather than a source of private wealth.[25] Various forms of land tenure stemming from centuries of Ottoman rule remained in place in Algeria, with different groups adhering to distinct practices of proprietorship. *Colons* typically ignored these complexities, framing their observations in simplified distinctions between a primitive tribal society and the individualism and private ownership constitutive of European selfhood.

In 1863, Napoleon III had pushed through measures aimed at dividing communally held lands and transforming Algerians into individual property holders. Just as the French Revolution had broken up provincial and church lands in an attempt to create modern proprietors in France, the *sénatus-consulte* of 1863 similarly intended to modernize Algerian land tenure by prescribing legal conditions for the sale and exchange of land between natives and settlers. In theory, the ruling was designed to protect native land rights from rapacious speculators and simplify the multiple Ottoman tax systems then in place. In reality, the reforms proved limited in scope and did little to protect native rights.[26] Perturbed by the government's feeble policies, critics persisted to levy allegations of sloth and waste against natives, holding out aggressive economic modernization and capitalist practices as the surest remedy to the feudalism and tribal "communism" ossifying North African society.

Under the military, Algeria was subject to what the editor of the *Progrès de l'Algérie*, Amand Favré, deemed the "inertia and lethargy sustained by the communist principle."[27] This communism "discouraged individual initiative" and encouraged the indolence and poverty familiar to tribal life.[28] The Arab tribe evoked all the connotations of the invidious "spectre rouge" that haunted Europe, and critics adeptly played upon this association, equating support for colonialism with the fight against socialism in France. Jules Favre drove the point home in 1866 when giving an address before the Corps législatif in which he accused Arab society of practicing "the most dangerous and destructive social system contrary to every type of individual activity." "It is communism," he charged, "the communism that certain people among us do not want to see implanted on the European continent."[29] In his view, Nativism was fundamentally flawed in its very principles and encouraged the same forms of moral barbarism and proletarian savagery that imperiled European civilization at home. Jules Duval shared a similar opinion. Bonapartist nationality polices promoted under the banner of tolerance and civilization were nothing short of catastrophic, both for the colony and the natives they claimed to protect. As he contended, "the salvation of the Arab *race* can only be achieved by sacrificing Arab *society*."[30]

Through these criticisms, *colons* and critics implicitly condemned their Nativist antagonists by drawing parallels between Arab society and the colonial administration. Much like the feudal and aristocratic Arabs, the "regime of the saber" abided by a martial ethos that respected only force and authority. It was hostile to liberty and conserved a petrified social order for personal gain. "After four successive revolutions, seventy-nine years after the abolition of privilege, is there not something abnormal and antiegalitarian in this organization from another age?" speculated Favré.[31] Not only was the military impugned for its authoritarian and illiberal comportment; its persistent opposition to colonial settlement within the Arab territories provided clear evidence of its disdain for modern civilization. The military was content to sit on the territory it possessed "without sacrificing a parcel of it to the monster it calls progress," one journalist exclaimed, adding: "We French citizens have not come to Algeria to move backward, to cede the path to the barbarians."[32] The liberal-minded writer Frédéric Morin went even further in his censure, labeling the military administration a "monstrous regime . . . a homicidal regime, a regime of ruin and death" that was completely at odds with modernity.[33] "The most imperfect civilian regime is worth more than the most perfect military regime," Duval summed up. "The latter is the past while the former the future."[34]

Binaries such as "primitive" and "modern," "barbaric" and "civilized" were salient terms of *colon* protest during the 1860s, effectively constructing an identity for the settler population as "pioneers of modern civilization" opposed doubly to military authority and Arab barbarism.[35] In contrast to the sterile and impoverished communities administered by the Arab Offices, the villages and farms built by settlers were "schools of civilization," Auguste Warnier claimed.[36] The journalist Joseph Guérin rhapsodized on the mission that the Europeans were destined to fulfill, asserting that the *colons* represented the very essence and embodiment of modern civilization in the French Orient. "The *colons* have a force more powerful than steam, more invincible than lightning. They are civilization [and] civilization does not regress."[37] As modern civilization incarnate, *colons* waxed lyrical on the material benefits and improvements that would result from an energetic policy of colonization. "In a third of a century," Duval boasted, "the French have built more towns, cleared more fields, planted more trees, carved out more canals, constructed more roads, and spread more ideas than the Arabs have in twelve centuries."[38] Unlike the Arabs who left the land barren and unproductive, French settlers promised to inaugurate a new era of commercial and agrarian productivity that would restore North Africa as the major grain-producing region it had once been under the Roman Empire.

Material concerns were not, however, the only prospect French colonization had to offer. Indeed, Great Britain was sharply criticized for its explicit concern with trade and commerce in acquiring its empire. Unlike the British, the French were engaged in "a work of national conquest" that subordinated profit making to a nobler mission: spreading civilization.[39] "Be convinced, the destiny that the future holds for Algeria is not that of a simple colony," affirmed one critic. "[Our] conquest is made in the name of progress and civilization."[40] Much like the messianic outlooks articulated by the Saint-Simonians and Nativists, *colons* professed that France had a civilizing mission to fulfill in the world as it established its empire of universal fraternity. Yet unlike that of the Nativists, this mission was the property of neither military commanders nor officers in the Arab Offices claiming a specialized knowledge of the *indigènes*. According to Joseph Guérin, it was "the *colons* alone" who would furnish the Arabs with a moral education, and for this reason it was "essential that [colonists] be numerous and penetrate into the hearts of the native populations."[41]

This "moral" education implied nothing short of radically reforming native tendencies and outlooks. Colonists were obliged to teach the Arabs how to be productive farmers and responsible landowners, casting off "the dead hand of feudalism" that consigned North Africa to permanent sterility, as Émile Thuillier put it.[42] This task necessitated breaking down traditional social hierarchies, abolishing outmoded forms of collective ownership, and creating a new type of individual befitting the dynamic agrarian capitalism endorsed by proponents of colonization.[43] "The emancipation of work and the dissolution of the tribe" were, according to the pro-*colon* publicist Arsène Vacherot, the essential ingredients in this "peaceful and indispensable revolution."[44] The revolutionary implications of colonial economic reform were hardly lost on critics. As one colonist boasted, "agriculture, the mother of liberty, dignity, and the robust and healthy virtues of the domestic hearth, will extend its salutary influence to [the Arabs]. They will become useful, honest, and moral citizens that will make the French family proud."[45] Drawing on a familiar language of citizenship, industry, and emancipation, *colons* tied their moral mission closely to the nation's revolutionary heritage, insisting, as Guérin did, that French colonization would transform savage Arab tribesmen into sedentary and productive individuals, "elevating them to the dignity of free men, the final aim of civilization for all countries."[46] Redolent of the Bonapartists' civilizing mission on the continent, *colon* critiques revealed a willingness to equate *civilisation* with core attitudes and values central to liberal ideology. Civilization meant individual initiative and private ownership; it promised economic development and mutually beneficial commercial interests.[47] It similarly translated the forcible uprooting and destruction of existing cultures into moral terms, obliging the imposition of such "civilizing" acts on a less-evolved and backward Muslim society.

Plans to discipline the natives and instill a work ethic in them may have found expression in lofty ideals and sentiments, but these rhetorical flourishes concealed a more troubling reality facing colonists: namely, the lack of a dominant European population in the colony. By the late 1850s, the European population consisted of nearly 190,000 inhabitants of which over 100,000 were French. These numbers paled in comparison to an indigenous population of over 2 million.[48] Immigration rates revealed, moreover, the unsettling fact that the French possessed little interest in leaving Europe for Africa. In 1857, over 10,000 French emigrated to foreign countries but less than 8,000 to Algeria. Rates for the following year were similarly disappointing.[49] French and European settlers continued to remain a small minority in the midst of an imposing Muslim population. As late as 1870, a colonial newspaper lamented the dearth of French compatriots to be found in the colony, writing, "unfortunately after forty years of occupation the inhabitants of the metropole have not shown themselves prepared to flock to Algeria en masse."[50] Sheer demographics made it difficult to rationalize the creation of a civilian government just as much as it did claiming a French identity for Algeria. To achieve these goals, *colons* would have to propose a solution mindful of Algeria's Muslim population even while simultaneously claiming a hegemonic role for Europeans in colonial society. Modernity offered a convincing ideological rationale and narrative for this objective, portending a "fusion of mores" and "unity of interests" as the modernization of North Africa's land and people proceeded under French stewardship.[51]

Whereas men like Lacroix and Urbain assailed assimilation as a racist policy that would aggravate existing social tensions, *colons* contended that it was, in fact, the Nativists who posed the greater threat. "On this earth where numerous indigenous races have lived enervated for centuries because they have remained hostile to one another and because different tribes have conserved the legacy of their hatreds and particular passions, the *colon* admirably understand the strength of concord and union," Fonvielle claimed in 1860.[52] Maintaining distinct communities would only perpetuate the ethnic and religious feuds that had long destabilized North Africa. More specifically, *colons* professed that the military's "systematic opposition" to fusion and its support for Arab nationality was a flagrant betrayal of French *nationalité*.[53] Was there a Bureau Basque or Bureau Corse in France to administer the populations in the provinces of the Pyrénées or Corsica, Devernois sarcastically asked? The idea was ludicrous.[54] *Unité*, that core tenet of French nationality, was just as much an ideological imperative as it was a strategic necessity. Without assimilation, there could be no *Algérie Française*. "The interest of the colony, the honor of France, and the triumph of civilization," declared Lambert in 1863, "demand that we search by all possible means to unify the diverse populations within a single people."[55]

In their struggle against Oriental primitivism, *colons* drew upon themes of modernization and *nationalité* prevalent within French national politics during the 1860s. These concepts were hardly unique to *colon* protest and often brought to light commonalities with their Nativist opponents that were marginalized for the sake of ideological consistency. Despite their differences, the Arab Kingdom and *Algérie Française* reflected a shared aspiration for Algerian modernization and an idea of France that transcended reductive ethnic and confessional affiliations. The fundamental divergence resided, however, in whether French *nationalité* would best be promoted through the association of Muslims and Europeans or the direct assimilation of North Africa's native populations.[56] For Jules Duval, a dedicated partisan of the *colon* cause, the choice was simple. Compulsive assimilation alone and the unity brought by a common *nationalité* offered the surest means of demonstrating France's great "cause to humanity" as it transformed a balkanized and stagnant Oriental world into a modern, progressive society.[57]

A writer and landowner with influential ties to the Parisian press, Duval stood as one of the most vociferous proponents of *colon* interests. Inspired by the ideas of the socialist Charles Fourier, he had come to Algeria in 1847 with the intention of founding an agricultural commune owned and operated by laborers. When the enterprise failed, Duval turned to journalism and politics, serving as a representative in the general council of Oran and editing a local newspaper, *L'Echo d'Oran*.[58] He fiercely opposed the Arab Kingdom policy on the grounds that it placed "Arabs at the level of the Europeans," a flagrant offense to "the superior intelligence, patriotism, work, national sentiment, and private interests" of the colonists.[59] A staunch defender of colonization, Duval saw the natives as a constant obstacle to economic modernization and a severe threat to the security of the European settlers. The tribes must either "be transformed or disappear" if the colony was to grow and prosper.[60] Only then would France be capable of fulfilling its mission in Africa, bringing order to the continent, and "raising monuments of civilization on the ruins of an Arab society crumbling into dust for a thousand years."[61]

For Duval, colonization was not simply an economic question, but a struggle between the forces of human progress and barbarism. "Colonization embraces at once moral, religious, and political interests," he wrote. "It founds new societies and concomitantly initiates savages and barbarians into the arts and civilization; it is the moral education of all young societies."[62] Man's incessant migration and continual need to exploit the natural world for his own productive ends motivated the colonial enterprise, and as "young and vigorous swarms," colonies constituted the field on which humanity's dynamic energy and desire for expansion were shaped and realized.[63] In his theories on settler colonialism, Duval saw colonies as "the progenitors of nations" and the essential first phase in a people's moral and social education.[64] They were the seeds that produced great nations, and for Duval the colonization of Algeria was never distinct from this purpose. In "pacifying" the warring clans scattered across North Africa and inducting them into civilized life, France was preparing the "mixed elements" of the colony for a "more intimate relationship" with the metropole, he believed.[65]

By their very nature, colonial societies possessed a hybridized quality consisting of various languages, religions, ethnicities, and interests.[66] Yet by founding schools, undertaking public works, and developing a viable economy, these "disparate elements" would "rapidly combine to form a living and sufficiently homogeneous body" that transcended natural differences, Duval posited.[67] "The special glory of Algeria," he extolled, "is [its] being the tomb of racial prejudices, national jealousies, religious hatreds, political parties, and all vain agitations."[68] Observing the festivities held in the colony on 13 June 1858, a day of state-sponsored celebration commemorating France's invasion of the Barbary Coast, Duval witnessed his vision of a unified Algerian society momentarily come to life. "In the joyous or grave gatherings, all the people of diverse origins, mores, dress, languages, races, and religions form only a single people: the Algerian people." Such gatherings and festivities exemplified to Duval "how tolerance and the admirable sociability of the French spirit" were capable of triumphing over old hatreds and prejudices. "[The] general reconciliation of religions and races is a legitimate hope of our epoch," he professed, and Algeria was the stage upon which this aspiration would be displayed for all to see.[69]

Through their opposition to the Nativists, *colons* and metropolitans found the means of articulating desires for an *Algérie Française* and framing their program in a language familiar to contemporaries. Assimilation and *rattachement*, rather than simply objectives in their own right, became intimately bound to a settler identity embodying modernity itself. In portraying the colonial administration as a relic of aristocracy and absolutism, activists made the case for a modern and Gallicized Algeria tied to France proper. "For us, Algeria should not be a colony but a second France and better still a part of France itself," declared Henri Verne.[70] This conviction rested on the assumption of a common culture and worldview shared among trans-Mediterranean coevals. By framing resistance to the Arab Kingdom as a struggle against Oriental primitivism, *colon* protestors lay claim to a modern identity that aimed to unify a diverse settler community and mobilize support for their cause of national integration. The universal pretentions evident in this vision of Algerian modernity consistently eclipsed the fact that "modern civilization" implied French civilization, condoning the brand of ethnic domination essential to sustaining a French Algeria. Yet in the terms of opposition employed by colonial elites during the 1860s, *Algérie Française* entailed only a question of whether North Africa would conform to the progress of modern time or remain mired in a barbaric past. The Algerian administration had revealed itself ill-disposed to bring modern society to fruition in North Africa. It was, therefore, up to the *colons* as partisans of colonization and modernization to come to its defense.

Algerian Republicanism and Colonial Citizenship

Colon protest took place against the backdrop of an evolving French Algerian press that was becoming increasingly central to the worldview and sociability of colonial elites. During the 1850s and 1860s, colonists promoted their cause through a growing number of newspapers, pamphlets, and petitions that circulated in the three civilian provinces and abroad. Upon arriving in the colony, Albert de Broglie compared the atmosphere of lively debate and discussion he found there to the early days of the Second Republic. "I believed I was dreaming or had gone back in time," he remarked with shock. Newspapers published polemics "that did not appear contained within any limits, not even those of polite discourse" while "conversation and publications possessed an energy and bravado" lacking in France.[71] On evening strolls through the heart of the governmental Marine quarter in 1860, the dramatist Ernest Feydeau reported that the merchants, soldiers, officials, and travelers congregating there had only one topic on their lips: "nothing else than the great question of *the future of the colony!*"[72] The late 1850s and early 1860s witnessed an "explosion of liberalism" in Algeria, as one *colon* claimed, that infused colonial life with a noticeably political character.[73]

The importance placed in colonial journalism derived from the political realities associated with French colonization itself. Colonists had no direct political representation in the French government and, therefore, no direct influence over colonial policymaking. Subject to the authority of the governor-general and, ultimately, Paris and the whims of the emperor, *colons* regularly protested against their lack of political rights and influence on policies. Auguste Warnier reiterated a familiar grievance in 1865 when criticizing the government's authoritarian attitude, complaining that "not a single colonist is asked for the slightest advice on questions concerning the future of the entire country."[74] The colonial administration's supposed disregard for the needs and interests of the settler community became a centerpiece of *colon* opposition as reformers held the government accountable for the slow pace of the colony's economic development, the troublingly low emigration rates, and the misuse of public funds for grandiose and impractical building projects in the major cities of the Tell Atlas region.[75]

If colonists could expect little sympathy from state and military officials, the same could also be said of metropolitan politicians and opinion leaders. In 1868, *Akhbar*'s Parisian correspondent chided the majority of deputies in the Corps législatif for the uninformed opinions and general disregard they revealed when it came to Algeria. "I do not fear I am going too far by claiming that in the Chamber there are not ten deputies who are familiar with [Algeria] or have bothered to study it," he reported.[76] This disinterest similarly extended to national newspapers as well. "Practically no organ of the Parisian press seems disposed to discuss our interests," Wilfrid de Fonvielle lamented in 1860. "They assume that they are of no concern to the French public."[77] These frustrations only further encouraged demands for the political rights enjoyed by compatriots across the Mediterranean. "Between the citizens of France and the citizens of the colonies," Jules Duval asked indignantly in 1869, "are we to presume that there exists such a difference in nature that one has the right of universal suffrage while the other only a privileged suffrage?"[78]

Unable to plead their case directly before the nation, colonists were obliged to rely upon metropolitan spokesmen to air their grievances, circumstances that necessitated courting public opinion and political allies through informal channels. This task, activists insisted, invested the colonial press with a specific mission and purpose. Journalists were obliged "to clarify public opinion and show things as they truly are," Joseph Guérin, the Algiers notable and future mayor of Sidi Moussa, explained in 1865.[79] Arnold Thomson, a regular contributor to the moderate *Akhbar*, was equally supportive of the role the Algerian press had in the colony, claiming the publicist was "to seek out and elucidate each one of the colonial questions and inspire thoughts in the diligent and intelligent part of the population."[80] In 1868, Émile Thuillier commended the efforts of his colleagues, remarking, "Algeria is recruiting new defenders each day." Yet he was also careful to reiterate the ongoing mission of Algerian journalism, reminding readers that "to draw people's attention, it is first essential that they understand [the colony]."[81]

The sense of unity and optimism conveyed by journalists often belied, however, a more complex reality. Censorship frequently made the hope of "clarifying" perceptions of Algerian society difficult. Colonial officials would fine or altogether suppress journals critical of the administration, imposing limits on the scope and tone of public discourse.[82] The spectrum of opinion found in the Algerian press was, moreover, far from uniform. In addition to the official state organ, *Le Moniteur algérien*, the only fairly regular newspaper in the colony during much of the nineteenth century was *Akhbar*, established in 1839 by Auguste Bourget. Bourget's success was due primarily to his political flexibility and willingness to work within the acceptable limits of public discourse set by the state without compromising the paper's overall independence.[83] More censorious journalists often chided Bourget for his moderation, and comparatively short-lived papers run by reform-minded liberals and anti-Bonapartist *transportés* like Thuillier considered it a duty to maintain an oppositional stance reflecting explicitly *colon* interests and opinions.[84] Journals such as the *Progrès de l'Algérie* and *Courrier de l'Algérie*—both of which tended to reflect republican attitudes—or Duval's pro-*colon L'Echo d'Oran* were typically the most critical of the colonial administration, and official efforts to mute criticism only further encouraged hostility. As one observer remarked in 1868: "Should you want to commend an act of state, send your prose to *Le Moniteur* or *Akhbar*; if you want to vent your spleen, send it to the *Courrier*."[85] Ideological differences aside, however, colonial journalists collectively saw themselves as spokesmen for settler interests and as mediators between the settler community and metropolitan policymakers. It was in the pages of colonial broadsheets and journals that *colon* identity was most effectively publicized and criticism of the government expressed.

Praise for the resourcefulness and tenacious spirit of the *colons* often accompanied more pessimistic appraisals of the state and its excessive interference in nearly all aspects of public life. From the beginning of the French occupation, the colonial administration and its staff of civil engineers had spearheaded the various public works projects and industrial ventures associated with Algerian modernization. Yet as various critics pointed out, these efforts could often be slow to materialize or incongruous with the practical needs of settler communities.[86] Colonists habitually complained about state restrictions on land purchases and the persistent interference of authorities in the daily activities of settlers.[87] In his observations of Algeria, Albert de Broglie noted that the values of "individual initiative" and the "spirit of enterprise" seemed feeble among the French colonists. Their "political institutions have habituated them over the years to being governed, administered, controlled, supervised, and protected at all times and on all points," he dismally concluded.[88] According to *Akhbar*, nine years later little had changed. "It seems Algerians can do nothing without the intervention of the government, and this intervention is indispensable to the execution of projects," the journal claimed.[89]

Critics complained that constant bureaucratic oversight encouraged settlers to remain idle and reliant on the state, and the effects of this dependency were most pronounced in the settler communities outside the cities. In 1858, Clément Duvernois sketched a depressing picture of rural colonial life, offering a tableau of poor farmers, barren fields, squalid towns filled with degrading cabarets, and streets populated by children shirking work. Travelers who visited only Algiers and Constantine—cities that received the lion's share of public funds and government attention— saw the newly laid roads and European houses and returned to France praising the administration's progress. "But," Duvernois countered, "if they even minutely examined the situation in the villages, they would lose the enthusiasm that had initially been inspired."[90] Rural Algeria was characterized by isolation, fields dotted with small shanty farms, debauchery, and penury, and this startling reality was the consequence of what Thuillier described as an egregious and ineffective "officialisme" smothering the colony.[91] "Here, where there is everything to be done," Andrieux warned, "centralization only serves to prevent everything from taking shape."[92]

Grievances over state policies were not merely complaints lodged against the colonial administration by angry settlers. The targets chosen by colons were strategic in nature and dovetailed nicely with the calls for decentralization emanating from prominent liberal and republican circles in the metropole. Algerian critiques of centralization were intended to portray the colony as an example par excellence of the shortcomings and impediments of the Bonapartist state and underscore the commonalities linking France and its North African periphery. The colon battle cry of "war on administrative centralization and bureaucracy!" was a sentiment shared by like-minded republican and liberal thinkers on the conti- nent, and such declarations encouraged an oppositional language that elided the conceptual boundaries traditionally distancing metropole and colony.[93] Much like liberal and republican critiques of centralization, moreover, colonial assessments of state power also provided a context against which desires for liberal reform, democratization, and political rights could be articulated, and *colons* rarely missed an opportunity to address such issues in their writings.

In editorials and political tracts, *colons* drew comparisons between "the spirit of liberty" and the practical work required for founding a prosperous and dynamic society in North Africa. Liberty, as the founder of the *Courrier de l'Algérie*, Charles de Guerle, informed his readers in 1862, was "the only true principle underlying the drive and progress of colonies."[94] "We ask for a greater freedom of action for our communes than in the mother country because here everything has to be created," explained a *colon* petition submitted to the senate in 1863. "Liberty is not to be feared and is necessary in the struggle against the numerous obstacles that nature offers against the action of man."[95] Only free and autonomous individuals were aptly suited for the arduous task of founding a new society in the colonial wilderness, and it was, therefore, unsurprising that reflections on liberty frequently translated into debates on the general health and vitality of French colonial society. In the opinion of one colonist, liberty was the most essential element in the growth and development of a settler community, warning that "without it, colonies wilt."[96]

Calls for reform focused attention on the necessity of civic participation and the need for liberalization at the local level of government. "[We must] open our hearts and spirits to liberty through the free choice of general and municipal councils," de Guerle explained, because it was at the departmental and communal levels that the decisions relevant to daily life were effectively made and implemented.[97] De Guerle's entreaty reflected a widespread desire on the part of colonial publicists to combat the debilitating influences of state power through the rehabilitation of municipal political life. Rather than constituting administrative entities akin to "companies and regiments" that knew only obedience, the Algerian municipalities would be "reborn" through the participation of citizens, Alexandre Lambert believed.[98] Liberty and individual initiative, rather than being abstract concepts, made up the cornerstone of any healthy society, obliging greater reflection on the more intimate contours of colonial life, government, and the local institutions that shaped them.

Like metropolitan republicans, *colons* attributed a particularly crucial role to the commune, the principal unit of French government. Much as Amand Favré claimed, the commune was the essential base of social organization, the "natural nucleus" of society. "Thanks to the commune, men coming from diverse points can undertake the apprenticeship of association to which they are destined and freely unite their efforts against the obstacles of nature."[99] The senator and Algerian landowner Ferdinand Barrot readily concurred when addressing the senate in 1863, claiming that the "municipal element" constituted "the first stage of all societies" and imparted the necessary education in self-governance and shared sociability without which society could not exist. In Barrot's opinion, the municipality was "the first guarantee of interests, the first element of the spirit of association and solidarity."[100] As the foundation of all social life, the commune provided an indissoluble link between the individual and the community, serving as the locale upon which social and commercial transactions came to shape common interests and associations. De Guerle proffered a familial metaphor in 1862, describing the commune as an "enlarged family." "Municipal life," he affirmed, "is what touches us at all points and all moments of our life."[101]

The central role attributed to local government extended far beyond the domain of commercial and social engagements. Algeria's diverse ethnonational composition remained a point of real concern, and not only regarding the questionable loyalties of certain populations. In a broader perspective, the ideological foundation of *Algérie Française* was at stake. *Colon* views on municipal government and citizenship remained, therefore, closely tied to desires for assimilation. Giving a speech before the *conseil général* of Constantine in 1865, the councilman Champroux expressed his support for communal organization in Algeria on the grounds that it would mark a progressive step toward "a solid political and administrative organization" in the colony. It was not only advisable, but essential in his opinion, since the commune provided "the first link attaching [an individual] to a new *patrie*. . . . In a colony composed of such diverse elements the commune becomes ever more necessary in uniting these elements."[102] Duval shared a similar perspective: "the municipality becomes the principal *patrie* for the majority of inhabitants and on its horizon they concentrate their affections, activity, and ambitions."[103] The idea of *Algérie Française*, colonists contended, must take root at the local level if it was to become a reality, and the commune was envisaged as the primary vehicle for shaping this French community on African soil.

If the "municipal principle . . . must penetrate into the heart and blood of the population," as Duval anticipated, the hope of encouraging integration among settlers also dictated cultivating the necessary "public mores." For Duval, the solution lay in allowing greater liberties at the municipal level through local elections. Municipal elections would provide the "education of the citizen" in the colony, nurturing an attachment to the *patrie* through civic engagement. "Without elections," he warned, "[the people] will see themselves as only a cog in a central administration estranged from their affections if not their interests."[104] In pleading his case for greater municipal freedoms in 1865, the journalist Montain-Lefloch argued that reform at the local level was paramount if colonists expected to regain representation at the national level, since it was through the commune that love for the *patrie* was born and the individual came to understand the "interests of the country." Only "by proving that the fibers of the most vibrant patriotism runs in us as in the most humble peasant of France," he claimed, would colonists win the right to elect deputies to the Corps législatif, and this could not be achieved without first liberating the communes from their administrative shackles, and developing citizens.[105]

While colonists looked back to the years of the Second Republic when Algerian deputies had sat in the National Assembly and appealed to a common body of rights shared with compatriots, Algerian citizenship was hardly a zero-sum game, especially given the government's Nativist leanings. As Urbain keenly observed, if common law was applied to the colony, "it would not be the natives who suffer."[106] Natives' demographic majority would, by necessity, eclipse the settlers, swallowing them up in a Muslim majority. To the alarm of colonists, moreover, by the mid-1860s government policy appeared to be moving toward the prospect of native enfranchisement. An official decree in late 1866 authorized the creation of special councils for Muslims, Jews, and foreigners, with supporters urging that, at least at the local level of society, "Muslims and Jews have a right to be represented just like the French."[107] The military, as Governor-General MacMahon made evident in an administrative circular, was coming to see native political participation as a "civilizing" vehicle capable of establishing a permanent link between the European and indigenous populations.[108]

Ardent defenders of *colon* civil and political rights, activists nonetheless stood firmly against extending political participation to North African natives. Addressing the issue directly in 1867, Arnold Thomson expressed fears that Muslims and Jews would vote along ethnic lines, warning that such a denouement would inflect Algerian politics with deep-rooted prejudices and hatreds.[109] One councilman in Constantine went as far as to claim that proportionate representation and democratic politics would result in "the despotism of material interests over moral interests" since to enfranchise the *indigène* majority would unquestionably mean abandoning the civilizing mission that ascribed a leading role to French and European settlers.[110] It was, furthermore, undeniable that the political status of Algerian natives in the colony would have a direct impact on the question of Algerian national representation overall. Addressing the issue before the Corps législatif in 1870, Jules Favre candidly spelled out the problem that native enfranchisement posed to Algerian national integration. If Muslims were allowed to participate in nominating deputies to the national legislature, France would be subject to what Favre described as an "invasion of the *indigène* element." "If the *indigène* element should be represented do you know how it will be? An *indigène* appearing in this body would be nominated by his conationals and would come to defend the principles that they defend on their soil."[111] Giving Muslims political power would not only undermine the French character of Algerian society; worse still, it would give them a voice before the nation, imperiling national unity and infecting French politics with a divisive tribalism.

The Maghrebi populations were deemed incapable of exercising the rights belonging to French citizens. While the senatorial ruling of 1865 recognized a distinction between *indigène* and *citoyen* on legal grounds, opponents of the government went further to insist that the practice of citizenship itself required specific intellectual and social qualifications that natives clearly lacked. This rationale was, by the 1860s, a familiar concept within French republican thinking, having been employed in the 1790s and again after 1848 to undermine political and civil liberties in the postemancipation Atlantic colonies. The energetic rights talk espoused by metropolitans and colonists during the years of the Second Empire demonstrated the resilience of liberal notions of *capacité* as well as that unique brand of republican racism that allowed for the existence of "particular laws" and exceptions so effective in excluding colonial subjects, nominal "foreigners," and undesirables from the political nation. The republican imperial nation-state may have consistently been imagined and legitimated through a rhetoric of universal and abstract rights, but this universality was persistently conditioned by a discourse of legal identification and assumed qualities exclusive to a Europeanized and primarily white citizenry.[112]

Even if *colons* and their supporters assured metropolitans that Algerian integration would not mean an Islamicized electorate, this hardly settled the issue of Algerian representation in the Corps légisalatif. For *colons* eager to regain the rights they had enjoyed prior to the Bonapartist seizure of power, the prospect that the current government would countenance such a measure appeared unlikely. As Thomson surmised, were Algeria to receive deputies in the Corps législatif they would vehemently oppose the government's Nativist policies. Why, therefore, would the Second Empire freely invite new members to fuel the growing opposition movement taking shape in the national legislature?[113] If Algeria was to secure deputies in the metropole it was evident that this aspiration could come about only through the victory of the liberal-republican platform endorsed by the Bonapartists' political rivals. The liberalization of the metropole was, *colons* inferred, closely tied to the success of administrative and liberal reform in the colony, establishing the context for a trans-Mediterranean opposition movement oriented around common principles of civic participation, decentralization, and the rights of citizens. "Algeria will float on the wind, find itself year in and year out between different systems," opined one critic in 1868, "until the day when a freer France gives more liberty to the colony and consults it on the important question of colonization."[114] The journalist Paul Capdeveille summed up the situation more robustly the following year in his appeal to support the metropolitan opposition. "Our plight is . . . intimately linked to that of France," he avowed. "Its triumph and its defeat will have here their inevitable corollary. Its interests are identical to ours and cannot be separated."[115]

From *Algérie Française* to *La France Transméditerranéenne*

In the autumn of 1868, Jules Favre appeared before a crowd in Algiers to deliver a much-anticipated speech. Addressing his audience as fellow "citizens" to loud applause, Favre went on to outline his hopes for the future of the colony and the French nation. "I am grateful that the defense of our cause has been entrusted to me," he declared. "I say *our* cause because I don't know what is meant by the Algerian question. Algeria is France and to deny this is to close our eyes to the truth. . . . Between us there is a bond that exists between all men who support a common idea and [this bond] is now strengthened at this very moment by our personal contact."[116] A prominent lawyer known for carefully selecting his cases to promote the young republican cause in France, Favre had earned a reputation as both a political trailblazer and tough critic of the Bonapartist government by the late 1860s. As with his tactful use of legal precedent and political opportunity, he was insightful enough to recognize the utility that the Algerian question held for the opposition movement and diligently emphasized themes of citizenship and national unity central to republican ideology in his Algerian speeches. Yet he was hardly being insincere when stressing the collective nature of this struggle, for by the end of the 1860s the cause of Algeria had become a collective concern and aspiration.

Throughout the decade, *colon* critics had worked to tailor metropolitan ideas to the unique contours and problems of colonial society, placing the Algerian question within a larger framework of national debates over state power, liberalization, and citizenship. In 1858, Clément Duvernois had foreshadowed Favre's rousing speech given in Algiers with his assertion that "since the conquest, political life in Algeria has been marked by numerous vicissitudes corresponding more or less to the events that have taken place in the metropole. . . . Algeria is not a colony. Nobody has considered it such for a long time."[117] In many ways, Duvernois's political career exemplified the complementary nature of colonial and national politics. The son of a French emigrant, he had received a formal education at the lycée d'Alger before taking up a career in Algeria as a political journalist. Through travel and correspondence during the 1850s and early 1860s, Duvernois situated himself at the nexus of an emerging trans-Mediterranean political culture by cultivating ties to prominent metropolitan opinion leaders such as Auguste Nefftzer, editor of the popular daily *Le Temps*, and the newspaper magnate Émile de Girardin.[118] Settling in Paris, Duvernois contributed articles to *Le Temps* on a semiregular basis between 1862 and 1864. Nefftzer, an influential publicist allied with the liberal-republican camp in the capital, openly gave his endorsement to the *colon* cause, deeming it "a movement whose importance cannot be mistaken."[119] Armed with a major Parisian daily that reached a broad audience of educated, middle-class readers, Duvernois continued his attacks on the colonial regime unabated, apprising metropolitans of the issues central to Algerian colonization and urging a "new path" for French North Africa that would give a voice to the disenfranchised settler community.[120] In the coming years, *Le Temps* increasingly dedicated greater attention to the Algerian question, whether by reprinting excerpts from the Algerian press, publishing articles written by colonial polemicists, or drawing attention to republican activities in Algeria and the Corps législatif.[121]

By the mid-1860s, French politics was assuming a conspicuous trans-Mediterranean character, one shaped and elaborated through journalism, advocacy, and parliamentary debate. In their effort to build a broad opposition platform against Napoleon III's imperial regime, republicans exhibited a willingness to turn the Algerian question to their own benefit. Criticism of Napoleonic despotism, although a centerpiece of the opposition platform, always proved exceedingly difficult to substantiate in light of the government's alleged commitment to revolutionary ideals and universal manhood suffrage. Yet as Favre's defense of *colon* interests made clear, Algeria offered an alternative theater in which the hypocrisy and pretensions of the detested regime could be laid bare. In an address before the Corps législatif in 1861, Favre drew attention to the disenfranchised citizens currently inhabiting France's North African colony and accused the Second Empire of reneging on its supposed democratic principles. "The right to elect representatives belongs to all Frenchmen who reside on French territory," he declared, adding that he awaited the day when the Algerian colonists could "march under the same banner" as their metropolitan compatriots and enjoy the common institutions and rights guaranteed to all French citizens. "Algeria and the colonies are French," Favre proclaimed among a mixture of applause and hissing from the assembled deputies, "and I ask why they are placed beyond this common right."[122]

Favre's attempts to portray Algeria as a microcosm of Bonapartist tyranny drew praise from activists and publicists in the colony who blandished him as "the illustrious defender of all just causes" and the "most noted orator of our century." In an open letter addressed to Favre in 1868, *Akhbar* thanked him for his continual support and commitment to the universal cause of freedom. "A day will come—and it is not far off thanks to your constant efforts—when these ideas of justice and liberty that you have expressed with such noble language and warm honesty will find a common place in France," the journal's Parisian correspondent wrote. "On this day, neither the eloquence of a minister skillfully sidestepping the issues of debate nor the hostility of an incompetent majority will be capable of hindering the triumph of law over force and civilization over ignorance and barbarism."[123]

In the late 1850s, Favre's stringent defense of civilian government in the colony could have been considered exceptional. Yet within a decade his efforts had proved instrumental in giving a voice to *colons* and transforming their plight into a national cause taken up by a small but growing number of opposition deputies. "Algeria finally begins to be known and appreciated by the metropole and our courage is working to bring about what up until now we have only imagined," exclaimed one critic in 1868.[124] In light of the flagrant violations to the nation's democratic and revolutionary ideals perpetrated by the Bonapartists, opposition spokesmen insisted they were obliged to speak on behalf of their silenced compatriots, fashioning themselves defenders of "public opinion" and "unofficial representatives" of all Frenchmen suffering under the yoke of Napoleonic despotism.[125] "It is our principal argument, and we will not stop repeating it," Jules Simon stressed in 1870, "that our overseas cocitizens are, at this moment, deprived of their liberties."[126]

Speaking in the name of disenfranchised Frenchmen not only offered opponents a means of contesting the Second Empire's apparent commitment to democracy; it also assisted in constructing a political identity for the opposition and the young republican movement. Republicans maintained that their commitment to the *colons* was not motivated by personal interest but rather by a dedication to universal values of justice and democracy. It was not the Algerian cause that the deputies explicitly sought to defend, Ernest Picard claimed, "but the cause of rights and justice, which desires that all parts of France be represented in [the national parliament]."[127] In construing support for Algerian liberty as a matter of conscience and principle, republicans sought to fashion a political identity for themselves rooted in respect for public opinion and liberal practices contrary to Bonapartist tyranny. "You place force in the arbitrary while I put it in opinion and law," Favre remarked sharply when confronting Bonapartist supporters in 1866. "You place force in the dictator while I put it in the regime of law."[128] Such arguments naturally extended to support for representative government and the influence of public opinion on political decision making, with opponents using their status as "unofficial representatives" of the colonial citizenry to indicate the necessity of overall liberal reform in France.

Employing the issue of Algerian representation to attack the democratic shortcomings of the imperial regime entailed, however, defining Algeria as part of the national body rather than a mere colonial appendage and affirming that Algerian settlers belonged to a French community extending beyond continental Europe. As the liberal Léopold Le Hon explained to his fellow deputies in 1870, "Algeria has a right to be represented [before the nation] and it will only see itself as completely French the day that its deputies come to sit among us."[129] Republican opinion leaders readily concurred, envisaging a national community of citizens that encompassed France's North African periphery and settler population. "France has always wanted to attach itself to Algeria," Favre insisted, "and it has understood perfectly that these two earths separated only by a French lake should be united."[130] With the rise of the opposition movement in the Corps législatif during the 1860s, Algeria quickly became a debate on the French nation itself. Ferdinand Barrot was not mistaken when in 1863 he claimed, "The Algerian question is posed in daily polemics with an eminently national character."[131] If Bonapartist statesmen extolled the government's respect for national sovereignty and democratic politics, republican and liberal deputies saw fit to correct this misrepresentation by reconceptualizing the contours of the nation and using the plight of Algerian colonists to expose the contradictory claims and practices that buttressed an illegitimate Napoleonic state.

Efforts to portray Algeria as a symbol of Bonapartist despotism and hypocrisy encouraged opponents to associate their own demands for liberty at home directly with the colonial opposition, validating assertions that France and North Africa were, indeed, engaged in a common political struggle. The issues of French liberty and the Algerian question were portrayed as two sides of a national resistance movement against arbitrary rule and power. In professing his support for the liberalization of Algeria's general councils in 1869, Favre tellingly inscribed the issue within a larger national context with his assertion that free departmental elections would realize "that true liberty, which it is necessary to assure in Algeria as in France."[132] The next year he went further, maintaining, "Algeria has constantly protested and protests still against personal power, and in this it has followed the movement of France in its sentiments, thoughts, and aspirations. Its heart has beat with ours."[133] Like Favre, Jules Duval interpreted the Algerian resistance as nothing less than "a new episode in the struggle between centralization and liberty" that had characterized French politics since the Revolution.[134]

In the growing consensus taking shape between metropolitans and *colons*, French elites were urged to imagine the nation in geographic and conceptual terms compatible with a republican imperial nation-state. France was a community of citizens that extended beyond the territorial limits of the continental metropole. This claim effectively deterritorialized French nationality and reconfigured it within a broader framework of universal rights and emancipation consistent with republican principles yet equally adaptable to the vision of *Algérie Française*, a national territory built upon an ethnopolitical colonial order.[135] These contradictions were products of the modernity and modernizing ideology that political elites claimed to represent. Trans-Mediterranean France proposed a basis for a common identity and imagined community opposed to the injustice of the past that threatened "to smother the modern world."[136] The Bonapartist state reviled by metropolitans as a remnant of absolutism found its relevant counterpart in a colonial administration personifying the "despotic spirit" of the old Orient that modern society could neither assimilate nor tolerate. "Does it not seem logical, even indispensable, to refrain from importing the faults of old societies into Africa, to not found a colony in decadence?" Fonvielle asked pointedly when speculating on Algeria's future. "Can something truly great be created without the enthusiasm of liberty?"[137] More caustic, Favre did not hesitate to carry these allegations directly into the chambers of the Corps législatif, denouncing Nativism and the Arab Kingdom as an abomination. French contact with the Orient was not expected to preserve an atrophied Oriental society but rather "disrupt its mores, change its habits, and lead [the Arabs] in a completely opposite direction."[138] The Second Empire and its military allies had failed in this goal, leaving a dispirited France to "kneel before the remains of barbarism" as modern civilization "regressed."[139]

Writing to Jules Ferry during a trip to Algeria in 1862, his friend Marcel Roulleaux informed him that "the military makes a sad government. . . . [It] is not suited for the evolution of the Arabs, not because it carries a saber but because it knows nothing and is infatuated with its arbitrary power."[140] Roulleaux's appraisal of military incompetence appeared vindicated in the coming years as a series of natural disasters and epidemics in the mid-1860s provided the opposition with new ammunition for their attacks against the colonial administration and Arab Kingdom. Beginning in 1866, locust blights, droughts, and poor harvests severely affected grain and cereal cultivation throughout the colony, with the most extreme cases of crop failure reported in the southern Arab territories ravaged by the military during periods of intermittent rebellion. With the price of barley more than tripling in some regions, famine soon devastated a significant portion of the native population residing outside the civilian provinces. Virulent outbreaks of cholera only compounded the misery already generated by natural disasters, with more than 86,000 natives dying from disease in 1867 and some 120,000 starving to death by 1868.[141] Catholic spokesmen led by the Archbishop Lavigerie wasted little time in exaggerating accounts of native hardship. Resentful of military rule and the limitations placed on the North African missions, Lavigerie made appeals to international Catholic networks for the purposes of collecting aid and mobilizing support for a stronger Christian influence in the colony. In doing so, he shaped a particular view of the crisis that saw Muslims resorting to cannibalism and other deplorable acts of savagery. Although inaccurate, these efforts to "Africanize" Algeria and demonstrate the inadequacies of the military government had a strong influence on public perceptions. As rumors of Arab raids on European farms and cannibalism began circulating in the press, military officials found it difficult to soften the demoralizing blow delivered by natural disaster and rising mortality rates.[142]

With the civilian provinces inhabited by Europeans remaining relatively insulated from the "catastrophe," *colon* activists saw fit to place blame for the crisis squarely on the military. "The great misery afflicting the *indigènes* has clearly exposed the vices of their nature and organization while showing the exact measure of vitality in our young European populations," Émile Thuillier gloated in 1868.[143] Famine and diseases clearly demonstrated the errors of preserving an archaic and defunct Arab society. Had the Arab territories been placed under a civilian administration dedicated to assimilation and developing settled agricultural production among the nomadic tribes, this deplorable state of affairs would have been avoided. Yet the military regime had persistently shielded the natives from modernity, leaving them to wallow in misery. According to one callous journalist, the famine exemplified the ineffectiveness of military rule as Arabs now died of hunger en masse "on a rich soil capable of feeding ten million European inhabitants!"[144] "The Arab Offices reap what they have sown," Jules Duval declared triumphantly. "They have celebrated and sought to conserve a society in which they are sultans. They have praised and supported their docile instruments, the *indigène* sheikhs. Today this society is crumbling into dust, roiled by famine and sickness, and the seigneurs of the tent reign over cadavers!"[145]

As the death toll rose throughout 1867, the military was forced to request a two million franc credit from the imperial government to supply the population with grain. Obtaining these emergency funds meant, however, submitting the issue to a budgetary vote in the Corps législatif where it would be subject to the criticism of the opposition deputies and exploited for the sake of national politics. Yet with the extent of the crisis growing and no tenable solution in sight, the military had little choice if it intended to salvage its reputation and assuage doubts regarding the viability of its antiassimilationist policies. The disease and famine decimating Algeria's population not only reflected poorly on the military but also called into question France's civilizing mission in North Africa as reports of the crisis circulated internationally thanks in large part to the efforts of Lavergerie and his Catholic allies. How could France claim to be spreading the benefits of civilization, critics demanded, if it allowed its colonial subjects to die of starvation and resort to bestial acts of cannibalism? Alleviating the problem as quickly as possible was not only a matter of recouping the military's tarnished image; it was, ultimately, a question of rehabilitating France's national honor and identity as a modern power. As the newspaper *Progrès de L'Algérie* informed its readers in the autumn of 1868, the Algerian crisis represented a pressing national concern: "for France it is a matter of not having five hundred thousand or more cadavers on its conscience."[146]

When the session of the Corps législatif opened in 1868, the opposition deputies used the convocation as a forum for their grievances as expected. Favre led the attack, alluding to the relative stability of the civilian provinces in contrast to the territories governed directly by the Arab Offices. Echoing the accusations levied by *colons*, the inveterate republican once again insisted that he spoke in the name of Algerian public opinion. "It is their voices that cross the Mediterranean and penetrate this palace to warn you, to press upon you not to continue the current state of affairs that is the cause of ruin, that multiplies catastrophes, that has made possible the death of over one hundred thousand people," he declared.[147] Civilian institutions and an energetic policy of assimilation were the remedy to the problem in his opinion, and until the military regime gave up its vain hope of shielding a moribund society from the regenerative forces of modern progress and allowed law and freedom to prevail over authority and barbarism the future of the colony would continue to remain uncertain.

Taking the floor, Baron David, leading spokesman for the Nativists in Paris, refuted the points made by the opposition and reaffirmed the military's dedication to civilization and alleviating the present catastrophe. "If you had had a civilian regime in Algeria during the current crisis you would have seen what happened!" he retorted. A civilian government dominated by the racist settler minority would have been content to sit back and watch idly as natives perished from hunger and disease.[148] Military officials attempted to parcel out blame for the woeful situation, emphasizing the constant political feuding incited by opponents that undermined the colonial administration's good intentions. General Lacretelle did not hide his disgust with the attempts to exploit the crisis for political ends, snapping: "The heart is saddened to see parties invariably pursue their hostile system in the presence of such extreme calamities!"[149] Yet while officials made appeals to patriotism, humanity, and patience in their defense of the military's Nativist policy, it was evident that by 1868 the toll of the catastrophe and the barbed criticisms of opponents had severely injured the prestige of the administration and placed the future of the Arab Kingdom in doubt.

With the elections of 1869 signaling a victory for the liberal-republican opposition and the Algerian cause attracting greater attention in the Corps législatif and metropolitan press, *colon* polemicists expressed a growing sense of optimism for their cause. "The apprehensions, fears, and black clouds" that loomed over Algeria were on the verge of "vanishing like a bad dream," Paul Capdevielle sanguinely assured.[150] The changing political atmosphere of the late 1860s and the promise of liberal reform made by the emperor were becoming evident in the declarations of prominent military officials. It was revealing when Baron David appeared before the Corps législatif in 1870 and "candidly and loyally" admitted to past errors in judgment. "I sincerely believed that only misfortune, oppression, and disaster would result from the contact of the two races," he confessed. "I have now come to recognize that the situation of the *indigènes* in the civilian territories is better when compared with those in the military territories." In his revised opinion, it was time to advance "a new system" based upon liberal principles and common rights.[151] Speaking before the Oranais general council, the commander of the province, General Deligny, similarly espoused the changing perspectives in the military administration, remarking that in his eyes "a radical regime change would be better than a return to an organization already condemned."[152]

With prominent military officials and government spokesmen admitting to the shortcomings and errors of the Nativist policy, it was evident that by 1870 the Arab Kingdom envisioned by Napoleon III was on the verge of becoming yet another failed colonial policy. Colonial polemicists and political opponents could both claim an active role in bringing about its destruction. Protesting against the "Arabophilic" designs of the Nativists and the emperor during the 1860s, *colons* and metropolitans had successfully managed to form a common front against the Second Empire in the final years of the regime. Placing the Algerian question in the larger context of national political concerns over liberty, sovereignty, and representational government, the grievances of *colons* and the liberal-republican opposition had come together to discredit the nationalist and modernizing identity of the Bonapartist state. The confluence of colonial and metropolitan interests and the formation of a common opposition front not only contributed to the waning popularity of the imperial government in France but also emboldened nationalists to press their case for Algerian integration, cementing a relationship between France and its North African frontier that would be nurtured and reinforced by republican statesmen in the wake of the Second Empire. Noting the emergence of a shared oppositional language and identity spanning metropole and colony in 1869, the journal *Akhbar* was correct to assert that an "uninterrupted current of people and affairs . . . [and] a constant exchange of ideas and sentiments" existed between France and Algeria. "Are there really two countries?" the newspaper asked. "Are they not rather different members of the same body, receiving life and pulsating movements from the same heart?"[153]

This assertion of a common Franco-Algerian people was indicative of the ways in which the politics of modernity had transformed colonial opposition under the Second Empire. In the Algerian question, republican opponents found a means of challenging Bonapartist modernity and exposing the illiberal facets of the imperial state. The colonists themselves had their part to play in this denouement. Colonial journalists and activists were instrumental in cultivating a brand of Algerian republicanism that successfully applied republican modernization to key issues focused on colonization and civilian government. In making their case for national inclusion and settler rights, *colons* persistently emphasized the strong link between colonization and modernization that lay at the heart of their program. They espoused the language of republican modernization and, in the process, furnished the basis for an idea of *la France transméditerranéenne* read in terms of a trans-Mediterranean republic, that single "body" animated by the same heart and sentiments. The "common struggle" remarked upon by metropolitans and colonists throughout the decade acquired saliency in the struggle for modern society itself. Condemning the Oriental barbarism and despotism that impeded Algerian modernity, opponents committed themselves to a modernizing ideology with both national and colonial implications. In arguing that colonists and metropolitans were, in fact, part of a single body, it was ultimately a shared vision of republican modernity that bound these communities together and provided the ideological content for imagining a French imperial nation-state as the embodiment of republican equality and fraternity.

Conclusion

The Second Empire and the Politics of Modernity

Observing the displays of French art at the Exposition Universelle in 1867, the art critic Théophile Thoré noted an impression of transition and change as he walked through the gallery hall examining the various exhibition pieces. "We are between two worlds," he wrote, "between a world that is ending and a world that is beginning."[1] Thoré's remark could have extended to the entirety of the Second Empire and two decades of Bonapartist rule. By the late 1860s, locomotives were facilitating travel and transportation throughout the country, telegraph lines now expedited the flow of communication, and mechanized production was turning out consumer goods at an exceptional pace; in almost every sector of national life under the Second Empire, what was understood as modernity was impinging upon the familiar world to which the French had long been accustomed. And yet despite these technological innovations and feelings of growing expectation, the years of the Second Empire remained nonetheless situated at the crossroads of modernity, a period trapped "between two worlds," as Thoré stated.

A republican journalist who spent the first decade of imperial rule in Brussels as a political exile, Thoré made an incisive critic, and his depiction of the Second Empire as a threshold between an old, expiring world and a modern world on the cusp of realization was revealing. Although expressing nothing but contempt for Louis Napoleon and his followers, opponents of the imperial regime could hardly dismiss the influence that Bonapartist industrial and economic policies had on the country, even if this recognition was given begrudgingly. Yet they remained unwilling to recognize the detested regime as the embodiment of the new and modern type of society hailed by imperial spokesmen. For republicans, modernity would only come with the founding of a durable republican government and the liberty and national sovereignty that it promised. If the modernizing initiative spearheaded by the Second Empire signaled France's entrance into the modern era, democratic opponents nonetheless insisted that the Bonapartists remained ill-equipped to bring this change to fruition and lead the nation to its proper destiny. As the positivist critic Hippolyte Stupuy claimed in 1870, under Napoleon III France marched along "a path almost complete" and resembled "a nation nearly free."[2] In the view of self-proclaimed democrats, the years of the Second Empire may have initiated a process toward a more modern type of world and society, but it could never fully represent or embody the modernity associated with France's democratic-revolutionary heritage.

In the atmosphere of the 1860s, criticism of imperial policies increasingly came to share the opinion that the imperial government was unprepared to deliver the supposed social and political institutions that a modern society required. Everywhere one looked, there existed a state of arrested development and unfilled expectations. Taking in the sight of Paris in the late 1850s, Charles Monselet contrasted the images of a beautified and modern capital touted by government officials with the actuality of demolition yards and debris-littered streets that fast-paced urbanization had produced. "It is no longer the old Paris, but it is not yet the new Paris either," he remarked soberly. "We are placed between memory and promise."[3] The Algerian notable August Vital would express the exact same sentiment in 1864 when assessing the government's colonial policies, writing: "We are, as they say in the military, an ass poised between two saddles, between the old organization that has had its time and that is no longer taken seriously by anyone and a new organization that is anticipated and promised but has not yet materialized."[4] Straddling two worlds, the government of Napoleon III stood accused of adopting palliatives and promoting half measures, seeking to please everyone while, in reality, pleasing nobody. "Half measures are dangerous," warned the author and republican critic Émile Zola when reflecting on the Second Empire in 1868. "They kill governments."[5] Such became the epitaph of the imperial regime.

This conception of the Second Empire as a liminal period poised between a dying past and an innovative future has remained one of the enduring myths of republican history and identity in France. Ostensibly modern in its social and economic orientation yet hostile to the representative and free institutions that a modern society demanded, the Second Empire became characterized as a hybrid of old and new forms that ultimately proved incompatible with the modernity of a democratic and republican France. This reading of the imperial period has not only served to cast the liberal-republican opposition as the champion of a modernity that would come into existence with the founding of a new republican government—the Third Republic—in 1870; it would equally provide the basis for a narrative and ideological discourse central to French republicanism over the next century, enshrining republicanism at the heart of a nominally "modern" French society defined within the context of a liberal and democratic state.

This mythology overlooks the fact that perceptions of the Second Empire as a threshold period between tradition and modernity constituted a strategy employed by political rivals set on denying the modern identity coveted by the imperial regime and rejecting the master narrative of Bonapartist modernity. Concepts of modern time and society were not necessarily reflections of a world in the throes of industrial and social transformation. They proved a vital means of rationalizing conflicting democratic and imperial aspirations of the nineteenth century. As French social elites came to terms with mass democracy and the contradictory values of colonialism, the idiom of modernity furnished a new discourse with both inclusive and exclusionary implications that was capable of organizing social hierarchies and power relationships along new lines. This style of representation encouraged a shift toward an identity regime grounded in conceptions of time and temporality that not only broke with established tenets of classical "bourgeois" liberalism but also sketched the contours of a novel social order in which modernity became the legitimacy for power and domination in a country ostensibly committed to equality and pluralism.

The Second Empire may have become the victim of its own politics, but the politics of modernity it inaugurated persisted into the coming decades. No matter how despicable the Bonapartist clan may have been for hot-blooded republicans loath to recognize the illegitimate Empire, it was difficult to refute that an entire generation of republicans received its political education under the rule of a Bonaparte. The Third Republic had the example of Napoleon III at its disposal and the tepid formalism of the Second Republic was not to be repeated. The civic festivities, demonstrations of patriotism, and international exhibitions that would be staged over the course of the Third Republic sought to transform the government into an iconic regime with a memory and deep roots in the country.[6] Republicans employed national celebrations and public spectacle to attach citizens to a democratic society that symbolically embodied the sovereignty of people and nation. These representations of society, whether described in terms of "nation," "people," or even "civilization," remained intimately tied to the modernizing language and discourses elaborated since the French Revolution. Modernity symbolized an end toward which French political ideologies projected themselves, and while elites increasingly employed the idioms of *nation*, *nationalité*, and *civilisation* in their speeches and writing, they were never divorced from an ideological vision of a modern France.

For both the Bonapartist leadership and their opponents, modernity constituted a means to political action and legitimacy. To this end, the binaries reinforcing a new elite sense of self at midcentury were only essential as long as they were politically useful. If marginalized republicans had been eager to paint the mass of rural voters as vestiges of the old world in the 1860s, this opinion was subject to revision once in power. As a chronic suspicion of the urban working classes and the threat they posed to the social order grew in the late nineteenth century, French political elites were compelled to rely on the support of the rural peasantry in sustaining a conservative democracy. The conventional image of the rural "savage" proved incongruous with elite objectives, and it was unsurprising that in the wake of the Paris Commune leading republicans endeavored to rehabilitate the image of the peasant and associate the countryside directly with the interests and progressive values of the "new social classes" (*nouvelles couches sociales*). The transformation—both real and imagined—of *la France profonde* under the Third Republic revealed the extent to which modernity was a construction shaped and reshaped by elites as the cultural representation of the archaic peasant was replaced with that of the modern citizen.[7]

Modernity furnished political elites with the language and symbols capable of translating political form into a real and living idea that communicated a vision of a unified community associated across space and time. To represent and give embodiment to this abstraction required, however, complimentary actions and "modernizing" gestures. The Bonapartist state proved especially adept at conjuring the modern through economic campaigns, building projects, and industrial exhibitions, yet the extent of its modernizing impulses extended far beyond these theaters. Modernization was a process broadly understood as the colonization of primitive spaces by modernity, and the colonial implications of this outlook illustrated the dynamic relations between metropole and colony that emerged during the period. While the years of republican rule in the late nineteenth and early twentieth centuries were instrumental in forging a mass colonial consciousness and transforming the *mission civilisatrice* into a national crusade, this does not negate the fact that the civilizing mission acquired a saliency during the years of Bonapartist rule that mutually structured and reinforced ongoing processes of nation and empire building. Nation and Empire, France and North Africa became central to the articulation of the new social imaginary that modernity anticipated. That a renewed French colonialism corresponded to the emergence of the postrevolutionary cult of the modern ensured that the "Algerian question" would occupy a central place in the debates over the meaning and import of modern society and French identity. This relationship between metropole and colony was strengthened over the years as the politics of modernity resonated through a society that was increasingly coming to see itself in national and imperial terms. The growing social and political networks encouraged by colonial migration and advancements in transport and communication entailed that French modernity was a trans-Mediterranean product.

Like the magic lantern shows that fascinated nineteenth-century spectators, visions of modernity were projected onto a North African world that to most Europeans appeared foreign and remote. These images diminished the distance between the Orient and their world, not only in terms of space and time but also in terms of the forms of identification it encouraged. In a political culture that valorized the modern, Algeria furnished a horizon on which claims to modernity were validated and contested, often with a furious violence. Through the cause of Algerian "regeneration," Napoleon III conveyed his government's modernizing ambitions and rationalized a nationality policy fraught with contradictions. For the Armée d'Afrique and Arab Offices, colonial modernization provided the legitimacy for military rule and authority once the "pacification" of Algeria had been achieved. Colonists hostile to the "Arabophilic" tendencies of the emperor and military equally pressed modernity into service and drew upon the new language of republican modernization and emancipation to fashion their own image of a French Algeria linked culturally and politically to Europe. Settler activism struggled to ensure that colonization would not simply be a metropolitan project monopolized by elites in Paris. In order to make this arrangement viable, however, the diverse settler population needed to obtain equality with its counterparts across the Mediterranean, demanding it in the name of civil justice and a common modern time and worldview shared with civilized men. It was this very same bond that offered the justification for ostracizing and dominating the primitive other in their midst. Modernity, as the French anthropologist Bruno Latour reminds us, is not merely a "break" in the regular passage of time, but "a combat in which there are victor and vanquished."[8]

When the Second Empire collapsed in 1870 due to a mix of domestic discontent and poorly executed foreign policy maneuvers, the link between the French metropole and Algeria would be strengthened by the new republican regime built on the ruins of the Bonapartist state.

Meeting with Algerian delegates in Tours in October 1870, the provisional republican government showed its willingness to meet *colon* demands, declaring an end to military rule in the colony and granting Algeria representation before the National Assembly. In the coming years, discriminatory legislation against the Muslim population—the infamous Code de l'indigénat—and recourse to harsh extralegal punitive measures would ensure the hegemony and privileged dominance of a small colonial elite composed of European settlers.[9] The retention of authoritarian administrative practices and desires on the part of the colonial government to maintain the boundaries between the native and European populations exposed dour misgivings on the part of administrators and politicians about fulfilling the goals of the nation's civilizing mission and elevating a backward Muslim people to the level of French citizens. If statesmen hailed a modern and republican France as a departure from the authoritarian and obstreperous policies of Bonapartist authoritarianism, Algeria persistently stood as a glaring reminder of the contradictions and paradoxes that French modernity embodied in practice.

Historians have criticized the colonial republic for reneging on its emancipatory promise. Yet it is worth considering to what extent this outcome was a direct product of the logic and ideology that underpinned the brand of republicanism born from the Second Empire. Young republicans always professed adherence to the spirit and heritage of 1789, even as they grappled with the legacy of factionalism and instability the French Revolution left. Looking back to their revolutionary forbearers, republicans were obligated to keep the spirit and memory of the Revolution alive for ideological reasons while seeking to bring an end to the era of revolutionary politics at home. Preserving the revolutionary élan and unifying the community around a shared national mission to modernize the primitive necessitated a colonial French republic. It was in the colonial domain that the modernizing work of the French Revolution could be continually actualized and symbolically conveyed. The colonies were a place for the channeling of these revolutionary and modernizing impulses in a country that had grown weary of radical policies and the instability they invited. Until the very end of the empire, French colonialism remained premised on the promise of a modernity that could never, in reality, be fulfilled. The social imaginary of a modern France continually required "primitive" objects to act upon and others against which the possibilities of the modern could be projected and brought into sharp relief, for a modern people could only be assured of its own modernity through recourse to a project that sustained and nurtured that identity.

Today, as the attributes of European modernity secure themselves firmly beyond the continent, Europe finds its historic claim to a universal modernizing project compromised. The proliferation of nation-states across former colonial empires, the industrialization of world economies and the establishment of global capitalist markets have relegated Europe to a partner in a larger vision of modernity shared with non-Western societies. Modernity, once seen as a particularly European or Occidental phenomenon, has, in the twenty-first century, acquired its own culture, logic, and attributes that can no longer be considered purely Western or European in character.[10] The advent of a postcolonial and globalized modernity entails the end of the European civilizing mission and with it the end of a particular idea of European selfhood and history. With Algerian independence in 1962, *la France transméditerranéenne* as it was understood ceased to exist, provoking a "postcolonial" France to redefine essential categories of nation and people and construct a new idea of Frenchness that, in many ways, is an ongoing project.[11]

NOTES

INTRODUCTION

1. Quoted in Fritzsche, *Stranded in the Present*, 127.
2. Taine, *Essais de critique et d'histoire*, 380. Translations are the author's unless otherwise noted.
3. Taine, *Notes on England*, 126.
4. Saint-Simon and Enfantin, *Œuvres de Saint-Simon et d'Enfantin*, 32:47.
5. Fournel, *Paris nouveau*, 77.
6. Monselet, *Les Ruines de Paris*, 2:43.
7. Baudelaire, "The Painter of Modern Life," *My Heart Laid Bare*, 37.
8. Littré, *Dictionnaire de la langue française*, 4:3932.
9. For example, see *La Presse*, 23 November 1853.
10. René Doumic, "La Manie de la modernité," *Revue des Deux Mondes* (1898), 148:925.
11. Roger Friedland and Deirdre Boden, "NowHere: An Introduction to Space, Time and Modernity," in *NowHere*, 2.
12. Paz, *Alternating Currents*, 161–62.
13. Cooper, *Colonialism in Question*, 113. See also Moore, *Industrialization and Labor*; Kerr et al., *Industrialism and Industrial Man*; Berman, *All That Is Solid Melts into Air*.
14. Gluck, "The End of Elsewhere," 677–79.
15. Camaroff, "Interview with John and Jean Camaroff," 3–4.
16. Chakrabarty, *Provincializing Europe*; Eisenstadt, "Multiple Modernities"; Rofel, *Other Modernities*.
17. Sagan, *Citizens and Cannibals*; Fehér, *The French Revolution*; Hunt, *Politics, Culture and Class*.
18. Quoted in Huet, *The Culture of Disaster*, 104.
19. Rabinow, *French Modern*; Berman, *All That Is Solid Melts into Air*; Hahn, *Scenes of Parisian Modernity*; Clark, *The Painting of Modern Life*; Forth and Accampo, *Confronting Modernity*.

20. Lynn Hunt has addressed this for the revolutionary period in *Politics, Culture and Class*.

21. Nicolet, *L'Idée républicaine en France*, 146. Among the most prominent examples of this historiography are: Halévy, *La Fin des notables*; Chastener, *L'Enfance de la Troisième République*; Goguel, *La Politique des partis*; Eugen Weber, "The Nineteenth-Century Fallout," in Best, *The Permanent Revolution*, 165.

22. Clark, "After 1848."

23. Hazareesingh, *From Subject to Citizen*; Nord, *The Republican Moment*; Truesdell, *Spectacular Politics*; Huard, *La Naissance du parti politique*.

24. See Charles-Robert Ageron, "Gambetta et la reprise de l'expansion coloniale," in *De l'Algérie "française"*, 39–68; Conklin, *A Mission to Civilize*; Girardet, *L'Idée coloniale en France*.

25. Bancel, Blanchard, and Vergès, *La République coloniale*, 98.

26. Frederick Cooper and Ann Laura Stoler, "Between Metropole and Colony: Rethinking a Research Agenda," in Cooper and Stoler, *Tensions of Empire*, 1–57; Horne, *A Social Laboratory for Modern France*; Wright, *The Politics of Design*; Dhombres and Dhombres, *Naissance d'un pouvoir*, 103–5.

27. Pierre Serna, "Every Revolution Is a War of Independence," in Desan, Hunt, and Nelson, *The French Revolution*, 172; Kumar, "Nation-States as Empires"; Melzer, *Colonizer or Colonized*; Trumbull, *An Empire of Facts*; Lejeune, *Les Sociétés de géographie*.

28. Said, *Culture and Imperialism*; Mackenzie, *Imperialism and Popular Culture*; Hall and Rose, *At Home with the Empire*; Chafer and Sackur, *Promoting the Colonial Idea*.

29. See Belmessous, *Assimilation and Empire*; Miller and Burger, *Nationalizing Empires*.

30. See Wilder, *The French Imperial Nation-State*.

31. For works signaling a change in this outlook, see Abi-Mershed, *Apostles of Modernity*; Sandrine Lemaire, Pascal Blanchard, and Nicolas Bancel, "Jalons d'une culture coloniale sous le Second Empire, 1851–1870," in Lemaire, Blanchard, and Bancel, *Culture coloniale en France*, 96–109; Pitts, *A Turn to Empire*.

32. Coller, *Arab France*, 116–17, 214–15.

33. Amselle, *Affirmative Exclusion*, 119.

34. Garrigus, *Before Haiti*; Dubois, *A Colony of Citizens*; Larcher, *L'autre citoyen*; Schloss, *Sweet Liberty*; Spieler, *Empire and Underworld*.

35. Coller, *Arab France*, 12–13, 218.

36. Sessions, *By Sword and Plow*, 324–25.

37. Shepard, *The Invention of Decolonization*, 19–55; Silverstein, *Algeria in France*, 52–67.

38. Hain, *A la nation, sur Alger*, 56.

39. See Marsh and Firth, *France's Lost Empires*.

40. Todd, "A French Imperial Meridian."
41. Jean-Robert Henry, "Introduction," in Hargreaves and Heffernan, *French and Algerian Identities*, 4.
42. Kale, *Legitimism*, 7.
43. Laclau, "Death and Resurrection," 316.
44. Brubaker and Cooper, "Beyond 'Identity,'" 20.
45. I borrow this term from Bauman and Gingrich, *Grammars of Identity/Alterity*.
46. This definition of community is derived from Clifford, *Routes*, 245.

1. IMAGINING THE MODERN COMMUNITY
1. Miravals, *Causeries parisiennes*, 149, 101.
2. Duruy, *Notes et souvenirs*, 1:204.
3. Renan, *The Future of Science*, 38.
4. Charles Baudelaire, "Exposition universelle, 1855," in *Art in Paris*, 126.
5. See Berman, *All That Is Solid Melts into Air*; Clark, *The Painting of Modern Life*; Harvey, *The Condition of Postmodernity*, 201–80.
6. As Jacques Le Goff has noted, temporal consciousness is not naturally given or implicit in and of itself. It is a construction dependent on a certain understanding of time that relies on an opposition between past and present. See *Histoire et mémoire*, 25.
7. Seigel, *Modernity and Bourgeois Life*, 5–6.
8. Saint-Simon and Enfantin, *Œuvres de Saint-Simon et d'Enfantin*, 33:28.
9. Shaw, *Time and the French Revolution*; Perovic, *The Calendar in Revolutionary France*, 3–16; François Furet, "The Tyranny of Revolutionary Memory," in Fort, *Fictions of the French Revolution*, 152–57; Marisa Linton, "Ideas of the Future in the French Revolution," in Crook, Doyle, and Forrest, *Enlightenment and Revolution*, 154–57; Koselleck, *Future's Past*.
10. Fritzsche, *Stranded in the Present*, 89–95.
11. Seigel, *Modernity and Bourgeois Life*, 15.
12. Rimbaud, "Farewell," in *A Season in Hell*, 89.
13. For Marx's interpretation of French society and politics at midcentury, see Marx, *Class Struggles in France 1848–1850* and the more analytical *The Eighteenth Brumaire*.
14. Maza, *The Myth of the French Bourgeoisie*, 3–4, 162–66.
15. Seigel, *Bohemian Paris*, 89–96.
16. Garrioch, *The Formation of the Parisian Bourgeoisie*, 266.
17. Michelet, *Le Peuple*, 132.
18. Quoted in Alexander, *Bonapartism and Revolutionary Tradition*, 3.
19. Rosanvallon, *Le Moment Guizot*, 99–114; Maza, *The Myth of the French Bourgeoisie*, 147–50.
20. Guizot, *Histoire parlementaire de France*, 1: xxi.

21. On French liberal ideology, see Rosanvallon, *Le Moment Guizot*, 99–114; Maza, *The Myth of the French Bourgeoisie*, 147–50; Pitt, "The Irrational Liberalism of Hippolyte Taine," 1040–41; Hulliung, *Citizens and Citoyens*, 47–50; Kahan, *Liberalism in Nineteenth-Century Europe*, 35–50.

22. AN 87 AP 15, "Discours prononcé par M. De Rémusat," 14 March 1834.

23. Quoted in Rosanvallon, *Le Moment Guizot*, 120.

24. Maza, *The Myth of the French Bourgeoisie*, 158–60.

25. Jennings, *French Anti-Slavery*, 24–27; Andrews, "Breaking the Ties That Bind," 497–504.

26. Kwon, "When Parisian Liberals Spoke for Haiti," 317–41; Kielstra, *The Politics of Slave Trade Suppression*.

27. Jennings, *French Anti-Slavery*, 146–49.

28. Schloss, "The February 1831 Slave Uprising."

29. Jennifer Pitts, "Republicanism, Liberalism and Empire in Postrevolutionary France," in Muthu, *Empire and Modern Political Thought*, 264–91; Pitts, *A Turn to Empire*.

30. Barrault, *Occident et Orient*, 223.

31. Sessions, *By Sword and Plow*, 84–87, 142–48.

32. Quoted in Shepard, *The Invention of Decolonization*, 20.

33. *La Presse*, 7 June 1838.

34. Eugène Lerminier, "De la conservation d'Alger," *Revue des Deux Mondes* (Paris, 1836), 6:611.

35. Sessions, *By Sword and Plow*, 184–85.

36. Enfantin, *Colonisation de l'Algérie*, 33.

37. Clancy-Smith, *Rebel and Saint*, 71.

38. Bory-de-Saint-Vincent, *Note sur la commission exploratrice*, 13.

39. Saint-Simon and Enfantin, *Œuvres de Saint-Simon et d'Enfantin*, 32:92.

40. Brower, *A Desert Named Peace*, 4.

41. Quoted in Popkin, *Press, Revolution, and Social Identities*, 2.

42. *Journal des Débats*, 10 July 1832.

43. See Chevalier, *Classes laborieuses et classes dangereuses*; Price, *People and Politics in France*, 278; Bullard, *Exile to Paradise*, 95.

44. Sessions, *By Sword and Plow*, 82–128.

45. Enfantin, *Colonisation de l'Algérie*, 457.

46. Harsin, *Barricades*, 273.

47. Quoted in Seigel, *Bohemian Paris*, 107.

48. Louis Blanc, "De l'abolition de l'esclavage aux colonies," *La Revue du Progrès* 1, no. 2 (1840): 16. See also: Jennings, *French Anti-Slavery*; Schloss, *Sweet Liberty*, 26–44; Pitts, *A Turn to Empire*, 165–239.

49. Schloss, *Sweet Liberty*, 227–28; Andrews, "Breaking the Ties," 524–26; Larcher, *L'Autre citoyen*, 70–95.

50. *Le National*, 24 February 1840.

51. Jouffroy d'Eschavannes, "Chronique d'Orient," *Revue de l'Orient* (Paris, 1848), 4:37.

52. Pierre Boyer, "La Vie politique et les élections à Alger," in Emerit, *La Révolution de 1848 en Algérie*, 43–46.

53. Société Algérienne, *Aux citoyens représentants de peuple à l'Assemblé Nationale*.

54. *Akhbar*, 6 April 1848.

55. Solms and Bassano, *Pétition à l'Assemblée Nationale*, 8.

56. Brossard, *A M. Louis Blanc*, 5.

57. Société Algérienne, *Aux citoyens représentants de peuple à l'Assemblé Nationale*.

58. Boyer, "La vie politique," 54–55.

59. *Akhbar*, 9 April 1848.

60. *Le Moniteur Universel*, 20 September 1848.

61. Harsin, *Barricades*, 294–95; Marx, *The Eighteenth Brumaire*, 22–26; Gould, *Insurgent Identities*, 47–53.

62. Lecouturier, *Paris incompatible*, 73; Bastiat, *Ce qu'on voit*, 39.

63. *Akhbar*, 12 June 1848.

64. *Le Moniteur Universel*, 20 September 1848. Also see Salinas, "Colonies without Colonists," 104–40.

65. Heffernan, "The Parisian Poor and the Colonization of Algeria"; Pilbeam, *The Saint Simonians*, 154–62.

66. Quoted in Mélonio, *Naissance et affirmation*, 211.

67. Quoted in Clark, *The Absolute Bourgeois*, 99. See also Clark, *The Painting of Modern Life*, 50–60; Miller, *The Bon Marché*, 3–4.

68. Rosanvallon, *Le Moment Guizot*, 347–49.

69. Quoted in Hanson, *Manet and the Modern Tradition*, 13.

70. Hugo, *Napoleon the Little*, 301.

71. Ballanche, "Essai sur les institutions sociales," *Œuvres*, 2:84.

72. Flaubert, *A Sentimental Education*, 325.

73. Kolakowski, *Modernity on Endless Trial*, 35.

74. Collins, *The Government and the Newspaper*, 91; Price, *A Social History*, 160, 215.

75. Flaubert, *Flaubert in Egypt*, 161.

76. See Fabian, *Time and the Other*, 23–30.

77. Thierry-Mieg, *Six semaines en Afrique*, 6, 102, 169.

78. Fritzsche, *Stranded in the Present*, 95.

79. *Bulletins de la Société d'Anthropologie de Paris* (Paris, 1861), 2:284.

80. Bullard, *Exile to Paradise*, 12–20.

81. Staum, *Labeling People*, 13–14.

82. Buchez, *Introduction à la science*, 139.

83. Matsuda, *The Memory of the Modern*, 12; Furet, "History and 'Savages,'" 4.

84. See Rogers, "Good to Think." For theories on identity formation in general, see Laclau, "Death and Resurrection," 316; Adamovsky, "Euro-orientalism," 591–92.

85. Pagden, "The Savage Critic," 33; Elias, *The Civilizing Process*, 38–40; Lucien Febvre, "Civilization: Evolution of a Word and a Group of Ideas," in Burke, *A New Kind of History*, 224–34; Muthu, "Conquest, Commerce and Cosmopolitanism in Enlightenment Political Thought," *Empire and Modern Political Thought*, 204–31.

86. Elias, *The Civilizing Process*, 50; Febvre, "Civilization," 224–34, 238.

87. Constant, *De la religion*, 2:6.

88. Alletz, *Génie du dix-neuvième siècle*, xxxvi.

89. Elias, *The Civilizing Process*, 50; Coller, *Arab France*, 29–32; Woolf, "French Civilization and Ethnicity in the Napoleonic Empire."

90. Guizot, *Histoire parlementaire de France*, 1:cxi.

91. Popkin, *Press, Revolution and Social Identities*, 70; Rosanvallon, *Le Moment Guizot*, 347–48.

92. Wilder, *The French Imperial Nation-State*, 124–29.

93. Edouard Hommaire de Hell, "Coup d'œil sur la condition de la classes noire dans les colonies françaises des Antilles," *Revue de l'Orient* (Paris, 1858), 8:254.

94. Edouard Hommaire de Hell, "Coup d'œil sur la condition de la classe noire," *Revue de l'Orient* (1859), 9:44.

95. Dubois, "The Price of Liberty," 385–86.

96. Drescher, *Capitalism and Antislavery*, 53–54.

97. Schmidt, *Abolitionnistes de l'esclavage*, 115–16

98. Lara, *La Liberté assassinée*.

99. Staum, *Labeling People*, 86–87.

100. Hommaire de Hell, "Coup d'œil," *Revue de l'Orient* (1859), 9:44.

101. Fabian, *Time and the Other*, 30–31.

102. Gérardo, *The Observations of Savage Peoples*, 63.

103. Senhaux, *La France et l'Algérie*, 175–76.

104. Robb, *The Discovery of France*, 17; Lehning, *Peasant and French*, 3–4.

105. Taine, *Carnets du voyage*, 58, 77.

106. Ténot, *Le Suffrage universel*, 13.

107. A. Molot, "L'Émigration européenne et le peuplement de l'Algérie," *Courrier de l'Algérie*, 25 January 1865.

108. See Belmessous, *Assimilation and Empire*.

109. Étourneau, *L'Algérie faisant appel*, 136.

110. Bullard, *Exile to Paradise*, 29.

111. Flaubert, *Madame Bovary*, 70.

112. *La Vie moderne*, 23 November 1859.

113. William Max Nelson, "Colonizing France: Revolutionary Regeneration and the First French Empire," in Desan, Hunt, and Nelson, *The French Revolution*, 73–85; Hodson, "Colonizing the *Patrie*."

114. See Abi-Mershed, *Apostles of Modernity*, 25.

115. Horner, *Voyage à la côte orientale*, 4.

116. *Annales du Sénat* (1861), 2:107.

117. Thomson, *Barbary and Enlightenment*; Bourguet et al., *L'Invention scientifique de la Mediterranée*.

118. Gallois, *A History of Violence*, 81–121; Brower, *A Desert Named Peace*, 22–23.

119. Morin, *Civilisation*, 71.

120. O'Brien, *Narratives of Enlightenment*, 156–60.

121. Guys, *Études sur les mœurs des Arabes*, 3.

122. Gautier, *Caprices et zigzags*, 309.

123. Monselet, *Les Ruines de Paris*, 2:91.

124. Quoted in Mélonio, *Naissance et affirmation*, 196.

125. Bullard, *Exile to Paradise*, esp. 94–96.

126. Lecouturier, *Paris incompatible*, 65.

127. Blackburn, *Normandy Picturesque*, 7.

128. Taine, *Carnets du voyage*, 43–44.

129. Duvivier, *L'Empire en province*, 16.

130. Maza, *The Myth of the French Bourgeoisie*, 6–7.

2. STATE MODERNIZATION

1. Taine, *Carnets du voyage*, 111–12.

2. Nicolet, *L'Idée républicaine en France*, 14.

3. See Pinkney, *Decisive Years in France*.

4. Landes, *The Unbound Prometheus*, 79, 236; Asselain, *Histoire économique*, 106–7.

5. Eckalbar, "The Saint-Simonians in Industry"; Price, *People and Politics in France*, 38–39.

6. Bonaparte, Address to the Senate and Corps législatif, 16 February 1857, *Discours*, 348.

7. Olivier Pétré-Grenouilleau, "Colonial Trade and Economic Development in France, Seventeenth to the Twentieth Centuries," in Emmer, Pétré-Grenouilleau, and Roitman, *A Deus ex Machina Revisited*, 254–55.

8. *Akhbar*, 23 December 1852.

9. Mayer, *The Recollections of Alexis de Tocqueville*, 69.

10. Christiansen, *Paris Babylon*, 96.

11. Taine, *Notes on England*, 164.

12. Guizot, *Du gouvernement de la France*, 152.

13. See Ménager, *Les Napoléon du peuple*; Hazareesingh, *The Legend of Napoleon*.

14. Quoted in Price, *The French Second Empire*, 15.

15. Price, *The French Second Empire*, 16–17; Bresler, *Napoleon III*, 222.

16. Napoleon III once famously declared: "What a government I have! The Empress is a legitimist, Napoleon-Jérôme a republican, Morny an Orléanist and I myself a socialist. Persigny is the only Bonapartist, but he is crazy."

17. Bonaparte, "Ideas of Napoleonism," *Political and Historical Works*, 1:349.
18. Bonaparte, *Des idées Napoléoniennes*, 11.
19. Quoted in Carmona, *Morny*, 141.
20. Williams, *Gaslights and Shadow*, 49.
21. Quoted in Bresler, *Napoleon III*, 112.
22. AN 44 AP 30, "Les Élections de 1848 d'après les correspodance inédites du Prince Louis-Napoléon et de M. de Persigny," letter dated 18 March 1848.
23. Quoted in Plessis, *De la fête imperial*, 75.
24. Quoted in Frédéric Salmon, "La 'Gauche avancée' en 1849 et en 1870," in Hamon, *Les Républicains sous le Second Empire*, 98.
25. Hazareesingh, *The Saint-Napoleon*; Lehning, *The Melodramatic Thread*, 41–42; Truesdell, *Spectacular Politics*, 54–56.
26. Bonaparte, "L'Idée Napoléonienne," *Political and Historical Works*, 2: 269.
27. Garrigues, *Les Hommes providentiels*; Hazareesingh, "A Common Sentiment," 308; Choisel, *Bonapartisme et Gaullisme*; Bluche, *Le Bonapartisme*; Rothney, *Bonapartism after Sedan*, 22.
28. *Le Temps*, 11 July 1862.
29. Bluche, *Le Bonapartisme*, 336.
30. AN 116 AP 1, "Rapport au président de la république," 1851.
31. AN 246 AP 17, "Rapport à l'Empereur sur la situation de l'instruction publique," September 1853.
32. Troismonts, *Napoléon III et la nationalité française*, 19.
33. Duc de Persigny, "Discours sur le rétablissement de l'Empire," in Delaroa, *Le Duc de Persigny et les doctrines*, 87, 99.
34. Bonaparte, "Analysis of the Sugar Question," *Political and Historical Works*, 2:36.
35. Bonaparte, "Ideas of Napoleonism," *Political and Historical Works*, 1:265.
36. AN 45 AP 1, "Réponse de l'Empereur à l'adresse du Corps législatif," 1861.
37. Bonaparte, "Ideas of Napoleonism," *Political and Historical Works*, 1:253.
38. Bonaparte, Lunch Speech in Rennes, 20 August 1858, *Discours*, 384.
39. Bonaparte, Letter to Prince Jérôme Bonaparte, 30 October 1858, *Discours*, 386.
40. Bonaparte, Address to the Senate and Corps législatif, 16 February 1857, *Discours*, 348.
41. AN 45 AP 1, "Discours prononcé par sa Majesté l'Empereur à l'ouverture de la session législative de 1858," 18 January 1858.
42. Vimercati, *Histoire de l'Italie*, xiii.
43. Bonaparte, Speech in Bordeaux, 9 October 1852, *Discours*, 243.
44. AN 45 AP 19, "Discours au concours régional de Roanne," May 1864.
45. Weber, *Peasants into Frenchmen*, 120–24.
46. Pinkney, *Napoleon III and the Rebuilding of Paris*, 23.
47. Thierry-Mieg, *Six semaines en Afrique*, 148.
48. Urbain, *L'Algérie française*, 35–36.

49. Saint-Simon, "De la physiologie appliqée à l'amélioration des institutions sociales," *Œuvres*, 5:177.

50. Saint-Simon, "Lettres d'un habitant de Genève à ses contemporains," in *Œuvres*, 1:43.

51. Saint-Simon, "L'Industrie," in *Œuvres*, 1:68–69.

52. Weill, "Les Saint-Simoniens"; Franck Yonnet, "La Structuration de l'économie et de la banque sous le Second Empire," in Coilly and Régnier, *Le Siècle des Saint-Simoniens*, 125–27; Eckalbar, "The Saint-Simonians in Industry," 83–96; Emerit, *Les Saint-Simoniens en Algérie*, 252–65. In general, see Pilbeam, *The Saint-Simonians*.

53. Antoine Picon, "L'Utopie-spectacle d'Enfantin," in Coilly and Régmoer, *Le Siècle des Saint-Simoniens*, 68–77.

54. Saint-Simon, *Œuvres de Saint-Simon*, 33:98.

55. Mélonio, *Naissance et affirmation*, 45.

56. Saint-Simon, *Œuvres de Saint-Simon*, 33:183.

57. Saint-Simon, *Œuvres de Saint-Simon*, 33:104.

58. Enfantin, *Colonisation de l'Algérie*, 192–93, 198.

59. Saint-Simon, *Œuvres de Saint-Simon*, 32:73.

60. Saint-Simon, *Œuvres de Saint-Simon*, 33:38.

61. Marcel Émerit, "Les Sources des idées sociales et coloniales de Napoléon III," *Revue d'Alger* (1945): 7–11.

62. Rey-Goldzeiguer, *Le Royaume Arabe*, 123.

63. Bonaparte, "Ideas of Napoleonism," in *Political and Historical Works*, 1:251.

64. Delaroa, *Le Duc de Persigny e les doctrines*, 163.

65. AN 44 AP 16, "Caisse des travaux publics," (1868).

66. Duc de Persigny, "Discours sur la politique extérieur de l'Empire," in Delaroa, *Le Duc de Persigny e les doctrines*, 101.

67. AN 44 AP 16, "Caisse des travaux publics," 1868.

68. Bonaparte, Speech at the Palais de Justice, 11 November 1849 *Discours*, 69.

69. See AN F1a 66, Circulaire du Ministère de l'agriculture du commerce et des travaux publics, 19 and 26 July 1856 (dams), Circulaire du Ministère de l'agriculture du commerce et des travaux publics, 14 June 1852 and 29 April 1854 (mines); AN F1a 68, Circulaire du Ministère de l'intérieur, 4 August 1852 (agriculture) and 14 March 1856 (population).

70. AN F1a 68, Circulaire du Ministère de l'intérieur, 4 March 1851.

71. AN F1a 49, "Circulaire du Ministère de l'agriculture du commerce et des travaux publics," 12 April 1867.

72. Plessis, *De la fête impériale*, 85–86.

73. Chevalier, *Éxposition Universelle de Londres*, 12.

74. Charles Lavollée, "Les Chemins des fer français en 1866 et leur influence sur la prospérité du pays," *Revue des Deux Mondes* (1866), 61:13.

75. Emerit, *Les Saint-Simoniens en Algérie*, 177–79; Plessis, *De la fête impériale*, 113–15.
76. AN F70 252, "Exposé de la situation de l'Empire," February 1861, 20.
77. Plessis, *De la fête impériale*, 115–16.
78. Yonnet, "La Structuration de l'économie," 125–34; Eckalbar, "The Saint-Simonians in Industry," 89–90; Cameron, *France and the Economic Development of Europe*, 147.
79. Hugonnet, *Français et arabes en Algérie*, 273.
80. Prochaska, *Making Algeria French*, 80–81.
81. Michel Levallois, "Essai de typologie des orientalistes Saint-Simoniens," in Levallois and Moussa, eds., *L'Orientalisme des Saint-Simoniens*, 102; Emerit, *Les Saint-Simoniens en Algérie*, 190–92.
82. Gautier, *Voyage en Algérie*, 107.
83. Quoted in Truesdell, *Spectacular Politics*, 87.
84. Bonaparte, Speech in Rouen, 11 August 1849 and Banquet Speech in the Jardin-d'hivre, 16 August 1850, *Discours*, 55, 90.
85. Bonaparte, "Ideas of Napoleonism," *Political and Historical Works*, 1:253.
86. *Le Constitutionnel*, 14 November 1865.
87. Miravals, *Causeries parisiennes*, 17.
88. Truesdell, *Spectacular Politics*, 120.
89. Horne, *A Social Laboratory for Modern France*, 56.
90. Sandrine Lemaire, Pascal Blanchard, and Nicolas Bancel, "Jalons d'une culture colonial sous le Second Empire (1851–1870)," in Lemaire, Blanchard, and Bancel, *Culture colonial en France*, 99–105; Çelik, *Displaying the Orient*, 2–3. For more general studies on colonial exhibitions in France and visual culture, see Evans and Sackur, *Empire and Culture*; Morton, *Hybrid Modernities*.
91. Duval, *L'Algérie et les colonies françaises*, 327–28.
92. There have been numerous works dealing with the urban projects of the imperial regime, inviting a plethora of interpretations as to the objectives and intentions of Napoleon III and the Second Empire. For major works, see Pinkney, *Napoleon III and the Rebuilding of Paris*; Jordan, *Transforming Paris*; Kirkland, *Paris Reborn*. For the costs associated with the rebuilding of Paris, see Pinkney, "Money and Politics in the Rebuilding of Paris, 1860–1870."
93. Claire Hancock, "Capitale du Plaisir: The Remaking of Imperial Paris," in Driver and Gilbert, *Imperial Cities*, 68–69.
94. Arbousse-Bastide, *A propos de tout quelque chose*, 15.
95. Charles Lovolée, "Statistique industrielle de Paris," *Revue des Deux Mondes* (1865), 55:1033.
96. Benjamin, *The Writer of Modern Life*; Clark, *The Painting of Modern Life*.
97. Fournel, *Paris nouveau*, 26.
98. Taine, *Carnets du voyage*, 111.

99. Fromentin, *Between Sea and Sahara*, 11.
100. Thierry-Mieg, *Six semaines en Afrique*, 41.
101. Augustin Marquand, "Alger et ses environs," *Akhbar*, 14 February 1869.
102. Oulebsir, *Les Usages du patrimoine*, 129–34.
103. *Papiers et Correspondance*, 1:381.
104. "La Fête de l'Empereur," *Moniteur de l'Algérie*, 17 August 1864.
105. Christiansen, *Paris Babylon*, 96–101; Marcel Roncayolo, "Logiques urbaines,"
    in Agulhon, *Histoire de la France urbaine*, 4:10.
106. Jordan, "Baron Haussmann and Modern Paris."
107. Christiansen, *Paris Babylon*, 96.
108. Charles Tilly and Lynn H. Lees, "The People of June, 1848," in Price, *Revolution
    and Reaction*, 176–77; Harvey, *Consciousness and the Urban Experience*, 167.
109. Fournel, *Paris nouveau*, 12.
110. Oulebsir, *Les Usages du patrimoine*, 10–11; Çelik, *Urban Forms*, 29–38.
111. Fromentin, *Between Sea and Sahara*, 12.
112. Gautier, *Voyage en Algérie*, 69.
113. Fromentin, "Fragments d'un journal de voyage," in *Œuvres*, 965.
114. Feydeau, *Alger*, 157.
115. Blackburn, *Normandy Picturesque*, 193.
116. Quoted in Price, *People and Politics in France*, 196.
117. See Truesdell, *Spectacular Politics*.
118. Hauterive, *Napoléon III et le Prince Napoléon*, 59.
119. See Guionnet, *L'Apprentissage*, 10–28; Hazareesingh, *From Subject to Citizen*,
    4–7.

3. CIVILIZING AND NATIONALIZING

1. Warmington, *Qu'est-ce que le Bonapartisme?* 84, 32.
2. See Birnbaum, *The Idea of France*.
3. Giddens, *The Consequences of Modernity*, 57.
4. Bonaparte, Address to the Senate, 9 October 1852, *Discours*, 245.
5. Bonaparte, Address to the Senate and Corps Législatif, 14 February 1853, *Discours*, 261.
6. Duc de Persigny, "Discours sur l'établissement de la liberté par l'Empire," in
    Delaroa, *Le Duc de Persigny e les doctrines*, 188.
7. AN 44 AP 16, "Proclamation de l'Empire, voyage du Midi," 1852.
8. *Annales du Sénat* (1862), 1:223.
9. See Lewis Namier's classic study, *1848*.
10. Zamoyski, *Holy Madness*, 329–30.
11. *Conquête et oppression*, 45.
12. For works examining the different manifestations of nationalism under the
    Second Empire, see Truesdell, *Spectacular Politics*, 3–5; Huard, *La Naissance du*

parti politique, 112; Hazareesingh, "A Common Sentiment," 310; Glikman, "Vœu populaire et bien public," 87–91.

13. Bonaparte, Address to the Army, 12 May 1859, *Discours*, 396.
14. Quoted in Clark, *The Absolute Bourgeois*, 11.
15. Guionnet, *L'Apprentissage*, 310.
16. Namier, *1848*, 199; Zamoyski, *Holy Madness*, 329–81.
17. Duvivier, *L'Empire en province*, 11.
18. Bonaparte, *Recueil historique*, 17.
19. Troismonts, *Napoléon III et la nationalité française*, 24.
20. Boinvilliers, *Nationalité*, 54.
21. *Les Temps*, 10 May 1863.
22. *Conquête et oppression*, 45–46.
23. Bell. *The Cult of the Nation*, 35–37, 199.
24. Voltaire, "Patrie," in Woolf, *Voltaire's Philosophical Dictionary*, 132.
25. For examples of postrevolutionary cosmopolitanism, see Girardin, *Conquête et Nationalité*, 46; *La Rive gauche*, 24 June 1866; Émile Littré, "Politique," *La Philosophie positive* (1867), 1:127–32.
26. Mélonio, *Naissance et affirmation*, 16–17.
27. Quoted in Birnbaum, *The Idea of France*, 57.
28. Hulliung, *Citizens and Citoyens*, 42–45; Rosanvallon, *La Démocratie inachevée*, 20–22; Schnapper, *Community of Citizens*, 3–4, 12; Pierre Guillaume, "L'Accession à la nationalité: le grand débat, 1882–1932," in Colas, Emeri, and Zylberberg, *Citoyenneté et nationalité*, 137–48.
29. See articles 7 and 8 of the Napoleonic Code.
30. Woolf, "French Civilization and Ethnicity," 105–7; Hazareesingh, *Political Traditions in Modern France*, 131.
31. Quoted in Darriulat, *Les Patriotes*, 228.
32. Cappot, *Les Nationalités*, 42.
33. Michelet, *The People*, 164.
34. Wahnich, *L'Impossible citoyen*.
35. Mondonico-Torri, "Aux origines du Code," 35. See also Rapport, *Nationality and Citizenship*.
36. Sahlins, *Unnaturally French*, 302–12.
37. Hulliung, *Citizens and Citoyens*, 49–50.
38. Taine, *Essais de critique et d'histoire*, 278.
39. Anderson, *Imagined Communities*, 193–95.
40. Gerson, *The Pride of Place*.
41. Taguieff, "Les Métamorphoses idéologique du racisme et la crise de l'anti-racisme," in *Face au Racisme*, 2:135–36.
42. Stuart Hall, "The Multi-Cultural Question," in Hesse, *Un/settled Multicultralisms*, 216.

43. Duc de Persigny, "Discours sur le rétablissement de l'Empire," in Delaroa, *Le Duc de Persigny e les doctrines*, 89.

44. Duc de Persigny, "Circulaire sur les élections de 1852," in Delaroa, *Le Duc de Persigny e les doctrines*, 39.

45. AN 45 AP 1, "Discours du Prince Louis-Napoléon," 29 March 1852.

46. *La Patrie*, 7 October 1864.

47. AN 44 AP 16, "Proclamation de l'Empire, Voyage du Midi," (1852).

48. AN 45 AP 11, "Circulair du 5 Octobre 1860."

49. Persigny, "Discours sur le rétablissement de l'Empire," 89–90.

50. AN 45 AP 19, "Discours au concour régional de Roanne," May 1864; Duc de Persigny, "Circulaire du comité de la rue Montmartre en vue des élections générales à l'Assemblée législative," in Delaroa *Le Duc de Persigny e les doctrines*, 34.

51. AN 44 AP 30, "Les Élections de 1848 d'après les correspondances inédites du Prince Louis-Napoléon et de M. de Persigny," 18 March 1848.

52. Bonaparte, Speech Inaugurating the Tours-Angers Railroad, 29 July 1849, *Discours*, 50.

53. Morny, "Quelques réflexions sur la politique actuelle," *Revue des Deux Mondes* (Paris, 1848), 21:151.

54. Gaboriaux, *La République en quête de citoyens*, 177.

55. Duc de Persigny, "Discours sur les principes politiques de l'Empire," in Delaroa, *Le Duc de Persigny e les doctrines*, 166.

56. Bonaparte, "The Revision of the Constitution," *Political and Historical Works*, 2:295.

57. Persigny, "Discours sur l'établissement de la liberté par l'Empire," 187.

58. Persigny, "Discours sur les principes politiques de l'Empire," 163.

59. Persigny, "Discours sur les principes politiques de l'Empire," 183–87. See also Morny, "Quelques réflexions sur la politique actuelle," *Revue des Deux Mondes* (1848), 21:160.

60. Persigny, "Discours sur l'établissement de la liberté par l'Empire," 187.

61. McMahon, *Enemies of the Enlightenment*, 141–45; Birnbaum, *The Idea of France*, 71–100. In general, see Hobsbawm, *Nations and Nationalism since 1780*, 40–44.

62. Bonaparte, "Projets d'articles," *Papiers et correspondance de la famille impériale*, 1:373.

63. Gary Wilder has noted this dualism as one of the many antinomies that formed the French imperial nation-state under the Third Republic. See *The French Imperial Nation-State*, 15–17.

64. *La Presse*, 7 May 1852.

65. Henry Chauvin, "Les Chefs arabes à Paris," *Revue de l'Orient* (Paris, 1852), 11:371.

66. Coller, *Arab France*, 116–17, 214–15; Shreier, "Napoléon's Long Shadow," 80–85.

67. "Proclamation de l'Empereur au people arabe," *Moniteur de l'Algérie*, 6 May 1865.

68. Quoted in Spillmann, *Napoléon III*, 54.

69. Oulebsir, *Les Usages du patrimoine*, 18–19.

70. Daudet, *Adventures prodigieuse de Tartarin*, 86.

71. Thierry-Mieg, *Six semaines en Afrique*, 406.

72. Prochaska, *Making Algeria French*, 65–71.

73. AN F19 10923, "Ministère de l'instruction publique et des cultes au Ministère de la guerre," 23 June 1851; "Directoire du Consistoire au Ministère de l'instruction publique et des cultes," 11 June 1851.

74. Abbé Bargès, "Notice sur la Cathédrale d'Alger en 1839," *Journal Asiatique* (Paris, 1841), 2:183.

75. Sellam, *La France et ses musulmans*, 144–46.

76. Alexis de Tocqueville, "Rapport fait à la Chambre des députés au nom de la commission chargée d'examiner le projet de loi relatif aux crédits extraordinaires demandés pour l'Algérie," in *Œuvres complètes*, 9:437.

77. *Conseil général de la province d'Oran*, vi.

78. Duvernois, *L'Algérie*, 146.

79. Thierry-Mieg, *Six semaines en Afrique*, 16.

80. Lacroix, *L'Algérie et la lettre*, 43.

81. Feydeau, *Alger*, 62.

82. Perkins, *Quaids, Captains and Colons*, 18–19; Frémeaux, *Les Bureaux arabes*, 22; François Leblanc de Prébois, "Gouvernement civil et Gouvernement militaire," *Akhbar*, 9 June 1864.

83. Emerit, *Les Saint-Simoniens en Algérie*, 54–56.

84. Enfantin, *Colonisation de l'Algérie*, 480.

85. Enfantin, *Colonisation de l'Algérie*, 35–36.

86. *Annales du Senat* (1863), 2:208.

87. *Annales du Senat* (1861), 2:108.

88. Frémeaux, *La France et l'Islam*, 37–48; Coller, *Arab France*, 31–32; Amselle, *Affirmative Exclusion*, 32–36.

89. Quoted in Sullivan, *Thomas-Robert Bugeaud*, 100.

90. Frémeaux, *Les Bureaux arabes*, 36–37; Charles-Robert Ageron, "La Politique Kabyle sous le Second Empire," in *De l'Algérie "française"*, 71–95.

91. Brett, "Legislating for Inequality," 442–43.

92. Lacretelle, *De l'Algérie*, 26, 28.

93. Hugonnet, *Souvenirs d'un chef*, 5, 10.

94. Voisin [Urbain], *L'Algérie pour les algériens*, 154.

95. Quoted in Levallois, "Introduction," *Les Écrits autobiographiques*, 13.

96. Quoted in Levallois, *Ismaÿl Urbain*, 187.

97. Urbain, "Notes autobiographiques," in Levallois, *Les Écrits autobiographiques*, 34, 35.

98. Urbain, "Notice chronologique," in Levallois, *Les Écrits autobiographiques*, 102.

99. Henri de Saint-Simon, "Lettres d'un habitant de Genève à ses contemporains," in Œuvres, 1:43.

100. See Émile Temime, "Rêves méditerranéens et présence française en Orient au milieu du XIXe siècle," in Levallois and Moussa, L'Orientalisme des Saint-Simoniens, 19–22; Michel Levallois and Philippe Régnier, "De l'Égypte à l'Algérie," in Coilly and Régnier, Le Siècle des Saint-Simoniens du Nouveau Christianisme au Canal de Suez, 108–12.

101. Barrault, Occident et Orient, 250.

102. Saint-Simon, Œuvres, 32: 14.

103. Temime, "Rêves méditerranéens," in L'Orientalisme des Saint-Simoniens, 21.

104. Saint-Simon, Œuvres, 33:113.

105. Barrault, Occident et Orient, 251.

106. Saint-Simon, Œuvres, 32:7.

107. Barrault, Occident et Orient, 254.

108. Enfantin, Colonisation de l'Algérie, 148.

109. Saint-Simon, Œuvres, 32:7.

110. Quoted in Levallois, Ismaÿl Urbain, 349.

111. Voisin [Urbain], L'Algérie pour les algériens, 10–11.

112. Urbain, "Des Arabes," Journal des Débats, 19 December 1837.

113. Voisin [Urbain], L'Algérie pour les algériens, 125–26.

114. Voisin [Urbain], L'Algérie pour les algériens, 15.

115. Voisin [Urbain], L'Algérie pour les algériens, 10.

116. Lacroix, L'Algérie et la lettre, 7.

117. Lacroix, L'Algérie et la lettre, 73.

118. Annales du Sénat (1868), 15:43.

119. Hugonnet, Souvenirs d'un chef, 44.

120. Lacretelle, De l'Algérie, 76.

121. Lacretelle, De l'Algérie, 50–51.

122. Urbain, "Des Arabes."

123. Turin, Affrontements culturels, 256, 280; Giedji, L'Enseignement indigène, 62; Abi-Mershed, Apostles of Modernity, 147–50; Frémeaux, Les Bureaux arabes, 22.

124. Annales du Sénat (1861), 2:107.

125. Voisin [Urbain], L'Algérie pour les algériens, 69, 15.

126. Voisin [Urbain], L'Algérie pour les algériens, 10.

127. Amselle, Affirmative Exclusion, 69; Abi-Mershed has also assessed the artificial designations made between colonial "association" and "assimilation," arguing that these two policies often coexisted and reinforced another. See Apostles of Modernity, 5.

128. Voisin [Urbain], L'Algérie pour les algériens, 9–12.

129. Lacroix, L'Algérie et la lettre, 43, 71.

130. Urbain, L'Algérie française, 72.

131. Abi-Mershed, *Apostles of Modernity*, 190–200.
132. "Discours de M. le général Yusuf," *Moniteur de l'Algérie*, 7 January 1864.
133. Quoted in Emerit, *Les Saint-Simoniens en Algérie*, 261.
134. Emerit, *Les Saint-Simoniens en Algérie*, 264–65; Levallois, *Ismaÿl Urbain*, 613; Oulebsir, *Les Usages du patrimoine*, 115; Rey-Goldzeiguer, *Le Royaume Arabe*, 127–28.
135. AN 234 AP 4, "Lettre de Sa Majesté l'Empereur," 6 February 1863.
136. AN 45 AP 1, anonymous news clipping, 6 May 1865.
137. Christelow, *Muslim Law Courts*, 134–37; Spillmann, *Napoléon III*, 99–100.
138. Urbain, *L'Algérie française*, 6.
139. Urbain, *L'Algérie française*, 46.
140. Quoted in Emerit, *Les Saint-Simoniens en Algérie*, 265.
141. Levallois, *Ismaÿl Urbain*, 621–23.
142. MacMahon, *Mémoires*, 303.
143. Quoted in Spillmann, *Napoléon III*, 58.
144. Voisin [Urbain], *L'Algérie pour les algériens*, 153.
145. Nouschi, *Correspondance du Docteur A. Vital*, 145.
146. Brett, "Legislating for Inequality," 454–56; Levallois, "Essai de typologie des orientalistes Saint-Simoniens," in Levallois and Moussa, *L'Orientalisme des Saint-Simoniens*, 108.
147. Urbain, *L'Algérie française*, 3.
148. Blévis, "Les Avatars," 575–79; Smith, "Citizenship in the Colony," 43–44.
149. *Annales du Sénat* (1862), 1:231.
150. Voisin [Urbain], *Algérie pour les algériens*, 15.
151. Persigny, "Discours sur le rétablissement de l'Empire," 99.
152. *Annales du Sénat* (1868), 15:62.
153. Bonaparte, Address to the Senate at Corps Législatif, 8 February 1859, *Discours*, 389–90.

4. THE CRUCIBLE OF MODERN SOCIETY

1. Bonaparte, Speech in Marseille, 26 September 1852, *Discours*, 239.
2. *Annales du Sénat* (1862), 1:230.
3. For the Second Empire's efforts at fostering good relations between the state and more liberal-oriented clerics, see Boudon, *Paris capitale*, 200–202, 347–50.
4. Broers, *Europe under Napoleon*, 81–86.
5. Bonaparte, Address to the Senate and Corps Législatif, 19 January 1858, *Discours*, 369.
6. Nouschi, *Correspondance du Docteur A. Vital*, 144.
7. See Hazareesingh, "A Common Sentiment," 308; Bierman, *Napoleon III*.
8. Veuillot, *L'Illusion libérale*, 57.

9. Reprinted in "Abd-el-Kader," *La Presse*, 11 January 1852.

10. Curtis, *Educating the Faithful*, 175.

11. Horvath-Peterson, *Victor Duruy*, 28–34; Anderson, *Education in France*, 15–19; Burrows, "Mission Civilisatrice," 120.

12. Mélonio, *Naissance et affirmation*, 204–5.

13. Weber, *Peasants into Frenchmen*, 303–39; Lehning, *Peasant and French*, 133–53.

14. Duruy, *Notes et souvenirs*, 1:226.

15. AN F70 253, "Exposé de la situation de l'Empire présenté au Sénat et au Corps législatif," January 1863, 76–77.

16. Duruy, *Notes et souvenirs*, 1:57, 223.

17. Wilson, *The Victorians*, 283.

18. Frémeaux, *Les Bureaux arabes*, 225.

19. Duruy, *Notes et souvenirs*, 1:56.

20. *Bulletin Officiel de l'Algérie et des colonies*, 31 August 1858.

21. Turin, *Affrontements culturels*, 25; Fanny Colonna, "Educating Conformity in French Colonial Algeria," in Cooper and Stoler, *Tensions of Empire*, 350; Lehning, *Peasant and French*, 3–4.

22. AN 246 AP 17, "Rapport à l'Empereur sur la situation de l'instruction publique," September 1853; Anderson, *Education in France*, 229.

23. Gallagher, *The Students of Paris*, 105.

24. Émile de Laveleye, "L'Instruction du peuple au XIXe siècle," *Revue des Deux Mondes* (1866), 62:993.

25. Coppa, *Pope Pius IX*, 47.

26. Moody, *Church and Society*, 37–38; Coppa, *Pope Pius IX*, 97–116.

27. Quoted in Williams, *Gaslights and Shadows*, 21.

28. Quoted in Anderson, *Education in France*, 114.

29. AN F17 9327, "Rapport sur la situation de l'instruction primaire dans le département du Jura," 1858–59.

30. Moody, "The French Catholic Press"; Williams, *Gaslights and Shadow*, 75.

31. Weisz, *The Emergence of Modern Universities*, 30; Horvath-Peterson, *Victor Duruy*, 37–38.

32. Moody, *Church and Society*, 139; Price, *The French Second Empire*, 198, 272–76.

33. AN 246 AP 17, "Rapport à l'Empereur sur la situation de l'instruction publiques," September 1853.

34. Quoted in Weisz, *The Emergence of Modern Universities*, 34.

35. AN 246 AP 17, "Rapport à l'Empereur sur la situation de l'instruction publiques," September 1853.

36. Quoted in Robert Fox, "Science, the University and the State in Nineteenth-Century France," in Geison, *Professions and the French State*, 87.

37. Quoted in Anderson, *Education in France*, 229.

38. Quoted in Weisz, *The Emergence of Modern Universities*, 79.

39. Maurian, *La Politique ecclésiastique*, 175; Case, *French Opinion*, 115–16; Boudon, *Paris capitale*, 155–59.

40. Price, *The French Second Empire*, 114.

41. *Le Temps*, 2 May 1861.

42. *Le Temps*, 23 April 1863.

43. Clancy-Smith, *Rebel and Saint*, 72–76, 92–97, 257; Frémeaux, *Les Bureaux arabes*, 114–22, 198; for works on Abd al-Qādir, see Danziger, *Abd al-Quadir*; Bouyerdene, *Abd el-Kader*.

44. *Annales du Sénat* (1865), 3:172.

45. Andrieux, "Le prolétariat et les indigènes," *Courrier de l'Algérie*, 4 May 1862.

46. Nouschi, *Correspondance du Docteur A. Vital*, 107.

47. Frémeaux, *Les Bureaux arabes*, 192–93; Giedji, *L'Enseignement indigène*, 40–42.

48. Quoted in Turin, *Affrontements culturels*, 119.

49. Geudj, *L'Enseignement indigène*, 52–57; Heggoy, "Education in French Algeria," 183.

50. Quoted in Frémeaux, *Les Bureaux arabes*, 203.

51. Alexis de Tocqueville, "Rapport fait à la chambre des députés au nom de la commission chargée d'examiner le projet de loi relatif aux crédits extraordinaires demandés pour l'Algérie," in Tocqueville, *Œuvres complètes*, 9:437.

52. Voisin [Urbain], *L'Algérie pour les algériens*, 40.

53. Turin, *Affrontements culturels*, 164.

54. *Bulletins de la Société d'Anthropologie de Paris* (1860), 1:298.

55. Urbain, *L'Algérie française*, 42, 62.

56. Fourmestraux, *Les Idées Napoléoniennes*, 16.

57. Lacretelle, *De l'Algérie*, 25.

58. Turin, *Affrontements culturels*, 181, 198. For an overview of the Bureaux Arabes in native education, see Frémeaux, *Les Bureaux arabes*, 191–208.

59. Giedji, *L'Enseignement indigène*, 59–62; Frémaux, *Les Bureaux arabes*, 198–99, 203–4.

60. Giedji, *L'Enseignement indigène*, 64; Emerit, *Les Saint-Simoniens en Algérie*, 294–95.

61. Quoted in Turin, *Affrontements culturels*, 279.

62. Quoted in Levallois, *Ismaÿl Urbain*, 352.

63. Abi-Mershed, *Apostles of Modernity*, 147–50; Frémeaux, *Les Bureaux arabes*, 223.

64. Turin, *Affontements culturels*, 256, 280.

65. Giedji, *L'Enseignement indigène*, 62.

66. Poujoulat, *Voyage en Algérie*, 96.

67. Arbousse-Bastide, *A propos de tout quelque chose*, 61.

68. Horner, *Voyage à la côte orientale*, 13.

69. Quoted in Spillmann, *Napoléon III*, 103.

70. *Le Moniteur Universel*, 5 July 1850.

71. Spillmann, *Napoléon III*, 103; Rey-Goldzeiguer, *Le Royaume Arabe*, 96–97.
72. Urbain, "Notes autobiographiques," in Levallois, *Les Écrits autobiographiques*, 50.
73. Nouschi, *Correspondance du Docteur A. Vital*, 274.
74. Émile Thullier, "Instruction primarie," *Courrier de l'Algérie*, 13 February 1868.
75. Duvernois, *L'Algérie*, 216.
76. *L'Echo d'Oran*, 7 January 1868.
77. Quoted in Abi-Mershed, *Apostles of Modernity*, 109.
78. Quoted in Turin, *Affrontements culturels*, 195.
79. Duvernois, *La Liberté de discussion*, 19–20.
80. Duvernois, "Les Réformes en Tunisie," *Revue de l'Orient* (1858), 7:83.
81. Duvernois, "L'Enseignement public en Algérie," *Revue de l'Orient* (1858), 8:187.
82. Lorcin, *Imperial Identities*, 33–34.
83. Verne, *De Bône à Hammam-Meskhoutine*, 111.
84. Fonvielle, *L'Empereur en Algérie*, 22.
85. Fonvielle, *L'Empereur en Algérie*, 21, 22.
86. Fonvielle, *L'Empereur en Algérie*, 22.
87. Duruy, *Notes et souvenirs*, 1:29.
88. Duvernois, "L'Enseignement public en Algérie," 186.
89. Duvernois, *L'Algérie*, 227.
90. Duvernois, "L'Enseignement public en Algérie," 185.
91. Ballue, *La Question algérienne*, 49.
92. Viel-Castel, *Mémoires*, 2:192.
93. Quoted in Price, *The French Second Empire*, 343.
94. Duruy, *Notes et souvenirs*, 1:29, 329.
95. Duruy, *Notes et souvenirs*, 1:197.
96. Horvath-Peterson, *Victor Duruy*, 71.
97. Schweitzer, *The Quest for the Historical Jesus*, 164–66.
98. Warman, *Ernest Renan*, 80–81.
99. Duruy, *Notes et souvenirs*, 1:194, 378; Nord, *The Republican Moment*, 34.
100. AN F17 4396, "Lettre du vice-recteur au Ministère de l'Instruction Publique," 2 April 1862.
101. AN F17 4396, "Lettre du vice-recteur au Ministère de l'Instruction Publique," 5 April 1862.
102. AN F17 4396, "Lettre du vice-recteur au Ministère de l'Instruction Publique," 14 March 1862, and "Lettre du Préfet de Police au Ministère de l'Instruction Publique," 31 March 1862.
103. Quinet, *Lettres d'exile*, 2:181.
104. *Congrès international des étudiants*, 450.
105. Quoted in Dammanget, "Introduction," Lafargue, *Le Droit à presses*, 14.
106. Dallas, *At the Heart of a Tiger*, 38–39.

107. Da Costa, *La Commune vécue*, 3:361.
108. Longuet, "La Génération nouvelle," *La Rive gauche*, 5 November 1865.
109. Longuet, "La Génération nouvelle."
110. AN 45 AP 18, "Cabinet de Préfet du police au Ministère d'État," January 1866.
111. Longuet, "La Génération nouvelle."
112. Quoted in Derfler, *Paul Lafargue*, 24.
113. Spitzer, *The Revolutionary Theories*, 60.
114. See Hutton, *The Cult of the Revolutionary Tradition*, 39–46; Bernstein, *Auguste Blanqui*, 258–67.
115. Charles Longuet, "La Tradition des écoles," *Les Écoles de France*, 31 January 1864.
116. Gallagher, *The Students of Paris*, 105.
117. *La Rive gauche*, 24 June 1866.
118. AN F17 4398, "Supplément au Journal des étudiants," 16 April 1867.
119. Spitzer, *The Revolutionary Theories*, 54; Derfler, *Paul Lafargue*, 26.
120. *Le Travail*, 2 March 1862.
121. *Le Constitutionnel*, 14 November 1865.
122. A. Rogeard, "Critique de l'idée de gouvernement," *La Rive gauche*, 5 November 1865.
123. AN F17 4398, "Supplément au journal des étudiants," 16 April 1867.
124. Gustave Tridon, "La Force," in *Œuvres diverses*, 114.
125. *La Rive gauche*, 5 November 1865.
126. *La Rive gauche*, 24 June 1866.
127. AN F17 4397, "Discours aux universités allemandes et italiennes," 1866.
128. AN F17 4398, "Supplément aux journaux des étudiants: Compte-rendu officiel du Congrès des étudiants," 14 April 1867.
129. AN 45 AP 18, "Lettre adressée aux journaux de Paris," 5 October 1865.
130. AN 45 AP 18, "Cabinet du Préfet du Police au Ministère d'État," January 1866.
131. *Congrès international des étudiants*, 146.
132. AN 45 AP 18, "Cabinet du Préfet du Police au Ministère d'État," January 1866.
133. *Le Pays*, 15 November 1865.
134. *La Gazette de France*, 15 November 1865.
135. *L'Opinion Nationale*, 24 December 1865.
136. Derfler, *Paul Lafargue*, 30–31.
137. See *Le Temps*, 9 December 1865.
138. *Le Temps*, 21 December 1865; Bernstein, *Auguste Blanqui*, 267; Derfler, *Paul Lafargue*, 30; Nord, *The Republican Moment*, 35.
139. Turin, *Affrontements culturels*, 198.
140. Taine, *Carnets*, 138.
141. Bonaparte, Speech Given during Military Ceremony, 21 March 1852, *Discours*, 229.
142. Veuillot, *L'Illusion libérale*, 60.

5. OLD ENDS AND NEW MEANS

1. Ollivier, *Journal*, 1:145.
2. Quinet, *Lettres d'exile*, 2:21.
3. Quoted in Hazareesingh, *Intellectual Founders of the Republic*, 242.
4. Hunt, *Politics, Culture and Class*, 26–28.
5. Harsin, *Barricades*, 215–18; Gould, *Insurgent Identities*, 37–38.
6. Marx, *The Eighteenth Brumaire*, 15.
7. Émile Littré, "La Révolution par M. Edgar Quinet," *La Philosophie positive* (1868), 3:384.
8. *Le Temps*, 13 October 1863.
9. Charle, *Histoire social de la France*, 130–33; Elwitt, *The Making of the Third Republic*, 7–10; Price, *People and Politics in France*, 234.
10. Garrigues, *La République*, 16–70.
11. Pilbeam, *Republicanism*, 271–74.
12. Furet, *Penser la Révolution Française*; Judt, "Rights in France"; Hulliung, *Citizens and Citoyens*, 42–44, 51–84.
13. See Berstein, *Les Cultures politiques*, 70–125.
14. Rosanvallon, *La Démocratie inachevée*, 301.
15. Nicolas Rousselliet, "La Culture politique libérale," in Berstein, *Les Cultures politiques en France*, 84–110.
16. Jainchill, *Reimagining Politics*, 12–13; Rosanvallon, *Le Moment Guizot*, 42–43.
17. Vacherot, *La Démocratie*, 48.
18. Jainchill, *Reimagining Politics*, 14–32.
19. Quoted in Rosanvallon, *Le Moment Guizot*, 36.
20. Claude Lefort, "Guizot théoricien du pouvoir," in Valensise, *François Guizot*, 96–98.
21. Adam, *Mes sentiments*, 34.
22. Quoted in Price, *The French Second Empire*, 350.
23. Quoted in Eros, "The Positivist Generation," 265.
24. Adam, *Mes sentiments*, 48.
25. See Gaillard, *Jules Ferry*, 136–38.
26. Quoted in Hazareesingh, *From Subject to Citizen*, 320.
27. Adam, *Mes premières armes*, 5.
28. Comte, *The Fundamental Principles*, 26.
29. Émile Littré, "La Philosophie positive—M. Auguste Comte et M. J. Stuart Mill," *Revue des Deux Mondes* (1866), 64:843.
30. Charles Dupont-White, "Le Positivisme," *Revue des Deux Mondes* (1865), 55:869.
31. Pierre-Joseph Proudhon, "De la création de l'ordre dans l'humanité," in *Œuvres complètes*, 7:253.
32. Quoted in Swart, *The Sense of Decadence*, 69.

33. Hippolyte Stupuy, "Un Pointe de politique positive," *La Philosophie positive* (1870), 6:470.
34. Félix Aroux, "Comment on devient positive," *La Philosophie positive* (1867), 1:70.
35. Mélonio, *Naissance et affirmation*, 45.
36. Stupuy, "Un Pointe de politique positive," 482.
37. Littré, "La Philosophie positive," 837.
38. Émile Littré, "A nos lecteurs et à notre nouvelle année," *La Philosophie positive* (1868), 3:1868.
39. Comte, *A General View*, 62.
40. Comte, *The Fundamental Principles*, 29.
41. Louis-Adolphe Bertillon, "De la mortalité parisienne," *La Philosophie positive* (1869), 4:445.
42. Comte, *A General View*, 98.
43. Émile Littré, "Du suffrage universel en France, considéré comme une expérience sociologique," *La Philosophie positive* (1869), 4:51.
44. Comte, *A General View*, 75.
45. Comte, *A General View*, 79–80.
46. Eros, "The Positivist Generation," 256.
47. Littré, *Conservation Révolution Positivisme*, 236.
48. Littré, *Du devoir de l'homme*, 24.
49. Littré, *Comte*, 588, 659; Aquarone, *The Life and Works of Émile Littré*, 34.
50. Émile Littré, "Politique," *La Philosophie positive* (1867), 1:141.
51. Stupuy, "Un Point de politique positive," 478.
52. Stupuy, "Un Point de politique positive," 478–81.
53. Stern, *Histoire de la révolution*, 1:xiii.
54. Quoted in Eros, "The Positivist Generation," 261.
55. Quoted in Hazareesingh, *From Subject to Citizen*, 173.
56. Littré, *Conservation Révolution Positivisme*, 315.
57. For contrasting views on the extent of Positivist influence on nineteenth-century republican thinkers, see Eros, "The Positivist Generation," 255–77; Patrice Decormeille, "La Philosophie politique républicaine sous le Second Empire," in Hamon, *Les Républicains sous le Second Empire*, 117.
58. Dupont-White, "Le Positivisme," 576.
59. Quinet, *La Révolution*, 772.
60. Quinet, *La Révolution*, 48, 59.
61. See the series of articles written by Alphonse Peyrat in *L'Avenir national*, 20 November 1865 and 3, 9, 12, and 18 January 1866.
62. Littré, "La Révolution, par M. Edgar Quinet," 384.
63. Saint-René Taillandier, "L'Histoire et l'idéal de la Révolution française à propos du livre de M. Edgar Quinet," *Revue des Deux Mondes* (1866), 63:453.
64. Robiquet, *Discours et opinions*, 101, 108.

65. Gaillard, *Jules Ferry*, 121–22.
66. Simon, *Le Devoir*, 362.
67. Ollivier, *Journal*, 1:274.
68. Quoted in Deschanel, *Gambetta*, 16.
69. Ollivier, *Journal*, 1:182.
70. Quoted in Hazareesingh, *Intellectual Founders of the Republic*, 135.
71. Simon, *La Politique radicale*, 5–6.
72. Stupuy, "Un Point de politique positive," 473.
73. AN 87 AP 15, "L'Élection des maires," 5 April 1865.
74. Littré, "La Révolution par M. Edgar Quinet," 395–96.
75. Taine, *Essais de critique et d'histoire*, 323.
76. Guizot, *Histoire des origines*, 1:9; Guizot, *Histoire parlementaire de France*, 1:cxxxv–cxxxvi.
77. Hulliung, *Citizens and Citoyens*, 48–50.
78. Laboulaye, *Le Parti libéral*, 6.
79. Quoted in Garrigues, *La République*, 26.
80. Charles de Rémusat, "Les Élections de 1863," *Revue des Deux Mondes* (1863), 46:276–77.
81. Laboulaye, *Le Parti libéral*, 150.
82. Duvernois, *Un Suicide politique*, 13.
83. Duvernois, *Le Couronnement de l'édifice*, 18.
84. Hauranne, *La Coalition libérale*, 67.
85. Hauranne, *La Coalition libérale*, 5–6.
86. Quoted in Garrigues, *La République*, 25.
87. Duvernois, *Le Couronnement de l'édifice*, 27.
88. Laboulaye, *Le Parti libéral*, v.
89. Roussellier, "La Culture politique libérale," in Berstein, *Les Cultures politique*, 74–75; Hulliung, *Citizens and Citoyens*, 59.
90. Laboulaye, *Le Parti libéral*, xv.
91. Pilbeam, *Republicanism*, 266.
92. "Chronique de la Quinzaine," *Revue des Deux Mondes* (1863), 43:233.
93. De Bray, "Liberté," *Courrier de l'Algérie*, 8 March 1868.
94. Arnold Thomson, "Les Élections," *Akhbar*, 6 September 1868.
95. AN 45 AP 19, clipping from *La Presse*.
96. *Le Temps*, 14 April 1863.
97. Quoted in Decormeille, "La Philosophie politique républicaine," 118.
98. Simon, *La Politique radicale*, 3–4.
99. Simon, *La Politique radicale*, 34.
100. Hulliung, *Citizens and Citoyens*, 77.
101. Laboulaye, *L'État et ses limites*, 154.
102. Stupuy, "Un point de politique positive," 484.

103. Quoted in Bertocci, *Jules Simon*, 149.

104. Pelletan, *Les Droits de l'homme*, 169.

105. Ollivier, *Journal*, 1:116.

106. Simon, *La Politique radicale*, 34.

107. As Ernesto Laclau notes, without confrontation there is no identity because identities require conflict for their constitution. "The Death and Resurrection," 316.

108. Ferry, *La Lutte électorale*, 6.

109. Prévost-Paradol, *La France nouvelle*, 298.

110. Laboulaye, *Le Parti libéral*, 117.

111. *Le Temps*, 11 May 1863.

112. Ténot, *Le Suffrage universel*, 31.

113. Quoted in Hanson, *Manet and the Modern Tradition*, 9.

114. Ollivier, *Journal*, 1:439.

115. Dupont-White, "L'Administration locale en France et Angleterre," *Revue des Deux Mondes* (1863), 45:181.

116. Huard, *La Naissance du parti politique*, 16–17.

117. Favre, *Discours parlementaires*, 3:699.

118. Decormeille, "La Philosophie politique républicaine," 116.

119. Quinet, *Lettres d'exile*, 2:48.

120. Favre, *Jules Favre à Constantine*, 26.

121. Babaud-Laribière, *Lettres Charentaises*, 2:133.

122. Quoted in Zeldin, *Emile Ollivier*, 38.

123. Quinet, *Lettres d'exile*, 2:82.

6. REPUBLICAN GOVERNMENT

1. Lecouturier, *Paris incompatible*, 70, 75–76.

2. Truesdell, *Spectacular Politics*, 18–19.

3. Duvernois, *Un Suicide politique*, 9.

4. Guizot, *Du gouvernement de la France*, 2.

5. Taine, *Carnets de voyage*, 172–73.

6. Perier, Bertillon, and Lagneau, "Questionaire sur l'anthropologie de la France," *Bulletins de la Société d'Anthropologie de Paris* (1861): 2:327–81. In more general terms, see Geary, *The Myth of Nations*, 19–22.

7. Rogers, "Good to Think," 316.

8. Bullard, *Exile to Paradise*, 99.

9. Weber, *Peasants into Frenchmen*, 233.

10. Cooper, *Colonialism in Question*, 116–17.

11. Ténot, *Le Suffrage universel*, 29.

12. Vacherot, *La Démocratie*, 63.

13. Quoted in Hulliung, *Citizens and Citoyens*, 75.

14. Laboulaye, *L'État et ses limites*, 85.
15. Agulhon, *The Republican Experiment*, 10–13; Berenson, *Populist Religion*, 48–73.
16. Gunn, "French Republicans and the Suffrage"; Darriulat, *Les Patriotes*, 210–11.
17. Berenson, *Populist Religion*, 219–26; Agulhon, *The Republican Experiment*, 85–94.
18. Margadant, *French Peasants in Revolt*, xvii, 3–39.
19. Ferry, *La Lutte électorale*, 9.
20. In some areas such as Strasbourg, Vierzon, and Bordeaux, it is estimated that some two-thirds of the electorate abstained from political participation during the 1850s, resulting in victories for official candidates favored by the government. See Pilbeam, *Republicanism*, 246–47.
21. Frédéric Salmon, "La 'Gaunche avancée' en 1849 et en 1870: le pourquoi de la chute," in Hamon, *Les Républicains sous le Second Empire*, 99–100.
22. Ténot, *Le Suffrage universel*, 9.
23. Quinet, *Lettres d'exile*, 2:218–19.
24. Grégoire Wyrouboff, "L'Enseignement libre," *La Philosophie positive* (1868), 2:147–49.
25. Vacherot, *La Démocratie*, xxvii.
26. Simon, *La Liberté*, 2:428.
27. Laboulaye, *Le Parti libéral*, 119, 299.
28. Ferry, *La Lutte électorale*, 16.
29. Ténot, *Le Suffrage universel*, 11.
30. Ferry, *La Lutte électorale*, 43.
31. Quoted in Robb, *The Discovery of France*, 20–21.
32. Wyrouboff, "L'Enseignement libre," 2:448.
33. Laboulaye, *L'État et ses limites*, 211.
34. Charles Dollfus, "Le Prolétariat de l'esprit," *Le Temps*, 29 April 1861.
35. Dollfus, "Le Prolétariat de l'esprit."
36. Quoted in Gunn, "French Republicans and the Suffrage," 40.
37. Vacherot, *La Démocratie*, 353.
38. Gunn, "French Republicans and the Suffrage," 34.
39. Taine, *Life and Letters*, 2:297–80.
40. Price, *People and Politics in France*, 185–97.
41. Laboulaye, *Le Parti libéral*, 119.
42. Hugo, *Napoleon the Little*, 301.
43. Ténot, *Le Suffrage universel*, 19.
44. Cottin, *Lettre à des électeurs*, 11–12.
45. Laboulaye, *L'État et ses limites*, 43.
46. Favre, *Discours parlementaires*, 3:222.
47. Girard, *Les Conseillers généraux*, 133; Hazareesingh, *From Subject to Citizen*, 40–42; Zeldin, *The Political System*, 20–26.

48. Favre, *Discours parlementaires*, 3:214.
49. Ponteil, *Les Institutions de la France*, 372–73; Nicolet, *L'Idée républicaine en France*, 147.
50. Dollfus, "Le prolétariat de l'esprit."
51. Quoted in Hazareesingh, *From Subject to Citizen*, 269.
52. Simon, *La Liberté*, 2:276.
53. *L'Europe*, 17 July 1865.
54. AN 45 AP 1, "Lettre de l'Empereur sur la décentralisation," 24 June 1863.
55. Duc de Persigny, "Rapport sur l'administration du ministère de l'intérieur," in Delaroa, *Le Duc de Persigny et les doctrines*, 52–54.
56. 45 AP 11, "Girande," 1864; 45 AP 5, "Note sur l'élection de Rochefort-Marennes," n. d.
57. 45 AP 5, "Ministère de l'Intérieur aux préfets," 15 March 1864.
58. See Abi-Mershed, *Apostles of Modernity*, 164–65; Dell'Osso, "The Ministry of Algeria."
59. *Bulletin Officiel de l'Algérie et des colonies*, 31 August 1858, 34–35.
60. *Bulletin Officiel de l'Algérie et des colonies*, 27 October 1858, 51.
61. *Bulletin Officiel de l'Algérie et des colonies*, 31 August 1858, 35.
62. 87 AP 15, "L'Élection des maires," 5 April 1865.
63. Ferry, *La Lutte électorale*, 23–24.
64. Barni, *Manuel Républicain*, 23.
65. For a detailed examination of the role decentralization and municipal concerns played in the political culture of the late Second Empire, see Hazareesingh, *From Subject to Citizen*.
66. Favre, *Discours parlementaires*, 3:796, 801.
67. Duvernois, *Un Suicide politique*, 20.
68. Duvernois, "L'État VII," *Le Temps*, 4 November 1863.
69. Duvernois, "L'État IV," *Le Temps*, 4 October 1863.
70. *Le Temps*, 10 September 1863.
71. *Le Temps*, 10 September 1863.
72. Laboulaye, *Le Parti libéral*, 107.
73. Ferry, *La Lutte électorale*, 40.
74. *Annales du Sénat* (1867), 2:250.
75. Duvernois, "L'État V," *Le Temps*, 10 October 1863.
76. Laboulaye, *L'État et ses limites*, 87.
77. Popkin, *Press, Revolution and Social Identities*, 59–69.
78. Simon, *La Politique radicale*, 93–94.
79. Charles Baudelaire, "My Heart Laid Bare," in *My Heart Laid Bare*, 203.
80. Duc de Persigny, "Rapport sur l'Administration du Ministère de l'intérieur," in Delaroa *Le Duc de Persigny et les doctrines*, 48.
81. Quoted in Rosanvallon, *La Démocratie inachevée*, 215.

82. Nicolas Rousellier, "La Culture politique libérale," in Berstein *Les Cultures politique*, 76–77; Hulliung, *Citizens and Citoyens*, 128.

83. Laboulaye, *Le Parti libérale*, 38.

84. Prévost-Paradol, *La France nouvelle*, 205.

85. Simon, *La Politique radicale*, 99.

86. AN 87 AP 15, "Discours de la loi de la presse," 19 February 1868.

87. Simon, *La Politique radicale*, 80.

88. Pelletan, *Les Droites de l'homme*, 145, 167.

89. "Programme," *Le Temps*, 25 April 1861.

90. Laboulaye, *L'État et ses limites*, 223.

91. Ténot, *Le Suffrage universel*, 19.

92. Quoted in Price, *People and Politics in France*, 177.

93. Vacherot, *La Démocratie*, 117.

94. *Annales de Sénat* (1870), 3:302.

95. Lévêque, *Histoire des forces politiques*, 339–41; Lehning, *To Be a Citizen*.

96. Adam, *Mes sentiments*, 202.

7. TRANS-MEDITERRANEAN REPUBLIC

1. Favre, *Plaidoyers et discours*, 1:467–84.

2. Quoted in Julien, *Histoire de l'Algérie contemporaine*, 340.

3. Quoted in Perrod, *Jules Favre*, 184.

4. Lorcin, *Imperial Identities*, 186; Gosnell, *The Politics of Frenchness*, 186–90.

5. Heffernan, "The Parisian Poor"; Salinas, "Colonies without Colonists," 104–40; Davis, "Turning French Convicts into Colonists."

6. Pierre Boyer, "La Vie politique et les élections à Alger," in Emerit, *La Révolution de 1848 en Algérie*, 61; Rey-Goldzieger, *Le Royaume Arabe*, 114–15.

7. Fonvielle, *L'Empereur en Algérie*, 12.

8. Dodman, "Un Pays pour la colonie," 778–83.

9. Julien, *Histoire de l'Algérie contemporaine*, 216–18, 419; Charles-Robert Ageron, "L'Évolution politique de l'Algérie sous le Second Empire," in *De l'Algérie "française"*, 104–9.

10. Nouschi, *Correspondance du Docteur A. Vital*, 78.

11. Lacroix, *L'Algérie et la lettre*, 2–3.

12. MacMahon, *Mémoires*, 314.

13. Auguste Warnier, "L'Algérie," *Akhbar* 31 August 1865.

14. "Pétition au Sénat," *L'Echo d'Oran*, 10 February 1863.

15. *L'Echo d'Oran*, 10 February 1863.

16. Prochaska, *Making Algeria French*, 11; Rey-Goldzieger, *Le Royaume Arabe*, 62–65.

17. For a favorable assessment of the military's role in the colony, see F. Paysant, "Question algérienne," *Akhbar*, 20 February 1870. For *colon* opposition to direct

assimilation with France, see Alexander Lambert, "Réponse à la lettre de M. J. Duval," *L'Echo d'Oran*, 15 January 1863, and "Envoi de délégués à Paris," *L'Echo d'Oran*, 5 February 1863; Paul Capdevielle, "Le Petite Église," *Courrier de l'Algérie*, 29 April 1870.

18. Alexandre Lambert, "La Nationalité arabe," *Akhbar*, 1 May 1864.

19. Arnold Thomson, "De l'assimilation," *Akhbar*, 15 November 1868.

20. Duval, *Réflexions*, 30.

21. Duval, *Réflexions*, 32.

22. Andrieux, "La Question algérienne devant la France," *Courrier de l'Algérie*, 21 January 1863.

23. Verne, *De Bône à Hammam-Meskhoutine*, 110.

24. Warnier, *L'Algérie devant l'Empereur*, 27.

25. Prochaska, *Making Algeria French*, 49–50.

26. Guignard, "Conservatoire ou révolutionnaire?"

27. Amand Favré, "Notre programme," *Progrès de l'Algérie*, 9 December 1867.

28. Arsène Vacherot, "L'Algérie sous l'Empire: les indigènes et la colonisation," *Revue des Deux Mondes* (1869), 83:181.

29. Favre, *Discours parlementaires*, 3:132.

30. Jules Duval, "La Misère arabe en Algérie," *L'Echo d'Oran*, 30 January 1868.

31. *Progrès de l'Algérie*, 11 July 1868.

32. J.-M. Junca, "L'Unité de juridiction," *L'Algérie nouvelle*, 25 June 1859.

33. Frédéric Morin, "Le Projet de sénatus-consulte sur l'Algérie," *Courrier de l'Algérie*, 27 February 1870.

34. Duval, *L'Algérie et les colonies françaises*, 71.

35. Étourneau, *L'Algérie faisant appel à la France*, 140, 180.

36. Warnier, *L'Algérie devant l'Empereur*, 271.

37. Joseph Guérin, "Pourquoi trembler?" *Akhbar*, 11 July 1865.

38. Duval, *Réflexions*, 26.

39. Thuillier, "Sur le rapport de S. Exc. Le gouverneur général de l'Algérie à l'Empereur," *Courrier de l'Algérie*, 16 May 1868.

40. Étourneau, *L'Algérie faisant appel*, 380.

41. Joseph Guérin, "De la nécessité d'attirer une population européenne nombreuse en ce pays," *Akhbar*, 11 May 1865.

42. *Courrier de l'Algérie*, 28 March 1868.

43. See Duvernois, *La Réorganisation de l'Algérie*, 19–21; Duvernois, *Le Temps*, 10 April 1863; Thomson, "De l'assimilation," *Akhbar*, 15 November 1868.

44. Arsène Vacherot, "L'Algérie sous l'Empire," *Revue des Deux Mondes* (1869), 83:182.

45. M. Mille-Noé, "Colonisation de l'Algérie," *L'Echo d'Oran*, 26 March 1863.

46. Joseph Guérin, "Les Colons sont les meilleurs amis des Arabes," *Akhbar*, 9 May 1865.

47. Nicolas Roussellier, "La Culture politique libérale," in Berstein, *Les Cultures politiques*, 99; John C. Camaroff, "Images of Empire, Contests of Conscience: Models of Colonial Domination in South Africa," in Cooper and Stoler, *Tensions of Empire*, 169–72; Goldstein, *The Post-Revolutionary Self*, 162–64, 180–81.

48. *Tableau de la situation*, 177, 188. The actual numbers for 1857 were cited at 188,827 total Europeans, of which 106,930 were of French origin. The native population numbered 2,344,813 inhabitants.

49. Desmaze, *Rapports à son Excellence*, 5, 19.

50. Delimone, "De l'immigration européenne et de la naturalisation," *Akhbar*, 3 April 1870.

51. Thomson, "De l'assimilation" *Akhbar*, 10 November 1868; Warnier, *L'Algérie devant l'Empereur*, 208, 68.

52. Fonvielle, *L'Empereur en Algérie*, 13.

53. Duvernois, *L'Algérie*, 126–27, 131.

54. Duvernois, *L'Algérie*, 252.

55. Alexandre Lambert, "Envoi de délégués à Paris," *L'Echo d'Oran*, 5 February 1863.

56. See Abi-Mershed, *Apostles of Modernity*; Amselle, *Affirmative Exclusion*.

57. Jules Duval, "L'Anniversaire du 13 juin en Algérie," *Revue de l'Orient* (1852), 12:92.

58. Girardet, *L'Idée colonial en France*, 43–45.

59. Duval, *Réflexions*, 13–14.

60. Duval, *l'Algérie et les colonies françaises*, 9.

61. Duval, *l'Algérie et les colonies françaises*, 37.

62. Duval, *Les Colonies et la politique coloniale*, xx.

63. Duval, *Réflexions*, 173.

64. Duval, *Réflexions*, 476.

65. Duval, *L'Algérie et les colonies françaises*, 66.

66. While noted by Duval, the intrinsically "hybridic" nature of colonial societies has been a subject of scrutiny among postcolonial theorists today. See Said, *Culture and Imperialism*, xxv; Bahbah, *The Location of Culture*.

67. Duval, *Les Colonies et la politique coloniale*, 465.

68. Duval, "L'Anniversaire du 13 juin en Algérie," *Revue de l'Orient* (1858), 12:97.

69. Duval, "L'Anniversaire du 13 juin en Algérie," (1858), 12:94, 97.

70. Verne, *La France en Algérie*, 37.

71. Broglie, *Une Réforme administrative*, 5–6.

72. Feydeau, *Alger*, 35.

73. Ernest Fonvielle, "La Conspiration du silence," *L'Algérie Nouvelle*, 12 February 1860.

74. Warnier, *L'Algérie devant l'Empereur*, 101.

75. See, for example, Joseph Guérin, "Le Chemin de fer," *Courrier de l'Algérie*, 4 June 1866; A. Molot, "Les Travaux publics et le budget," *Courrier de l'Algérie*, 13 January 1865; *Courrier de l'Algérie*, 30 July 1862; Verne, *La France en Algérie*, 38; Joseph Guérin, "De la nécessité d'attirer une population européenne nombreuse en ce pays," *Akhbar*, 11 May 1865.

76. *Akhbar*, 21 July 1868.

77. Wilfred de Fonvielle, "A la presse française," *L'Algérie Nouvelle*, 2 February 1860.

78. Duval, *L'Algérie et les colonies françaises*, 309.

79. Guérin, "Pourquoi trembler?"

80. Thomson, "De l'assimilation," *Akhbar*, 10 November 1868.

81. Émile Thuillier, "L'Algérie au Corps législatif," *Courrier de l'Algérie*, 7 June 1868.

82. Delord, *Histoire du Second Empire*, 4:658; Duvernois, *La Liberté de discussion*, 5.

83. Rey-Goldzeiguer, *Le Royaume Arabe*, 65–66.

84. Duvernois, *L'Akhbar et les novateurs téméraires*.

85. Desprez, *Alger naguère et maintenant*, 297.

86. See Guérin, "Le Chemin de fer"; Andrieux, "Langueur de l'Algérie, ses causes et le moyen d'y remédier," *Courrier de l'Algérie*, 25 May 1862; J-M. Junca, "L'Unité de juridiction," *L'Algérie Nouvelle*, 25 June 1859; Arnold Thomson, "L'Agriculture algérienne," *Akhbar*, 4 July 1867; A. Molot, "Les Travaux publics et le Budget," *Courrier de l'Algérie*, 13 January 1865.

87. Clément Duvernois, "Question algérienne," *L'Echo d'Oran*, 15 March 1863.

88. Broglie, *Une Réforme administrative en Afrique*, 137.

89. *Akhbar*, 13 June 1869.

90. Duvernois, *L'Algérie*, 144–45.

91. Thuillier, "Echos de l'opinion publique," *Courrier de l'Algérie*, 9 April 1868.

92. Andrieux, "Langueur de l'Algérie, ses causes et le moyen d'y remédier," *Courrier de l'Algérie*, 25 May 1862.

93. Andrieux, "Le Prolétariat et les indigènes," *Courrier de l'Algérie*, 4 May 1862.

94. De Guerle, "Un Moyen de colonisation," *Courrier de l'Algérie*, 27 July 1862.

95. "Pétition au Sénat," *L'Echo d'Oran*, 10 February 1863.

96. *Courrier de l'Algérie*, 10 July 1862.

97. De Guerle, "Un Moyen de colonisation," *Courrier de l'Algérie*, 27 July 1862.

98. Alexandre Lambert, "Les Élections départementales et la décentralisation," *Akhbar*, 16 June 1864.

99. Favré, "Notre programme."

100. *Annales du Sénat* (1863), 2:251.

101. *Courrier de l'Algérie*, 30 July 1862.

102. "Délibérations du conseil général," *Rapports sur le Budget*, 175.

103. Duval, *Les Colonies et la politique coloniale*, 456.

104. Duval, *L'Algérie et les colonies françaises*, 72–73.
105. Montain-Lefloch, "Nécessité de la politique," *Courrier de l'Algérie*, 10 November 1865.
106. Voisin [Urbain], *L'Algérie pour les algériens*, 128–29.
107. *Annales du Sénat* (1868), 7:174; Ageron, "L'Évolution politique," 118.
108. *Moniteur de l'Algérie*, 4 July 1867.
109. Arnold Thomson, "De l'exécution du décret sur les élections," *Akhbar*, 28 April 1867.
110. "Délibérations de conseil général," *Rapports sur le budget*, 404.
111. *Annales du Sénat* (1870), 2:536–37.
112. Wilder, *The French Imperial Nation-State*, 14–16; Spieler, *Empire and Underworld*, 149–51; Blévis, "Les Avatars," 566–67.
113. Arnold Thomson, "Nos affaires," *Akhbar*, 18 April 1869.
114. *L'Echo d'Oran*, 11 January 1868.
115. Paul Capdevielle, "Le 29 Novembre!" *Courrier de l'Algérie*, 30 November 1869.
116. *Le Temps*, 6 November 1868.
117. Duvernois, *L'Algérie*, 259, 239.
118. See Émile Girardin, "Civilisation de l'Algérie," *L'Algérie Nouvelle*, 14 February 1860; Duvernois, *Un suicide politique*.
119. A. Nefftzer, "Question algérienne," *Le Temps*, 19 February 1863.
120. *Le Temps*, 25 January 1864. See also *Le Temps*, 8 February 1862, 10 April 1863, 11 September 1863, 16 September 1863, and 31 December 1863.
121. See, for example, M. Étourneau, "Lettres d'Algérie," *Le Temps*, 23 September 1867; *Le Temps*, 2 October 1864, and 6 November 1868.
122. *Annales du Sénat* (1861), 2:95, 99, 96.
123. *Akhbar*, 21 July 1868.
124. Nicolas, "Alger," *L'Echo d'Oran*, 16 January 1868.
125. See Léopold Le Hon's address in *Annales du Sénat* (1870), 2:463; Favre, *Discours parlementaires*, 3:141; Robiquet, *Discours et opinions*, 335.
126. *Annales du Sénat* (1870), 3:11.
127. *Annales du Sénat* (1870), 4:529.
128. Favre, *Discours parlementaires*, 3:71.
129. *Annales du Sénat* (1870), 2:468.
130. Favre, *Discours parlementaires*, 3:549.
131. *Annales du Sénat* (1863), 2:243.
132. *Annales du Sénat* (1869), 2:403.
133. Favre, *Discours parlementaires*, 3:767.
134. Duval, *Réflexions*, 175.
135. Blévis, "Les Avatars," 573–79.
136. Duval, *L'Algérie et les colonies françaises*, 96.
137. Fonvielle, *L'Empereur en Algérie*, 14–15.

138. Favre, *Discours parlementaires*, 3:487.
139. Favre, *Discours parlementaires*, 3:132–33.
140. Quoted in Gaillard, *Jules Ferry*, 599–600.
141. Ageron, "L'Évolution politique," 121–23; Lorcin, *Imperial Identities*, 87.
142. Taithe, "La Famine de 1866–1868."
143. *Courrier de l'Algérie*, 8 April 1868.
144. *L'Echo d'Oran*, 4 February 1868.
145. Jules Duval, "Comment découvrir la vérité algérienne," *Progrès de L'Algérie*, 30 June 1868.
146. *Progrès de L'Algérie*, 10 September 1868.
147. Favre, *Discours parlementaires*, 3:548.
148. *Annales du Sénat* (1868), 15:36.
149. Lacretelle, *De l'Algérie*, 12.
150. Paul Capdevielle, "Les Trios grandes journées," *Courrier de l'Algérie*, 15 March 1870.
151. *Annales du Sénat* (1870), 2:496.
152. *Conseil Général de la Province d'Oran*, xv.
153. *Akhbar*, 13 June 1869.

CONCLUSION

1. Théophile Thoré, "Exposition Universelle de 1867," in *Salons de W. Bürger*, 2:385.
2. Hippolyte Stupuy, "Un Point de politique positive," *La Philosophie positive* (1870), 6:470.
3. Monselet, *Les Ruines de Paris*, 1:256.
4. Nouschi, *Correspondance du Docteur A. Vital*, 118.
5. *La Tribune*, 20 December 1868.
6. Lehning, *Peasant and French*, 60; Hazareesingh, "A Common Sentiment," 286.
7. Lehning, *Peasant and French*, 2–3, 208–10; Gaboriaux, *La République en quête de citoyens*, 337–39.
8. Latour, *We Have Never Been Modern*, 10.
9. Charles-Robert Ageron, "L'Évolution politique de l'Algérie sous le Second Empire," in *De l'Algérie "française"*, 132–33; Frémigacci, "L'État colonial français"; Merle, "Retour sur le régime."
10. Gluck, "The End of Elsewhere," 677–79; Djaït, *Europe and Islam*, 102–3, 167.
11. Shepard, *The Invention of Decolonization*; Silverstein, *Algeria in France*, 67.

BIBLIOGRAPHY

ARCHIVAL AND MANUSCRIPT MATERIALS
Archives Nationales (Paris) (AN)
Official Papers
    F1a 49, Ministry of Interior circulars
    F1a 66–68, Ministry of Agriculture, Commerce and Public Works circulars
    F12 5000–5004, Local Exhibitions
    F17 2909–11, Scientific Commission for Mexican Expedition
    F17 4396–98, Reports on Academic Discipline
    F19 10923–25, Ministry of Public Instruction and Religion
    F17 9327, Departmental Reports on Primary Instruction
    F70 252, Exposés on the Situation of the Empire
Private Papers
    Papiers Persigny 44 AP 16, 27, 30
    Papiers Rouher 45 AP 1, 5, 11, 18, 19
    Papiers Simon 87 AP 9, 15, 16
    Papiers Morny 116 AP 1, 2
    Papiers Bugeaud 225 AP 2
    Papiers Pelessier 234 AP 4
    Papiers Fortoul 246 AP 17

PUBLISHED WORKS
Abi-Mershed, Osama W. *Apostles of Modernity: Saint-Simonians and the Civilizing Mission in Algeria*. Stanford CA: Stanford University Press, 2010.
Adam, Juliet. *Mes premières armes: littéraires et politiques*. Paris: Alphonse Lemerre, 1904.
———. *Mes sentiments et nos idées avant 1870*. Paris: Alphonse Lemerre, 1905.
Adamovsky, Ezequiel. "Euro-orientalism and the Making of the Concept of Eastern Europe in France, 1810–1880." *Journal of Modern History*, 77 (September 2005): 591–628.

Ageron, Charles-Robert. *De l'Algérie "française" à l'Algérie algérienne*. Paris: Bouchene, 2005.

Agulhon, Maurice, ed. *Histoire de la France urbaine*. 4 vols. Paris: Seuil, 1983.

——. *La République au village: les populations du Var de la Révolution à la Seconde République*. Paris: Seuil, 1979.

——. *The Republican Experiment, 1848–1852*. Translated by Janet Lloyd. Cambridge: Cambridge University Press, 1983.

Alexander, R. S. *Bonapartism and Revolutionary Tradition in France: The Fédérés of 1815*. Cambridge: Cambridge University Press, 1991.

Alletz, Édouard. *Génie du dix-neuvième siècle, ou Esquisse des progrès de l'esprit humain depuis 1800 jusqu'à nos jours*. Paris: Paulin, 1843.

Amselle, Jean-Loup. *Affirmative Exclusion: Cultural Pluralism and The Rule of Custom in France*. Ithaca NY: Cornell University Press, 2003.

Anderson, Benedict. *Imagined Communities: Reflections on the Origin and Spread of Nationalism*. London: Verso, 1983.

Anderson, R. D. *Education in France, 1848–1870*. Oxford: Clarendon Press, 1975.

Andrews, Naomi J. "Breaking the Ties That Bind: French Romantic Socialism and the Critique of Liberal Slave Emancipation." *Journal of Modern History* 85, no. 3 (September 2013): 489–527.

Annales du Sénat et du Corps législatif. Paris: L'Administration du Moniteur Universel, 1852–70.

Aquarone, Stanislas. *The Life and Works of Émile Littré, 1801–1888*. Leyden: A. W. Sythoff, 1958.

Arbousse-Bastide, Antoine-François. *A propos de tout quelque chose, ou mes impressions à Paris*. Paris: Meyrueis, 1857.

Armand, Lévy. *L'Empereur Napoléon III et les principautés roumaines*. Paris: E. Dentu, 1858.

Asselain, Jean-Charles. *Histoire économique de la révolution industrielle à la première guerre mondiale*. Paris: Presses de la Fondation Nationale des Sciences Politiques, 1985.

Aux citoyens représentants de peuple à l'Assemblé Nationale. Paris: Imprimerie Centrale de Napoléon Chaix, 1848.

Babaud-Laribière, Léonide. *Lettres Charentaises*. 2 vols. Marseille: Lafitte, 1979.

Bahbah, Homi K. *The Location of Culture*. London: Routledge, 2004.

Ballanche, Pierre-Simon. *Œuvres*. 6 vols. Paris: Bureau de l'Encyclopédie des Connaissances Utiles, 1833.

Ballue, Arthur. *La Question algérienne à vol d'oiseau*. Marseille: J. Doucet, 1869.

Bancel, Nicolas, Pascal Blanchard, and Françoise Vergés. *La République colonial*. Paris: Hachette, 2003.

Barni, Jules. *Manuel Républicain*. Paris: Germer Baillière, 1872.

Barrault, Émile. *Occident et Orient: Études politiques, morales, religieuse*. Paris: A. Poigin, 1835.

Bastiat, Frédéric. *Ce qu'on voit et ce qu'on ne voit pas ou l'économie politique en une leçon*. Paris: Guillaumin, 1850.

Baudelaire, Charles. *Art in Paris: 1845–1862*. Translated by Jonathan Mayne. London: Phaidon, 1965.

——. *My Heart Laid Bare and Other Prose Writings*. Translated by Norman Cameron. New York: Haskell House, 1975.

Bauman, Gerd, and Andre Gingrich, eds. *Grammars of Identity/Alterity*. Oxford: Oxford University Press, 2004.

Bell, David A. *The Cult of the Nation in France: Inventing Nationalism, 1680–1800*. Cambridge MA: Harvard University Press, 2001.

Belmessous, Saliha. *Assimilation and Empire: Uniformity in French and British Colonies, 1541–1954*. Oxford: Oxford University Press, 2013.

Benjamin, Walter. *The Writer of Modern Life: Essays on Charles Baudelaire*. Cambridge MA: Harvard University Press, 2006.

Berenson, Edward. "Making a Colonial Culture? Empire and the French Public, 1880–1940." *French Politics, Culture and Society* 22, no. 2 (Summer 2004): 127–49.

——. *Populist Religion and Left-Wing Politics in France, 1830–1852*. Princeton NJ: Princeton University Press, 1984.

Berman, Marshall. *All That Is Solid Melts into Air: The Experience of Modernity*. New York: Penguin, 1988.

Bernstein, Samuel. *Auguste Blanqui and the Art of Insurrection*. London: Lawrence and Wishart, 1971.

Berstein, Serge, ed. *Les Cultures politiques en France*. Paris: Seuil, 1999.

Bertocci, Philip A. *Jules Simon: Republican Anticlericalism and Cultural Politics, 1848–1886*. Columbia: University of Missouri Press, 1978.

Best, Geoffrey, ed. *The Permanent Revolution: The French Revolution and Its Legacy, 1789–1989*. Chicago: University of Chicago Press, 1988.

Bierman, John. *Napoleon III and His Carnival Empire*. New York: St. Martin's Press, 1988.

Birnbaum, Pierre. *The Idea of France*. Translated by M. B. Debevoise. New York: Hill and Wang, 2001.

Blackburn, Henry. *Normandy Picturesque*. London: S. Low, Son and Marston, 1870.

Blanqui, Louis Auguste. *Instructions pour une prise d'armes, L'Éternité par les asters, hypothèse astronomique, et austres textes*. Paris: Société encyclopédique française, 1972.

Blévis, Laure. "Les Avatars de la citoyenneté en Algérie coloniale ou les paradoxes d'une catégorisation." *Droit et Société* 48 (2001): 557–81.

Bluche, Frédéric. *Le Bonapartisme: Aux origines de la droite autoritaire*. Paris: Nouvelles Editions Latines, 1980.

Boinvilliers, Edouard. *Nationalité*. Paris: E. Duverger, 1853.

Bonaparte, Louis Napoleon. *Des idées Napoléoniennes*. Translated by James A. Dorr. New York: D. Appleton, 1859.

———. *Discours, messages et proclamations de l'Empereur*. Paris: Henri Plon, 1860.

———. *The Political and Historical Works of Louis Napoleon Bonaparte*. 2 vols. New York: Howard Fertig, 1972.

———. *Recueil historique des pensées, opinions, discours, proclamations, lettres et beaux traits de Napoléon III*. Paris: Appert et Vavasseur, 1858.

Bory-de-Saint-Vincent, Jean Baptiste. *Note sur la commission exploratrice et scientifique d'Algérie*. Paris: Cosson, 1838.

Boudon, Jacques-Olivier. *Paris capitale religieuse sous le Second Empire*. Paris: CEFR, 2001.

Bourguet, Marie-Noëlle, Bernard Lepetit, Daniel Normand and Maroula Sinarellis, eds. *L'Invention scientifique de la Méditerranée: Egypte, Morée, Algérie*. Paris: Éditions de l'École des hautes études en sciences sociales, 1998.

Bouyerdene, Ahmed. *Abd el-Kader: L'harmonie des contraires*. Paris: Seuil, 2008.

Bresler, Fenton. *Napoleon III: A Life*. New York: Carroll and Graf, 1999.

Brett, Michael. "Legislating for Inequality in Algeria: The Senatus-Consulte of 14 July 1865." *Bulletin of the School of Oriental and African Studies* 51, no. 3 (1988): 440–61.

Broers, Michael. *Europe under Napoleon, 1799–1815*. London: Arnold, 1996.

Broglie, A. de. *Une Réforme administrative en Afrique*. Paris: H. Dumineray, 1860.

Brossard, Amédée-Hippolyte. *A M. Louis Blanc: de la nécessité des colonies agricoles considérées dans leur rapport avec l'organisation du travail*. Paris: Lange Lévy, 1848.

Brower, Benjamin Claude. *A Desert Named Peace: The Violence of France's Empire in The Algerian Sahara, 1844–1902*. New York: Columbia University Press, 2009.

Brubaker, Roger, and Frederick Cooper. "Beyond 'Identity.'" *Theory and Society* 29 (2000): 1–47.

Buchez, Philippe. *Introduction à la science de l'histoire ou science du développement de l'humanité*. Paris: Paulin, 1833.

Bullard, Alice. *Exile to Paradise: Savagery and Civilization in Paris and the South Pacific, 1790–1900*. Stanford CA: Stanford University Press, 2000.

Bulletin Officiel de l'Algérie et des colonies. Paris: Imprimaire de Schiller, 1858–60.

Bulletins de la Société d'Anthropologie de Paris. Paris: Victor Masson, 1860–70.

Burke, Peter, ed. *A New Kind of History: From the Writings of Lucien Febvre*. New York: Harper and Row, 1973.

Burrows, Matthew. "'Mission Civilisatrice': French Cultural Policy in the Middle East, 1860–1914." *Historical Journal* 29, no. 1 (March 1986): 109–35.

Camaroff, John, "Interview with John and Jean Camaroff." *NAB: Newsletter of African Studies at Bayreuth University* 1, no. 1 (2002): 3–6.

Cameron, Rondo E. *France and the Economic Development of Europe, 1800–1914*. Princeton NJ: Princeton University Press, 1961.

Cappot, Jean-Gabriel. *Les Nationalités*. Paris: Michel Lévy Frères, 1855.

Carmona, Michel. *Morny: le vice-empereur.* Paris: Fayard, 2005.

Case, Lynn M. *French Opinion on War and Diplomacy during the Second Empire.* Philadelphia: University of Pennsylvania Press, 1944.

Çelik, Zeynep. *Displaying the Orient: Architecture of Islam at Nineteenth-Century's World Fairs.* Berkeley: University of California Press, 1992.

―――. *Urban Forms and Colonial Confrontations: Algiers under French Rule.* Berkeley: University of California Press, 1997.

Chafer, Tony, and Amanda Sackur, eds. *Promoting the Colonial Idea in France: Propaganda and Visions of Empire in France.* New York : Palgrave Macmillan, 2001.

Chakrabarty, Dipesh. *Provincializing Europe: Postcolonial Thought and Historical Difference.* Princeton NJ: Princeton University Press, 2000.

Charle, Christophe. *Histoire social de la France au XIXeme siècle.* Paris: Seuil, 1991.

Chastener, Jacques. *L'Enfance de la Troisième République 1870–1879.* Paris: Hachette, 1952.

Chateaubriand, René François de. *Mémoires d'outre-tombe.* 3 vols. Paris: Le Livre de Poche, 1973.

Chevalier, Louis. *Classes laborieuses et classes dangereuses à Paris pendant la première moitié du XIXe siècle.* Plon: Paris, 2002.

Chevalier, Michel. *Éxposition Universelle de Londres en 1851.* Paris: L. Mathias, 1851.

Choisel, Francis. *Bonapartisme et Gaullisme.* Paris: Albatros, 1987.

Chomsky, Noam. *Necessary Illusions: Thought Control in Democratic Societies.* Boston: South End Press, 1989.

Christelow, Allen. *Muslim Law Courts and the French Colonial State in Algeria.* Princeton NJ: Princeton University Press, 1985.

Christiansen, Rupert. *Paris Babylon: The Story of the Paris Commune.* New York: Viking, 1995.

Çinar, Alev, and Thomas Bender, eds. *Urban Imaginaries: Locating the Modern City.* Minneapolis: University of Minnesota Press, 2007.

Clancy-Smith, Julia A. *Rebel and Saint: Muslim Notables, Populist Protest, Colonial Encounters, Algeria and Tunisia, 1800–1904.* Berkeley: University of California Press, 1994.

Clark, Christopher. "After 1848: The European Revolution in Government." *Transactions of The Royal Historical Society* 22 (December 2012): 171–97.

Clark, T. J. *The Absolute Bourgeois: Artists and Politics in France, 1848–1851.* Berkeley: University of California Press, 1973.

―――. *The Painting of Modern Life: Paris in the Art of Manet and His Followers.* New York: Knopf, 1985.

Clifford, James. *Routes: Travel and Translation in the Late Twentieth Century.* Cambridge MA: Harvard University Press, 1997.

Coilly, Nathalie, and Philippe Régnier, eds. *Le Siècle des Saint-Simoniens.* Paris: Bibliothèque Nationale, 2006.

Colas, Dominique, Claude Emeri, and Jacques Zylberberg, eds. *Citoyenneté et nationalité.* Paris : Presses Universitaires de France, 1991.

Coller, Ian. *Arab France: Islam and the Making of Modern Europe, 1798-1831.* Berkeley: University of California Press, 2010.

Collins, Irene. *The Government and the Newspaper, 1813-1881.* Oxford: Oxford University Press, 1959.

Comte, Auguste. *The Fundamental Principles of the Positive Philosophy.* Translated by Paul Descours. London: Watts, 1905.

———. *A General View of Positivism.* Translated by J. H. Bridges. London: Trubner, 1865.

Congrès international des étudiants: Compte rendu official et intégral. Brussels: Imprimerie Bauvais, 1866.

Conklin, Alice L. *A Mission to Civilize: The Republican Idea of Empire in France and West Africa, 1895-1930.* Stanford CA: Stanford University Press, 1997.

Conquête et oppression, Nationalité et liberté. Paris: E. Dentu, 1860.

Conseil Général de la Province d'Oran: Rapports de M. le Préfet et procès-verbaux des séances. Oran: Adolphe Perrier, 1863-1870.

Constant, Benjamin. *De la religion.* 2 vols. Paris: Béchet Ainé, 1825.

Cooper, Frederick. *Colonialism in Question: Theory, Knowledge, History.* Berkeley: University of California Press, 2005.

Cooper, Frederick, and Ann Laura Stoler, eds. *Tensions of Empire: Colonial Cultures in a Bourgeois World.* Berkeley: University of California Press, 1997.

Coppa, Frank J. *Pope Pius IX: Crusader in A Secular Age.* Boston: Twayne, 1979.

Cottin, Paul. *Lettre à des électeurs: un député en Algérie.* Paris: A. Le Chévalier, 1868.

Crook, Malcolm, William Doyle, and Alan Forrest, eds. *Enlightenment and Revolution.* Cornwall: Ashgate, 2004.

Curtis, Sarah A. *Educating the Faithful: Religion, Schooling and Society in Nineteenth-Century France.* DeKalb: Northern Illinois University Press, 2000.

———. "Supply and Demand: Religious Schooling in Nineteenth-Century France." *History of Education Quarterly* 39, no. 1 (Spring 1999): 51-72.

Da Costa, Gaston. *La Commune vécue.* 3 vols. Paris: Maison Quantin, 1905.

Dallas, Gregor. *At the Heart of a Tiger: Clemenceau and his World, 1841-1929.* New York: Carroll and Graf, 1993.

Danziger, Raphael. *Abd al-Quadir and the Algerians: Resistance to the French and Internal Consolidation.* New York: Holmes and Meier, 1977.

Darmesteter, Madame James. *The Life of Ernest Renan.* London: Methuen, 1898.

Darriulat, Philippe. *Les Patriotes: la gauche républicaine et la nation, 1830-1870.* Paris: Seuil, 2001.

Daudet, Alphonse. *Adventures prodigieuse de Tartarin de Tarascon.* Paris: Le Livre de Poche, 1997.

Davis, Stacey Renee. "Turning French Convicts into Colonists: The Second Empire's Political Prisoners in Algeria, 1852-1858." *French Colonial History* 2 (2002): 93-113.

Delaroa, Joseph. *Le Duc de Persigny et les doctrines de l'Empire*. Paris: Henri Plon, 1865.

Dell'Osso, Monica. "The Ministry of Algeria and the Colonies, 12 June 1858–24 November 1860: An Experiment in Civil Government." PhD dissertation, University of Virginia, 1989.

Delord, Taxile. *Histoire du Second Empire*. 5 vols. Paris: Librairie Germer Baillère, 1973.

Derfler, Leslie. *Paul Lafargue and the Founding of French Marxism, 1842–1882*. Cambridge MA: Harvard University Press, 1991.

Desan, Suzanne, Lynn Hunt, and William Max Nelson. *The French Revolution in Global Perspective*. Ithaca NY: Cornell University Press, 2013.

Deschanel, Paul. *Gambetta*. London: William Heinemann, 1920.

Desmaze, Charles. *Rapports à son Excellence le Ministre de l'Intérieur sur l'émigration*. Paris: Imprimerie impériale, 1859.

Desprez, Charles. *Alger naguère et maintenant*. Algiers: Imprimerie du Courrier de l'Algérie, 1868.

Dhombres, Nicole, and Jean Dhombres. *Naissance d'un pouvoir: Sciences et savants en France, 1793–1824*. Paris: Payot, 1989.

Djaït, Hichem. *Europe and Islam*. Translated by Peter Heinegg. Berkeley: University of California Press, 1985.

Dodman, Thomas. "Un pays pour la colonie: Mourir de nostalgie en Algérie française, 1830–1880." *Annales, histoire, sciences sociales* 3 (July–September 2011): 743–84.

Drescher, Seymour. *Capitalism and Antislavery: British Mobilization in Comparative Perspective*. Oxford: Oxford University Press, 1986.

Driver, Felix, and David Gilbert, eds. *Imperial Cities: Landscape, Display and Identity*. Manchester: Manchester University Press, 1999.

Dubois, Laurent. *A Colony of Citizens: Revolution and Slave Emancipation in the French Caribbean, 1787–1804*. Chapel Hill: University of North Carolina Press, 2004.

———. "The Price of Liberty: Victor Hugues and the Administration of Freedom in Guadeloupe, 1794–1798." *William and Mary Quarterly* 56, no. 2 (April 1999): 363–92.

Duruy, Victor. *Notes et souvenirs*. 2 vols. Paris: Hachette, 1901.

Duval, Jules. *L'Algérie et les colonies françaises*. Paris: Librairie Guillaumin, 1879.

———. *Les Colonies et la politique coloniale de la France*. Paris: Arthur Bertrand, 1864.

———. *Notre Pays*. Paris: Hachette, 1867.

———. *Réflexions sur la politique de l'Empereur en Algérie*. Paris: Challamel Ainé, 1866.

Duvernois, Clément. *L'Akhbar et les novateurs téméraires: Lettre à M. A. Bourget*. Algiers: Dubos Frères, 1858.

———. *L'Algérie: Ce qu'elle est, ce qu'elle doit être*. Algiers: Dubos Frères, 1858.

———. *La Liberté de discussion: lettre à M. Levert préfet d'Alger* Algiers: Dubos Frères, 1860.

———. *La Réorganisation de l'Algérie: Lettre à S. A. I. le Prince Napoléon*. Algiers: Dubos Frères, 1858.

——. *Le Couronnement de l'édifice: Liberté démocratique.* Paris: E. Dentu, 1860.

——. *Un Suicide politique: Lettre à Émile de Girardin.* Paris: E. Dentu, 1861.

Duveyrier, Charles. *Civilisation et la démocratie française.* Paris: Bureaux de l'Encyclopédie, 1865.

Duvivier, J. H. *L'Empire en province.* Paris: E. Dentu, 1861.

Eckalbar, John C. "The Saint-Simonians in Industry and Economic Development." *American Journal of Economics and Sociology* 38, no. 1 (January 1979): 83–96.

Eisenstadt, S. N. "Multiple Modernities." *Daedalus* 129, no. 1 (Winter 2000): 1–29.

Elias, Norbert. *The Civilizing Process.* Translated by Edmund Jephcott. New York: Urizen, 1978.

Elwitt, Stanford. *The Making of the Third Republic: Class and Politics in France, 1868–1884.* Baton Rouge: Louisiana State University Press, 1975.

Emerit, Marcel, ed. *La Revolution de 1848 en Algérie.* Paris: Larose, 1949.

——. *Les Saint-Simoniens en Algérie.* Paris: Faculté des Lettres d'Alger, 1941.

Emmer, P. C., O. Pétré-Grenouilleau, and J. V. Roitman, eds. *A Deus ex Machina Revisited: Atlantic Colonial Trade and European Economic Development.* Leiden: Brill, 2006.

Enfantin, Prosper. *Colonisation de l'Algérie.* Paris: P. Bertrand, 1843.

Eros, John. "The Positivist Generation of French Republicanism." *Sociological Review* 3, no. 1 (July 1955): 255–77.

Étourneau, M. *L'Algérie faisant appel à La France.* Paris: Grassart, 1867.

Evans, Martin, and Amanda Sackur, eds. *Empire and Culture: The French Experience, 1830–1940.* New York: Palgrave Macmillan, 2004.

Fabian, Johannes. *Time and the Other: How Anthropology Makes Its Object.* New York: Columbia University Press, 1983.

Falloux, Alfred de. *Mémoires d'un royaliste.* 2 vols. Paris: Perrin, 1888.

Favre, Jules. *Discours parlementaires.* 4 vols. Paris: E. Plon, 1881.

——. *Jules Favre à Constantine.* Paris: Challamel, 1870.

——. *Plaidoyers et discours du bâtonnat.* 3 vols. Paris: Marescq Aîné, 1893.

Fehér, Ferenc, ed. *The French Revolution and the Birth of Modernity.* Berkeley: University of California Press, 1990.

Ferry, Jules. *La Lutte électorale en 1863.* Paris: E. Dentu, 1863.

Feydeau, Ernest. *Alger: Étude.* Paris: Editions Bouchene, 2003.

Flaubert, Gustave. *Flaubert in Egypt.* Translated by Francis Steegmuller. New York: Penguin, 1996.

——. *Madame Bovary.* Translated by Lowell Bair. New York: Bantam, 1989.

——. *A Sentimental Education.* Translated by Douglass Parmée. Oxford: Oxford University Press, 1989.

Fonvielle, Wilfrid de. *L'Empereur en Algérie.* Paris: E. Dentu, 1860.

Fort, Bernadette, ed. *Fictions of the French Revolution.* Evanston, IL: Northwestern University Press, 1991.

Forth, Christopher E., and Elinor Accampo, eds. *Confronting Modernity in Fin-de-Siècle France: Bodies, Minds and Gender.* New York: Palgrave Macmillan, 2010.

Foucault, Michel. *The Order of Things: An Archeology of the Human Sciences.* New York: Vintage, 1994.

Fourmestraux, Eugène. *Les Idées Napoléoniennes en Algérie.* Paris: Challamel Ainé, 1866.

Fournel, Victor. *Paris nouveau et Paris futur.* Paris: J. Lecoffre, 1865.

Frémeaux, Jacques. *La France et l'Islam depuis 1789.* Paris: Presses Universitaires de France, 1991.

———. *Les Bureaux arabes dans l'Algérie de la conquête.* Paris: Denöel, 1993.

Frémigacci, Jean. "L'État colonial français, du discours mythique aux réalités 1880–1940." *Matériaux pour l'Histoire de Norte Temps* 32–33 (1993): 27–35.

Friedland, Roger, and Deirdre Boden, eds. *NowHere: Space, Time, and Modernity.* Berkeley: University of California Press, 1994.

Fritzsche, Peter. *Stranded in the Present: Modern Time and the Melancholy of History.* Cambridge MA: Harvard University Press, 2004.

Fromentin, Eugène. *Between Sea and Sahara: An Algerian Journal.* Translated by Blake Robinson. Athens: Ohio University Press, 1999.

———. *Œuvres completes.* Paris: Gallimard, 1984.

Furet, François. "History and 'Savages.'" *Rain* 8 (May–June 1975): 4–6.

———. *Penser la Révolution Française.* Paris: Gallimard, 1978.

Gaboriaux, Chloé. *La République en quête de citoyens: Les républicains français face au bonapartisme rural, 1848–1880.* Paris: Les Presses de Science Po, 2010.

Gaillard, Jean-Michel. *Jules Ferry.* Paris: Fayard, 1989.

Gallagher, John G. *The Students of Paris and the Revolution of 1848.* Carbondale: Southern Illinois University Press, 1980.

Gallois, William *A History of Violence in the Early Algerian Colony.* London: Palgrave Macmillan, 2013.

Garrigues, Jean. *La République des hommes d'affaires, 1870–1900.* Paris: Aubier, 1997.

———. *Les Hommes providentiels: histoire d'une fascination française.* Paris: Seuil, 2012.

Garrigus, John. *Before Haiti: Race and Citizenship in French Saint-Domingue.* New York: Palgrave Macmillan, 2006.

Garrioch, David. *The Formation of the Parisian Bourgeoisie, 1690–1830.* Cambridge MA: Harvard University Press, 1996.

Gautier, Théophile. *Caprices et zigzags.* Paris: Victor Lecou, 1852.

———. *Voyage en Algérie.* Paris: La Boîte à Documents, 1989.

Geary, Patrick. *The Myth of Nations: The Medieval Origins of Europe.* Princeton: Princeton University Press, 2003.

Geison, Gerald L., ed. *Professions and the French State, 1700–1900.* Philadelphia: University of Pennsylvania Press, 1984.

Gellner, Ernest. *Nations and Nationalism.* Oxford: Blackwell, 1983.

Gérardo, Joseph-Marie de. *The Observations of Savage Peoples*. Berkeley: University of California Press, 1969.

Gerson, Stéphane. *The Pride of Place: Local Memories and Political Culture in Nineteenth-Century France*. Ithaca NY: Cornell University Press, 2003.

Giddens, Anthony. *The Consequences of Modernity*. Stanford CA: Stanford University Press, 1990.

Giedji, Eliau Gaston. *L'Enseignement indigène en Algérie au cours de la colonisation, 1832–1962*. Paris: Editions des Ecrivains, 2000.

Girard, Louis. *Les Conseillers généraux en 1870*. Paris: Presses Universitaires de France, 1967.

Girardet, Raoul. *L'Idée coloniale en France de 1871 à 1962*. Paris: Hachette, 1972.

Girardin, Émile de. *Conquête et Nationalité*. Paris: Michel Lévy, 1859.

Glikman, Juliette. "Vœu populaire et bien public, 1852–1870." *Parlement[s]: Revue d'histoire politique* 4 (2008): 84–97.

Gluck, Carol. "The End of Elsewhere: Writing Modernity Now." *American Historical Review* 116, no. 2 (June 2011): 676–87.

Goguel, François. *La Politique des partis sous la Troisième République*. Paris: Seuil, 1956.

Goldstein, Jan. *The Post-Revolutionary Self: Politics and Psyche in France, 1750–1850*. Cambridge MA: Harvard University Press, 2005.

Gosnell, Jonathan K. *The Politics of Frenchness in Colonial Algeria, 1930–1954*. Rochester NY: University of Rochester Press, 2002.

Gould, Roger V. *Insurgent Identities: Class Community and Protest in Paris from 1848 to the Commune*. Chicago: University of Chicago Press, 1995.

Greenfield, Liah. *Nationalism: Five Roads to Modernity*. Cambridge MA: Harvard University Press, 1992.

Guignard, Didier. "Conservatoire ou révolutionnaire? Le sénatus-consulte de 1863 appliqué au régime foncier d'Algérie." *Revue d'histoire du XIXe siècle* 41 (2010): 81–95.

Guionnet, Christine. *L'Apprentissage de la politique moderne: les elections municipales sous le Monarchie de Juillet*. Paris: Harmattan, 1997.

Guizot, François. *Du gouvernement de la France depuis la Restauration et du ministère actuel*. Paris: Libraire Français de l'Avocat, 1820.

——— . *Histoire de la civilisation en Europe depuis la chute de l'Empire romain jusqu'à la Révolution française*. Paris: Hachette, 1985.

——— . *Histoire des origines du gouvernement représentatif et des institutions politiques de l'Europe depuis la chute de l'Empire romain jusqu'au XIXe siècle*. 2 vols. Paris: Didier, 1880.

——— . *Histoire parlementaire de France*. 5 vols. Paris: Michel Lévy, 1863.

Gunn, J. A. W. "French Republicans and the Suffrage: The Birth of the Doctrine of False Consciousness." *French History* 22, no. 1 (March 2008): 28–50.

Guys, Henri. *Études sur les mœurs des Arabes et sur les moyens d'amener ceux de l'Algérie à la civilisation*. Paris: E. Dentu, 1866.

——. *Français et arabes en Algérie*. Paris: Challamel, 1860.

Hahn, H. Hazel. *Scenes of Parisian Modernity: Culture and Consumption in the Nineteenth Century*. New York: Palgrave Macmillan, 2010.

Hain, Victor-Armand. *A la nation, sur Alger*. Paris: Imprimerie de Lachevardiere, 1832.

Halévy, Daniel. *La Fin des notables*. Paris: Grasset, 1930.

Hall, Catherine, and Sonya O. Rose, eds. *At Home with the Empire: Metropolitan Culture and the Imperial World*. Cambridge: Cambridge University Press, 2007.

Hamon, Léo, ed. *Les Républicains sous le Second Empire*. Paris: Editions de la Maison des Sciences de l'Homme, 1993.

Hansen, Eric C. *Disaffection and Decadence: A Crisis in French Intellectual Thought, 1848–1898*. Washington, DC: University Press of America, 1982.

Hanson, Anne Coffin. *Manet and the Modern Tradition*. New Haven CT: Yale University Press, 1977.

Hargreaves, Alec G., and Michael J. Heffernan, eds. *French and Algerian Identities from Colonial Times to the Present: A Century of Interaction*. Lewiston NY: Edwin Mellen, 1993.

Harrigan, Patrick J. *Mobility, Elites, and Education in French Society of the Second Empire*. Ontario: Wilfred Laurier University Press, 1980.

Harsin, Jill. *Barricades: The War of The Streets in Revolutionary Paris, 1840–1848*. New York: Palgrave, 2002.

Harvey, David. *The Condition of Postmodernity*. Oxford: Oxford University Press, 1990.

——. *Consciousness and the Urban Experience*. Baltimore: Johns Hopkins University Press, 1985.

Hauranne, Ernest Duvergier de. *La Coalition libérale*. Paris: Armand le Chevalier, 1969.

Hauterive, Ernest d', ed. *Napoléon III et le Prince Napoléon: Correspondance inédite*. Paris: Calmann-Lévy, 1925.

Hazareesingh, Sudhir. "'A Common Sentiment of National Glory': Civic Festivities and French Collective Sentiment under the Second Empire." *Journal of Modern History* 76 (June 2004): 280–311.

——. *From Subject to Citizen: The Second Empire and the Emergence of Modern French Democracy*. Princeton NJ: Princeton University Press, 1998.

——. *Intellectual Founders of the Republic: Five Studies in Nineteenth-Century French Political Thought*. Oxford: Oxford University Press, 2001.

——. *The Legend of Napoleon*. London: Granata Press, 2004.

——. *Political Traditions in Modern France*. Oxford: Oxford University Press, 1994.

——. *The Saint-Napoleon: Celebrations of Sovereignty in Nineteenth-Century France*. Cambridge MA: Harvard University Press, 2004.

Heffernan, Michael J. "The Parisian Poor and the Colonization of Algeria during the Second Republic." *French History* 3, no. 4 (1989): 377–403.

Heggoy, Alf Andrew. "Education in French Algeria: An Essay on Cultural Conflict." *Comparative Education Review* 17, no. 2 (June 1973): 180–97.

Hesse, Barnor, ed. *Un/settled Multicultralisms: Diasporas, Entanglements, Disruptions.* London: Zed Books, 2001.

Hobsbawm, Eric. *Nations and Nationalism since 1780: Programme, Myth, Reality.* Cambridge: Cambridge University Press, 1992.

Hodson, Christopher. "Colonizing the *Patrie*: An Experiment Gone Wrong in Old Regime France." *French Historical Studies* 32, no. 2 (Spring 2009): 193–222.

Horne, Janet. *A Social Laboratory for Modern France: The Musée Social and the Rise of the Welfare State.* Durham NC: Duke University Press, 2002.

Horner, R. P. *Voyage à la côte orientale d'Afrique pendant l'année 1866.* Paris: Gaume Frères, 1872.

Horvath-Peterson, Sandra. *Victor Duruy and French Education: Liberal Reform in the Second Empire.* Baton Rouge: Louisiana State University Press, 1984.

Huard, Raymond. *La Naissance du parti politique en France.* Paris: Presse de la Fondation Nationale des Sciences Politique, 1996.

Huet, Marie-Hélène. *The Culture of Disaster.* Chicago: University of Chicago Press, 2012.

Hugo, Victor. *Napoleon the Little.* New York: Sheldon, 1870.

Hugonnet, Ferdinand. *Français et Arabes en Algérie.* Paris: Challamel Ainé, 1860.

———. *Souvenirs d'un chef de Bureau arabe.* Paris: Michel Lévy, 1858.

Hulliung, Mark. *Citizens and Citoyens: Republicans and Liberals in America and France.* Cambridge MA: Harvard University Press, 2002.

Hunt, Lynn. *Politics, Culture and Class in the French Revolution.* Berkeley: University of California Press, 1984.

Hutton, Patrick H. *The Cult of the Revolutionary Tradition: The Blanquists in French Politics, 1864–1893.* Berkeley: University of California Press, 1981.

Inkeles, Alex, and David Smith, *Becoming Modern.* Cambridge MA: Harvard University Press, 1974.

Jainchill, Andrew. *Reimagining Politics after the Terror: The Republican Origins of French Liberalism.* Ithaca NY: Cornell University Press, 2008.

Jainchill, Andrew, and Samuel Moyn, "French Democracy between Totalitarianism and Solidarity: Pierre Rosanvallon and Revisionist Historiography." *Journal of Modern History* 76 (March: 2004): 107–54.

Jennings, Lawrence C. *French Anti-Slavery: The Movement for the Abolition of Slavery in France, 1802–1848.* Cambridge: Cambridge University Press, 2000.

Jordan, David P. "Baron Haussmann and Modern Paris." *American Scholar* 61, no. 1 (Winter 1992): 100–114.

———. *Transforming Paris: The Life and Times of Baron Haussmann.* New York: Maxwell Macmillan, 1995.

Judt, Tony. "Rights in France: Reflections on the Etiolation of a Political Language." *Tocqueville Review* 14 (1993): 67–108.

Julien, Charles-André. *Histoire de l'Algérie contemporaine: La conquête et les débuts de la colonisation, 1827–1871.* Paris: Presses Universitaires de France, 1964.

Kahan, Alan. *Liberalism in Nineteenth-Century Europe: The Political Culture of Limited Suffrage*. New York: Palgrave Macmillan, 2003.

Kale, Steven D. *Legitimism and the Reconstruction of French Society, 1852–1883*. Baton Rouge: Louisiana State University Press, 1992.

Katznelson, Ira, and Aristide R. Zolberg, eds. *Working-Class Formation: Nineteenth-Century Patterns in Western Europe and the United States*. Princeton NJ: Princeton University Press, 1986.

Kerr, Clark, John T. Dunlop, Frederick Harrison, and Charles Myers. *Industrialism and Industrial Man: The Problems of Labor and Management in Industrial Growth*. Cambridge MA: Harvard University Press, 1960.

Kielstra, Paul Michael. *The Politics of Slave Trade Suppression in Britain and France, 1814–1848*. New York: Palgrave Macmillan, 2000.

Kirkland, Stephane. *Paris Reborn: Napoleon III, Baron Haussmann and the Quest to Build a Modern City*. New York: Picador, 2013.

Kolakowski, Leszek. *Modernity on Endless Trial*. Chicago: University of Chicago Press, 1990.

Koselleck, Reinhart. *Future's Past: On the Semantics of Historical Time*. Translated by Keith Tribe. Cambridge MA: MIT Press, 1985.

Kumar, Krishan. "Nation-States as Empires, Empires as Nation-States: Two Principles, One Practice?" *Journal of Theory and Society* 39 (2010): 119–43.

Kwon, Yun Kyoung. "When Parisian Liberals Spoke for Haiti: French Antislavery Discourses on Haiti under the Restoration, 1814–1830." *Atlantic Studies* 8, no. 3 (September 2011): 317–41.

Laboulaye, Édouard. *Le Parti libéral*. Paris: Charpentier, 1863.

——— . *L'État et ses limites suivi d'essais politique*. Paris: Charpentier, 1868.

Laclau, Ernesto. "The Death and Resurrection of the Theory of Ideology." *MLN* 112, no. 3 (April 1997): 297–321.

Lacretelle, Charles Nicolas. *De l'Algérie au point de vue de la crise actuelle*. Paris: Challamel Ainé, 1868.

Lacroix, Frédéric. *L'Algérie et la lettre de l'Empereur*. Paris: Challamel, 1863.

Lafargue, Paul. *Le Droit à presses*. Paris: François Maspero, 1972.

Landes, David S. *The Unbound Prometheus: Technological Change and Industrial Development in Western Europe from 1750 to the Present*. Cambridge: Cambridge University Press, 2003.

La Question d'Orient au point de vue français et catholique. Paris: Charles Douniot, 1864.

Lara, Oruno D. *La Liberté assassinée: Guadeloupe, Guyane, Martinique, et la Réunion en 1848–1856*. Paris: Harmattan, 2005.

Larcher, Silyane. *L'Autre citoyen: L'idéal républicain et les Antilles après l'esclavage*. Paris: Armand Colin, 2014.

Latour, Bruno. *We Have Never Been Modern*. Translated by Catherine Porter. Cambridge MA: Harvard University Press, 1993.

Leblois, L. *Discours prononcé en l'Église du Temple-Neuf à Strasbourg*. Strasbourg: Frédéric-Charles Heitz, 1860.

Lecouturier, Henri. *Paris incompatible avec la République*. Paris: Desloges, 1848.

Lefort, Claude. *Democracy and Political Theory*. Cambridge: Polity Press, 1988.

——. *The Political Forms of Modern Society*. Cambridge: Polity Press, 1986.

Le Goff, Jacques. *Histoire et mémoire*. Paris: Gallimard, 1988.

Lehning, James R. *The Melodramatic Thread: Spectacle and Political Culture in Modern France*. Bloomington: University of Indiana Press, 2007.

——. *Peasant and French: Cultural Contact in Rural France during the Nineteenth Century*. Cambridge: Cambridge University Press, 1995.

——. *To Be a Citizen: The Political Culture of the Early Third Republic*. Ithaca NY: Cornell University Press, 2001.

Lejeune, Dominique. *Les Sociétés de géographie en France et l'expansion coloniale au XIXe siècle*. Paris: Michel Albin, 1993.

Lemaire, Sandrine, Pascal Blanchard, and Nicolas Bancel, eds. *Culture coloniale en France de la Revolution française à nos jours*. Paris: CNRS Editions, 2008.

Levallois, Anne, ed. *Les Écrits autobiographiques d'Ismayl Urbain: Homme de couleur, Saint-Simonien et Musulman, 1812-1884*. Paris: Maisonneuve et Larose, 2005.

Levallois, Michel. *Ismaÿl Urbain: Une autre conquête de l'Algérie*. Paris: Maisonneuve et Larose, 2001.

Levallois, Michel, and Sarga Moussa, eds. *L'Orientalisme des Saint-Simoniens*. Paris: Maisonneuve et Larose, 2006.

Lévêque, Pierre. *Histoire des forces politiques en France, 1789-1880*. Paris: Armand Colin, 1992.

Littré, Émile. *Comte et la Philosophie Positive*. Paris: Bureaux de la philosophie Positive, 1877.

——. *Conservation Révolution Positivisme*. Paris: Ledrange, 1852.

——. *Dictionnaire de la langue française*. 6 vols. Versailles: Partenaires livres, 2004.

——. *Du devoir de l'homme envers lui-même et envers ses semblables*. Paris: Loge la Clémente Ainé, 1906.

Lorcin, Patricia M. E. *Imperial Identities: Stereotyping, Prejudice and Race in Colonial Algeria*. London: I. B. Tauris, 1995.

Mackenzie, John M. *Imperialism and Popular Culture*. Manchester: Manchester University Press, 1986.

MacMahon, Patrice de. *Mémoires: Souvenirs d'Algérie*. Paris: Plon, 1923.

Margadant, Ted W. *French Peasants in Revolt: The Insurrection of 1851*. Princeton NJ: Princeton University Press, 1979.

Marsh, Kate, and Nicola Firth, eds. *France's Lost Empires: Fragmentation, Nostalgia and la fracture coloniale*. Plymouth: Lexington Books, 2011.

Marx, Karl. *Class Struggles in France*. London: Martin Lawrence, 1895.

———. *The Eighteenth Brumaire of Louis Bonaparte*. New York: International Publishers, 1998.

Matsuda, Matt K. *The Memory of the Modern*. Oxford: Oxford University Press, 1996.

Maurian, Jean. *La Politique écclésiastique du Second Empire, 1852–1869*. Paris: Félix Alcan, 1930.

Mayer, J. P. *The Recollections of Alexis de Tocqueville*. New York: Columbia University Press, 1949.

Maza, Sarah. *The Myth of the French Bourgeoisie: An Essay on the Social Imaginary, 1750–1850*. Cambridge MA: Harvard University Press, 2003.

McMahon, Darrin M. *Enemies of the Enlightenment: The French Counter-Enlightenment and the Making of Modernity*. Oxford: Oxford University Press, 2001.

Mélonio, Françoise. *Naissance et affirmation d'une culture nationale: La France de 1815 à 1880*. Paris: Seuil, 1998.

Melzer, Sara. *Colonizer or Colonized: The Hidden Stories of Early Modern French Culture*. Philadelphia: University of Pennsylvania Press, 2012.

Ménager, Bernard. *Les Napoléon du peuple*. Paris: Aubier, 1988.

Merle, Isabelle. "Retour sur le régime de l'indigénat: genèse et contradictions des principes répressifs dans l'empire français." *French Politics, Culture and Society* 20, no. 2 (Summer 2002): 77–99.

Michelet, Jules. *Le Peuple*. Paris: Flammarion, 1974.

———. *The People*. Translated by G. H. Smith. New York: D. Appleton, 1846.

Miller, Alexei, and Stefan Berger, eds. *Nationalizing Empires*. Budapest: Central European University Press, 2015.

Miller, Michael B. *The Bon Marché: Bourgeois Culture and the Department Store, 1869–1920*. Princeton NJ: Princeton University Press, 1981.

Miravals, Raimond de. *Causeries parisiennes*. Dragignan: P. Gimbert, 1867.

Mitchell, Timothy, ed. *Questions of Modernity*. Minneapolis: University of Minnesota Press, 2000.

Mondonico-Torri, Cécile. "Aux origines du Code de la nationalité en France." *Le Mouvement Social* 171 (April–June 1995): 31–46.

Monselet, Charles. *Les Ruines de Paris*. 4 vols. Paris: L. de Potter, 1857.

Montalembert, Charles de. *Discours de M. le Comte de Montalembert*. 3 vols. Paris: Jacques Lecoffre, 1860.

———. *L'Église libre dans l'État libre*. Dijon: L'Échelle de Jacob, 2006.

Moody, Joseph N. *Church and Society: Catholic Social and Political Thought and Movements, 1789–1950*. New York: Arts, 1953.

———. "The French Catholic Press in the Education Conflict of the 1840s." *French Historical Studies* 87 (1972): 394–415.

Moore, Wilbert E. *Industrialization and Labor: Social Aspects of Economic Development*. Ithaca NY: Cornell University Press, 1951.

Morin, René. *Civilisation: Unité*. Saumur: P. Godet, 1854.

Morton, Patricia A. *Hybrid Modernities: Architecture and Representation at the 1931 Colonial Exposition, Paris*. Cambridge MA: Harvard University Press, 2000.

Musset, Alfred de. *The Confession of a Child of the Century*. Westport CT: Hyperion, 1978.

Muthu, Sankar, ed. *Empire and Modern Political Thought*. Cambridge: Cambridge University Press, 2012.

Namier, Lewis. *1848: The Revolution of Intellectuals*. Oxford: Oxford University Press, 1992.

Nicolet, Claude. *L'Idée republicaine en France*. Paris: Gallimard, 1982.

Nord, Philip. *The Republican Moment: Struggles for Democracy in Nineteenth-Century France*. Cambridge MA: Harvard University Press, 1995.

Nouschi, André, ed. *Correspondance du Docteur A. Vital avec I. Urbain*. Paris: Larose, 1959.

O'Brien, Karen. *Narratives of Enlightenment: Cosmopolitan History from Voltaire to Gibbon*. Cambridge: Cambridge University Press, 1997.

Ollivier, Émile. *Journal, 1846–1869*. 2 vols. Paris: René Juillard, 1961.

Oulebsir, Nabila. *Les Usages du patrimoine: monuments, musées et politique coloniale en Algérie, 1830–1930*. Paris: Editions de la Maison des Sciences de l'Homme, 2004.

Pagden, Anthony. "The Savage Critic: Some European Images of the Primitive." *Yearbook of English Studies* 13 (1983): 32–45.

Papiers et correspondance de la famille impériale. 2 vols. Paris: Garnier Frères, 1871.

Paz, Octavio. *Alternating Currents*. Translated by Helen Lane. New York: Viking, 1973.

Pelletan, Eugène. *Le Monde marche: lettres à Lamartine*. Paris: Pagnerre, 1857.

———. *Les Droits de l'homme*. Paris: Pagnerre, 1867.

Perkins, Kenneth J. *Quaids, Captains and Colons: French Military Administration in the Colonial Maghrib, 1844–1934*. New York: Africana, 1981.

Perovic, Sanja. *The Calendar in Revolutionary France: Perceptions of Time in Literature, Culture, Politics*. Cambridge: Cambridge University Press, 2012.

Perrod, Pierre Antoine. *Jules Favre: Avocat de la liberté*. Lyon: La Manufacture, 1988.

Pilbeam Pamela M. *Republicanism in Nineteenth-Century France, 1814–1871*. New York: St. Martin's Press, 1995.

———. *The Saint Simonians in Nineteenth-Century France: From Free Love to Algeria*. New York: Palgrave Macmillan, 2014.

Pinkney, David H. *Decisive Years in France, 1840–1847*. Princeton NJ: Princeton University Press, 1986.

———. "Money and Politics in the Rebuilding of Paris, 1860–1870." *Journal of Economic History* 17, no. 1 (March 1957): 45–61.

———. *Napoleon III and the Rebuilding of Paris*. Princeton NJ: Princeton University Press, 1958.

Pitt, Alan. "The Irrational Liberalism of Hippolyte Taine." *The Historical Journal*, 41:4 (December 1998): 1035–53.

Pitts, Jennifer. *A Turn to Empire: The Rise of Imperial Liberalism in France and Britain.* Princeton NJ: Princeton University Press, 2005.

Plessis, Alain. *De la fête imperial au mur des fédérés, 1852–1871.* Paris: Seuil, 1979.

———. *La Politique de la Banque de France de 1851 à 1870.* Geneva: Droz, 1985.

Ponteil, Félix. *Les Institutions de la France de 1814 à 1870.* Paris: Presses Universitaires de France, 1966.

Popkin, Jeremy D. *Press, Revolution, and Social Identities in France, 1830–1835.* University Park: Pennsylvania State University Press, 2002.

Poujoulat, Jean-Joseph François. *Études africaines.* 2 vols. Paris: Imprimeurs-Unis, 1847.

———. *Voyage en Algérie.* Paris: Vermot, 1861.

Prévost-Paradol, Lucien Anatole. *La France nouvelle.* Paris : Michel Lévy, 1868.

Price, Roger. *The French Second Empire: An Anatomy of Political Power.* Cambridge: Cambridge University Press, 2001.

———. *The Modernization of Rural France: Communications, Networks and Agricultural Market Structures in Nineteenth-Century France.* New York: St. Martin's Press, 1983.

———. *People and Politics in France, 1848–1870.* Cambridge: Cambridge University Press, 2004.

———, ed. *Revolution and Reaction: 1848 and the Second French Empire.* London: Croom Helm, 1975.

———. *A Social History of Nineteenth-Century France.* New York: Holmes and Meier, 1987.

Prochaska, David. *Making Algeria French: Colonization in Bône, 1870–1920.* Cambridge: Cambridge University Press, 1990.

Proudhon, Pierre-Joseph. *Œuvres complètes.* 14 vols. Paris: Marcel Rivière, 1924.

Quinet, Edgar. *La Révolution.* Paris: Velin, 1987.

———. *Lettres d'exile.* 3 vols. Paris: Calmann Lévy, 1885.

Rabinow, Paul. *French Modern: Norms and Forms of the Social Environment.* Chicago: University of Chicago Press, 1989.

Rapport de préfet et délibérations du conseil général: Province de Constantine. Constantine: Veuve Guende, 1861–70.

Rapport, Michael. *Nationality and Citizenship in Revolutionary France: The Treatment of Foreigners, 1789–1799.* Oxford: Oxford University Press, 2000.

Rapports sur le Budget et procès-verbaux des Délibérations du conseil général. Constantine: Veuve Guende, 1865.

Renan, Ernest. *The Future of Science.* Boston: Roberts Brothers, 1893.

Rey-Goldzeiguer, Annie. *Le Royaume Arabe: La politique algérienne de Napoléon III, 1861–1870.* Algiers: Société Nationale d'Editions et de Diffusion, 1977.

Rimbaud, Arthur. *A Season in Hell.* Translated by Louise Varèse. New York: New Directions, 1961.

Robb, Graham. *The Discovery of France: A Historical Geography from the Revolution to the First World War*. New York: Norton, 2007.

Robiquet, Paul, ed. *Discours et opinions de Jules Ferry*. Paris: Armand Colin, 1893.

Rofel, Lisa. *Other Modernities: Gendered Yearnings in China after Socialism*. Berkeley: University of California Press, 1999.

Rogers, Susan Carol. "Good to Think: The 'Peasant' in Contemporary France." *Anthropological Quarterly* 60, no. 2 (April 1987): 56–63.

Rosanvallon, Pierre. *La Démocratie inachevée: histoire de la souveraineté du peuple en France*. Paris: Gallimard, 2000.

———. *Le Moment Guizot*. Paris: Gallimard, 1985.

Ross, Kristin. *Fast Cars, Clean Bodies: Decolonization and the Reordering of French Culture*. Cambridge MA: MIT Press, 1995.

Rothney, John. *Bonapartism after Sedan*. Ithaca NY: Cornell University Press, 1969.

Sagan, Eli. *Citizens and Cannibals: The French Revolution, the Struggle for Modernity and the Origins of Ideological Terror*. Lanham, MD: Rowman and Littlefield, 2001.

Sahlins, Peter. *Unnaturally French: Foreign Citizens in the Old Regime and After*. Ithaca NY: Cornell University Press, 2004.

Said, Edward. *Culture and Imperialism*. New York: Knopf, 1993.

Saint-Simon, Henri de. *Œuvres de Claude-Henri de Saint-Simon*. 6 vols. Paris, Anthropos, 1966.

Saint-Simon, Henri de, and Prosper Enfantin. *Œuvres de Saint-Simon et d'Enfantin*. 47 vols. Aalen: O. Zeller, 1963–64.

Salinas, Claire. "Colonies without Colonists: Colonial Emigration, Algeria and Liberal Politics in France, 1848–1870." PhD dissertation, Stanford University, 2005.

Schafer, Tony, and Amanda Sackur, eds. *Promoting the Colonial Idea: Propaganda and Visions of Empire in France*. New York: Palgrave, 2002.

Schloss, Rebecca Hartkopf. "The February 1831 Slave Uprising in Martinique and the Policing of White Identity." *French Historical Studies* 30, no. 2 (Spring 2007): 203–36.

———. *Sweet Liberty: The Final Days of Slavery in Martinique*. Philadelphia: University of Pennsylvania Press, 2009.

Schmidt, Nelly. *Abolitionnistes de l'esclavage et reformateurs des colonies*. Paris: Éditions Karthala, 2000.

Schnapper, Dominique. *Community of Citizens: On the Modern Idea of Nationality*. Translated by Séverine Rosée. New Brunswick NJ: Transactions, 1998.

Schweitzer, Albert. *The Quest for the Historical Jesus*. Minneapolis: Fortress Press, 2001.

Seigel, Jerrold. *Bohemian Paris: Culture, Politics and The Boundaries of Bourgeois Life, 1830–1930*. Baltimore: Johns Hopkins University Press, 1986.

———. *Modernity and Bourgeois Life: Society, Politics and Culture in England, France and Germany since 1750*. Cambridge: Cambridge University Press, 2012.

Sellam, Sadek. *La France et ses musulmans: un siècle de politique musulmane, 1995–2005*. Paris, Fayard, 2006.

Senhaux, Henri de. *La France et l'Algérie*. Paris: Challamel Ainé, 1872.

Sessions, Jennifer E. *By Sword and Plow: France and the Conquest of Algeria*. Ithaca NY: Cornell University Press, 2011.

Shaw, Matthew. *Time and the French Revolution: The Republican Calendar, 1789–Year XIV*. London: Boydell and Brewer, 2001.

Shepard, Todd. *The Invention of Decolonization: The Algerian War and the Remaking of France*. Ithaca NY: Cornell University Press, 2006.

Shreier, Joshua. "Napoléon's Long Shadow: Morality, Civilization and Jews in France and Algeria, 1808–1870." *French Historical Studies* 30, no. 1 (Winter 2007): 77–103.

Silverstein, Paul A. *Algeria in France: Transpolitics, Race and Nation*. Bloomington: Indiana University Press, 2004.

Simon, Jules. *La Liberté*. 2 vols. Paris: Hachette, 1859.

———. *La Politique radicale*. Paris: Librairie Internationale, 1868.

———. *Le Devoir*. Paris: Hachette, 1863.

Smith, Andrea L. "Citizenship in the Colony: Naturalization Law and Legal Assimilation in Nineteenth-Century Algeria." *Polar* 11, no. 1 (1996): 33–50.

Solms, E. de, and E. de Bassano. *Pétition à l'Assemblée Nationale: Projet de Colonisation de l'Algérie par l'association*. Paris: Édouard Proux, 1848.

Spieler, Miranda Frances. *Empire and Underworld: Captivity in French Guiana*. Cambridge MA: Harvard University Press, 2012.

Spillmann, Georges. *Napoléon III et le Royaume Arabe d'Algérie*. Paris: Académie des Sciences d'Outre-Mer, 1975.

Spitzer, Alan B. *The Revolutionary Theories of Louis Auguste Blanqui*. New York: Columbia University Press, 1957.

Staum, Martin S. *Labeling People: French Scholars on Society, Race and Empire, 1815–1848*. Montreal: McGill-Queen's University Press, 2003.

Stern, Daniel. *Histoire de la révolution de 1848*. 2 vols. Paris: Charpentier, 1862.

Stora, Benjamin. *La Gangrène et l'oubli: la mémoire de la guerre d'Algérie*. Paris: La Découverte, 1991.

Sullivan, Anthony Thrall. *Thomas-Robert Bugeaud, France and Algeria, 1789–1849: Politics, Power and the Good Society*. Hamden CT: Archon, 1983.

Suny, Ronald Grigor, and Terry Martin, eds. *A State of Nations: Empire and Nation-Making in the Age of Lenin and Stalin*. Oxford: Oxford University Press, 2001.

Swart, Koenraad W. *The Sense of Decadence in Nineteenth-Century France*. The Hague: Martinus Nijhoff, 1964.

Tableau de la situation des Établissements français dans l'Algérie. Paris: Imprimerie impériale, 1856–63.

Taguieff, Pierre-André, ed. *Face au Racisme: Les moyens d'agir*. 2 vols. Paris: La Découverte, 1991.

Taine, Hippolyte. *Carnets du voyage: Notes sur la province, 1863–1865*. Paris: Hachette, 1913.

———. *Essais de critique et d'histoire.* Paris: Hachette, 1900.

———. *Life and Letters of H. Taine.* Translated by R. L. Devonshire. 3 vols. Westminster: Archibald Constable, 1902–8.

———. *Notes on England.* Translated by Edward Hyams. London: Thames-Hudson, 1957.

Taithe, Bertrand. "La famine de 1866–1868: anatomie d'un catastrophe et construction médiatique d'un événement." *Revue d'Histoire du XIXe Siècle* 41 (2010): 113–27.

Ténot, Eugène. *Le Suffrage universel et les paysans.* Paris: Librarie Centrale, 1865.

Thierry-Mieg, Charles. *Six semaines en Afrique.* Paris: Michel Lévy, 1861.

Thomson, Ann. *Barbary and Enlightenment: European Attitudes toward the Maghreb in the 18th Century.* London: Brill, 1989.

Thoré, Théophile. *Salons de W. Bürger, 1861 à 1868.* 2 vols. Paris: Renouard, 1870.

Tiffin, Chris, and Alan Lawson, eds. *De-scribing Empire: Post-Colonialism and Textuality.* London: Routledge, 1994.

Tocqueville, Alexis de. *Œuvres complètes.* 9 vols. Paris: Michel Lévy, 1866.

———. *Sur l'Algérie.* Paris: Flammarion, 2003.

Todd, David. "A French Imperial Meridian, 1814–1870." *Past and Present* 210 (February 2011): 155–86.

Tridon, Gustave. *Œuvres diverses de Gustave Tridon.* Paris: Allemane, 1891.

Troismonts, Charles Piel de. *Napoléon III et la nationalité française.* Paris: Michel Lévy, 1853.

Truesdell, Matthew. *Spectacular Politics: Louis-Napoleon Bonaparte and the Fête Impériale, 1849–1870.* New York: Oxford University Press, 1997.

Trumbull, George R. *An Empire of Facts: Colonial Power, Cultural Knowledge and Islam in Algeria, 1870–1914.* Cambridge: Cambridge University Press, 2009.

Turin, Yvonne. *Affrontements culturels dans l'Algérie colonial: écoles, médecines, religion, 1830–1880.* Algiers: Entreprise Nationale du Livre, 1983.

Twain, Mark. *The Innocents Abroad.* New York: Signat, 1966.

Urbain, Ismael. *L'Algérie française: Indigènes et immigrants.* Paris: Challamel Ainé, 1862.

Vacherot, Étienne. *La Démocratie.* Brussels: A. Lacroix, 1860.

Vaillant, J.-A. *Nationalité et patriotisme.* Paris: E. Dentu, 1855.

Valensise, Marina, ed. *François Guizot et le culture politique de son temps.* Paris: Gallimard, 1991.

Verne, Henri. *De Bône à Hammam-Meskhoutine: Étude sur la question algérienne.* Lyon: H. Storck, 1869.

———. *La France en Algérie.* Paris: Charles Douniol, 1869.

Veuillot, Louis. *L'Illusion libérale.* Versailles: Editions de Paris, 2005.

———. *Mélanges religieux, historiques, politiques et littéraires.* 6 vols. Paris: L. Vivès, 1857.

Viel-Castel, Horace de. *Mémoires sur le règne de Napoléon III.* 6 vols. Paris: Le Prat, 1979.

Vimercati, César. *Histoire de l'Italie en 1848–49*. Paris: Noblet, 1858.

Voisin, Georges [Urbain, Ismael]. *L'Algérie pour les algériens*. Paris: Michel Lévy, 1861.

Wahnich, Sophie. *L'Impossible citoyen: L'étranger dans le discours de la Révolution Française*. Paris: Albin Michel, 1997.

Warman, H. W. *Ernest Renan: A Critical Biography*. London: Althone, 1964.

Warmington, Edward. *Qu'est-ce que le Bonapartisme?* Paris: Ledoyen, 1852.

Warnier, Auguste. *L'Algérie devant l'Empereur*. Paris: Challamel Ainé, 1865.

Weber, Eugen. *Peasants into Frenchmen: The Modernization of Rural France, 1870–1914*. Stanford CA: Stanford University Press, 1976.

Weill, Georges. "Les Saint-Simoniens sous Napoleon III." *Revue des Études Napoléoniennes* 3 (1913): 391–406.

Weisz, George. *The Emergence of Modern Universities in France, 1863–1914*. Princeton NJ: Princeton University Press, 1983.

Wilder, Gary. *The French Imperial Nation-State: Negritude and Colonial Humanism between the World Wars*. Chicago: University of Chicago Press, 2005.

Williams, Roger L. *Gaslights and Shadow: The World of Napoleon III, 1852–1970*. New York: Macmillan, 1957.

Wilson, A. N. *The Victorians*. London: Arrow Books, 2003.

Wright, Gwendolyn. *The Politics of Design in French Colonial Urbanism*. Chicago: University of Chicago Press, 1991.

Woolf, H. I., ed. *Voltaire's Philosophical Dictionary*. London: Allen and Unwin, 1923.

Woolf, Stuart. "French Civilization and Ethnicity in the Napoleonic Empire." *Past and Present* 124 (August 1989): 96–120.

Zamoyski, Adam. *Holy Madness: Romantics, Patriots, and Revolutionaries, 1776–1871*. New York: Viking, 1999.

Zeldin, Theodore. *Emile Ollivier and the Liberal Empire of Napoleon III*. Oxford: Clarendon Press, 1963.

———. *The Political System of Napoleon III*. London: Macmillan, 1958.

Žižek, Slavoj. *The Sublime Object of Ideology*. London: Verso, 1989.

INDEX

Abd al-Qādir: and relations with Napoleon III, 119; and resistance to French, 128

abolitionism, 23, 29

About, Edmond, 148

Adam, Juliette, 159, 160

Algeria, 10, 25, 28, 32, 83, 97, 254; and the "Algerian question," 11, 83, 95, 210, 212, 238, 251; and decentralization, 198, 229–30; and famine, 240–42; and French Algeria (*Algérie Française*), 13, 94, 212, 214, 215, 221–24, 230–31, 239; and French colonialism, 11, 13, 29–30, 47, 56, 98, 106, 107, 110, 115, 211; and French invasion of, 24–26, 96, 99; and general councils, 199, 229, 230, 238; and land tenure, 216–17; and modernization, 71–72, 75, 135, 218–19; and religious conflict, 102, 128–29, 133, 134; and republicanism, 30–31, 210–11, 232–33, 235–38, 243–44, 252–53

Algiers (Algeria), 32, 75, 76, 132

Allain-Targé, Henri, 206

Alletz, Édouard, 41

anthropology, 39, 185

anticlericalism, 117, 191; and Algeria, 135, 137; and atheism, 146; and student activism, 145

antiquity, 16, 44

Arab Kingdom (*Royaume Arabe*), 111–12, 113, 119, 131, 243; and opposition to, 133, 134, 212, 213–14, 215, 217, 222, 239

Arab Offices (*Bureaux Arabes*), 107, 134; and creation of, 100; and criticism of, 209, 218, 241, 242; and education, 131

Arabs, 39, 44, 47–48, 78, 93, 98, 99, 106, 110, 122, 134, 240; and feudalism, 216; and tribalism, 217, 220. *See also* nationality

Arbousse-Bastide, Antoine, 75

Armée d'Afrique, 27, 33, 93, 98, 119; and Algeria, 100, 107, 130, 218

Aroux, Félix, 161

Atlantic, the, 22, 24, 27, 29; and French imperialism, 9, 10, 11, 25. *See also* slavery

Babaud-Laribière, Léonide, 181

Ballanche, Pierre-Simon, 36

Barbarism, 26, 47, 48, 84; and Algerian natives, 218; and poverty, 27

Bardoux, Agénor, 172

Barni, Jules, 154, 200

Barrault, Émile, 24, 103, 104

Barrot, Ferdinand, 230, 238

Baudelaire, Charles, 2, 5, 16, 29, 203
Baulle, Arthur, 138
Ben Abdullah, 209
Berbers, 97, 108
Bertillon, Louis-Adolphe, 162
Billaut, Adolphe, 115, 117
Blackburn, Henry, 50, 78
Blanc, Louis, 29, 193
Blanqui, Louis Auguste, 144
Blanquists, 143, 146, 158; and Liège congress, 147–48
Bonaparte, Jérôme Napoleon, 82; and Algeria, 76, 79, 122; and Algerian ministry, 198–99, 212
Bonaparte, Louis-Napoleon (Napoleon III), 59–62, 63, 64, 79, 81, 82, 90, 116, 150, 181, 188, 203, 247; and Algeria, 83, 93, 95, 101, 110, 111–12, 198, 211, 217; and Catholics, 117–18, 124, 128; and modernization, 3, 54, 70, 72–73; and Muslims, 118, 119, 128; and nationality, 84, 85, 91; and Saint-Simonianism, 68–69; and the second republic, 57–58, 84, 184, 189
Bonaparte, Napoleon (Napoleon I), 1, 10, 23, 41, 61, 99; and the Concordat, 118. *See also* First Napoleonic Empire
Bonapartism, 57, 61–62, 81, 89, 114–15; and civilization, 63–64, 78, 90, 200; and modernity, 13, 62–63, 150–51, 184, 249, 251; and nationalism, 82–83, 92; and religion, 117; and unity, 82, 84
Bory-de-Saint-Vincent, Jean Baptiste, 26
Bourbon dynasty, 20
bourgeoisie, 20, 28, 34, 41–42; and modernity, 17, 18, 51, 249–50; and

July Monarchy, 27; and politics, 21–22, 172
Bourget, Auguste, 226–27
Broglie, Albert de, 224, 227
Brossard, Amédée-Hippolyte, 31
Brunet, Jacques Charles, 32
Buchez, Philippe, 39
Bugeau, Thomas Robert, 100

Capdeveille, Paul, 234, 243
Cappot, Jean-Gabriel, 86
Casse, Germaine, 146, 158
Catholicism: and Algeria, 96–97, 133, 134, 240–41; and education, 124; and politics, 125; and Second Napoleonic Empire, 117–18 centralization, 187, 200, 227–28. *See also* Second Napoleonic Empire
Changarnier, Nicolas Theodule, 136
Charon, Viala, 99
Chassériau, Charles Frédéric, 76
Chauvin, Henry, 93
Chevalier, Michel, 70, 192
citizenship, 29, 34–35, 42, 86, 92, 207; and Algeria, 220, 230–32, 237; and civic participation, 187, 195, 206, 230–31; and empire, 22–23, 29–31, 43, 210, 233; and municipal government, 200–01, 202, 229–30; and Muslims, 112, 113–14, 231–32; and political rights, 21, 94, 112, 233
civilization, 7, 15, 24, 26, 34, 39, 40–42, 43, 45, 48–49, 52, 66, 97, 186, 214; and "civilizing mission," 8, 25, 30, 32, 46, 48, 64, 76, 93, 99, 101, 220, 241, 251; and religion, 117
Clemenceau, Georges, 142, 143.
Code de l'indigénat, 253
colonialism, 6, 74; and Algeria, 30, 32, 47, 78, 97, 98, 99, 103–05, 111; and the Atlantic, 22–23, 210, 233; and

assimilation, 31, 94, 211–12, 214, 221–24, 230–31; and Catholicism, 96, 97, 240; and education, 123, 130, 131, 134–35, 136, 138, 150; and France, 11, 12; and internal colonization, 186; and reform, 42, 134–35, 229–30, 238; and Second Napoleonic Empire, 12, 71–72, 105–112; and the social question, 34, 50

colonists: and Algeria, 13, 30, 32, 98, 212; and the Atlantic, 22–23, 29–30; and *colon* identity, 214–15, 218, 227; and *colon* opposition, 134, 136–37, 151, 213, 216, 218, 223–24, 225, 228, 239–40; and emigration, 220–21; and relations with natives, 133–39, 218–20; and republican politics, 211, 233–34

commune, 195; and Algeria, 229–30; and French government, 203

communism, 217

Comte, Auguste, 159–62, 165, 166, 175, 180. *See also* Positivism

Constant, Benjamin, 40

Constantine (Algeria), 26, 32, 44, 113, 213

Corps législatif, 70, 116, 139, 156, 165, 178, 196, 200, 202, 205, 209, 217, 225, 231, 232, 238, 241, 242

cosmopolitanism, 9, 86, 94

Costa, Gaston da, 143

Couchery, Adolphe, 159

Crédit Mobilier, 71

Daudet, Alphonse, 96

Daumier, Honoré, 35

David, Jérôme Frédéric, 110; and Algeria, 107, 108, 129, 242; and views on Arabs, 47, 99

Declaration of Rights of Man and Citizen, 22

Deligny, Édouard-Jean-Étienne, 97, 243

democracy, 6, 7, 21, 34–35, 173–74, 186–87; and universal manhood suffrage, 29, 34, 53, 88, 90, 175, 187, 193

D'Eschavannes, Jouffroy, 30

D'Hautpoul, Alphonse Henri, 134

Doctrinaires, 20, 21, 26, 156, 172, 174. *See also* liberalism

Doineau, Auguste, 209

Dollfus, Charles, 193

Doumic, René, 3

Dupont-White, Charles, 160, 166, 179

Duruy, Victor: and Algeria, 122, 137–38; and education reform, 121–22, 139, 141, 149; and Exposition Universelle, 15, 73

Duval, Jules, 74, 215, 218, 227, 239; and colonial citizenship, 226, 230–31; and opinion on Arabs, 217, 241; and views on colonialization, 222–23

Duvergier, Ernest, 172

Duvernois, Clément: and Algerian colonization, 97, 136; and anti-Islamic sentiment, 136; and colonial education, 135; and colonial journalism, 201, 235; and colonial opposition, 138, 221, 228; and liberal opposition, 155, 171–72, 174, 201–02

education: and Catholic opposition, 141, 148; and the Church, 120; and collèges arabe-française, 132–33; and colonialism, 123; and Islam, 128, 131–132; and secularism, 136–37; and student radicalism, 141

egalitarianism, 14, 21, 23, 34; and republican ideology, 155

Egypt, 41, 48, 99–100

empire, 6, 8, 24, 29, 39, 50, 251–52; and the Atlantic, 23, 25, 42–43, 233; and North Africa, 10, 11, 25, 63, 151.

industrial revolution, the, 5
Islam, 48, 49, 108, 119; and Algeria, 96, 130; and education, 129, 136. *See also* Muslims

Jacobins, 22, 143, 144, 147, 159, 168, 169. *See also* republicanism
Jaincot, Gustave, 148
Jihad, 25, 128
journalism: and Algeria, 214, 224–27; and liberalism, 203–04; and student organizations, 142–43.
Jouvencel, Paul de, 39
Judaism: and French Jews, 94; and Algerian Jews, 113, 232
July Monarchy, the, 21, 26, 27–28, 29, 34, 54, 57, 61, 70, 84, 154, 158; and Algeria, 24; and Atlantic colonies, 22–23; and politics, 187
June Days (1848), 33, 50, 56, 84, 124, 183; and legacy of, 154, 167

Kabylia (Algeria), 71, 128
Kant, Immanuel, 40

laborers, 77; and colonialism, 33–34, 50
Laboulaye, Édouard, 175, 176, 192, 205; and liberty, 195; and "new liberalism," 171
Lacretelle, Charles Nicolas, 107, 242
Lacroix, Frédéric, 110, 213; and Algerian natives, 98, 106
Lafargue, Paul, 145, 147
Lambert, Alexandre, 214, 215, 229
Lavigerie, Charles, 240, 241; and Algiers bishopric, 133–34
Lavollée, Charles, 75
Lecouturier, Henri, 50, 183
Le Hon, Léopold, 238
Lerminier, Eugène, 25

liberalism, 20, 21–22, 34, 35, 170; and Algeria, 225, 229–30, 238; and imperialism, 22–23, 24, 28; and liberty, 173–74; and nationality, 87, 88; and political change, 156, 170, 171; and relation to republicanism, 156–57; and social outlooks, 27, 41–42, 49, 171; and universal manhood suffrage, 172–73, 175, 193
Liège, and student congress, 146–47, 148
Littré, Émile, 3, 166, 167, 169; and *La Philosophie positivie*, 164; and positivism, 160, 161, 162, 163; and republican ideology, 155, 165, 170, 180
Longuet, Charles, 142; and the "new generation," 143, 144, 148, 158
Louvre, the, 96

MacMahon, Patrice de, 113, 213, 232
Maghreb. *See* North Africa
Magnin, Joseph, 203
Malon, Benoît, 142
Mamluk, 99
Manet, Édouard, 5
Margueritte, Jean-Auguste, 130
Marlet, Hippolyte, 86
Marquand, Augustin, 76
Martinique, 23, 24, 30
Marx, Karl, 4, 19, 20, 154; and Marxism, 19
Mediterranean, 12, 214; and French imperialism, 10, 12, 30
Michelet, Jules, 20, 87
Miravals, Raimond de, 15, 16, 73
missionaries, 47, 96; and Algeria, 133
modernism, 5
modernity, 2–5, 56, 250, 252; and identity, 37–38, 40, 49, 51–52; and

Second Napoleonic Empire, 7, 8, 12, 14, 53–54, 90, 115; and Algeria, 12, 13, 58, 63, 76, 95, 198–200, 212–13; and the business community, 60, 71; and censorship, 203–04, 226–27; and centralization, 92, 196–97, 227–28; and church-state relations, 118, 119, 120, 125, 127, 140, 150; and decentralization, 197–98, 200; and education policies, 121, 123, 126, 131, 139, 149–50; and Italian policy, 127; and liberty, 82, 89, 91; and modernization, 55, 64–65, 69–70, 72–73, 79, 194, 247; and nationalism, 83, 127; and nationality policies, 83, 85, 88–89, 95, 111; and opposition to, 155, 195, 202, 238–39, 243–44; and peace, 63–64; and peasant vote, 189; and sovereignty, 89–90, 173, 195; and revolution, 82, 114, 181

Second Republic, 29–30, 42, 88, 125, 154; and Algeria, 31, 98, 224, 231; and Atlantic, 29–30; and collapse of, 183–84; and the countryside, 188; and *quarante-huitards*, 139, 142, 154, 190; and the "social question," 32–33, 34

Senhaux, Henri de, 44

Sieyès, Emmanuel-Joseph, 86

Simon, Jules, 168, 169, 176, 191, 203, 237; and defense of free press, 205; and liberalization, 174, 202

slavery, 22–23, 42; and emancipation, 22–23, 29–30, 43, 210

socialism, 59, 250

Société Algérienne, 31

Société de Saint-Vincent-de-Paul, 127

Stern, Daniel (Marie de Flavigny), 165; and republican salons, 153, 154, 156

Stupuy, Hippolyte, 161, 169, 248; and positive philosophy, 164–65

Sufism, 25, 128

Taine, Hippolyte, 1, 44, 50, 53, 55, 56, 75, 87, 185; and liberalism, 150, 170

Talabot, Paulin, 72

Talleyrand, Charles Maurice de, 20

temporality, 16–17, 18, 35, 39–40, 43

Ténot, Eugène, 45, 178, 186, 206; and views on the provinces, 190, 192, 195

Theirs, Adolphe, 168

Thierry-Mieg, Charles, 39, 65, 76, 96, 98

Third Republic, 6, 9, 168, 172, 207, 249, 250–51; and opportunism, 159; and public education, 121

Thomson, Arnold, 173, 226, 232, 233

Thoré, Théophile, 178, 247

Thuillier, Émile, 134, 226, 227, 241

Tocqueville, Alexis de, 56

Tridon, Gustave, 143, 146

Troismonts, Charles Piel de, 62, 85

United States, 13, 19

universalism, 14, 42, 52, 87, 233

Urbain, Ismael, 66, 101, 110, 112, 114, 231; and colonization, 105; and ideological outlook, 102, 115; and Muslim education, 130, 132; and native policy, 105–06, 107, 109, 113; and religious conflict, 134; and Saint-Simonianism, 102–103

urbanization, 5, 49, 53, 74–75, 77; and colonialism, 75–77

Vacherot, Arsène, 220

Vacherot, Étienne, 157, 186, 193, 207

Verne, Henri, 137, 216, 224

Veuillot, Louis, 118, 151

Vimercati, César, 64

Vital, Auguste, 113, 129, 213, 248

Voltaire, 85

Warmington, Edward, 81
Warnier, Auguste, 218, 225; and
  criticism of Nativism, 214
Wyrouboff, Grégoire, 191

young republicans, 154, 155, 159, 180,
  207. *See also* republicanism
Yusuf Vantini, 110
Zola, Émile, 249

The French Colonial Mind, Volume 2: Violence, Military Encounters, and Colonialism
Edited and with an introduction by Martin Thomas

Beyond Papillon: The French Overseas Penal Colonies, 1854–1952
Stephen A. Toth

Madah-Sartre: The Kidnapping, Trial, and Conver(sat/s)ion of Jean-Paul Sartre and Simone de Beauvoir
Written and translated by Alek Baylee Toumi
With an introduction by James D. Le Sueur

To order or obtain more information on these or other University of Nebraska Press titles, visit nebraskapress.unl.edu.